The ....rch-
...........searched
...........n by **Henry**
...........**man** (far left) and
Joel Newton (right)
accompanied by **Daisy**.
This second edition was
rewalked and updated by
Joel Newton.

Born in Poole, Dorset,
JOEL NEWTON, first discovered the South-West
Coast Path whilst on a
family holiday to Corn-
wall in the spring of 2007.
Later that same year, feel-
ing somewhat jaded by everyday life (in reality, he had little else to do), Joel
found himself on a bus to Minehead with a bag that he would soon discover
was far too heavy. Six weeks later he arrived in Falmouth sun-drunk, blistered,
happy and with a newfound love for walking national trails. This passion led
to Joel ambling along Offa's Dyke, West Highland Way, Great Glen Way,
Cotswold Way, Two Moors Way, South Downs Way, Dales Way and stretches
of the Pennine Way amongst other paths. Sitting in a café in Hastings, East
Sussex, in 2011, a stranger who was there (stroking a puppy) admitted that he
was the author of the guidebook Joel was reading: Trailblazer's *Hadrian's Wall
Path*. They got talking and in 2012, Joel, Henry Stedman (the stranger) and
Daisy (the puppy, by now a dog) walked, researched and co-authored
Trailblazer's three-part series to the South-West Coast Path. Since then Joel has
written the Trailblazer guide *Thames Path* and travelled and trekked in South-
east Asia. This, the second edition of *Exmoor and North Devon Coast Path*, is
Joel's fifth book. When not walking he lives and works in Hastings.

Born in Chatham, Kent, **HENRY STEDMAN** has been writing guidebooks for
over 20 years and is the author or co-author of half a dozen titles, including
Trailblazer's *Kilimanjaro*, *Dolomites*, *Coast to Coast Path*, *Dales Way* and
Hadrian's Wall Path as well as guides for Bradt and Rough Guides.

  When not travelling or writing, Henry lives in the UK editing other people's guidebooks, maintaining his Kilimanjaro website and arranging climbs on
the mountain through his company, Climb Mount Kilimanjaro.

  DAISY is Henry's dog, though any assumption that ownership equates with
control is entirely wrong in this instance. Two parts trouble to one part Parson's
Jack Russell, together with her two human companions Daisy managed to walk
the entire South-West Coast Path – indeed, for every five miles that they completed, Daisy did about ten.

Authors

Exmoor & North Devon Coast Path (SWCP Part 1)

First edition: 2012; this second edition 2017

Publisher Trailblazer Publications
The Old Manse, Tower Rd, Hindhead, Surrey, GU26 6SU, UK
info@trailblazer-guides.com, ⌨ www.trailblazer-guides.com

British Library Cataloguing in Publication Data
A catalogue record for this book is available from the British Library

ISBN 978-1-905864-86-7

© **Trailblazer** 2012 & 2017: Text and maps

Series Editor: Anna Jacob-Hood
Editor & layout: Anna Jacob-Hood **Proofreading**: Jane Thomas
Cartography: Nick Hill **Index**: Daniel McCrohan **Photographs (flora)**: © Bryn Thomas
All other photographs: © Joel Newton (unless otherwise indicated)

Acknowledgements

Thank you to Zoe, Daisy, little Henry and big Henry for letting me stay at Little Squirrels
whilst I researched and wrote the bulk of this book (and, of course, for getting me into this
game in the first place!) and to Pat and Ted who kept an eye on (and fed) me when I was
there. Thank you also to Gavin Green for putting me up whilst I finished the book.

On the trail, of the numerous people that I met, who had suggestions, discussed experiences, or helped me out, two deserve a special mention: Nick Goodwin for the shared dinners, pints, puddings, tips and conversation; and Thirza Goaman, who let me stay at her
hostel for far longer than the average walker ever would … and twice!

Thank you to the following for their assistance with the first edition of this book or for
their contributions to this new edition: Mary Breeds, Tim Prosser, Jos Smith, Eric & Fiona
Greenslade, Michael Stanbury, Helen Older, Jeff Handley, Tony Maynard-Smith, Bryan
Gray, Keri & Pauline, Morten Planer, Gabi Blauer, Elissa Klapper and Isabel Heycock.

Finally, thank you to Bryn Thomas, Anna Jacob-Hood, Nick Hill and everyone at
Trailblazer for their hard work on this new edition.

A request

The author and publisher have tried to ensure that this guide is as accurate and up to date
as possible. Nevertheless, things change. If you notice any changes or omissions that should
be included in the next edition of this book, please write to Trailblazer (address above) or
email us at ⌨ info@trailblazer-guides.com. A free copy of the next edition will be sent to
persons making a significant contribution.

Warning: coastal walking and long-distance walking can be dangerous

Please read the notes on when to go (pp13-16) and outdoor safety (pp56-9). Every effort
has been made by the author and publisher to ensure that the information contained herein
is as accurate and up to date as possible. However, they are unable to accept responsibility
for any inconvenience, loss or injury sustained by anyone as a result of the advice and information given in this guide.

Updated information will be available on: ⌨ www.trailblazer-guides.com

Photos – Front cover and this page: Ilfracombe from the path to Hillsborough.
Overleaf: The sands and pebbles of Northam Burrows Country Park (see p171).

Printed in China; print production by D'Print (☎ +65-6581 3832), Singapore

★ trailblazer

EXMOOR &
North Devon
COAST PATH

SW COAST PATH PART 1 – MINEHEAD TO BUDE

68 large-scale maps & guides to 30 towns and villages

PLANNING – PLACES TO STAY – PLACES TO EAT

HENRY STEDMAN & JOEL NEWTON

TRAILBLAZER PUBLICATIONS

Contents

INTRODUCTION
Exmoor and North Devon Coast Path

PART 1: PLANNING YOUR WALK
Practical information for the walker

Budgeting 28

Itineraries

What to take

Getting to and from the path

PART 2: MINIMUM IMPACT WALKING & OUTDOOR SAFETY
Minimum impact walking

Outdoor safety

PART 3: THE ENVIRONMENT & NATURE
Flora and fauna

PART 4: ROUTE GUIDE AND MAPS

Contents

ABOUT THIS BOOK

This guidebook contains all the information you need. The hard work has been done for you so you can plan your trip from home without the usual pile of books, maps and guides.

When you're all packed and ready to go, there's comprehensive public transport information to get you to and from the trail and 68 detailed maps and town plans to help you find your way along it.

The guide includes:

● All standards of accommodation with reviews of campsites, hostels, B&Bs, guesthouses and hotels
● Walking companies if you want a guided or self-guided tour, and a baggage-carrying service if you just want your luggage carried
● Itineraries for all levels of walkers
● Answers to all your questions: when to go, degree of difficulty, what to pack, and how much the whole walking holiday will cost
● Walking times in both directions and GPS waypoints
● Cafés, pubs, tearooms, takeaways, restaurants and shops for buying supplies
● Rail, bus & taxi information for all villages and towns along the path
● Street plans of the main towns and villages both on and off the path
● Historical, cultural and geographical background information

❏ MINIMUM IMPACT FOR MAXIMUM INSIGHT

Man has suffered in his separation from the soil and from other living creatures ... and as yet he must still, for security, look long at some portion of the earth as it was before he tampered with it.
Gavin Maxwell, *Ring of Bright Water*, 1960

Why is walking in wild and solitary places so satisfying? Partly it is the sheer physical pleasure: sometimes pitting one's strength against the elements and the lie of the land. The beauty and wonder of the natural world and the fresh air restore our sense of proportion and the stresses and strains of everyday life slip away. Whatever the character of the countryside, walking in it benefits us mentally and physically, inducing a sense of well-being, an enrichment of life and an enhanced awareness of what lies around us.

All this the countryside gives us and the least we can do is to safeguard it by supporting rural economies, local businesses, and low-impact methods of farming and land-management, and by using environmentally sensitive forms of transport – walking being pre-eminent.

In this book there is a detailed and illustrated chapter on the wildlife and conservation of the region and a chapter on minimum-impact walking, with ideas on how to tread lightly in this fragile environment; by following its principles we can help to preserve our natural heritage for future generations.

About this book

INTRODUCTION

This book covers the first 124½ miles (200.3km) of the South-West Coast Path (hereafter known as SWCP), Britain's longest national trail. The trail in this book starts at Minehead in Somerset and, after navigating the whole of North Devon's coastline, ends just across the border at Bude in Cornwall.

This book covers the first 124½ miles of the 630-mile South-West Coast Path

Together with the two other books in this 'mini-series', the entire length of this 630-mile-long coast path is covered.

This first section of the path is also by some distance the shortest of the three. But size isn't everything, as they say, and there's plenty here to tempt the discerning walker. Look at a map of the British Isles and this part of the coastal path – meandering as it does along some of Britain's most exquisite shoreline, backed by a vast swathe of green, a verdant outlook unbroken save for tiny villages and hamlets scattered here and there – is a logical place to go for an amble. That vast swathe of green is Exmoor National Park, the most delightful of

The trail takes you through numerous villages such as picturesque Clovelly.

wildernesses and one through which the route saunters along the coastal cliffs for 34 miles and includes Great Hangman, at 318m (1043ft) the highest point on the entire trail. Nor does the fun stop there for no sooner does the path leave the park than it immediately joins the North Devon coast, luxuriating in its designation as an Area of Outstanding Natural Beauty (AONB). It is here you'll find enormous beaches stretching for miles; Braunton Burrows, part of a UNESCO Biosphere Reserve and the largest sand dune system in the country; plenty of pretty little historical towns and gorgeous villages where one can rest and recuperate, including the breathtaking harbour of Clovelly; and we haven't even mentioned the walk around Hartland Peninsula, the toughest, most isolat-

Clearly, God was in a rumbustious mood when He designed this gorgeous little corner of England

ed and the most spectacular walking – in most experts' opinions – on the entire SWCP. Clearly, God was in a rumbustious mood when He designed this gorgeous little corner of England.

The North Devon AONB continues all the way to the border with Cornwall, though this book actually finishes just across the border at Bude – a more logical end to a walk, with fine accommo-

dation, good restaurants in which to celebrate and half-decent (by the standards of the South-West at least!) transport links back to the everyday world.

Sounds perfect doesn't it? A dozen days or so of walking along romantic, windswept cliffs, through Elysian fields and sylvan valleys, a small yet vital part of a mammoth odyssey around England's most idiosyncratic corner. But such rewards are not gained easily; for one thing, the weather in this blessed corner of England takes a perverse pleasure in its unpredictability – though boy, it does have more than its fair share of good weather too, especially compared to the rest of the UK. But there's also some hard walking to be done; by many people's estimates, this is actually the toughest leg of the entire SWCP, with plenty of fiercely undulating sections guaranteed to torment calf muscles and sap morale. Indeed, it can't be denied that there are a couple of days that will truly test your mettle.

> **This is actually the toughest leg of the entire South-West Coast Path**

But then again, few if any will disagree that the obstacles and difficulties this path presents to those who dare to pit themselves against it, are far out-weighed by its compensations.

History

The Somerset and North Devon section of the South-West Coast Path is the youngest part, having only been created and added to the rest of the path in 1978 – five years after the Cornish section was declared open. The entire path, however, including this section, existed way before its designation as a national trail, having been used by the coastguard for centuries to protect against smugglers and aid maritime safety. The nature of the coastguard's job meant that the path had to follow the cliff-tops closely to provide their officers with far-reaching views over land and sea – and to allow them to visit every beach and cove along the way. By chance, these are the exact same qualities that discerning walkers look for in a coastal path!

Left: The start of the trail in Minehead is marked with a sculpture of a giant hand holding a South-West Coast Path map.

INTRODUCTION

❏ THE SOUTH-WEST COAST PATH

Typing 'Minehead to Poole Harbour, Dorset' into Googlemaps, reveals that travelling between the two can be completed in a matter of 2½ hours by car, along a distance of 98.1 miles. Even walking, along the most direct route, takes only around 28 hours, so Googlemaps says, with the path an even shorter one at just 88.2 miles.

It is these two points that are connected by the South-West Coast Path (SWCP). This most famous – and infamous – of national trails is, however, a good deal longer than 89.3 miles. Though estimates as to its exact length vary – and to a large part are determined by which of the alternative paths one takes at various stages along the trail – the most widely accepted estimate of the path is that it is about 630 miles long (1014km). That figure, however, often changes due to necessary changes in the path caused by erosion and other factors.

So why, when you could walk from Minehead to South Haven Point in just 29 hours, do most people choose to take 6-8 weeks? The answer is simple: the SWCP is one of the most beautiful trails in the UK. Around 70% of those 630 miles are spent either in national parks, or regions that have been designated as Areas of Outstanding Natural Beauty. The variety of places crossed by the SWCP is extraordinary too: from sunkissed beaches to sandy burrows, holiday parks to fishing harbours, esplanade to estuary, on top of windswept cliffs and under woodland canopy, the scenery that one travels through along the length of SWCP has to be the most diverse of any of the national trails. Of course, maintaining such a monumental route is no easy task. A survey in 2000 stated that the trail boasted 2473 signposts and waymarks, 302 bridges, 921 stiles, and 26,719 steps. These figures are, of course, out of date now, though they do still give an idea of both how long the trail is, and how much is involved in building and maintaining it to such a high standard. The task of looking after the trail falls to a dedicated team from the official body, Natural England. Another important organisation, and one that looks after the rights of walkers is the South West Coast Path Association (see box p40), a charity that fights for improvements to the path and offers advice, information and support to walkers. They also campaign against many of the proposed changes to the path and help to ensure that England's right-of-way laws which ensure that the footpath is open to the public – even though it does, on occasion, pass through private property – are fully observed.

History of the path

In 1948 a government report recommended the creation of a footpath around the entire South-West peninsula to improve public access to the coast which, at that time, was pretty dire. It took until 1973 for the Cornwall Coast Path to be declared officially open and another five years for the rest of the South-West Coast Path to be completed. The section covered in this book, North Devon and Exmoor, is the first part that most coastal walkers complete, though it was actually the last section to be opened to the public, in 1978.

The origins of the path, however, are much older than its official designation. Originally, the paths were established – or at least adopted, there presumably being coastal paths from time immemorial that connected the coastal villages – by the local coastguard in the 19th century, who needed a path that hugged the shoreline closely to aid them in their attempts to spot and prevent smugglers from bringing contraband into the country. The coastguards were unpopular in the area as they prevented the locals from exploiting a lucrative if illegal activity, to the extent that it was considered too dangerous for them to stay in the villages; as a result, the authorities were obliged to build special cottages for the coastguards that stood (and, often, still stand) in splendid isolation near the path – but well away from the villages.

How long do you need?

People take about 10-11 days to complete the walk; count on a fortnight away in total to give you time to travel there and back. Of course, if you're fit there's no reason why you can't go a little faster, if that's what you want to do, and finish the walk in eight days or even less, though you will end up having a differ-

People take about 10-11 days to complete the walk; count on a fortnight away in total

ent sort of walk to most of the other people on the trail. For, whilst theirs is a fairly relaxing holiday, yours will be more of a sport. What's more, you won't have much time to laze in the sun on the beaches, scoff scones in tearooms, visit an attraction or two, or sup local beers under the shade of a pub parasol – which

---

The lifeboat patrols also used the path to look out for craft in distress (and on one famous occasion used the path to drag their boat to a safe launch to rescue a ship in distress – see p98). When the coastguards' work ended in 1856, the Admiralty took over the task of protecting England's shoreline and thus the paths continued to be used.

The route – Minehead (Somerset) to Poole Harbour (Dorset)

The SWCP officially begins at Minehead in Somerset (its exact starting point marked by a sculpture of a giant hand holding a map, see p9), heads west right round the bottom south-west corner of Britain then shuffles back along the south coast to South Haven Point, overlooking Poole Harbour in Dorset.

On its lengthy journey around Britain's south-western corner the SWCP crosses national parks such as Exmoor as well as regions that have been designated as Areas of Outstanding Natural Beauty (including North, South and East Devon as well as Cornwall and Dorset) or Sites of Special Scientific Interest (Braunton Burrows being just one example – an area that also enjoys a privileged status as a UNESCO Biosphere Reserve), and even a couple of UNESCO World Heritage sites, too, including the Jurassic Coast of East Devon and Dorset and the old mining landscape of Cornwall and West Devon.

Other features passed on the way include: the highest cliffs on mainland Britain (at Great Hangman – also the highest point on the coast path at 318m/1043ft, with a cliff-face of 244m); the largest sand-dune system in England (at Braunton Burrows); England's most westerly point (at Land's End) and Britain's most southerly (at the Lizard); the 18-mile barrier beach of Chesil Bank; one of the world's largest natural harbours at Poole; and even the National Trust's only official nudist beach at Studland!

The path then ends at South Haven Point, its exact finish marked by a second SWCP sculpture. The path also takes in four counties – Somerset, Devon, Cornwall and Dorset, and connects with over fifteen other long-distance trails; the southern section from Plymouth to Poole also forms part of the 3125-mile long European E9 Coastal Path that runs on a convoluted route from Portugal to Estonia.

(cont'd overleaf)

INTRODUCTION

❏ **THE SOUTH-WEST COAST PATH** (cont'd from p11)

Walking the South-West Coast Path

In terms of difficulty, there are those people who, having never undertaken such a trail before, are under the illusion that coastal walking is a cinch; that all it involves is a simple stroll along mile after mile of golden, level beach, the walker needing to pause only to kick the sand out from his or her flip-flop or buy another ice-cream.

The truth, of course, is somewhat different, for coastal paths tend to stick to the cliffs above the beaches rather than the beaches themselves (which is actually something of a relief, given how hard it is to walk across sand or shingle). These cliffs make for some spectacular walking but – given the undulating nature of Britain's coastline, and the fact the course of the SWCP inevitably crosses innumerable river valleys, each of which forces the walker to descend rapidly before climbing back up again almost immediately afterwards – some exhausting walking too. Indeed, it has been estimated that anybody who completes the entire SWCP will have climbed more than four times the height of Everest (35,031m to be precise, or 114,931ft) by the time they finish!

Given these figures, it is perhaps hardly surprising that most people take around eight weeks to complete the whole route, and few do so in one go; indeed, it is not unusual for people to take years or even decades to complete the whole path, taking a week or two here and there to tackle various sections until the whole trail is complete.

does rather beg the question as to why you've come here in the first place! There's nothing wrong with this approach, of course – *chacun à son goût*, as the French probably say. However, what you **mustn't do is try to push yourself too fast, or too far**. That road leads only to exhaustion, injury or, at the absolute least, an unpleasant time.

When deciding how long to allow for the walk, those intending to camp and carry their own luggage shouldn't underestimate just how much a heavy pack

See pp32-3 for some suggested itineraries covering different walking speeds

can slow them down. On pp32-3 there are some suggested itineraries covering different walking speeds.

If you have only a few days, don't try to walk it all; concentrate instead on one area such as the coast path through Exmoor, the beaches around Woolacombe and Croyde, or the more low-key estuary path along a disused railway from Braunton to Westward Ho!. Or you can really challenge yourself by taking on the trail between lovely Clovelly and Bude.

How difficult is the path?

The South-West Coast Path (SWCP) is just a (very, very) long walk, so there's no need for crampons, ropes, ice axes, oxygen bottles or any other climbing paraphernalia. All you need to complete the walk is some suitable clothing, a bit of money, a rucksack full of determination and a half-decent pair of calf muscles.

That said, the part of the SWCP that is covered by this book is reputed to be the most challenging section, with plenty of steep ups-and-downs. It is also a fairly wild walk in places – to cross Exmoor National Park is to traverse one of the remotest corners of the country. There are also plenty of places on the regular trail where it would be possible to fall from a great height, even if you strayed from the path by only a few metres. Still, with the path well signposted (see pp17-18) all the way along and the sea keeping you company for the entire stretch, it's difficult to get lost (though it's always a good idea to take a compass or GPS unit, just in case).

As with any walk, you can minimise the risks by preparing properly. Your greatest danger on the walk is likely to be from the weather, which can be so unpredictable in this corner of the world, so it is vital that you dress for inclement conditions and always carry a set of dry clothes with you.

When to go

SEASONS

'My shoes are clean from walking in the rain.' **Jack Kerouac**

Britain is a notoriously wet country and South-West England does nothing to crush that reputation. Few walkers manage to complete the walk without suffering at least one downpour; two or three per walk are more likely, even in summer. That said, it's equally unlikely that you'll spend a week in the area and not see any sun at all, and even the most cynical of walkers will have to admit that, during the **walking season** at least, there are more sunny days than showery ones. The season, by the way, starts at Easter and builds to a crescendo in August, before steadily tailing off in October. Few people attempt the entire path after the end of October though there are still plenty of people on day walks. Many places close in November for the winter.

Below: Sundown, Combe Martin. Heading west you should get some fabulous sunsets.

There is one further point to consider when planning your trip. Firstly, remember that most people set off on the trail at a weekend. This means that you'll find the trail quieter **during the week** and as a consequence you may find it easier to book accommodation.

Spring

Find a dry fortnight in springtime (around the end of March to mid June) and you're in for a treat. The wild flowers are coming into bloom, lambs are skipping in the meadows and the grass is green and lush. Of course, finding a dry week in spring is not easy but occasionally there's a mini-heatwave at this time. Another advantage with walking at this time is that there will be fewer walkers and finding accommodation is relatively easy, though do check that the hostels/B&Bs are open. Easter is the exception; it's the first major holiday in the year when people flock to the coast.

Summer

Summer, on the other hand, can be a bit *too* busy, at least in the towns and tourist centres, and over a weekend in August can be both suffocating and insufferable. Still, the chances of a prolonged period of sunshine are of course higher at this time of year than any other, the days are much longer, and all the facilities and public transport are operating. Our advice is this: if you're flexible and want to avoid seeing too many people on the trail, avoid the school holidays, which basically means ruling out the tail end of July, all of August and the first few days of September. Alternatively, if you crave the company of other walkers summer will provide you with the opportunity of meeting plenty, though do remember that you **must book your accommodation in advance**, especially if staying in B&B-type accommodation. However, you'll need to factor in that most such places only accept advance bookings for two nights in the summer. Despite the higher than average chance of sunshine, take clothes for any eventuality – it will probably still rain at some point.

Autumn

September is a wonderful time to walk; many tourists have returned home and the path is clear. I think that the weather is usually reliably sunny too, at least at the beginning of September, though I'll admit I don't have any figures to back this claim. The first signs of winter will be felt in October but there's nothing really to deter the walker. In fact there's still much to entice you, such as the colours of the heathland, which come into their own in autumn; a magnificent blaze of brilliant purples and pinks, splashed with the occasional yellow flowers of gorse (it is more usual in spring but can thrive in autumn). By the end of October, however, the weather will begin to get a little wilder and the nights will start to draw in. The walking season is almost at an end and most campsites and some B&Bs and hostels may close.

Winter

November can bring crisp clear days which are ideal for walking, although you'll definitely feel the chill when you stop on the cliff tops for a break. Winter temperatures rarely fall below freezing but the incidence of gales and storms definitely increases. You need to be fairly hardy to walk in December and January and you may have to alter your plans because of the weather. By February the daffodils and primroses are already appearing but even into March it can still be decidedly chilly if the sun is not out.

While winter is definitely the low season with many places closed, this can be more of an advantage than a disadvantage. Very few people walk at this time of year, giving you long stretches of the trail to yourself. When you do stumble across other walkers they are as happy as you to stop and chat. Finding B&B accommodation is easier as you rarely have to book more than a night ahead (though it is still worth checking in advance as some B&Bs close out of season), but if you are planning to camp, or are on a small budget, you will find places to stay much more limited.

WEATHER

Before departing on your walk, tell yourself this: at some point on my walk it is going to **rain**. That's not to say it will, but at least if it does you won't be too disappointed and will hopefully have come prepared for this, clothes-wise. Besides, walking in the rain can be fun, at least for a while: the gentle drumming of rain on hood can be quite relaxing, the path is usually quiet, and if it really does chuck it down at least it provides an excuse to linger in tearooms and have that extra scone. And as long as you dress accordingly and take note of the safety advice given on pp56-9, walking in moderate rain is no more dangerous than walking at any other time – though do be careful, particularly on exposed sections, if the path becomes slippy or the wind picks up.

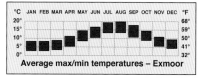
Average max/min temperatures – Exmoor

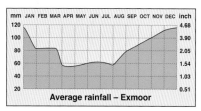
Average rainfall – Exmoor

DAYLIGHT HOURS

If walking in winter, autumn or even early spring, you must take account of how far you can walk in the available light. It won't be possible to cover as many miles as you

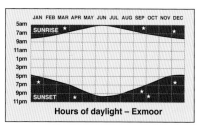
Hours of daylight – Exmoor

would in summer. Conversely, in the summer months there is enough available light until at least 9pm – so don't use that as an excuse for finishing your day's walk early! Remember, too, that you will get a further 30-45 minutes of usable light before sunrise and after sunset depending on the weather.

❑ FESTIVALS AND ANNUAL EVENTS

Before leaving home it may be wise to be aware of any cultural events that could turn your peaceful seaside stroll into something resembling the Rio Carnival! You may wish to consider either avoiding or participating in the following events whilst planning your walk.

June

● **Grand Victorian & Steampunk Festival** (🖳 www.visitilfracombe.co.uk) sees locals and visitors dress up in Victorian costumes to celebrate Ilfracombe's past.

● **GoldCoast Oceanfest** (🖳 goldcoastoceanfest.co.uk) Ostensibly a weekend music festival in Croyde Bay though with as much emphasis on sport, especially surfing.

● **Barnstaple Fringe Theatre Festival** (🖳 www.theatrefest.co.uk) Over 100 performances from numerous theatre companies taking place over four days in late June.

● **Braunton's Festival of music, dance and literature** Held around 26 June to celebrate St Brannock's Day. See p146.

July

● **Minehead & Exmoor Music Festival** (🖳 www.mineheadmusicfestival.org) Four concerts featuring the Festival Orchestra spread out over a week in late July.

● **Samphire Festival** (🖳 samphirefestival.com) An independent music and arts festival held in Exmoor National Park (Porlock Hill) over three days in early July.

August

● **Combe Martin Carnival** (🖳 www.visitcombemartin.com) Annual week-long event held in mid August with raft and wheelbarrow races as well as fireworks and a much-anticipated parade.

● **Bude Jazz Festival** (🖳 www.jazzfestivalbude.co.uk) Another week-long festival featuring top UK and international musicians.

● **Ilfracombe Carnival** (🖳 www.visitilfracombe.co.uk)   A procession of floats parades though the town on the August bank holiday weekend.

September

● **Appledore Book Festival** (🖳 www.appledorebookfestival.co.uk) Held over a week in late September, this festival attracts many highly regarded authors to the stage.

● **The Doone Run** (🖳 www.facebook.com/doonerun) See box p106.

● **Barnstaple Fair** (🖳 www.barnstapletowncouncil.co.uk/barnstaple-fair.asp) Held for four days beginning on the Wednesday before 20th September with carnivals and processions culminating in a firework 'extravaganza'.

● **Combe Martin Music Festival** (🖳 www.visitcombemartin.com) Takes place over four weekends in September aiming to showcase numerous different musical styles.

● **Clovelly Lobster and Crab Feast** (🖳 www.clovelly.co.uk) Family day out with lobster and crab dishes cooked on the quay.

This list is by no means comprehensive. For further information on other festivals in the area visit: 🖳 www.visitdevon.co.uk, or 🖳 www.exmoor.com.

If continuing along the SWCP you'll find the fun continues over the border in Cornwall (🖳 www.cornwall.gov.uk) too and if still wanting to walk there is a Walking Week in Boscastle (🖳 www.visitboscastleandtintagel.com/events) in late March. Further details on festivals around the Cornish Coast can be found in Trailblazer's guide to *Cornwall Coast Path*, part of this series of books for the SWCP.

Opposite: From Harscott High Cliff (see p198), first sightings of Cornish sand.
Overleaf: Walking towards Great Hangman from Heddon Valley. (Photo © Henry Stedman).

PLANNING YOUR WALK

Practical information for the walker

ROUTE FINDING

For most of its length the coast path is well signposted. At confusing junctions the route is usually indicated by a finger-post sign with 'coast path' written on it. At other points, where there could be some confusion, there are wooden waymark posts with an acorn symbol and a yellow arrow to indicate in which direction you should head. The waymarking is the responsibility of the local authorities along the trail who have a duty to maintain the path. Generally they do a good job but occasionally you will come across sections of the trail where waymarking is ambiguous, or even non-existent, but with the detailed trail maps and directions in this book and the fact that you always have the sea to one side it would be hard to get really lost.

Using GPS with this book

Given the above, modern Wainwrights may scoff while more open-minded walkers will accept that GPS technology can be an inexpensive, well-established if non-essential navigational aid. In no time at all a GPS receiver with a clear view of the sky will establish your position and altitude in a variety of formats, including the British OS grid system, to within a few metres.

The maps in the route guide include numbered waypoints; these correlate to the list on pp206-7, which gives the latitude/longitude position in a decimal minute format as well as a description. Where the path is vague, or there are several options, you will find more waypoints. You can download the complete list of these waypoints for free as a GPS-readable file (that doesn't include the text descriptions) from the Trailblazer website: ⌨ www.trailblazer-guides.com (click on GPS waypoints).

It's also possible to buy state-of-the-art digital mapping to import into your GPS unit, assuming that you have sufficient memory

---

(**Opposite**) Looking east along the Exmoor coastline from near Heddon's Mouth. (Photo © Henry Stedman).

capacity, but it's not the most reliable way of navigating and the small screen on your pocket-sized unit will invariably fail to put places into context or give you the 'big picture'.

Bear in mind that the vast majority of people who tackle this path do so perfectly well without a GPS unit. Instead of rushing out to invest in one, consider putting the money towards good-quality waterproofs or footwear instead.

ACCOMMODATION

The route guide (Part 4) lists a fairly comprehensive selection of places to stay along the length of the trail. You have two main options: camping or using B&Bs and hotels. There is, perhaps, a third option too, that of staying in hostels, though there aren't many on this stretch of the coast path and sometimes they are too far from the path to be a realistic alternative. Few people stick to just one of these options the whole way, preferring, for example, to camp most of the time but spend every third night in a guesthouse, or perhaps use hostels where possible but splash out on a B&B every once in a while.

Note that when booking accommodation that is far from the path, remember to ask if a pick-up and drop-off service is available (usually only B&Bs provide this service); at the end of a tiring day it's nice to know a lift is available to take you to your accommodation rather than having to traipse another two or three miles off the path to get to your bed for the night. (This is particularly true at the end of this section of the SWCP, around Hartland Point, where there are only a few B&Bs and they are usually a fair walk from the path – and the walking is arduous enough as it is around this peninsula.)

The facilities' table on pp30-1 provides a quick snapshot of what type of accommodation is available in each of the towns and villages along the way, while the tables on p32 and p33 provide some suggested itineraries.

Camping

There are campsites all the way along the South-West Coast Path. That said, few people choose to camp every night. You're almost bound to get at least one night where the rain falls relentlessly, soaking equipment and sapping morale, and it is then that most campers opt to spend the next night drying out in a hostel or B&B. There are, however, many advantages with camping; it's more economical, for a start (see opposite).

There are only two stretches of the SWCP described in this book where there is not a campsite (at least nearby) at the end of your day's walk – Westward Ho! and Clovelly. The longest stretch of the Exmoor and North Devon Coast Path not to feature a campsite is that between Abbotsham (Greencliff and Westacott farms), approximately three miles south of Westward Ho!, and Stoke (half a mile inland from Hartland Quay): totalling twenty miles in all; meaning that if you are intending to spend at least one night between duvet and sheet Clovelly would be the place to do so. If you are intent on spending every night outdoors Clovelly, Appledore and Hartland are all linked by public transport (see pp48-50), meaning that with a little planning (services are limited and somewhat convoluted), it is possible to return to/move on to the last/next campsite by bus.

Campsites vary; some are just a quiet corner of a farmer's field, while others are full-blown caravan sites with a few spaces put aside for tents; since their main customers are families on their annual holidays, backpackers are often low on their list of priorities. All the campsites in this book have showers, although, as with the quality of the site, the standard of their facilities can also vary. Camping is an option at YHA Elmscott (see p194) but there is space for only three tents. Note, too, that **wild camping** (ie not in a regular campsite) **is not allowed**.

Camping is not an easy option; the route is wearying enough without carrying your accommodation around with you. Should you decide to camp, therefore, we advise you to look into employing the baggage-transfer company mentioned on p27, though this does, of course, mean it will cost more and that you will lose a certain amount of freedom as you have to tell the company, at least a day before, of your next destination – and stick to it – so that you and your bag can be reunited every evening.

Rates for camping vary from site to site. Most of the sites in this book have a special rate for coastal-path hikers with small 'one-man' tents (£5-23); however, depending on the season, at some you may end up paying for a full pitch (which can be over double the price – even up to £50 for a pitch!).

Note: despite every effort being made to keep this book up-to-date things can change quickly. **You should always contact the campsites that you are planning to stay at to ensure that they are still open/accepting tents.**

Hostels

The Exmoor and North Devon Coast Path is not well served by hostels – there are large swathes where hostels don't exist – so it isn't really feasible to stay in hostels every night. Only two YHA hostels remain open: Minehead, and Elmscott, near Hartland Quay, and even the Minehead one is too far from the path to be of much use. There are, however, good independent hostels at Minehead, Ilfracombe, Croyde and Bude.

Most hostels have dorm rooms (sleeping up to seven people) and private rooms some of which are en suite but mostly facilities are shared. They also have a whole range of facilities from drying rooms to internet access and/or wi-fi as well as fully equipped kitchens for guests to use. Some have a shop selling emergency groceries, snacks and souvenirs. Hostels are good places to meet fellow walkers, swap stories and compare blisters.

If you are travelling in April/May or September you may find some hostels entirely taken over by school groups, leaving walkers shut out. Contact the YHA or the relevant hostel to find out the exact opening dates. Finally, the cost of staying in a hostel (around £16-20pp for a dorm bed, plus an additional £3pp per night for non-members of the YHA), once breakfast has been added on, is in most instances not that much cheaper than staying in a B&B. Contact the **Youth Hostels Association of England and Wales** (YHA; ☎ 0800 019 1700 or ☎ 01629-592700, 🖳 www.yha.org.uk) for details of membership and also to book hostels.

Bed and breakfast accommodation

Bed and Breakfasts (B&Bs) are a great British institution and many of those along the South-West Coast Path are absolutely charming.

Nearly all the B&Bs on this route have either en suite rooms or rooms with private facilities; only a few have rooms with shared facilities. The rooms usually contain either a double bed (known as a double room), or two single beds (known as a twin room). Some rooms sleep three (Tr) or four people (Qd); these are often called family rooms. Generally this means there is a double bed (which two people may need to share) with one or two single beds, or bunk beds.

Note that in winter some B&Bs close; for those that stay open, make sure that beforehand they will have their heating in your room turned on!

An evening meal (usually £15-20) is often provided at the more remote or bigger places, but almost always needs to be booked at least 24 hours in

❑ Should you book your accommodation in advance?

When walking any section of the South-West Coast Path it's essential that you have your night's accommodation booked by the time you set off in the morning, whether you're planning to stay in a hostel or a B&B. Nothing is more deflating than to arrive at your destination at the day's end only to find that you've then got to walk a further five miles or so, or even take a detour, because everywhere in town is booked.

That said, there's a certain amount of hysteria regarding the booking of accommodation, with many websites, B&Bs and other organisations suggesting you book at least six months in advance. Whilst it's true that the earlier you book the more chance you have of getting precisely the accommodation you require, booking so far in advance does leave you vulnerable to changing circumstances. Booking a full six months before setting foot on the trail is all very well if everything goes to plan but if you break your leg just before you're due to set off or, God forbid, there's another outbreak of foot and mouth, all you're going to end up with is a lot of lost deposits. By not booking so far in advance, you give yourself the chance to shift your holiday plans to a later date should the unforeseen arise.

In my experience, the lack of **B&B-style accommodation** is not as bad as some suggest, at least not outside the high season (ie the summer period coinciding with the long school holidays in the UK). Outside this period, and particularly in April/May or September, as long as you're flexible and willing to take what's offered, with maybe even a night or two in a hostel if that's all there is, you should get away with booking just a few nights in advance, or indeed just the night before. The exceptions to this rule are at weekends and in the high season, when everywhere is busy; at these times you should book as soon as you can, especially if you want to stay in a particular place. However, it is essential to be aware that most places require a minimum booking of two nights unless the booking is near the actual date required.

Campers, however, have more flexibility and can often just turn up and find a space there and then, though ringing in advance can't hurt. The exception is at Bude, where you should phone well in advance especially at weekends and in summer.

If staying in **hostels**, the same applies though do be careful when travelling out of high season as sometimes hostels are fully booked by school or other groups and shut altogether from around November to Easter. Once again, it's well worth phoning at least one night before and well before that if it's a weekend, to make sure the hostel isn't fully booked.

advance. (Note that if you have any dietary requirements – eg if you're vegetarian, or need a gluten-free meal, you should mention this when requesting the meal.) Alternatively, if you want to eat out, there's nearly always a pub or restaurant nearby or, if it's far, the B&B owner may give you a lift to and from the nearest place with food.

The difference between a B&B and a **guesthouse** is minimal, though some of the better guesthouses are more like hotels, offering evening meals and a lounge for guests. **Pubs** and **inns** also offer bed and breakfast accommodation and prices are generally no more than in a regular B&B. **Hotels** usually *do* cost more than B&Bs, however, and some might be a little incensed by a bunch of smelly walkers turning up and treading mud into their carpet. Most on the South-West Coast Path, however, are used to seeing walkers and welcome them warmly.

Rates Proprietors quote their **tariffs** either on a **per person** (pp) basis, or **per room**. Room rates are the same whether one or two people share. Accommodation in this guide starts at around £25pp (assuming two people are sharing) for the most basic B&Bs rising to around £50pp for the most luxurious places. Most charge around £30-40pp. Prices in hotels start at around £35pp; however, sometimes rates are for the room only and breakfast is additional. Solo walkers should take note: single rooms are not so easy to find and you will often end up occupying a double/twin room and are likely to have to pay a single occupancy supplement (from £10).

Most places now have their own website and offer online/email **booking** but for some you will need to phone. Note, that it can be worth contacting the proprietors direct as this may lead to better rates than via an online booking agent. Most places ask for a deposit (about 50%) which is generally non-refundable if you cancel at short notice. Some places may charge 100% if the booking is for one night only, or they may require a stay of at least two nights (see box opposite). Always let the owner know as soon as possible if you have to cancel your booking so they can offer the bed to someone else.

Airbnb
The rise and rise of Airbnb (🖥 www.airbnb.co.uk) has seen private homes and apartments opened up to overnight travellers on an informal basis. While accommodation is primarily based in cities, the concept is spreading to tourist hotspots in more rural areas, but do check thoroughly what you are getting and the precise location. While the first couple of options listed may be in the area you're after, others may be too far afield for walkers. At its best, this is a great way to meet local people in a relatively unstructured environment, but do be aware that these places are not registered B&Bs, so standards may vary, and prices may not necessarily be any lower than the norm.

FOOD AND DRINK

Breakfast and lunch
Stay in a B&B and you'll be filled to the gills with a cooked **English breakfast**. This usually consists of a bowl of cereal followed by a plateful of eggs, bacon,

sausages, mushrooms, tomatoes and possibly baked beans or black pudding, with toast and butter, and all washed down with coffee, tea and/or juice. Enormously satisfying the first time you try it, by the fourth or fifth morning you may start to prefer a lighter continental breakfast. If you have had enough of these cooked breakfasts and/or plan an early start, ask if you can have a packed lunch instead of breakfast. Your landlady or hostel can usually provide a **packed lunch** at an additional cost (unless it's in lieu of breakfast), though of course there's nothing to stop you preparing your own lunch (but do bring a penknife if you plan to do this), or going to a pub (see opposite) or café.

Remember, to plan ahead: certain stretches of the walk are virtually devoid of eating places (the stretch from Porlock Weir to Lynmouth/Lynton, and from Combe Martin to Ilfracombe, or the final stretch from Hartland Quay to Bude) so read ahead about the next day's walk in Part 4 to make sure you never go hungry.

Cream teas

Whatever you do for lunch, don't forget to leave some room for a cream tea (see box below) or two, a morale, energy and cholesterol booster all rolled into one delicious package: a pot of tea accompanied by scones served with cream and jam, and sometimes a cake or two. The jury is out on whether you should put the jam on first or the cream but either way do not miss the chance of at least one cream tea.

❏ **Traditional food in Somerset and Devon**

● **Somerset** As a major centre of farming and fishing, it's not surprising that the South-West is a major supplier of food to the rest of Britain and can boast some pretty fine local specialities. In Somerset – literally, 'Land of the Summer People' – fruit is unsurprisingly bountiful with **apples**, the main ingredient for their legendary cider (see box opposite) particularly renowned. However, the **cheeses** of Somerset are perhaps its most famous export, with the name Cheddar used throughout the world, though only The Cheddar Gorge Cheese Company actually produces the cheese within the parish of Cheddar.

● **Devon** Say 'Devon' to most Brits and in addition to images of sparkling coastlines and rolling hills, the county's name will also conjure up the delights of **clotted cream** – best enjoyed as part of a traditional **cream tea** with a scone or two and some whortleberry jam. This is an Exmoor speciality, **whortleberry** being the local name for wild bilberry (though they go by several other names including blueberry, heidelberry, huckleberry, hurtleberry and wimberry) and locally they're called 'worts' or 'urts'. **Dairy products** as a whole are plentiful in this corner of the country including delicious yoghurts and ice-cream.

In the sea, South Devon **crab** is reputed to be the tastiest in the world and smoked eels are a speciality in these parts too. Other **fish** caught in the Bristol Channel include thornback ray, bass, conger, dogfish, flounder, whiting, dab pout, cod and codling. There's also shellfish: lobsters, crabs, scallops, langoustines, clams and mussels, which are often fished for from the smaller coastal villages.

Even if you're on a tight budget the ubiquitous **fish & chips** can be satisfying if cooked with fresh fish. At the other end of the scale there are plenty of restaurants around the coast offering mouth-watering dishes concocted from locally caught fish.

Evening meals

Pubs are as much a feature of the walk as seagulls and sheep, and in some cases the pub is as much a tourist attraction as any Roman fort or ruined priory. The Ship Inn at Porlock, The Rising Sun at Lynmouth, The Hunters Inn, nestled in the Heddon Valley, The Pack o' Cards at Combe Martin, harbour-side Red Lion Hotel at Clovelly, 14th-century Bush Inn at Morwenstow ... the list goes on.

❏ BEERS AND CIDERS

Beers The process of brewing beer is believed to have been in Britain since the Neolithic period and is an art local brewers have been perfecting ever since. Real ale is beer that has been brewed using traditional methods. Real ales are not filtered or pasteurised, a process which removes and kills all the yeast cells, but instead undergo a secondary fermentation at the pub which enhances the natural flavours and brings out the individual characteristics of the beer. It's served at cellar temperature with no artificial fizz added unlike keg beer which is pasteurised and has the fizz added by injecting nitrogen dioxide.

Based in the Somerset town of Wiveliscombe on the border of the national park, **Exmoor Ale**s (🖳 www.exmoorales.co.uk) produces five permanent ales, including Exmoor Stag and Exmoor Beast (6.6%), named after Exmoor's most famous modern mystery (see box p66), and five seasonal ales. Nearby, **Cotleigh Brewery** (🖳 www .cotleighbrewery.com) was originally based in Devon but moved to Wiveliscombe after just one year of trading. They brew around half a dozen real ales, each named after a member of the local avifauna such as Barn Owl or Buzzard. Next door, Devon is well served with breweries with, according to a CAMRA study, 28 micro-breweries operating within its borders including **Barum Brewery** (🖳 www.barumbrewery.co .uk), a tiny brewery based at Reform Inn in Pilton near Barnstaple. They are responsible for the dangerously strong 6.6% ABV Barnstablasta!

Country Life Brewery (🖳 www.countrylifebrewery.co.uk) is in The Big Sheep attraction at Abbotsham, nr Bideford; you can watch the brewing process and pick up a couple of bottles of tipples such as Black Boar (4.5%) or Old Appledore Ale (3.7%). Further west along the trail, **Forge Brewery** (🖳 www.forge-brewery.co.uk) in Hartland is continuing a proud tradition of brewing that was started by the Augustinian monks at the abbey. They have nine real ales to choose from. **FatBelly Ales** (🖳 the cottageinnlynton.co.uk/fatbelly-ales) is based at The Cottage Inn in Lynmouth.

Ciders A pint of cider on this section of the walk is pretty much as obligatory as blisters. Somerset in particular is known for its cider farms with: **Sheppy's** (🖳 shep pyscider.com) at Bradford-on-Tone; **Torre Cider** (🖳 www.torrecider.co.uk) at Washford, Watchet; **Parson's Choice Cider** (🖳 www.parsonschoicecider.co.uk) at West Lyng; **Perry's Cider** (🖳 www.perryscider.co.uk) of Ilminster; **Hecks** (🖳 www .heckscider.com) at Street, and **The Somerset Cider Brandy Co** (🖳 www.cider brandy.co.uk) at Martock – though none is particularly near the path. Across the border, **Ostlers** (🖳 ostlerscidermill.co.uk) is a family-run cider mill based in Goodleigh near Barnstaple, Devon, that churns out scrumpy ciders, vinegars and chutneys.

Scrumpy, or rough cider, is a particular form of cider, easy to differentiate from the weaker, more mass-market keg ciders, being cloudy, fizz-free and with bits floating in it too! The only thing to remember before drinking scrumpy is that it should be done in moderation – it's powerful stuff. After you've drunk it, you'll be lucky to remember anything at all.

PLANNING YOUR WALK

Most pubs have become highly attuned to the desires of walkers and offer lunch and evening meals (often with a couple of local dishes and almost always a few vegetarian, and now also vegan and gluten-free, options), some locally brewed beers, a garden to relax in on hot days and a roaring fire to huddle around on cold ones. The standard of the food varies widely, though is usually served in big portions, which is often just about all walkers care about at the end of a long day. In many of the villages the pub is the only place to eat out. Note that pubs may close in the afternoon, especially in the winter months, so check

---

❏ **Information for foreign visitors**

● **Currency** The British pound (£) comes in notes of £100, £50, £20, £10 and £5, and coins of £2 and £1. The pound is divided into 100 pence (usually referred to as 'p', pronounced 'pee') which come in silver coins of 50p, 20p, 10p and 5p, and copper coins of 2p and 1p.

● **Money** Up-to-date **rates of exchange** can be found on 🖳 www.xe.com/currency converter, at some post offices, or at any bank or travel agent. **Travellers' cheques** can be cashed only at banks, foreign exchanges and some of the large hotels; it is probably better to use a debit card or bring cash.

● **Business hours** Most **village shops** are open Monday to Friday 9am-5pm and Saturday 9am-12.30pm, though some open as early as 7.30/8am; many also open on Sundays but not usually for the whole day. Occasionally you'll come across a local shop that closes at lunchtime on one day during the week, usually a Wednesday or Thursday; this is a throwback to the days when all towns and villages had an 'early closing day'. **Supermarkets** are open Monday to Saturday 8am-8pm (sometimes longer) and on Sunday from about 9am to 5 or 6pm, though main branches of supermarkets generally open 10am-4pm or 11am-5pm.

Main **post offices** generally open Monday to Friday 9am-5pm and Saturday 9am-12.30pm; **banks** typically open at 9.30/10am Monday to Friday and close at 3.30/4pm, though in some places both post offices and banks may open only two or three days a week and/or in the morning, or limited hours, only. **ATMs (cash machines)** located outside a bank, shop, post office or petrol station are open all the time, but any that are inside will be accessible only when that place is open. However, ones that charge, such as Link machines, may not accept foreign-issued cards.

Pub hours are less predictable as each pub may have different opening hours. However, most pubs on the Path open daily 11am-11pm (some close at 10.30pm on Sunday) but **some close in the afternoon**. The last entry time to most **museums and galleries** is usually half an hour, or an hour, before the official closing time.

● **National holidays** Most businesses in the South-West are shut on 1 January, Good Friday (March/April), Easter Monday (March/April), first and last Monday in May, last Monday in August, 25 December and 26 December.

● **School holidays** State-school holidays in England are generally as follows: a one-week break late October, two weeks over Christmas and the New Year, a week mid February, two weeks around Easter, one week at the end of May/early June (to coincide with the bank holiday at the end of May) and five to six weeks from late July to early September. Private-school holidays fall at the same time, but tend to be slightly longer.

● **Documents** If you are a member of a National Trust organisation in your country bring your membership card as you should be entitled to free entry to National Trust properties and sites in the UK. See also p39.

in advance if you are hoping to visit a particular one, and also if you are planning lunch there as food serving hours can change.

That other great British culinary institution, the **fish 'n' chip shop**, can be found in virtually every town on the trail. As well as the chippies, there are other **takeaways** (Chinese, Indian etc) in the larger towns en route.

Buying camping supplies

There is a grocery shop of some description in most of the places along the route, though most are small (and often combined with the post office) and

- **EHICs and travel insurance** Although Britain's National Health Service (NHS) is free at the point of use, that is only the case for residents. All visitors to Britain should be properly insured, including comprehensive health coverage. The European Health Insurance Card (EHIC) entitles EU nationals (on production of the EHIC card so ensure you bring it with you) to necessary medical treatment under the NHS while on a temporary visit here. For details, contact your national social security institution. However, this is not a substitute for proper medical cover on your travel insurance for unforeseen bills and for getting you home should that be necessary. Also consider cover for loss and theft of personal belongings, especially if you are camping or staying in hostels, as there will be times when you'll have to leave your luggage unattended.
- **Weights and measures** In Britain, milk is sold in pints (1 pint = 568ml), as is beer in pubs, though most other liquid including petrol (gasoline) and diesel is sold in litres. Distances on road and path signs are given in miles (1 mile = 1.6km) rather than kilometres, and yards (1yd = 0.9m) rather than metres. The population remains divided between those who still use inches (1 inch = 2.5cm), feet (1ft = 0.3m) and yards and those who are happy with millimetres, centimetres and metres; you'll often be told that 'it's only a hundred yards or so' to somewhere, rather than a hundred metres or so. Most food is sold in metric weights (g and kg) but the imperial weights of pounds (lb: 1lb = 453g) and ounces (oz: 1oz = 28g) are frequently displayed too. The weather – a frequent topic of conversation – is also an issue: while most forecasts predict temperatures in Celsius (C), many people continue to think in terms of Fahrenheit (F; see the temperature chart on p15 for conversions).
- **Smoking** The ban on smoking in public places relates not only to pubs and restaurants, but also to B&Bs, hostels and hotels. These latter have the right to designate one or more bedrooms where the occupants can smoke, but the ban is in force in all enclosed areas open to the public – even if they are in a private home such as a B&B. Should you be foolhardy enough to light up in a no-smoking area, which includes pretty well any indoor public place, you could be fined £50, but it's the owners of the premises who carry the can if they fail to stop you, with a potential fine of £2500.
- **Time** During the winter, the whole of Britain is on Greenwich Meantime (GMT). The clocks move one hour forward on the last Sunday in March, remaining on British Summer Time (BST) until the last Sunday in October.
- **Telephone** From outside Britain the international country access code for Britain is ☎ 44 followed by the area code minus the first 0, and then the number you require. Within Britain, to call a landline number with the same code as the landline phone you are calling from, the code can be omitted. If your mobile phone is registered overseas, consider buying a local SIM card to keep costs down. See also box p39.
- **Emergency services** For police, ambulance, fire or coastguard dial ☎ 999 or ☎ 112.

whether you'll be able to find precisely what you went in for is highly unlikely. If self-catering, therefore, your menu for the evening will depend upon what you found in the store that day. Part 4 details what shops are on the path.

Drinking water

On a hot day in some of the remoter parts after a steep climb or two you'll quickly dehydrate, which is at best highly unpleasant and at worst mightily dangerous. Always carry water with you and in hot weather drink 3-4 litres a day. Don't be tempted by the water in the streams; if the cow or sheep faeces in the water don't make you ill, the chemicals from the pesticides and fertilisers used on the farms almost certainly will. Using iodine or another purifying treatment will help to combat the former, though there's little you can do about the latter. It's a lot safer to fill up from taps instead.

MONEY

There are several banks on the trail, most equipped with an **ATM** (cash machine/cashpoint). You'll also find ATMs in many shops and stores though these often charge around £1.75 to withdraw money. The only place where you need to be careful is from Westward Ho! to Bude where there are no ATMs on the path (the nearest place to get money being Hartland, 2½ miles inland). Make sure you take enough cash out at Westward Ho!. Another way of getting money in your hand is to use the **cashback system**: find a store that will accept a debit card and when you are paying for whatever you are buying (usually a minimum of £5) ask them to advance cash against the card you are using.

Not all local stores, pubs and B&Bs accept credit or debit cards so it is essential to carry plenty of cash with you, though do keep it safe and out of sight (preferably in a moneybelt).

Using the Post Office for banking

Several banks have agreements with the Post Office (PO) allowing customers to make cash withdrawals free of charge using a debit card at branches throughout the country. Given that many towns and villages have post offices this is a very useful facility. However, check with the Post Office Helpline (☎ 0345-611 2970, 🖳 www.postoffice.co.uk/branch-finder) that your bank has an agreement with the post office and that the post offices en route are still open and have an ATM. If using the website put in the place name and you will be told if there is a PO there or nearby as well as the opening days/hours and services.

OTHER SERVICES

There is **internet access** in the libraries along the trail as well as at several shops and other private enterprises. Many pubs, restaurants and B&Bs also have wi-fi, useful for those who've brought their own laptop/mobile. In addition to a grocery store some villages and most towns have a **launderette**, **chemist/pharmacy**, **public toilets** and a **phone box**. There are **outdoor equipment shops** in Minehead, Porlock, Combe Martin, Woolacombe, Barnstaple and Bude.

WALKING COMPANIES

It is, of course, possible to turn up with your boots and backpack at Minehead and just start walking, with little planned save for your accommodation (see box on p20). The following companies, however, are in the business of making your holiday as stress-free and enjoyable as possible.

Baggage transfer

For those who don't fancy being burdened while on the path, it is possible to arrange to have your luggage transferred to the end of each day's destination. The main baggage company on the SWCP is the aptly named **Luggage Transfers** (☎ 01326-567247, ☎ 0800-043 7927, 🖳 www.luggagetransfers.co .uk), who cover the whole of the path, charging from £7.50 per bag for a two-bag transfer (max weight 25kg per piece of luggage); any journey can be quoted for. They deliver anywhere including campsites (as long as you have rung the campsite by the night before to give your name).

Alternatively, some of the **taxi** firms listed in this guide can provide a similar service within a local area if you want a break from carrying your bags for a day or so. Also, don't rule out the possibility of your B&B/guesthouse owner taking your bags ahead for you; plenty of them are glad to do so. Depending on the distance they may make no charge at all, or charge £10-15; this may be less than a taxi so is worth enquiring about.

Self-guided holidays

Useful for those who simply don't have the time to organise their trip, several companies now offer what are known as self-guided holidays, where your accommodation, transport at the start/end of the walk and baggage transportation along the trail are arranged for you.

Unless specified, all the companies below offer walks on the whole South-West Coast Path (SWCP) and they can tailor-make holidays if required. Detailed information and maps are also provided as a matter of course, thereby allowing you to just turn up and start marching!

● **Absolute Escapes** (☎ 0131-240 1210, 🖳 www.absoluteescapes.com; Edinburgh) Only offer walks on the other parts of the SWCP but can tailor make a holiday for this section of the SWCP.
● **Contours** (☎ 01629-821900, 🖳 www.contours.co.uk; Derbyshire) They divide the SWCP into 10 sections and their itineraries from Minehead to Westward Ho! last six, seven and eleven days. They offer dog-friendly hikes.
● **Encounter Walking Holidays** (☎ 01208-871066, 🖳 encounterwalkingholi days.com; Cornwall) Specialise in assisting overseas walkers along the route.
● **Explore Britain** (☎ 01740-650900, 🖳 www.explorebritain.com; Co Durham) Walks include Minehead to Barnstaple (6 days) and Minehead to Woolacombe (5 days).
● **Footpath Holidays** (☎ 01985-840049, 🖳 www.footpath-holidays.com; Wilts) Arrange a 6-day Exmoor Coast walk from Minehead to Instow, and a 5-day section along the North Devon Coast from Instow to Bude.

- **Let's Go Walking!** (☎ 01837-880075, 🖳 www.southwestcoastpathwalking holidays.com; Devon) Offers 8-day walks (Minehead to Barnstaple & Barnstaple to Crackington Haven (Cornwall), with an optional trip to Lundy Island.
- **Load off your back** (☎ 01707-386800, 🖳 www.loadoffyourback.co.uk; Herts) The 'self-guiding' arm of Ramblers Walking Holidays offers a range of itineraries.
- **Macs Adventure** (☎ 0141-530 5409, 🖳 www.macsadventure.com; Glasgow) Have walks covering the whole SWCP including Minehead to Westward Ho! (6-7 days) and Westward Ho! to Padstow (6-8 days).
- **Nearwater Walking Holidays** (☎ 01326-279278, 🖳 www.nearwaterwalking holidays.co.uk; Truro) Walks covering the whole path as well as sections.
- **The Walking Holiday Company** (☎ 01600-713008, 🖳 www.thewalkinglholi daycompany.co.uk; Monmouth) SWCP north section from Minehead to St Ives (Cornwall) in 6-8 walking days
- **Walk the Trail** (☎ 01326-567252, 🖳 www.walkthetrail.co.uk; Cornwall) Have walks from Minehead to Westward Ho! and Westward Ho! to Bude with itineraries to suit all levels of walking ability.
- **Westcountry Walking Holidays** (☎ 03303-501348, 🖳 www.westcountry-walking-holidays.com; Norfolk) Specialise in walking holidays in south-west England and offer a range of itineraries to suit all requirements and abilities.

Group/guided walking tour

This is ideal for those who want the extra safety, security and companionship that comes with walking in a group. Accommodation, meals, transport to and from the trail, baggage transfer – all of these are usually included in the price.

- **HF Holidays** (☎ 0345-470 7558, 🖳 www.hfholidays.co.uk; Herts) Offers guided walks to various parts of the SWCP including the 7-night Somerset & North Devon Coast Path (Minehead to Croyde).

Budgeting

England is not a cheap place to go travelling and the accommodation providers on the South-West Coast Path are more than used to seeing tourists and charge accordingly. You may think before you set out that you are going to try to keep your budget to a minimum by camping every night and cooking your own food but it's a rare walker who sticks to this rule. Besides, the B&Bs and pubs on the route are amongst the path's major attractions and it would be a pity not to sample the hospitality in at least some of them.

If the only expenses of this walk were accommodation and food, budgeting for the trip would be a piece of cake. Unfortunately, in addition there are all the little **extras** that push up the cost of your trip: getting to and from the path, beer, cream teas, stamps and postcards, internet access, buses here and there, baggage carriers, phone calls, laundry, souvenirs, entrance fees ... it's surprising how much all of these things add up.

CAMPING

Coastal-path hikers with small 'one-man' tents may be charged anything from £5 to £23 depending on the campsite. You could survive on less than £15 per person (pp) if you use the cheapest campsites, don't visit a pub, avoid all the museums and tourist attractions in the towns, cook all your own food from staple ingredients and generally have a pretty miserable time of it. Even then, unforeseen expenses will probably nudge your daily budget above this figure. Include the occasional pint, and perhaps a pub meal every now and then, and the figure will be nearer £20-30pp a day.

HOSTELS

Rates at the (independent and YHA) hostels on or near the path range from £13pp to £30pp, although YHA rates depend on whether or not you are a member. These rates don't usually include breakfast but you may be able to order one for around £5; which means that, overall, it can cost around £30-40pp per day, or £40-50pp to live in a little more comfort and enjoy the odd beer or two.

B&Bs, PUBS, GUESTHOUSES AND HOTELS

[See also pp20-1] B&B rates start at £25pp per night but can be at least twice this, particularly if you are walking alone and are thus liable to pay single supplements. Add the cost of lunch and dinner and you should reckon on about £40-45pp minimum. Staying in a guesthouse or hotel will push the minimum up to £55-60pp.

Itineraries

To help you plan your walk the **colour maps** at the back of the book have **profile charts**; there is also a **distance chart** and a **planning map**.

The **table of village/town facilities** (pp30-1) gives a run-down on the essential information you will need regarding accommodation possibilities and services.

SUGGESTED ITINERARIES

The itineraries in the boxes on p32 and on p33 are based on different accommodation types (camping or B&B-style accommodation), each divided into three options depending on your walking speed. They are only suggestions so feel free to adapt them. Don't forget to **add on your travelling time** before and after the walk.
(cont'd on p32)

PLANNING YOUR WALK

VILLAGE AND

Place name (Places in brackets are a short walk off the path)	Distance from previous place § approx miles/km	Bank/ ATM ≠ (Cash machine)*	Post Office	Tourist Information Centre (TIC) National Park Centre (NPC)
Minehead	0	✔	✔	TIC
Bossington	**6/9.7**			
(Porlock)	(1.25/2)	✔	✔	TIC
Porlock Weir	**3/4.8**			
Countisbury	**10.75/17.3**			
Lynmouth	**1.5/2.4**	✔		NPC
Lynton	**0.25/0.4**	✔	✔	TIC
Combe Martin	**13.5/21.7**	✔	✔	TIC
Watermouth	**2/3.2**			
Hele	2.75/4.4			
Ilfracombe	**1/1.6**	✔	✔	TIC
Lee Bay (& Lee)	**3/4.8** (0.25/0.4)			
Woolacombe	**5.5/8.8**	✔	✔	TIC
Croyde	**6.25/10.1**	✔	✔	
Saunton	**2.25/3.6**			
Braunton	**6.25/10.1**	✔	✔	TIC
Chivenor	**1.25/2**			
Barnstaple	**3.75/6**	✔	✔	TIC
Fremington Quay	**2.5/4**			
Instow	**5/8**	✔±	✔	
Bideford (& East-the-Water)	**2.75/4.4**	✔	✔	TIC
(Northam)	1.25/2			
Appledore	**2.25/3.6**	±	✔	TIP
Westward Ho!	**4.75/7.6**	✔	✔	
(Abbotsham)	(1.5/2.4)			
Clovelly (& Higher Clovelly)	**11/17.7** (0.75/1.25)			VC
Hartland Quay	**10.5/16.9**			
(Stoke)	(0.5/0.8)			
(Hartland)	(2.5/4)	✔±	✔	
(Elmscott)	(2/3.2)			
(Morwenstow)	(8/12.9)			
Bude	**15.5/24.9**	✔	✔	TIC

TOTAL DISTANCE   **124.5 miles/200.3km**

§ The distances between a place **and the previous place** *on* the path are given in brackets; distances in **bold** are between places directly on the trail.

TOWN FACILITIES

Eating Place ✔=one ✔✔=two ✔✔✔=three + (✔)=seasonal	Food Store	Campsite * means campsite is a short distance away	Hostels YHA/ H (Ind Hostel)	B&B-style accommodation ✔=one ✔✔=two ✔✔✔=three+	Place name (Places in brackets are a short walk off the path)
✔✔✔	✔	✔	YHA/H	✔✔	**Minehead**
✔				✔	**Bossington**
✔✔✔	✔	✔≠		✔✔✔	(**Porlock**)
✔✔✔	✔			✔✔	**Porlock Weir**
✔				✔	**Countisbury**
✔✔✔	✔			✔✔✔	**Lynmouth**
✔✔✔	✔	✔≠		✔✔✔	**Lynton**
✔✔✔	✔	✔		✔✔✔	**Combe Martin**
✔		✔		✔	**Watermouth**
✔✔	✔				**Hele**
✔✔✔	✔		H	✔✔	**Ilfracombe**
✔✔					(Lee &) **Lee Bay**
✔✔✔	✔	✔		✔✔✔	**Woolacombe**
✔✔✔	✔	✔	H	✔✔✔	**Croyde**
✔✔		✔≠		✔✔✔	**Saunton**
✔✔✔	✔			✔✔✔	**Braunton**
✔✔	✔	✔			**Chivenor**
✔✔✔	✔			✔✔	**Barnstaple**
✔					**Fremington Quay**
✔✔✔	✔			✔✔	**Instow**
✔✔✔	✔			✔✔✔(E-t-W &)	**Bideford**
		✔		✔✔✔	(**Northam**)
✔✔✔	✔			✔✔✔	**Appledore**
✔✔✔	✔			✔✔✔	**Westward Ho!**
✔		✔≠			(**Abbotsham**)
✔✔✔		✔ (limited hours)		✔✔✔	(HC &) **Clovelly**
✔		✔≠		✔	**Hartland Quay**
				✔✔✔	(**Stoke**)
✔✔✔	✔			✔✔✔	(**Hartland**)
		✔	YHA	✔	(**Elmscott**)
✔✔				✔	(**Morwenstow**)
✔✔✔	✔	✔≠	H	✔✔✔	**Bude**

✔≠   (Greencliff/Westacott Farm 0.5/0.8)

≠ **ATM** ✔ ATM (cash machine/cashpoint) available;   ✔ ATM but charges for use
±   cashback available

PLANNING YOUR WALK

(cont'd from p29) If using public transport to get to the start and end of the walk see the **public transport map and service details and map** on pp48-50. Once you have an idea of your approach turn to Part 4 for detailed information on accommodation, places to eat and other services in each village and town on the route. Also in Part 4 you will find summaries of the route to accompany the detailed trail maps.

CAMPING

	Relaxed		Medium		Fast	
Night	**Place**	**Approx Distance** miles/km	**Place**	**Approx Distance** miles/km	**Place**	**Approx Distance** miles/km
0	Minehead	0	Minehead	0	Minehead	0
1	Porlock*	7.25/11.7	Porlock*	7.25/11.7	Lynton*	22/35.4
2	Lynton*	15.25/24.5	Lynton*	15.25/24.5	Watermouth	16/25.75
3	Watermouth	16/25.75	Combe Martin	14/22.5	Woolacombe	12.25/19.7
4	Woolacombe	12.25/19.7	Woolacombe	14.25/22.9	Chivenor	16/25.7
5	Croyde	6.25/10.1	Saunton*	10.5/16.5	Appledore*	18/29
6	Chivenor	9.75/15.7	Chivenor	9.5/15.3	Clovelly*	16.25/26.2
7	Appledore*	18/29	Appledore*	18/29	H'land Quay*	12/19.3
8	Abbotsham*	8.75/14.1	Clovelly*	16.25/26.2	Bude*	16/25.7
9	Clovelly*	8.5/13.7	Hartland Quay*	11/17.7		
10	Hartland Quay*	11/17.7	Bude*	16/25.7		
11	Bude*	16/25.7				

* Note: In this chart we have included in the mile counts an approximate figure for places where the campsite is out of town. For example, the campsite at **Lynton** is half a mile outside the town, so that those who are staying there have to walk half a mile further to reach it – and another half-mile the next day to return to the path.

The other places where this is relevant are: **Porlock** (quarter of a mile to Sparkhayes Farm Campsite from path); **Saunton** (two miles to Lobb Campsite from path); **Appledore** (Marshford Campsite one mile from Appledore; half a mile from SWCP, see Map 37); **Abbotsham** (Greencliff and Westacott farms half a mile from SWCP); **Clovelly** (campers will need to return to Appledore or catch Stagecoach 319 on to Hartland and walk two miles to Stoke); **Hartland Quay** (half a mile to Stoke Barton Farm from path); **Bude** (from the SWCP at Bude Beach (Cerenety campsite one mile; Upper Lynstone campsite three-quarters of a mile).

❏ Woolacombe to Westward Ho! – two or three stages?

Between Woolacombe and Westward Ho! there are nearly 40 miles of mostly flat and easy walking. For this reason, some choose to cover the miles in just two stages. Whilst doing so means you will get back to the more spectacular parts of the SWCP faster, you also risk exhausting yourself before the final three days to Bude, which are very strenuous indeed. Completing these 40 miles over a longer period of time will allow you to thoroughly explore the towns and villages on the way. There is plenty of accommodation en route so a plethora of itineraries is possible (see above and opposite).

This book splits the journey into three sections, but it can be divided into just two stages, or four or more.

STAYING IN B&B-STYLE ACCOMMODATION

	Relaxed		Medium		Fast	
Night	Place	Approx Distance miles/km	Place	Approx Distance miles/km	Place	Approx Distance miles/km
0	Minehead	0	Minehead	0	Minehead	0
1	Porlock Weir	9/14.5	Porlock Weir	9/14.5	Lynmouth	21.25/34.2
2	Lynmouth	12.25/19.7	Lynmouth	12.25/19.7	Ilfracombe	19.5/31.3
3	Combe Martin	13.75/22.1	Combe Martin	13.75/22.1	Croyde	14.75/23.7
4	Ilfracombe	5.75/9.3	Woolacombe	14.25/22.9	Barnstaple	13.5/21.7
5	Woolacombe	8.5/13.7	Braunton	14.75/23.7	W'ward Ho!	18.5/29.8
6	Saunton	8.5/13.7	Instow	12.5/20.1	Clovelly	11/17.7
7	Barnstaple	11.25/18.1	Westward Ho!	11/17.7	H'land Quay	10.5/16.9
8	Instow	7.5/12.1	Clovelly	11/17.7	Bude	15.5/25
9	Appledore	6.25/10.1	Hartland Quay	10.5/16.9		
10	Westward Ho!	4.75/7.6	Morwenstow	8/12.9		
11	Clovelly	11/17.7	Bude	7.5/12.1		
12	Hartland Quay	10.5/16.9				
13	Morwenstow	8/12.9				
14	Bude	7.5/12.1				

WHICH DIRECTION?

It's more common for walkers attempting the entire trail to start from Minehead and head west. This is also the logical way to walk and thus the way we have chosen to describe the route in Part 4. If this is your first taste of the South-West Coast Path – but think you may like to do it all one day – obviously this is the way to head, with the Cornwall section next up. Furthermore, many will argue that Bude is a more picturesque place to celebrate the end of your walk than Minehead!

That said, this may of course be the final leg of your walk on the South-West Coast Path and thus Bude to Minehead would probably be the way to go. What's more, the prevailing wind usually comes from the west, so by walking in this direction you'll find you have the weather behind you, pushing you on rather than driving in your face. If you prefer to swim against the tide of popular opinion and walk west to east you should find it easy to use this book too.

THE BEST DAY AND WEEKEND WALKS

Trying to pick one particular section that is representative of the entire trail is impossible because each is very different. The wilds of Exmoor, the beaches of Woolacombe and Croyde, the estuaries of Bideford and Barnstaple, and the windswept cliff-top beauty of Hartland – each region enjoys its own character and to think that, by visiting one, you have a flavour of the entire region, is erroneous. That said, if you don't have the time to walk the entire route the following will allow you to savour at least some of the joys of the Exmoor and

PLANNING YOUR WALK

North Devon Coast Path. The main obstacle to preparing a short itinerary of a few days or less along the coast path is the lack of regular transport connections to towns and villages on the way. For example, on possibly the most spectacular part of the entire SWCP, Clovelly to Bude, public transport is scarce and it is thus very difficult to divide this section into day walks. However, if you have three days spare this section is both achievable and most definitely worth it!

All of the routes below are designed to link up with public transport (see pp48-50) at both their start and finish.

❏ **Other trails**

Whilst the SWCP follows the coastline of Exmoor, other walking trails meander through its interior and some, at points, cross over or join the coastal path.

● **The Coleridge Way** (🖥 www.visit-exmoor.co.uk/coleridge-way)   Starting in Nether Stowey, where Coleridge lived from 1797, The Coleridge Way crosses 36 miles of the Quantock Hills, Brendon Hills and Exmoor, ending in Porlock (where the Man who notoriously interrupted the writing of the poet's *Kubla Khan* originated).

In 1956 the Quantock Hills was the first area of England to be designated an Area of Outstanding Natural Beauty (AONB). The trail is well-serviced by pubs and tea-rooms.

● **The Tarka Trail** (🖥 www.northdevonbiosphere.org.uk/the-tarka-trail.html) Following in the paw-steps of Henry Williamson's famous *Tarka the Otter*, this 180-mile path runs in the shape of a figure-of-eight and centres on Barnstaple. It joins the SWCP at Lynton and colludes with it as far south as Bideford.

The stretch between Braunton and Meeth is part of Sustrans' National Cycle Network, and there's a section where you even take a train! Whilst the chances of seeing an otter are slim there is an abundance of other wildlife to be seen.

● **The Two Moors Way/Erme-Plym Trail** (🖥 www.devon.gov.uk/twomoorsway .pdf) The Erme-Plym Trail begins in Wembury on the South Devon coast and travels as far north as Ivybridge where The Two Moors Way begins. Climbing onto Dartmoor can be strenuous but the effort is worth it.

The trail then heads north, traversing the length of Dartmoor to Drewsteignton before passing through Morchard Bishop and Witheridge, eventually entering Exmoor from the south before culminating in Lynmouth. Splendid scenery and real solitude are just two of the joys of this trip.

● **The Samaritans Way** (🖥 www.samaritansway-southwest.org.uk) Beginning at Clifton Suspension Bridge in Bristol this 100-mile jaunt heads south through the Mendip Hills to Glastonbury before turning west and passing through the Quantock Hills and Exmoor to end in Lynton.

For those after a really long walk, The Samaritans Way can be joined to The Cotswold Way via The River Avon trail which runs from Bath to Bristol.

● **West Somerset Coast Path** (WSCP; 🖥 www.somerset.gov.uk; use the website's search function to find the link to a pdf booklet about the path) Significantly shorter than the SWCP, the WSCP travels approximately 25 miles from the tiny settlement of Steart, via the Quantock Hills AONB, passing both Watchet harbour and Dunster beach en route to Minehead; meaning, that if you wish to, you could make the SWCP even more of a challenge!

Day walks
Minehead to Porlock   (7½ miles/12km; see pp79-89)
A splendid introduction to Exmoor with varied terrain, tremendous views out to
sea as well as the option of an alternative rugged route. Parts of this walk are
quite tough – although the hardest part may well be turning back and going
home after just one day.

Lynton to Combe Martin   (13½ miles/22.1km; see pp105-17)
You may wish to get up early for this one, a long and strenuous day's walk that
will truly whet your appetite for both Exmoor and the coastal path. Highlights
include the extraordinary Valley of Rocks as well as the SWCP's highest point
– Great Hangman.

Woolacombe to Croyde   (6¼ miles/10km; see pp134-40)
A moderate to easy day's walk that could be completed in one morning. There
is the option of either walking through Woolacombe Warren or making your
way along the beach before both paths unite for a stroll around Baggy Point: the
views from here over Croyde Bay and Saunton Sands are terrific.

Croyde to Braunton   (8¾ miles/14km; see pp140-8)
Ambling hand-in-hand with the Tarka Trail around Saunton Down and through
the Braunton Burrows, this is an easy to moderate day's walk.

Bideford to Westward Ho!   (8¼ miles/13.2km; see pp164-75)
An easy day's walk that includes both the lovely village of Appledore – an ideal
location for lunch – and Northam Burrows Country Park.

Weekend walks – 2-3 days
● **Exmoor: Porlock Weir to Combe Martin**(26 miles/41.8km; see pp92-117)
A strenuous couple of days with an overnight stop in Lynmouth/Lynton; this
section offers some of the best walking in England – fact!
● **Beaches and Burrows: Ilfracombe to Braunton (23½ miles/38km; see
pp120-48)** This is a relatively easy couple of days; highlights include the
beaches of Woolacombe and Saunton as well as Braunton Burrows.
● **The best of the best: Westward Ho! to Bude (37 miles/59.5km; see pp172-
205)** A long, strenuous and truly spectacular three-day walk, but the scenery is
some of the best on the entire SWCP. Highlights include the village of Clovelly
and the remarkably dramatic views of the sunset over the Atlantic at Hartland
Quay.

SIDE TRIPS

The South-West Coast Path cuts through some of the richest walking territory
in the UK and there are plenty of opportunities for short (or long) diversions off
the trail. Such trips are beyond the scope of this book but a glance at the box
opposite and an Ordnance Survey map will give you some idea of the other
walks available.

PLANNING YOUR WALK

What to take

'When you have worn out your shoes, the strength of the shoe leather has passed into the fiber of your body. I measure your health by the number of shoes and hats and clothes you have worn out.' **Ralph Waldo Emerson**

Deciding how much to take can be difficult. Experienced walkers know that you should take only the bare essentials but at the same time you must ensure you have all the equipment necessary to make the trip safe and comfortable.

KEEP YOUR LUGGAGE LIGHT

Experienced backpackers know that there is some sort of complicated formula governing the success of a walk, in which the enjoyment of the walk is inversely proportional to the amount carried.

Carrying a heavy rucksack slows you down, tires you out and gives you aches and pains in parts of the body that you never knew existed. It is imperative, therefore, that you take a good deal of time packing and that you are ruthless when you do; if it's not essential, don't take it.

HOW TO CARRY IT

If you are using the baggage-transfer service (see p27), you must comply with their regulations regarding the weight and size of the luggage you wish them to carry.

Even if you are using this service, you will still need to carry a small **daypack**, filled with those items that you will need during the day: water bottle or pouch, this book, map, sun-screen, sun hat, wet-weather gear, some food, camera, money and so on.

If you have decided to forego the services of the baggage carrier you will have to consider your **rucksack** even more carefully. Ultimately its size will depend on where you are planning to stay and how you are planning to eat. If you are camping and cooking for yourself you will probably need a 65- to 75-litre rucksack, which should be large enough to carry a small tent, sleeping bag, cooking equipment, crockery, cutlery and food. Those not carrying their home with them should find a 40- to 60-litre rucksack sufficient.

When choosing a rucksack, make sure it has a stiffened back and can be adjusted to fit your own back comfortably. Don't just try the rucksack out in the shop: take it home, fill it with things and then try it out around the house and take it out for a short walk. Only then can you be certain that it fits. Make sure the hip belt and chest strap (if there is one) are fastened tightly as this helps distribute the weight more comfortably with most of it being carried on your hips. Carry a small daypack inside the rucksack, as this will be useful to carry things in when leaving the main pack at the hostel or B&B.

One reader wrote in with the eminently sensible advice of taking a **water-proof rucksack cover**. Most rucksacks these days have them 'built in' to the sack, but you can also buy them separately for less than a tenner. Lining your bag with a **bin liner** is another sensible, cut-price idea. Finally, it's also a good idea to keep everything wrapped in plastic bags inside the rucksack; I usually place all these bags inside a bin-bag which then goes inside the rucksack. That way, even if it does pour with rain, everything should remain dry.

FOOTWEAR

Boots
Only a decent pair of strong, durable walking boots is good enough to survive the rigours of the South-West Coast Path. Don't be tempted by a spell of hot weather into bringing something flimsier. Make sure, too, that your boots provide good ankle support, for the ground can occasionally be rough and stony and twisted ankles are commonplace. Make sure your boots are waterproof as well: these days most people opt for a synthetic waterproof lining (Gore-Tex or similar), though a good-quality leather boot with dubbin should prove just as reliable in keeping your feet dry.

In addition, many people bring an extra pair of shoes or trainers to wear off the trail. This is not essential but if you are using the baggage-transfer service and you've got room in your luggage, why not?

Socks
If you haven't got a pair of the modern hi-tech walking socks the old system of wearing a thin liner sock under a thicker wool sock is just as good. Bring a few pairs of each.

CLOTHES

In a country notorious for its unpredictable climate it is imperative that you pack enough clothes to cover every extreme of weather, from burning hot to bloomin' freezing.

Modern hi-tech outdoor clothes come with a range of fancy names and brands but they all still follow the basic two- or three-layer principle, with an inner base layer to transport sweat away from your skin, a mid-layer for warmth and an outer layer to protect you from the wind and rain.

A thin lightweight **thermal top** of a synthetic material is ideal as the base layer as it draws moisture (ie sweat) away from your body. Cool in hot weather and warm when worn under other clothes in the cold, pack at least one thermal top. Over the top in cold weather a mid-weight **polyester fleece** should suffice. Fleeces are light, more water-resistant than the alternatives (such as a woolly jumper), remain warm even when wet and pack down small in rucksacks; they are thus ideal walking gear.

Over the top of all this a **waterproof jacket** is essential. 'Breathable' jackets cost a small fortune (though prices are falling all the time) but they do prevent the build-up of condensation.

Leg wear

Many walkers find walking trousers an unnecessary investment. Any light, quick-drying trouser should suffice. Jeans are heavy and dry slowly and are thus not recommended. A pair of waterproof trousers *is* more than useful, however, while on really hot sunny days you'll be glad you brought your shorts. Thermal **long johns** take up little room in a rucksack and could be vital if the weather starts to close in.

Gaiters are not essential but, again, those who bring them are always glad they did, for they provide extra protection when walking through muddy ground and when the vegetation around the trail is dripping wet after bad weather.

Underwear

Three or four changes of underwear is fine. Any more is excessive, any less unhygienic. Because backpacks can cause bra straps to dig painfully into the skin, women may find a **sports bra** more comfortable.

Other clothes

You may like to consider a woolly **hat** and **gloves** – you'd be surprised how cold it can get up on the cliffs even in summer. A **sun hat** (see p59) is vital given the strength of the sun sometimes.

TOILETRIES

Once again, take the minimum. **Soap**, **towel**, a **toothbrush** and **toothpaste** are pretty much essential (although those staying in B&Bs will find that most provide soap and towels anyway). Some **toilet paper** could also prove vital on the trail, particularly if using public toilets (which occasionally run out).

Other items: **razor**; **deodorant**; **tampons/sanitary towels** and a high factor **sun-screen** should cover just about everything.

FIRST-AID KIT

A small first-aid kit could prove useful for those emergencies that occur along the trail. This kit should include **aspirin** or **paracetamol**; **plasters** for minor cuts; Compeed, **Second Skin** or some other treatment for blisters; a **bandage** or elasticated joint support for supporting a sprained ankle or a weak knee; **antiseptic wipes**; **antiseptic cream**; **safety pins**; **tweezers** and **scissors**.

❏ **Canine companions**

The South-West Coast Path is a dog-friendly path and many are the rewards that await those prepared to make the extra effort required to bring their best friend along the trail. However, you shouldn't underestimate the amount of work involved in bringing your pooch to the path. Indeed, just about every decision you make will be influenced by the fact that you've got a dog. The best starting point is to study the advice in the appendix on pp208-10, and the village & town facilities table (pp30-1) so you can plan where to stay and eat, and where to buy food for your mutt.

Henry Stedman

PLANNING YOUR WALK

> **❏ Mobile phone reception and internet connections on the trail**
> While many people view their walk in this remote corner of England as an escape
> from the modern world, for some people a decent connection with the outside world
> is vital. In our research we found EE (🖳 ee.co.uk) provided the best coverage for
> mobile and (up to) 4G internet connections (with Vodaphone pretty good too).
>
>   Those who need to stay in touch online, and who are taking a laptop, may like to
> consider investing in a dongle (a small device that plugs into a USB port and connects
> your computer to the internet) – though most accommodation options, cafés and pubs
> offer wi-fi.

GENERAL ITEMS

Essential

Everybody should have a **map**, **torch**, **water bottle or pouch**, **spare batteries**,
penknife, **whistle** (see p57 for details of the international distress signal), some
emergency food and a **watch** (preferably with an alarm to help you make an
early start each day). Those with weak knees will find a **walking pole** or **sticks**
essential. Those who've also walked in Scotland will recognise the importance
of taking **insect repellent** to ward off midges, though they're not so bad here.
Sun screen, however, is vital; see p59.

   A **mobile phone** (see box above) is invaluable too – and reception is usually
pretty good – for arranging a lift from the path to the B&B, booking a table at
a restaurant etc; just don't forget the charger! If you know how to use it properly
you'll also find a **compass** handy.

Useful items and luxuries

Suggestions here include a **book** for days off or on train and bus journeys, a
camera, a pair of **sunglasses**, **binoculars** and a **radio or iPod**.

   National Trust and English Heritage **membership cards**, as well as stu-
dent (ISIC) and YHA hostel cards could save you money on the trail. Some
sort of ID, such as a driving licence, might also prove useful.

CAMPING GEAR

Campers will find a sleeping bag essential. A two- to three-season bag should
suffice for summer. In addition, they will also need a decent bivvy bag or tent, a
sleeping mat, fuel and stove, cutlery/pans, a cup and a scrubber for washing up.

MONEY

ATMs (cash machines) are fairly common along the Exmoor and North Devon
Coast Path as are banks and post offices (see p26). However, not everybody
accepts **debit** or **credit cards** as payment – though many B&Bs and most
restaurants now do. As a result, you should carry a fair amount of **cash** with
you, just to be on the safe side. Crime on the trail is thankfully rare but it's
always a good idea to carry your money safely in a **moneybelt**.

❑ SOURCES OF FURTHER INFORMATION

Online information

● 🖳 www.nationaltrail.co.uk/south-west-coast-path The official and most useful website to Britain's longest national trail. Good for background information on the trail and has the latest news on the path, details about river crossings and army ranges, as well as lots of information on accommodation, suggested itineraries and distance and timing calculators.

● 🖳 www.southwestcoastpath.org.uk The site for the **South-West Coast Path Association (SWCPA)**, a registered charity that exists to support users of the path. Many of the features on the official site are replicated here – distance calculators, river-crossing details etc – though there is much more detail here too. The Association is also very active politically, pressurising government bodies to ensure that the path is highly maintained along its length. Membership is available at £20/25 for single/joint memberships for UK residents (£25 for both single and joint membership for non-UK residents) and includes a free copy of their guidebook and twice-yearly newsletters.

● 🖳 www.southwestcoastalpath.co.uk Unusual website that concentrates on day walks along short stretches of the Coast Path. Also includes information on accommodation, pubs and restaurants.

● 🖳 www.exmoor-nationalpark.gov.uk The official site of the Exmoor National Park – home to both the country's longest wooded coastline and its highest tree!

● 🖳 www.northdevon-aonb.org.uk Official website of the North Devon Areas of Outstanding Natural Beauty. Good for background information on the geology, flora and fauna of the region.

Tourist information centres (TICs)

As one of the busiest tourist areas of the country, it is no surprise to find that the South-West is well served by tourist information centres with all manner of locally specific information. Most also provide an accommodation-booking service (in many cases a 10% deposit is payable which is deducted from the final bill and sometimes there's a booking charge as well). Centres close to this section of the coastal path are: **Minehead** (see p75); **Lynton** (see p104); **Combe Martin** (see p115); **Ilfracombe** (see p123); **Woolacombe** (see p141); **Braunton** (see p146); **Barnstaple** (see p152); **Bideford** (see p164) and **Bude** (see p202).

There is also a **National Park Centre** in Lynmouth (see p100).

Organisations for walkers

● **The Backpackers' Club** (🖳 www.backpackersclub.co.uk) A club aimed at people who are involved or interested in lightweight camping through walking, cycling, skiing and canoeing. They produce a quarterly magazine, provide members with a comprehensive advisory and information service on all aspects of backpacking, organise weekend trips, offer discounts for maps and at outdoor stores, and also publish a farm-pitch directory. Membership is £15 a year.

● **The Long Distance Walkers' Association** (🖳 www.ldwa.org.uk) Membership (£13 a year) includes a copy of their journal *Strider* three times per year giving details of challenge events and local group walks as well as articles on the subject. Members also receive a discount on maps.

● **Ramblers** (🖳 www.ramblers.org.uk) Looks after the interests of walkers throughout Britain. They publish a large amount of useful information including their quarterly *Walk* magazine (£3.60 to non-members). The website also has a discussion forum. Annual membership costs £34.50/45.50/20.50 individual/joint/concessionary.

MAPS

It would be perfectly possible to walk long stretches of the coastal path unaided by map or compass. Just keep the sea to your right (or left, depending on which way you're heading) and you can't go too far off track. The **hand-drawn maps in this book**, which cover the trail at a scale of 1:20,000, should provide sufficient aid in areas where navigation is slightly more problematic.

Nevertheless, having other maps will paint a more fulfilling picture of your surroundings and will allow you to plan much more effectively for any accommodation or other facilities that lie off the trail. **Ordnance Survey** (OS; ⌨ www.ordnancesurvey.co.uk) produce their maps to two scales: the 1:25,000 Explorer series in orange and the 1:50,000 Landranger in pink (which is less useful for walking purposes). Alongside the paper versions OS also produce an 'Active' edition of both which is 'weatherproof' (covered in a lightweight protective plastic coating).

Those needed for the stretch of the SWCP covered by this book are as follows: Explorer: Outdoor Leisure (OL) 9 Exmoor; 139 Bideford, Ilfracombe and Barnstaple; 126 Clovelly and Hartland, and 111 Bude, Boscastle and Tintagel. The fourth map is really essential only if you plan to continue past Bude, as the section of path missing between Map 126 and Bude is only about a mile or two of fairly uneventful walking. If you don't feel that such precise cartography is needed the Landranger may be sufficient; of the 14 to cover the SWCP you will need the following three to cover the initial 115 miles: 181 Minehead and Brendon Hills; 180 Barnstaple and Ilfracombe; and 190 Bude and Clovelly.

While it may be extravagant to buy all these maps, Ramblers (see box opposite) allows members to borrow them for a small charge. Alternatively, members of Backpackers are entitled to discounts. Some public libraries in the UK also have OS maps that can be borrowed by library members.

Harvey Maps (⌨ www.harveymaps.co.uk) produce a series of maps that cover all the designated National Trails to a scale of 1:40,000. For full coverage of the SWCP you will need three, but if you are intending to walk the section covered by this book just Map One (Minehead to St Ives) will suffice. This of course will save on weight and cost compared to buying the four OS maps, though the OS has more detail and will show you what is further inland.

For those who like the comfort of having an OS map with them, but are not overly concerned by what is too far away from the trail, a great companion to this guidebook, is **AZ**'s (⌨ www.az.co.uk) adventure booklet: *South West Coast Path 1: North Devon & Somerset*, which includes Ordnance Survey mapping (scale 1:25,000) of the trail described in this book. There are a further four in AZ's SWCP series.

Digital maps

There are numerous software packages that provide Ordnance Survey (OS) maps for a PC, smartphone, tablet or GPS. Maps are supplied by direct download over the internet. The maps are then loaded into an application, also available by download, from where you can view them, print them and create routes

on them. **Memory Map** (🖳 www.memory-map.co.uk) sell OS 1:25,000 mapping covering the whole of the UK for £50.

Both OS and Harvey maps can also be obtained online from **Anquet** (🖳
www.anquet.com).

For a subscription of £3.99 for one month or £23.99 for a year (on their current offer) **Ordnance Survey** (see p41) let you download and then use their UK
maps (1:25,000 scale) on a mobile or tablet without a data connection for a specific period.

RECOMMENDED READING

Below is a by no-means exhaustive but hopefully helpful introduction to some
of the literature available in regards to the SWCP and, in particular, the Exmoor
and North Devon coast.

Guidebooks

If you're willing to also carry separate maps, undoubtedly the most detailed
guide to the accommodation, tide tables and other useful information on the
entire SWCP is the South West Coast Path Association's companion to the path,
called simply **The South-West Coast Path** and currently priced at £15.
Alongside this annual guide they also produce and sell pamphlets for each section which can be found in tourist information centres en route or ordered via
post or online for £2; see 🖳 www.southwestcoastpath.org.uk for details.

Flora and fauna

For identifying obscure plants and peculiar-looking beasties as you walk,
Collins and New Holland publish a pocket-sized range to Britain's natural rich-
es. The Collins Gem series are tough little books; current titles include guides
to *Trees*, *Birds*, *Mushrooms*, *Wild Flowers*, *Wild Animals*, *Insects* and
Butterflies.

In addition, for any budding crustacean connoisseur there is a *Seashore*
book; there is also handbook to the *Stars*, which could be of particular interest
for those who are considering sleeping under them.

Also in the Collins series, there's an adapted version of Richard Mabey's
classic bestseller *Food for Free* – great for anyone intent on getting back to
nature, saving the pennies, or just with an interest in what's edible outside of a
supermarket. You could also consult *Wild Food: Foraging for Food in the Wild*,
written by Jane Eastoe and published by the National Trust.

New Holland's Concise range covers much the same topics as the Gem
series and comes in a waterproof plastic jacket and include useful quick reference foldout charts. Both series contain a wealth of information.

If you have a smart phone it's worth investigating the rapidly increasing
range of flora and fauna identification apps that are becoming available.

Autobiography and fiction

With the Falklands War imminent Mark Wallington set off to walk the SWCP
in an attempt to impress a girl that he had met at a party. Accompanied by the

more-loathed-than-loved Boogie the dog, man and beast survive all that the path can throw at them on a diet of tinned soup and Kennomeat. *Travels with Boogie: 500 Mile Walkies* is Wallington's humorous account of his time spent on the trail. If you have walked and camped or have ever walked a long distance with a dog many of the author's anecdotes will ring true – a light-hearted and thoroughly enjoyable read.

Another dog goes walking in *Two feet, four paws*, Spud Talbot-Ponsonby's tale of her time circumnavigating Britain (Chapter 15: Bristol to Boscastle is the relevant chapter to this section of the SWCP).

Unsurprisingly, more poetic than both is Simon Armitage's *Walking Away*, the poet, playwright, and novelist's account of his time walking and reciting odes along the SWCP between Minehead and Land's End; remarkably funny, I would advise reading this after your trek rather than before.

For fans of English rock band Mott the Hoople there is former member Overend Watts' account of his time on the trail: *The Man Who Hated Walking: The South West Coast Path*. I imagine all the young dudes will like this one.

The Tarka Trail is a local path named after Henry Williamson's much-loved *Tarka the Otter*, just one of many books in which Williamson's extraordinary ability to evoke the Devonshire countryside gilds every page. Perhaps the most famous book, however, is the most dense 19th-century classic, *Lorna Doone: A Romance of Exmoor*, by Richard Doddridge Blackmore. Margaret Drabble's witty 1998 novel *The Witch of Exmoor* is also set near the Lyn Valley.

Possibly the only piece of fiction to inspire the name of an English village, *Westward Ho!* (see p172) is a Spanish Armada adventure-romp written by Charles Kingsley.

History

Hope Bourne had four books published during her 91-year lifetime that vividly describe life in the wilds of Devon, beginning with 1963's *Living on Exmoor* and ending with 1993's *My Moorland Life*.

One thousand years of farming, quarrying and the Home Guard are crammed into Felicity Goodall's *Lost Devon*, which is good for those with an interest in the lost heritage of the county; while for those interested in the development of the moor's landscape and archaeology, *The Field Archaeology of Exmoor* by Hazel Riley and Robert Wilson-North is published by English Heritage.

A broader, more conventional historical summary can be found in Mary Siraut's *Exmoor: The Making of an English Upland*. Local historian Dennis Corner has written several books on the local area including *Porlock in those Days*.

Derrick Warren's *Curious Devon* examines the quirkier side of the county, while for something a little darker there's John Van Der Kiste's *Grim Almanac of Devon* that recounts 366 of the county's more macabre episodes.

Getting to and from the Coast Path

Given that it is one of the most popular holiday destinations in the UK, the South-West is surprisingly poorly served by public transport connections. Indeed, getting to the start of your walk can be quite laborious – and returning home at the end can be equally painful.

Those who wish to take a train will soon discover that neither Minehead nor Bude has a mainline rail connection. The best way to get to Minehead by train is to go to Taunton, Barnstaple, or Tiverton Parkway. Barnstaple, Exeter and Okehampton are best for Bude; see opposite for more details.

National Express coach services only go to Minehead in the summer months and also serve the Butlins there rather than the centre of town and the

PLANNING YOUR WALK

❑ **GETTING TO BRITAIN**

● **By air** Exeter (🖳 www.exeter-airport.co.uk); Bristol (🖳 www.bristolairport.co .uk), Southampton (🖳 www.southamptonairport.com) and Bournemouth (🖳 www .bournemouthairport.com) have international flights though mostly from Europe only; for details on Newquay Airport see p46. However, none of these airports is well connected to Minehead (or Bude), so for this reason London's Heathrow (🖳 www .heathrow.com) may be the most convenient.

See box p46 for details of National Express coach services from Heathrow, Exeter and Bristol. There are also rail services between Bristol Temple Meads (take a bus from the airport) and Taunton. From Heathrow you can take the Heathrow Express (🖳 www.heathrowexpress.com) to Paddington and from there take a train to Taunton (see box opposite). From Taunton you can catch Buses of Somerset No 28 service (see box p48) to Minehead at the start of the trail.

● **Eurostar** (🖳 www.eurostar.com) operates a high-speed passenger service via the Channel Tunnel between Paris, Brussels and Lille and London. The Eurostar terminal in London is at St Pancras International station with connections to the London Underground and to all other main railway stations in London. Trains to Somerset and Devon leave from Paddington station.

For more information about rail services to Britain contact **Railteam** (🖳 www .railteam.eu).

● **From Europe by coach** Eurolines (🖳 www.eurolines.com) have a wide network of long-distance bus services connecting over 500 destinations in 25 European countries to London (Victoria Coach Station). Visit the Eurolines website for details of services from your country. Check carefully: often, once expenses such as food for the journey are taken into consideration, it doesn't work out much cheaper than flying, particularly when compared to the prices of some of the budget airlines.

● **From Europe by car** Ferries operate on several routes between mainland Europe and Britain. Look at 🖳 www.ferrysavers.com or 🖳 www.directferries.com for a full list of companies and services.

Eurotunnel (🖳 www.eurotunnel.com) operates '**le shuttle**' train service for vehicles via the Channel Tunnel between Calais and Folkestone.

fare is quite expensive. A service to Bude only operates weekly on a Saturday mid-June to early September. See pp46-7 for options for coach travel.

Given the above, the temptation to drive (see p47) to the start of your walk is understandable. This may be the most convenient way to get there but it will also probably be the most expensive and you may not feel comfortable abandoning your car in a car park (see also p47 for details of long-stay parking) for a couple of weeks. Nor have we mentioned the ecological considerations of driving.

NATIONAL TRANSPORT

By train

Neither Minehead or Bude is served by a regular rail service (though see box below). **Taunton**, however, *is* well connected by rail (Bristol is less than an hour away, Exeter half an hour and even London Paddington is within a two-hour journey) and there are regular bus services (Buses of Somerset No 28) from there on to Minehead (1½hrs). This journey is, whilst slow, enjoyable: if you have already travelled by train from London, or indeed any other metropolis, you will feel life pleasantly decelerating around you as you approach the northern end of Exmoor.

❏ **Rail services**
Note: not all stops are listed.
● London to Penzance via Reading, Taunton, Exeter, Plymouth & Bodmin Parkway, Mon-Sat approx 12/day, Sun approx 8/day, some services go via Bristol, some call at Tiverton Parkway.
● Cardiff to Taunton via Bristol (some services continue to Tiverton Parkway, Exeter & Plymouth), Mon-Fri 1/hr, Sat & Sun no direct services.
● Glasgow/Edinburgh to Plymouth via Newcastle, York, Leeds, Birmingham, Bristol, Taunton, Tiverton Parkway & Exeter, Mon-Sat 7-day, Sun 5/day for the full route.
● Exeter to Barnstaple (The Tarka Line), Mon-Sat 1/hr, Sun 6/day.

The West Somerset Railway Arriving in Minehead by rail is undoubtedly the most attractive way of arriving (apart from walking from Porlock, of course!), the steam train chuffing its way through the rolling Somerset countryside before terminating its journey right in the centre of town, just a few steps from the seafront and only a couple of hundred metres from the start of the SWCP itself.

Unfortunately, the only train service that operates a service to/from Minehead is the West Somerset Railway (⌨ www.west-somerset-railway.co.uk). It may be one of the most picturesque services imaginable – but it's also one of the most pointless, in that it doesn't go anywhere particularly useful. Running between Minehead and Bishops Lydeard, on the way to Taunton, the railway offers a choice of transportation by either steam or diesel, the entire journey taking around 1¼ hours to cover the 20 miles.

If you're determined that this is how you want to arrive, Bishops Lydeard is a half-hour bus ride from Taunton on Buses of Somerset's 28 service (see box p48). The train operation's regularity differs daily so it would be wise to check the website (or phone ahead) for up-to-date timetabling information.

PLANNING YOUR WALK

As for the other end of the walk, the nearest railway stations to Bude are at Exeter, Okehampton and Barnstaple, and each boasts some sort of bus service to Bude (see pp48-50).

Barnstaple is actually the only location on the path that *is* served by a regular rail service, though it's a 3½-hour journey from London, two hours from Taunton and a good 80 minutes from Exeter. The quickest way from Barnstaple to Minehead (2hrs) is to take a bus to Lynton (Filers Travel's No 309/310) and then their, or Quantock's, No 300 to Minehead; the 300, however only operates between mid July and early September meaning that during the rest of the year you'll need to pay for a taxi from Lynton to Minehead (approximately £40).

From Barnstaple there is a limited service (Stagecoach No 85) to Bude. Alternatively Stagecoach's No 319 to Hartland connects with their 219 service to Bude but none of these operates on a Sunday; see pp48-50 for details.

National Rail (☎ 03457-484950, 🖳 www.nationalrail.co.uk) is the best source of rail information. The lines throughout the South-West are run by **Great Western Railway** (☎ 03457-000125, 🖳 www.gwr.com). **Arriva Cross Country Trains** (🖳 www.crosscountrytrains.co.uk) also run services linking the Midlands, North and Scotland with the South-West.

Finally, one tip for when buying **tickets**: it's always worth checking the fares on the relevant train company's website or 🖳 www.thetrainline.com – you'll normally find significant reductions, especially if booking 8-12 weeks in advance and also if you are able to travel on a particular service. However, be aware of additional charges such as a booking fee, or for using a debit/credit card.

If you plan to take a bus when you arrive consider getting a **plusbus** (🖳 www .plusbus.info) ticket and if you want to book a taxi **Traintaxi**'s website (🖳 www .traintaxi.co.uk) gives details of the companies operating at railway stations.

By coach

Although coach travel can take significantly longer than getting a train and is susceptible to traffic jams – especially in the summer months when the South-West

---

❏ **National Express coach services**
Note: not all stops are listed.
324 Huddersfield to Exeter via Leeds, Sheffield, Birmingham & Bristol (1/day)
328 Birmingham to Plymouth via Bristol & Taunton (1/day)
336 Birmingham to Exeter via Bristol & Taunton (1/day)
339 Birmingham to **Westward Ho!** via Cheltenham, Bristol, Taunton, Barnstaple, **Fremington**, **Instow**, **Bideford** & **Northam** (1/day)
406 London Victoria to Taunton via Heathrow Airport & Weston-super-Mare, 1/day
501 London Victoria to Taunton via Heathrow Airport & Reading 3/day
502 London Victoria to **Ilfracombe** via Heathrow Airport, Taunton, **Barnstaple** & **Braunton** (2/day plus mid July to early Sep Fri-Mon 1-2/day)
502 London Victoria to **Westward Ho!** via Heathrow Airport, Taunton, **Barnstaple**, **Fremington**, **Instow** & **Bideford** (2/day, but continues to **Bude** Sat only mid June to early Sep)
532 Edinburgh to Plymouth via Glasgow, Carlisle, Taunton & Exeter, 1/day
672 Bristol to **Minehead** Butlin's, July to Sep 2/week (Mon & Fri)

is choked with tourists – it is generally cheaper than train travel and can, on some of today's newer coaches, also be far more salubrious than coach travel of old.

National Express (see box opposite; 🖳 www.nationalexpress.com) runs several services to Taunton (from here take Buses of Somerset No 28 to Minehead); services also go to Barnstaple, Bideford and Ilfracombe and in the summer months from Bristol to Minehead Butlins, which is about a mile from the town centre.

However, it is not easy to reach Bude by coach. There is a seasonal service (Saturday only) from London and several services to Westward Ho! but it is not easy to get to Bude from there. Your best bet is to travel to Exeter and from there take Stagecoach's No 6/6A service (see box p50).

Megabus (🖳 uk.megabus.com), part of Stagecoach, is a cheap and expanding bus company but its only useful services are to Exeter and Newquay from where you still have quite a journey to the Path!

By car

Driving to the start of the path raises as many questions as it does answers: Where do you leave your car while you're walking? Will it be safe? And how are you going to get back to it at the end of your trip? Furthermore, given the ever-rising price of fuel and the fact that you'll probably have to pay to leave your car somewhere, taking your car will almost certainly be the least financially viable option.

For those who do decide to drive, a great way to look at the varying options in regards to **route planning** is to use the AA's website and route planner (🖳 www.theaa.com/route-planner/index.jsp).

Both Minehead and Bude have **long stay parking**. This involves paying cash into a machine (usually) for your first seven days and then paying for longer online or via your phone, or completing the whole arrangement online. For up-to-date information on prices and processes for organising this and for which car parks you can use in Minehead consult 🖳 www.westsomersetonline .gov.uk; for Bude see 🖳 www.cornwall.gov.uk.

One idea that is popular with drivers is to park in Barnstaple (the railway station has long-term parking where you can pay (about £3.50 per day) for seven days and update it by phone if necessary. The advantage with parking in Barnstaple is that your vehicle is left at a point approximately half-way along the trail – allowing you to leave items in the car and pick them up when you walk past – or jump in and drive home if you've found the walking too taxing! It also means you won't have quite such an arduous journey to get back to the car from Bude at the end of the trip.

By air

In addition to the airports mentioned in the box on p44, there is the option of flying (mostly domestic flights) into Newquay (🖳 www.newquaycornwallairport .com). However, Newquay lies 70 miles along the coast from Bude. What's more, it isn't particularly well placed even for Bude (and not really a realistic option for Minehead) – a bus between Newquay and Bude takes at least three hours.

PLANNING YOUR WALK

LOCAL TRANSPORT

Bus services

All places along the trail (or at least those with inhabitants) boast at least some sort of bus service except for Hartland Quay, the penultimate stop on the path. (From here you'll need to walk 2½ miles inland to Hartland to catch a bus.) Nearly all the buses servicing points on the trail run at least once a day (usually more) Monday to Saturday, which makes the chances of getting stuck somewhere on one of those days gratifyingly slim – you may just have to wait a while. However, it is not the same on a Sunday as many services are seasonal.

The main problem with public transport in the area is the time it takes to get anywhere. Things are further complicated by the fact that local buses have been organised by county, meaning that while Minehead and Bude may have good connections within their respective counties (Somerset and Cornwall), they have pretty lousy connections with their neighbour Devon, which means that if you want to cross a county border you've often got to change buses somewhere along the way.

Planning ahead is a must as services change and may have been cut. Note, that other than in the school summer holidays there is no direct service between Lynton/Lynmouth and Combe Martin or between Lynton/Lynmouth and Porlock/Porlock Weir. Also note that Filers No 300 service doesn't operate on a Saturday.

Timetables for the services should be available for free at bus stations and tourist information centres (the North Devon booklet covers most services) and can also be found online on either the relevant company's website or 🖥 www .travelinesw.com.

❑ BUS SERVICES

Buses of Somerset (☎ 0345 602 0121, 🖥 www.firstgroup.com/somerset)
10 **Minehead to Porlock Weir** via Porlock, Mon-Fri 5/day
28 **Taunton to Minehead** via Bishops Lydeard, Mon-Sat 2/hr, Sun approx 1/hr

Filers Travel (☎ 01271-863819, 🖥 www.filers.co.uk)
31 **Ilfracombe to Mortehoe** via Woolacombe, Mon-Fri 6/day, Sat 4/day
300 Lynmouth to Ilfracombe via Lynton, Combe Martin, Watermouth & Hele, mid July-early Sep Mon-Fri 2/day (connects with Quantock's 300 service)
300 Minehead to Ilfracombe via Porlock, Lynmouth, Lynton, Combe Martin, Watermouth & Hele, mid July-early Sep Sun 1/day plus 1/day Minehead to Lynmouth (see also Quantock Heritage)
301 Combe Martin to Barnstaple via Berrynarbor & Ilfracombe, Mon-Sat 9-11/day
302 Ilfracombe to Woolacombe, end May to mid Sep Sun/bank hol Mons 8/day
303 Barnstaple to Woolacombe via Chivenor, Velator, Braunton & Mortehoe, Mon-Sat 4-5/day
309 Lynton to Barnstaple via Martinhoe Cross, Mon-Sat 2/day
310 Lynton to Barnstaple via Blackmoor Gate, Mon-Fri 11/day, Sat 8/day (3-4/day start/end in Lynmouth)

(cont'd on p50)

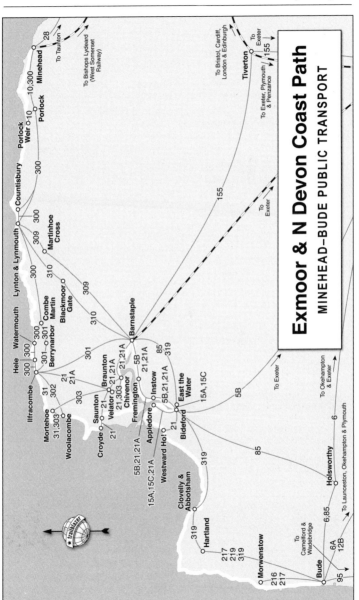

Exmoor & N Devon Coast Path
MINEHEAD–BUDE PUBLIC TRANSPORT

PLANNING YOUR WALK

❏ **BUS SERVICES** *(cont'd from p48)*

First (🖳 www.firstgroup.com/cornwall)
95   Bude to Wadebridge via Camelford, Mon-Sat 6/day

Quantock Heritage (🖳 www.quantockheritage.com)
300 Minehead to Lynmouth via Porlock & Countisbury, mid July to early Sep
    daily 2/day

Stagecoach (🖳 www.stagecoachbus.com)
5B   Exeter to Barnstaple via Bideford, Instow & Fremington, Mon-Sat 8-10/day
6   Bude to Exeter via Holsworthy & Okehampton, Mon-Sat 7/day, Sun and bank
      holidays 2/day
6A   Bude to Exeter via Launceston & Okehampton, Mon-Sat 4/day, Sun 1/day
15A East-the-Water to Appledore via Bideford & Northam,
      Mon-Fri 9/day, Sat 11/day
15C East-the-Water to Appledore via Bideford & Northam, Mon-Sat 11/day,
      3/day start/end in **Barnstaple**
      (**note** the services operate on a slightly different route and start in/continue to
      Barnstaple in the early morning/evening)
21   (called North Devon Wave) Ilfracombe to Bideford via Braunton, Chivenor,
      Barnstaple, Fremington & Instow, Mon-Sat 1-2/hr, Sun 1/hr continues to
      Westward Ho! via Northam
      Croyde to Westward Ho! via Saunton Sands, Braunton, Chivenor, Barnstaple,
      Fremington, Instow, Bideford & Northam, Mon-Sat 1/hr
      Croyde to Barnstaple, May-Sep Sun 5/day
      Braunton to Westward Ho! via Chivenor, Barnstaple, Fremington, Instow,
      Bideford & Northam, Mon-Sat 1/hr
21A Ilfracombe to Appledore via Braunton, Chivenor, Barnstaple, Fremington,
      Instow, East-the-Water & Bideford, Sun & Bank Hols 1/hr
85   Barnstaple to Holsworthy via Bideford, Mon-Sat 4-5/day, 1-2/day continue to
      Bude in the afternoon and start in Bude in the morning
155 Exeter to Barnstaple via Tiverton, Mon-Sat 5-6/day
216/217 Morwenstow to Bude, Mon-Sat 1/day
217/219 Hartland to Bude, Mon-Tue & Thur-Sat 5/day
319 Barnstaple to Hartland via Bideford, Abbotsham & Clovelly, Mon-Sat 4/day,
      1/day continues to Bude and another 1/day goes from Bideford to Hartland; the
      319 connects with the 219 service (see above).

Plymouth Citybus Service (☎ 01752-662271, 🖳 www.plymouthbus.co.uk)
12B   Launceston to Bude, Mon-Sat 6/day; this connects at Launceston with the
      No 12 service to Plymouth (Mon-Sat 12/day, Sun 6/day)

MINIMUM IMPACT & OUTDOOR SAFETY

Minimum impact walking

By visiting this rural corner of England you are having a positive impact, not just on your own wellbeing but on local communities as well. Your presence brings money and jobs into the local economy and also pride in, and awareness of, the region's environment and culture.

However, the environment should not just be considered in terms of its value as a tourist asset. Its long-term survival and enjoyment by future generations will only be possible if both visitors and local communities protect it now. The following points are made to help you reduce your impact on the environment, encourage conservation and promote sustainable tourism in the area.

ECONOMIC IMPACT

Support local businesses

Rural businesses and communities in Britain have been hit hard in recent years by a seemingly endless series of crises. Most people are aware of the countryside code – not dropping litter and closing the gate behind you are still as pertinent as ever – but in light of the economic pressures there is something else you can do: **buy local**.

Look and ask for local produce (see box p22) to buy and eat; not only does this cut down on the amount of pollution and congestion that the transportation of food creates (the so-called 'food miles'), but also ensures that you are supporting local farmers and producers; the very people who have moulded the countryside you have come to see and who are in the best position to protect it. If you can find local food which is also organic so much the better.

It's a fact of life that money spent at local level – perhaps in a market, or at the greengrocer, or in an independent pub – has a far greater impact for good on that community than the equivalent spent in a branch of a national chain store or restaurant. While no-one would advocate that walkers should boycott the larger supermarkets, which after all do provide local employment, it's worth remembering that businesses in rural communities rely heavily on visitors for their very existence. If we want to keep these shops and post offices, we need to use them.

ENVIRONMENTAL IMPACT

A walking holiday in itself is an environmentally friendly approach to tourism. The following are some ideas on how you can go a few steps further in helping to minimise your impact on the environment while walking the South-West Coast Path.

Use public transport whenever possible

While we recognise that public transport along this section of the South-West Coast Path is not ideal, it is preferable to using private cars as it benefits everyone: visitors, locals and the environment.

Never leave litter

Leaving litter shows a total disrespect for the natural world and others coming after you. As well as being unsightly, litter can be harmful to wildlife, pollutes the environment and can be dangerous to farm animals. Please carry a plastic bag so you can dispose of your rubbish in a bin in the next village. It would be very helpful if you could pick up litter left by other people too.

● **Is it OK if it's biodegradable?** Not really. Apple cores, banana skins, orange peel and the like are unsightly, encourage flies, ants and wasps and ruin a picnic spot for others. Using the excuse that they are natural and biodegradable just doesn't cut any ice. When was the last time you saw a banana tree in England?

● **The lasting impact of litter** A piece of orange peel left on the ground takes six months to decompose; silver foil 18 months; a plastic bag 10 years; clothes 15 years; and an aluminium can 85 years.

Respect all wildlife

Care for all wildlife you come across along the path; it has as much right to be there as you. As tempting as it may be to pick wild flowers, leave them in place so the next person who passes can enjoy them too. Don't break branches off or damage trees in any way.

If you come across wildlife, keep your distance and don't watch for too long. Your presence can cause considerable stress, particularly if the adults are with young, or in winter when the weather is harsh and food is scarce. Young animals are rarely abandoned. If you come across young birds, keep away so that their mother can return.

Outdoor toiletry

As more and more people discover the joys of walking in the natural environment issues such as how to go to the loo outdoors rapidly gain importance. How many of us have shaken our heads at the sight of toilet paper strewn beside the path, or even worse, someone's dump left in full view? Human excrement is not only offensive to our senses but, more importantly, can infect water sources.

Where to go The coast path is a high-use area and many habitats will not benefit from your fertilisation. As far as 'number twos' are concerned try whenever possible to use public toilets. There is no shortage of public toilets along the coast path and they are all marked on the trail maps. However, there are those times when the only time is now. If you have to go outdoors help the environment to deal with your deposit in the best possible way by following a few simple guidelines:

● **Choose your site carefully** It should be at least 30 metres away from running water and out of reach of the high tide and not on any site of historical or archaeological interest. Carry a small trowel or use a sturdy stick to dig a small hole about 15cm (6") deep to bury your faeces in. Faeces decompose quicker when in contact with the top layer of soil or leaf mould; by using a stick to stir loose soil into your deposit you will speed decomposition up even more. Do not squash it under rocks as this slows down the decomposition process. If you have to use rocks as a cover make sure they are not in contact with your faeces.

● **Pack out toilet paper and tampons** Toilet paper, tampons and sanitary towels take a long time to decompose whether buried or not. They can easily be dug up by animals and may then blow into water sources or onto the trail. The best method for dealing with these is to pack them out. Put the used item in a paper bag placed inside a plastic bag and dispose of it at the next toilet.

ACCESS

Britain is a crowded cluster of islands with few places where you can wander as you please. Most of the land is a patchwork of fields and agricultural land and the environment through which the Exmoor & North Devon Coast Path marches is no different. However, there are countless public rights of way (see below), in addition to the main trail, that criss-cross the land.

This is fine, but what happens if you feel a little more adventurous and want to explore the moorland, woodland and hills that can also be found near the walk? Access to the countryside has always been a hot topic in Britain. In the 1940s soldiers coming back from the Second World War were horrified and disgruntled to find that landowners were denying them the right to walk across the moors; ironically the very country that they had been fighting to protect. The battle was finally won in 2005 as new legislation (see p56) came into force granting public access to thousands of acres of Britain's wildest land.

All those who enjoy access to the countryside must respect the land, its wildlife, the interests of those who live and work there and other users; we all share a common interest in the countryside. Knowing your rights and responsibilities gives you the information you need to act with minimal impact.

Rights of way

As a designated National Trail (see box p55) the coast path is a public right of way. A public right of way is either a footpath, a bridleway or a byway. The SWCP is a footpath for almost all its length which means that anyone has the legal right to use it on foot only.

Rights of way are theoretically established because the owner has dedicated them to public use. However, very few paths are formally dedicated in this way. If members of the public have been using a path without interference for 20 years or more the law assumes the owner has intended to dedicate it as a right

❏ THE COUNTRYSIDE CODE

The countryside is a fragile place which every visitor should respect. The Countryside Code, originally described in the 1950s as the Country Code, was revised and relaunched in 2004, in part because of the changes brought about by the CRoW Act (see p56); it was updated again in 2012, 2014 & 2016. The Code seems like common sense but sadly some people still appear to have no understanding of how to treat the countryside they walk in. An adapted version of the 2016 Code (💻 www.gov.uk/gov ernment/publications/the-countryside-code/the-countryside-code), launched under the logo 'Respect. Protect. Enjoy.', is given below:

Respect other people

● **Consider the local community and other people enjoying the outdoors** Be sensitive to the needs and wishes of those who live and work there. If, for example, farm animals are being moved or gathered keep out of the way and follow the farmer's directions. Being courteous and friendly to those you meet will ensure a healthy future for all based on partnership and co-operation.

● **Leave gates and property as you find them and follow paths unless wider access is available** A farmer normally closes gates to keep farm animals in, but may sometimes leave them open so the animals can reach food and water. Leave gates as you find them or follow instructions on signs. When in a group, make sure the last person knows how to leave the gates. Follow paths unless wider access is available, such as on open country or registered common land (known as 'open access land'). Leave machinery and farm animals alone – if you think an animal is in distress try to alert the farmer instead. Use gates, stiles or gaps in field boundaries if you can – climbing over walls, hedges and fences can damage them and increase the risk of farm animals escaping. The path is well supplied with stiles where it crosses field boundaries. If you have to climb over a gate because you can't open it always do so at the hinged end. Also be careful not to disturb ruins and historic sites.

Minimise erosion by not cutting corners or widening the path.

Protect the natural environment

● **Leave no trace of your visit and take your litter home** Take special care not to damage, destroy or remove features such as rocks, plants and trees. Take your litter with you (see p52); litter and leftover food doesn't just spoil the beauty of the countryside, it can be dangerous to wildlife and farm animals.

Fires can be as devastating to wildlife and habitats as they are to people and property – so be careful with naked flames and cigarettes at any time of the year.

● **Keep dogs under effective control** This means you should keep your dog on a lead or in sight at all times, be aware of what it's doing and be confident it will return to you promptly on command. Across farmland dogs should always be kept on a short lead; during lambing time they should not be taken at all. Always clean up after your dog and get rid of the mess responsibly – 'bag it and bin it'. (See also box p38 and pp208-10).

Enjoy the outdoors

● **Plan ahead and be prepared** You're responsible for your own safety: be prepared for natural hazards, changes in weather and other events. Wild animals, farm animals and horses can behave unpredictably if you get too close, especially if they're with their young – so give them plenty of space. Check the weather forecasts and tide times. See also p58.

● **Follow advice and local signs** Get to know the signs and symbols used in the countryside to show paths and open countryside. In some areas there may be temporary diversions in place. Take notice of these and other local trail advice.

of way. If a path has been unused for 20 years it does not cease to exist; the guiding principle is 'once a highway, always a highway'.

On a public right of way you have the right to 'pass and repass along the way' which includes stopping to rest or admire the view, or to consume refreshments. You can also take with you a 'natural accompaniment' (!) which includes a dog, but it must be kept under close control (see box opposite).

Farmers and land managers must ensure that paths are not blocked by crops or other vegetation, or otherwise obstructed, that the route is identifiable and the surface is restored soon after cultivation. If crops are growing over the path you have every right to walk through them, following the line of the right of way as closely as possible. If you find a path blocked or impassable you should report it to the appropriate highway authority. Highway authorities are responsible for maintaining footpaths. In Somerset and North Devon the highway authorities are Somerset and North Devon county councils respectively. The council is also the surveying authority with responsibility for maintaining the official definitive map of public rights of way.

Wider access
The access situation to land around the coast path is a little more complicated. Trying to unravel and understand the seemingly thousands of different laws and acts is never easy in any legal system. Parliamentary Acts give a right to walk over certain areas of land such as some, but by no means all, common land and some specific places such as Dartmoor and the New Forest. However, in other places, such as Bodmin Moor and many British beaches, right of access is not written in law. It is merely tolerated by the landowner and could be terminated at any time.

Some landowners, such as the Forestry Commission, water companies and the National Trust, are obliged by law to allow some degree of access to their land. Land covered by schemes such as the Environmental Stewardship Scheme

❏ National trails
There are 15 national trails in England and Wales. According to the National Trail website (💻 www.nationaltrail.co.uk), the definition of a National Trail 'is a long-distance path (or, in one case, bridleway) for walking, cycling and horse-riding through the finest landscapes in the two countries'. (Scotland, by the way, has its own equivalent, called Long Distance Routes, of which there are four.) In total they cover around 2500 miles (4000km) of pathways, of which the SWCP is the longest by far in the UK; the next longest, the Pennine Way, is a mere 268 miles/429km. The Pennine Way was also the first national trail to be opened, back in 1965.

Each National Trail has been made by linking existing paths together to form one long-distance path, rather than by creating new paths. All of them have a dedicated officer charged with maintaining, improving and promoting the trail. They in turn are helped by the local Highways Authorities, landowners and volunteers who all help in keeping the Trails to a usable standard. Funding for the Trails comes from Natural England and Natural Resources Wales, as well as local highway authorities and other funding partners.

MINIMUM IMPACT & OUTDOOR SAFETY

or Countryside Stewardship Scheme, gives landowners a financial incentive to manage their land for conservation and to provide limited public access. There are also a few truly altruistic landowners who have allowed access over their land and these include organisations such as the RSPB, the Woodland Trust, and some local authorities. Overall, however, access to most of Britain's countryside is forbidden to Britain's people, in marked contrast to the general rights of access that prevail in other European countries.

Right to roam

For many years groups such as Ramblers (see box p40) and the British Mountaineering Council (⌨ www.thebmc.co.uk) campaigned for new and wider access legislation. This finally bore fruit in the form of the Countryside and Rights of Way Act of November 2000, colloquially known as the CRoW Act, which granted access for 'recreation on foot' to mountain, moor, heath, down and registered common land in England and Wales. In essence it allows walkers the freedom to roam responsibly away from footpaths, without being accused of trespass, on about four million acres of open, uncultivated land.

On 28 August 2005 the South-West became the sixth region in England/Wales to be opened up under this act; however, restrictions may still be in place from time to time – check the situation on ⌨ www.gov.uk/right-of-way-open-access-land/use-your-right-to-roam. Natural England (see p61) has mapped the new agreed areas of open access and they are also clearly marked on all the latest Ordnance Survey Explorer (1:25,000) maps. In the future it is hoped that the legislation can be extended to include other types of land such as cliff, foreshore, woodland, riverside and canal side.

Outdoor safety

AVOIDANCE OF HAZARDS

Swimming

If you are not an experienced swimmer or familiar with the sea, plan ahead and swim only at beaches where there is a lifeguard service, such as Woolacombe, Croyde and Saunton. On such beaches you should swim between the red and yellow flags as this is the patrolled area. Don't swim between black and white chequered flags as these areas are only for surfers. A red flag indicates that it is dangerous to enter the water. If you are not sure about anything ask one of the lifeguards; after all they are there to help you.

If you are going to swim at unsupervised beaches never do so alone and always take care. Some beaches are prone to strong rips. Never swim off headlands or near river mouths as there may be strong currents. Always be aware of changing weather conditions and tidal movement. The South-West has a huge tidal range and it can be very easy to get cut off by the tide.

If you see someone in difficulty do not attempt a rescue until you have contacted the coastguard (see below). Once you know help is on the way try to assist the person by throwing something to help them stay afloat. Many beaches have rescue equipment in red boxes should you find yourself needing it.

Walking alone
If you are walking alone you must appreciate and be prepared for the increased risk. Take note of the safety guidelines below.

Safety on the Coast Path
Sadly every year people are injured walking along the trail, though usually it's nothing more than a badly twisted ankle. Parts of Exmoor can be pretty remote, however, and it certainly pays to take precautions when walking. Abiding by the following rules should minimise the risks:

● Avoid walking on your own if possible.
● Make sure that somebody knows your plans for every day you are on the trail. This could be the place you plan to stay in at the end of each day's walk or a friend or relative whom you have promised to call every night. That way, if you fail to turn up or call, they can raise the alarm.
● If the weather closes in suddenly and fog or mist descends and you become uncertain of the correct trail, do not be tempted to continue. Just wait where you are and you'll find that mist often clears, at least for long enough to allow you to get your bearings. If you are still uncertain and the weather doesn't look like improving, return the way you came to the nearest point of civilisation and try again another time when conditions have improved.
● Always fill your water bottle or pouch at every available opportunity (don't empty it until you are certain you can fill it again) and ensure you have some food such as high-energy snacks.
● Always carry a torch, compass, map, whistle and wet-weather gear with you; a mobile phone can be useful though you cannot rely on getting good reception (see p39).
● Wear strong sturdy boots with good ankle support and a good grip, not trainers.
● Be extra vigilant with children.

Dealing with an accident
● Use basic first aid to treat the injury to the best of your ability.
● Try to attract the attention of anybody else who may be in the area. The **international distress (emergency) signal** is six blasts on a whistle, or six flashes with a torch.
● If possible leave someone with the casualty while others go to get help. If there are only two people, you have a dilemma. If you decide to get help, leave all spare clothing and food with the casualty.
● In an emergency dial ☎ 999 and ask for the coastguard. They are responsible for dealing with any emergency that occurs on the coast or at sea. Make sure you know exactly where you are before you call.
● Report the exact position of the casualty and their condition.

WEATHER AND WEATHER FORECASTS

The trail suffers from extremes of weather so it's vital that you always try to find out what the weather is going to be like before you set off for the day. It is a good idea to pay attention to **wind and gale warnings**. The wind on any coastline can get very strong and if it is strong it is advisable not to walk, particularly if you are carrying a pack which can act as a sail. If you are on a steep incline or above high cliffs it is also dangerous.

Even if the wind direction is inland it can literally blow you right over (unpleasant if there are gorse bushes around!), or if it suddenly stops or eddies (a common phenomenon when strong winds hit cliffs) it can cause you to lose your balance and stagger in the direction in which you have been leaning, ie towards the cliffs!

Another hazard on the coast is **sea mist or fog** which can dramatically decrease visibility. If a coastal fog blows over take extreme care where the path runs close to cliff edges.

Most hotels, some B&Bs and TICs will have pinned up somewhere a summary of the **weather forecast**. Alternatively, you can get a forecast through 🖳 www.bbc.co.uk/weather, or 🖳 www.metoffice.gov.uk/public/weather.

Pay close attention to the weather forecast and alter your plans for the day accordingly. That said, even if the forecast is for a fine sunny day, always assume the worst and pack some wet-weather gear.

BLISTERS

It is important to break in new boots before embarking on a long walk. Make sure the boots are comfortable and try to avoid getting them wet on the inside. Air your feet at every opportunity, keep them clean and change your socks regularly; using talcum powder can help to keep them dry. If you feel any hot spots, stop immediately and apply a few strips of zinc oxide tape and leave it on until it is pain free or the tape starts to come off.

If you have left it too late and a blister has developed you should surround it with Compeed or any other blister kit to protect it from abrasion. Popping it can lead to infection. If the skin is broken keep the area clean with antiseptic and cover with a non-adhesive dressing material held in place with tape.

HYPOTHERMIA

Also known as exposure, this occurs when the body can't generate enough heat to maintain its normal temperature, usually as a result of being wet, cold, unprotected from the wind, tired and hungry. It is usually more of a problem in upland areas such as on the moors. Hypothermia is easily avoided by wearing suitable clothing, carrying and eating enough food and drink, being aware of the weather conditions and checking the morale of your companions.

Early signs to watch for are feeling cold and tired with involuntary shivering. Find some shelter as soon as possible and warm the victim up with a hot drink and some chocolate or other high-energy food. If possible give them another warm layer of clothing and allow them to rest until feeling better.

If allowed to worsen, strange behaviour, slurring of speech and poor coordination will become apparent and the victim can quickly progress into unconsciousness, followed by coma and death. Quickly get the victim out of any wind and rain, improvising a shelter if necessary. Rapid restoration of bodily warmth is essential and best achieved by bare-skin contact: someone should get into the same sleeping bag as the patient, both having stripped to their underwear, putting any spare clothing under or over them to build up heat. Send urgently for help.

HYPERTHERMIA

Hyperthermia occurs when the body generates too much heat, eg heat exhaustion and heatstroke. Not ailments that you would normally associate with England, these are serious problems nonetheless.

Symptoms of **heat exhaustion** include thirst, fatigue, giddiness, a rapid pulse, raised body temperature, low urine output and, if not treated, delirium and finally a coma. The best cure is to drink plenty of water. The darker your urine the more you should drink.

Heatstroke is more serious. A high body temperature and an absence of sweating are early indications, followed by symptoms similar to hypothermia (see p58) such as a lack of coordination, convulsions and coma. Death will follow if treatment is not given instantly. Sponge the victim down, wrap them in wet towels, fan them and get help immediately.

SUNBURN

The sun in the South-West can be very strong. The way to avoid sunburn is to stay wrapped up but that's not really an option. What you must do, therefore, is to wear a hat and smother yourself in sunscreen (with a minimum factor of 15); apply it regularly throughout the day.

Don't forget your lips, nose, the back of your neck and even under your chin to protect you against rays reflected from the ground.

MINIMUM IMPACT & OUTDOOR SAFETY

3

THE ENVIRONMENT & NATURE

Flora and fauna

With a varied topography that encompasses a full range of land-scapes from windblasted moor to wetland marsh, hogback cliffs to wooded valleys, muddy estuaries to mobile sand dunes, you can begin to appreciate why the South-West can boast such a rich and varied countryside, with several unique species of flora and thriving populations of mammals and birds that, elsewhere in the UK, struggle to survive.

The following is not in any way a comprehensive guide – if it were, you would not have room for anything else in your rucksack – but merely a brief run-down of the more commonly seen flora and fauna on the trail, together with some of the rarer and more spectacular species.

TREES

For a moorland region Exmoor boasts some surprisingly fine patches of woodland. The most interesting species is the **oak** (family name *Quercus*), which was originally planted as coppice or scrub and supports more kinds of insect than any other tree in Britain. In Exmoor the most prolific species of oak is sessile oak (*Quercus petraea*). Oak woodland is a diverse habitat and not exclusively made up of oak.

Other trees that flourish here include **downy birch** (*Betula pubescens*), its relative the **silver birch** (*Betula pendula*), **holly** (*Ilex aquifolium*) and **hazel** (*Corylus avellana*) which has traditionally

❏ Oak leaves showing galls
Oak trees support more kinds of insects than any other tree in Britain and some affect the oak in unusual ways. Some of these insects affect the oak in interesting ways: the eggs of gall-flies, for example, cause growths known as galls on the leaves. Each of these contains a single insect. Other kinds of gall-flies lay eggs in stalks or flowers, leading to flower galls, growths the size of currants.

❑ CONSERVATION SCHEMES – WHAT'S AN AONB?

It is perhaps the chief joy of this walk that much of it is spent in either a national park or an Area of Outstanding Natural Beauty (AONB). But what exactly are these designations and what protection do they actually confer?

National Parks

The highest level of landscape protection is the designation of land as a **National Park** (🖳 www.nationalparks.gov.uk). There are 15 in Britain of which nine are in England (including, of course, Exmoor National Park on this trail). This designation recognises the national importance of an area in terms of landscape, biodiversity and as a recreational resource. It does not signify national ownership and these are not uninhabited wildernesses, making conservation a knife-edged balance between protecting the environment and the rights and livelihoods of those living in the park.

Areas of Outstanding Natural Beauty

The second level of protection is **Area of Outstanding Natural Beauty** (AONB; 🖳 www.landscapesforlife.org.uk); there are 46 AONBs in the UK, 33 wholly in England. Much of the South-West Coast Path crosses land covered by either this designation or its close relative **Heritage Coasts**, of which there are currently 43 in England and Wales. The primary objective of AONBs is conservation of the natural beauty of a landscape. As there is no statutory administrative framework for their management, this is the responsibility of the local authority within whose boundaries they fall. It is of course one of the joys of this part of the South-West Coast Path that much of the last half of the walk is spent in the **North Devon AONB**, which includes the Heritage Coasts of North Devon and Hartland. Out at sea, **Lundy** is also a heritage coast and it is the only Marine Conservation Zone.

National Nature Reserves and Sites of Special Scientific Interest

The next level of protection includes **National Nature Reserves** (NNRs) and **Sites of Special Scientific Interest** (SSSIs). There are 224 NNRs in England of which three are in Exmoor National Park, with Hawkcombe Wood, near Porlock, the closest to the trail (Dunkery Woods and Tarr Steps are the others in the park). Hawkcombe Wood achieved its status largely because of its insect colonies, including fritillary butterflies. Outside the park and east of Bude lies Dunsdon Farm, which achieved its status due to its Culm grassland pasture that's typical of this region.

There are over 4100 **SSSIs** in England. The **Coastal Heaths of Exmoor** cover an area of 1758 hectares (4343 acres) and boast several rare plants including two species of whitebeam. SSSIs are a particularly important designation as they have some legal standing. They are managed in partnership with the owners and occupiers of the land who must give written notice before initiating any operation likely to damage the site and who cannot proceed without consent from **Natural England** (🖳 www.gov.uk/government/organisations/natural-england), the single body responsible for identifying, establishing and managing National Parks, Areas of Outstanding Natural Beauty, National Nature Reserves, Sites of Special Scientific Interest, and Special Areas of Conservation.

Special Area of Conservation (SAC) is an international designation which came into being as a result of the 1992 Earth Summit in Rio de Janeiro, Brazil. This European-wide network of sites is designed to promote the conservation of habitats, wild animals and plants, both on land and at sea. At the time of writing 235 land sites in England had been designated as SACs. *(cont'd on p62)*

THE ENVIRONMENT & NATURE

Conservation and campaigning organisations *(cont'd from p61)*
These voluntary organisations started the conservation movement in the mid-19th century and are still at the forefront of developments. Independent of government and reliant on public support, they can concentrate their resources either on acquiring land which can then be managed purely for conservation purposes, or on influencing political decision-makers by lobbying and campaigning.

Managers and owners of land include well-known bodies such as the **National Trust** (NT; ⌨ www.nationaltrust.org.uk) that owns over 600 miles of coastline including three sites on the Exmoor coastline (Holnicote, Watersmeet, West Exmoor Coast) and other sites on the Devon coast such as Croyde, Woolacombe and Mortehoe, and Bideford Bay and Hartland; the **Royal Society for the Protection of Birds** (RSPB; ⌨ www.rspb.org.uk), and the **Council for the Protection of Rural England** (CPRE; ⌨ www.cpre.org.uk) and **Woodland Trust** (⌨ www.woodland trust.org.uk).

There is also **The Wildlife Trusts** (⌨ www.wildlifetrusts.org), the umbrella organisation for the 47 wildlife trusts in the UK that manage nature reserves and run marine conservation projects.

been used for coppicing (the periodic cutting of small trees for harvesting).

In addition to Monterey cypress, Scots and Corsican pine, Sitka spruce and Douglas fir are some of the non-native species that have been planted by the landowners of Exmoor down the centuries. Most of the woodland on Exmoor is owned by the Forestry Commission, the Woodland Trust and the National Trust.

FLOWERS

There are said to be around 800 species of wild plants within Exmoor National Park. Spring is the time to come and see the spectacular displays of colour on the South-West Coast Path, when most of the flowers are in bloom. Alternatively, arrive in August and you'll see the heathers carpeting patches of the moors in a blaze of purple flowers.

Woodland and hedgerows

From March to May **bluebells** (*Hyacinthoides non-scripta*) proliferate in some of the woods along the trail, providing a wonderful spectacle. The white **wood anemone** (*Anemone nemorosa*) – wide open flowers when sunny, closed and drooping when the weather's dull – and the yellow **primrose** (*Primula vulgaris*) also flower early in spring.

Red campion (*Silene dioica*), which flowers from late April, can be found in hedgebanks along with **rosebay willowherb** (*Epilobium augustifolium*) which also has the name fireweed due to its habit of colonising burnt areas.

In scrubland and on woodland edges you will find **bramble** (*Rubus fruticosus*), a common vigorous shrub responsible for many a ripped jacket thanks to its sharp thorns and prickles. Blackberry fruits ripen from late summer to autumn.

Fairly common in scrubland and on woodland edges is the **dog rose** (*Rosa canina*) which has a large pink flower, the fruits of which are used to make rose-hip syrup.

Look out, too, on the water in streams or rivers for the white-flowered **water crow-foot** (*Ranunculus penicillatus pseudofluitans*) which, because it needs unpolluted, flowing water, is a good indicator of the cleanliness of the stream.

Other flowering plants to look for in wooded areas and in hedgerows include the tall **foxglove** (*Digitalis purpurea*) with its trumpet-like flowers, **forget-me-not** (*Myosotis arvensis*) with tiny, delicate blue flowers, and **cow parsley** (*Anthriscus sylvestris*), a tall member of the carrot family with a large globe of white flowers which often covers roadside verges and hedgebanks.

Heathland and scrubland

There are three species of heather. The most dominant is **ling** (*Calluna vulgaris*) with tiny flowers on delicate upright stems. The other two species are **bell heather** (*Erica cinera*) with deep purple bell-shaped flowers and **cross-leaved heath** (*Erica tetralix*) with similarly shaped flowers of a lighter pink, almost white colour. Cross-leaved heath prefers wet and boggy ground. As a result, it usually grows away from bell heather which prefers well-drained soils.

Heather is an incredibly versatile plant which is put to many uses. It provides fodder for livestock, fuel for fires, an orange dye and material for bedding, thatching, basketwork and brooms. It is still sometimes used in place of hops to flavour beer and the flower heads can be brewed to make good tea. It is also incredibly hardy and thrives on the denuded hills, preventing other species from flourishing. Indeed, at times highland cattle are brought to certain areas of the moors to graze on the heather, allowing other species a chance to grow.

Not a flower but worthy of mention is the less attractive species **bracken** (*Pteridium aquilinum*), a vigorous non-native fern that has invaded many heathland areas to the detriment of native species.

Grassland

There is much overlap between the hedge/woodland-edge habitat and that of pastures and meadows. You will come across **common birdsfoot-trefoil** (*Lotus corniculatus*), **Germander speedwell** (*Veronica chamaedrys*), **tufted** and **bush vetch** (*Vicia cracca* and *V. sepium*) and **meadow vetchling** (*Lathyrus pratensis*) in both. Often the only species you will see in heavily grazed pastures are the most resilient.

Of the thistles, in late summer you should come across the **melancholy thistle** (*Cirsium helenoides*) drooping sadly on roadside verges and hay meadows; unusually, it has no prickles on its stem. The **yellow rattle** is aptly named as its dry seedpods rattle in the wind; this is a good indication for farmers that it is time to harvest the hay.

Other widespread grassland species include **harebell** (*Campanula rotundifolia*), delicate yellow **tormentil** (*Potentilla erecta*) and **devil's-bit scabious**

(*Succisa pratensis*). Also keep an eye out for orchids such as the **fragrant orchid** (*Gymnaadenia conopsea*) and **early purple orchid** (*Orchis mascula*).

Dunes

Dunes are formed by wind action creating a fragile, unstable environment. Among the first colonisers is **marram grass** (*Ammophila arenaria*) which is able to withstand drought, exposure to wind and salt spray and has an ability to grow up through new layers of sand that cover it. Other specialist plants are **sea holly** (*Eryngium maritimum*), **sea spurge** (*Euphorbia paralias*) and **sea bindweed** (*Calystegia soldanella*). The one thing that these seemingly indomitable plants can't tolerate is trampling by human feet; stay on the path which is nearly always well marked through dunes.

MAMMALS

The South-West is blessed with wildlife and three species of mammals are particularly associated with the region. The largest population of **red deer**, *Cervus Elaphus*, lives on Exmoor – one of only three places where the herds are resident in England. Red deer, Britain's biggest wild animal, are nevertheless shy by nature and tend to flee at the approach of people.

There is a very slim chance that a stag may charge during the rutting (mating) season when their behaviour can be unpredictable, though there is no record of this ever happening on Exmoor. They are largely nocturnal and your best chance of seeing them is at dusk when they move out of their woodland coverts to feed. Stags and hinds live separately for most of the year, mingling properly only during the mating season of October and November.

Also at home on the moor are the famous **Exmoor ponies**, a very ancient breed that resembles the miniature breeds of Asia more than any other native British horse. These ponies are hardy and also largely wild or feral, though in the past they were trained to work in mines, on farms or for shepherding. There have never been many of them and during WWII their numbers collapsed to around 50. Today there are more than 500 adult breeding females (most on Exmoor), though a relatively small gene pool – after all, all today's ponies are descended from those 50 – means that they are still on the endangered list.

The third species for which the South-West is renowned is the **otter** (*Lutra lutra*). With Devon the home of the author Henry Williamson – author of *Tarka the Otter* – the county is proud to be associated with this most graceful of British carnivores and even has a Tarka Trail (see box p34). It wasn't always like this, however, and for much of the 20th century (and before) the otter was persecuted because it was (wrongly) believed to have an enormously detrimental effect on fish stocks.

Indeed, the otter was hunted with dogs up until 1977 and the Culmstock Otter Hounds were a regular sight in Exmoor National Park, particularly in the Exe and Barle valleys. Thankfully, today the otter is enjoying something of a renaissance due to some concerted conservation efforts. At home both in saltwater and freshwater, they are a good indicator of an unpolluted environment and Exmoor in particular is enjoying a resurgence in otter numbers; there are

Bell Heather
Erica cinerea

Heather (Ling)
Calluna vulgaris

Thrift (Sea Pink)
Armeria maritima

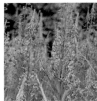

Rosebay Willowherb
Epilobium angustifolium

Common Vetch
Vicia sativa

Forget-me-not
Myosotis arvensis

Rowan (tree)
Sorbus aucuparia

Spear Thistle
Cirsium vulgare

Red Campion
Silene dioica

Early Purple Orchid
Orchis mascula

Foxglove
Digitalis purpurea

Sea Holly
Eryngium maritimum

Common Dog Violet
Viola riviniana

Common Centaury
Centaurium erythraea

Honeysuckle
Lonicera periclymemum

Ramsons (Wild Garlic)
Allium ursinum

Germander Speedwell
Veronica chamaedrys

Herb-Robert
Geranium robertianum

Lousewort
Pedicularis sylvatica

Self-heal
Prunella vulgaris

Scarlet Pimpernel
Anagallis arvensis

Sea Campion
Silene maritima

Bluebell
Hyacinthoides non-scripta

Hogweed
Heracleum sphondylium

Dog Rose
Rosa canina

Meadow Buttercup
Ranunculis acris

Gorse
Ulex europaeus

Tormentil
Potentilla erecta

Birdsfoot-trefoil
Lotus corniculatus

Ox-eye Daisy
Leucanthemum vulgare

Common Ragwort
Senecio jacobaea

Primrose
Primula vulgaris

Cowslip
Primula veris

Colour photos (following pages)

● **C4 Top left**: After the steep climb, take a well-deserved break to enjoy the tremendous views back over the Heddon Valley. **Right**: The Lynton and Lynmouth Cliff Railway (see p102), with Foreland Point in the distance. **Bottom**: The riverside at Lynmouth (see p98).
● **C5 Left**: Looking east, across Lee Bay. **Top right**: Culbone Church (see p93). **Bottom right**: The local lifeboat shelters in the estuary to the Taw and Torridge rivers; across the water the southern end of Braunton Burrows can be seen.
● **C6 Top**: Woolacombe's award-winning beach. **Right**: *Verity*, Damien Hirst's sculpture (see p120), gazes out over the Bristol Channel from Ilfracombe. **Bottom**: Ilfracombe.
● **C7 Left**: After a hard day's walk, Clovelly's steeply cobbled streets can be a challenge (see p180). **Right (top)**: Staunton Court, visible from the alternative route out of Staunton Sands. (Photo © Henry Stedman). **Middle**: South of Hartland Quay, you'll experience mile-upon-majestic-mile of cliff-top walking. **Bottom left**: A matter of metres from Cornwall you'll pass the hut of the writer, Ronald Duncan (see p194). **Bottom right**: Wherever you look, the views from Hartland Quay are tremendous; Lundy Island in the distance.

C6

now known to be at least 23 residing in Exmoor – a healthy number, given the size of the territory an otter requires. Trivia fans may like to know that the final, climactic scene of the 1979 film version of *Tarka* was set on Instow Beach in North Devon. The author Henry Williamson was taken seriously ill during filming and is said to have died during the filming of the last scene.

Seeing any of these animals requires patience and no little amount of luck. One creature that you will definitely see along the walk, however, is the **rabbit** (*Oryctolagus cuniculus*). Timid by nature, most of the time you'll have to make do with nothing more than a brief and distant glimpse of their white tails as they race for the nearest warren at the sound of your footfall. Because they are so numerous, however, the laws of probability dictate that you will at some stage during your walk get close enough to observe them without being spotted; trying to take a decent photo of one, however, is a different matter.

If you're lucky you may also come across **hares** (*Lepus europaeus*), often mistaken for rabbits but much larger, more elongated and with longer ears and back legs. There are populations of hares all over the arable parts of Exmoor, though nowhere is it common.

Like the otter, the **water vole** (*Arvicola terrestris*) has both been a major character in a well-known work of fiction (in this case 'Ratty' from Kenneth Grahame's classic children's story *Wind in the Willows*), and has suffered a devastating drop in its population. Their numbers had originally declined due to the arrival in the UK countryside of the mink from North America, which successfully adapted to living in the wild after escaping from local fur farms. Unfortunately, the mink not only hunts water voles but is small enough to slip inside their burrows. Thus, with the voles afforded no protection, the mink was able to wipe out an entire riverbank's population in a matter of months. (Incidentally, this is another reason why protecting the otter is important: they kill mink.) A programme is now in place in which the water vole and its habitat is not only protected but the mink are being trapped and killed.

Another native British species that has suffered at the hands of a foreign invader – and indeed has now disappeared altogether from Exmoor and this part of the South-West – is the red squirrel (*Sciurus vulgaris*), a small, tufty-eared native that has been usurped by its larger cousin from North America, the **grey squirrel** (*Sciurus carolinensis*). The nearest place to see the red squirrel is at Poole Harbour – at the very end of the South-West Coast Path!

(Opposite) Top left: The robins at Kitnors Tearooms in Bossington (see p84) are particularly friendly, although it is likely to be your scone rather than your company they're after. **Top right**: Grey heron are common along the East Lyn River. **Middle**: The feral goats that inhabit the Valley of the Rocks (see p106), near Lynmouth, have been here for many centuries and are now a mix of breeds including the Cheviot (an ancient British breed) and the Swiss Saanen. (Photo © Henry Stedman). **Bottom**: Great views but no meat on the bones atop the summit of Great Hangman (see p112), at 318m/1043ft the highest point on the entire South-West Coast Path. (Photo © Henry Stedman).

Other creatures you might see include the ubiquitous **fox** (*Vulpes vulpes*), now just as at home in the city as it is in the countryside. While generally considered nocturnal, it's not unusual to encounter a fox during the day too, often lounging in the sun near its den.

❏ **The Beast of Exmoor**
Red deer, ponies, otters, badgers... Exmoor isn't short of wildlife to observe and admire. Ask the people of Britain, however, what animal they most associate with the park and the chances are many will mention a creature that only a handful of people have ever seen – and which, officially at least, doesn't even exist.

That creature is the Beast of Exmoor. Sightings of a large, panther-like animal roaming the moors of North Devon were first reported back in the 1970s and reached their peak in 1983 when a sheep farmer in South Molton claimed that over a hundred of his herd had been killed in the space of just three months, their throats in each case having savagely been ripped from them. As speculation about the nature of the beast reached fever-pitch, there were reports of 'copycat' (!) sightings of similar creatures from as far away as Kent and Scotland.

At first the authorities were inclined to take the reports seriously and in response to the attacks on livestock, the Ministry of Agriculture sent in a troop of marines with high-powered rifles to hunt and kill any animal that fitted the description of a large cat between four and eight feet from nose to tail, that tended to crouch low to the ground but which had the ability to leap over six-foot-tall fences, and which was either black, tan or dark grey in colour.

Their mission proved unsuccessful, however, and the commanding officer – possibly with his tongue lodged in his cheek at the time – asserted that, if the creature did exist, it used the surrounding cover of hedges and woods with an almost 'human-like intelligence'.

News that the marines had returned to their barracks clearly reached the creature, for reports of sheep deaths on the moor continued to rise, with 200 sheep killings attributed to the beast in 1987. There was even more good news for the Beast in the mid-1990s when the authorities, growing ever-more sceptical at the lack of any hard evidence of its existence, concluded that there was, in fact, no Beast of Exmoor. In their opinion, all alleged sightings were either the product of mistaken identifications of the more 'mundane' members of Exmoor's animal kingdom (eg domestic cats, dogs and even sheep), or deliberate hoaxes. It was a point of view that was given added credence in 2009 when a carcass washed up on North Devon turned out not to be the body of the beast, but a badly decomposed seal; and again in 2010 when photos of the beast appeared on the front pages of various tabloids – before it was discovered that the photographer had been doctoring his pictures using Photoshop.

Today, the more sober followers of the story have concluded that, if there ever was a Beast of Exmoor, there isn't one now (panthers live for only about 15 years on average). But there remains the distinct possibility that such a creature did once prowl the moors. Experts of 'phantom' or cryptozoological cats (to give them their proper title) point to a fad in the 1960s and 1970s to keep wild cats as pets. Given that in 1976 the Dangerous Wild Animals Act effectively outlawed this practice, it is highly possible that one of these large cats either escaped – or was deliberately released – by its owner into the wild.

But while the creature may not exist anymore, it does, of course, live on in popular memory, folklore – and as a particularly potent concoction of Exmoor Ales Brewery whose Beast of Exmoor Ale weighs in at an impressive 6.6% ABV!

Another creature of the night you may *occasionally* see in the late afternoon is the **badger** (*Meles meles*). Relatively common throughout the British Isles, these sociable mammals with their distinctive black-and-white striped muzzles live in large underground burrows called setts, appearing around sunset to root for worms and slugs.

One creature that is strictly nocturnal, however, is the **bat**, of which there are 17 species in Britain, all protected by law. Your best chance of spotting one is at dusk while there's still enough light in the sky to make out their flitting forms as they fly along hedgerows, over rivers and streams and around street lamps in their quest for moths and insects. The commonest species in Britain is the **pipistrelle** (*Pipistrellus pipistrellus*).

In addition to the above, keep a look out for other fairly common but little seen species such as the carnivorous **stoat** (*Mustela erminea*), its diminutive cousin the **weasel** (*Mustela nivalis*), the **hedgehog** (*Erinaceus europaeus*) – these days, alas, most commonly seen as roadkill – and any number of species of **voles**, **mice** and **shrews**.

REPTILES

The **adder** (*Vipera berus*) is the only poisonous snake of the three species found in Britain. They pose very little risk to walkers – indeed, you should consider yourself extremely fortunate to see one, providing you're a safe distance away. They bite only when provoked, preferring to hide instead. The venom is designed to kill small mammals such as mice, voles and shrews, so deaths in humans are very rare but a bite can be extremely unpleasant and occasionally dangerous to children or the elderly. You are most likely to encounter them in spring when they come out of hibernation and during the summer when pregnant females warm themselves in the sun. They are easily identified by the striking zigzag pattern on their back. Should you be lucky enough to encounter one, (they enjoy basking on clifftops and on the moors) enjoy it but leave it undisturbed.

The **grass snake** (*Natrix natrix*) is the largest British species, growing up to four feet in length. Olive-grey in colour with short black bars down each side and orange or yellow patches just below the head, they are harmless, relying not on venom or biting for defence but instead give off a foul odour if disturbed. It is pretty scarce in the south-west but can be found in damp places on Exmoor.

The **slow-worm** (*Anguis fragilis*) must be one of the more unusual creatures in the British Isles – a reptile that is called a worm, looks like a snake but is actually a legless lizard! Silver-grey with a dark line down the centre of the back and along each side, it is common on Exmoor and in North Devon in general, where it feeds on slugs, worms and insects.

SEA LIFE

The high cliffs are also a great place from which to look out over the sea. Searching for seals is an enjoyable and essential part of cliff walking. You'll spot lots of grey lobster-pot buoys before your first seal, but it's worth the effort.

THE ENVIRONMENT & NATURE

❑ **Reporting wildlife sightings**
Report basking shark sightings to the website of the Marine Conservation Society (🖥 www.mcsuk.org). Remember to note any tags you've spotted. Reports are greatly appreciated.

If you see any of the other larger marine creatures such as dolphins, whales or seals you can report them online through Seaquest Southwest, part of the Devon Biodiversity Records Centre (🖥 www.dbrc.org.uk). With any report give the location, number and the direction they were heading in.

If you come across a stranded marine animal like a dolphin or porpoise, don't approach it but contact either British Divers' Marine Life Rescue (☎ 01825-765546, 🖥 www.bdmlr.org.uk) or the RSPCA hotline (☎ 0300-123 4999).

Atlantic grey seals (*Halichoerus grypus*) relax in the water, looking over their big Roman noses with doggy eyes, as interested in you as you are in them. Twice the weight of a red deer, a big bull can be over 200kg. On calm sunny days it's possible to follow them down through the clear water as they dive, as elegant in their element as they are clumsy on land. Seals generally come ashore only to rest, moult their fur, or to breed. The main centre where seals 'haul out' – come up on the rocks – is Lundy Island (see box p122). Indeed, Devon is a sort of frontier for the seals, as they rarely haul out east of here until you reach Norfolk.

A cliff-top sighting of Britain's largest fish is also a real possibility, but is more chilling than endearing! **Basking sharks** (*Cetorhinus maximus*) can grow to a massive eleven metres and weigh seven tonnes, and their two fins, a large shark-like dorsal fin followed by a notched tail fin, are so far apart it takes a second look to be convinced it's one fish. But these are gentle giants, cruising slowly with open jaws, filtering microscopic plankton from the sea. You are most likely to see one during late spring and summer when they feed at the surface during calm, warm weather. Look out for the coloured or numbered tags, which have been put on for research into this sadly declining species, and report them to the address given in the box above.

Taking a longer view and with some good luck, you may see **harbour porpoises** (*Phocoena phocoena*) and **bottlenose dolphins** (*Tursiops truncatus*); the former are particularly prevalent in Ilfracombe. Other cetaceans you may catch a glimpse of are: **Risso's dolphins** (*Grampus griseus*), **common dolphins** (*Delphinus delphis*), **striped dolphins** (*Stenella coeruleoalba*), **orcas** or **killer whales** (*Orcinus orca*) and **pilot whales** (*Globicephala melaena*). However, be warned, they are fiendishly difficult to tell apart: a brief glimpse of a fin is nothing like the 'whole animal' pictures shown in field guides.

BIRDS

In and around the fishing villages

The wild laugh of the **herring gull** (*Larus argentatus*) is the wake-up call of the coast path. Perched on the rooftops of the stone villages, they are a reminder of the link between people and wildlife, the rocky coast and our stone and concrete towns and cities. Shoreline scavengers, they've adapted to the increasing waste thrown out by human society. Despite their bad reputation it's worth taking a closer look at these fascinating, ubiquitous birds. How do they keep their pale grey and white plumage so beautiful feeding on rubbish?

Nobel-prize-winning animal behaviourist Nikko Tinbergen showed how the young pecking at the red dot on their bright yellow bills triggers the adult to regurgitate food. In August the newly fledged brown young follow their parents begging for food. Over the next three years they'll go through a motley range of plumages, more grey and less brown each year till they reach adulthood. But please don't feed them and do watch your sandwiches and fish & chips – they are quite capable of grabbing food from your hand.

The village harbours are a good place for lunch or an evening drink after a hard day on the cliffs. Look out for the birds which are equally at home on a rocky shore or in villages, such as the beautiful little black-and-white **pied wagtail** (*Motacilla alba*) with its long, bobbing tail.

Also looking black from a distance as they strut the beach are **jackdaws** (*Corvus monedula*). Close up, however, they are beautiful with a grey nape giving them a hooded look and shining blue eyes. They are very sociable: you will often see them high up in the air in pairs or flocks playing tag or performing acrobatic tricks.

Small, dark brown and easy to miss, the **rock pipit** (*Anthus petrosus*) is one of our toughest birds, as it feeds whilst walking on the rocks between the land and the sea. They nest in crevices and caves along the rocky coastline.

Seen on or from the sea cliffs

Walking on the coastal path leads you into a world of rock and sea, high cliffs with bracken-clad slopes, exposed green pasture, dramatic drops and headlands, sweeping sandy beaches and softer country around the estuaries. Stunning **stonechats** (*Saxicola torquata*) with black, white and orange colouring are common on heath and grassy plains where you may hear their distinctive song, which is not dissimilar to two stones being clacked together. Twittering **linnets** (*Carduelis cannabina*) with their bright red breasts and grey heads fly ahead and perch on gorse and fences. The vertiginous swoops of the path mean it's often possible to be at eye level or even look down on birds and mammals. Watch for **kestrels** (*Falco tinnunculus*), hovering on sharp brown wings, before plummeting onto their prey.

At eye level the black 'moustache' of the powerful slate-grey-backed **peregrine** (*Falco peregrinus*) is sometimes visible. At a glance it can be mistaken for a pigeon, its main prey. But the power and speed of this, the world's fastest bird, soon sets it apart. In the late summer whole families fly over the cliffs. In mid winter look for them over estuaries where they hunt ducks and waders. Despite the remote fastness of the cliffs, peregrine have suffered terribly. Accidental poisoning by the pesticide DDT succeeded where WWII persecution for fear they would kill carrier pigeons failed, and they were almost extinct in this region by the end of the 1960s. Its triumphant return means not only a thriv-

GUILLEMOT
L: 450mm/18"

ing population on its traditional sea cliffs, but more and more nesting in our cities on man-made cliffs, such as tower blocks and cathedrals.

Cliff ledges, a kind of multi-storey block of flats for birds, provide nesting places safe from marauding land predators such as foxes and rats. It's surprising just how close it's possible to get to **fulmars** (*Fulmarus glacialis*), which return to their nesting ledges in February for the start of the long breeding season that goes on into the autumn. Only in the depth of winter are the cliffs quiet. Fulmars are related to albatrosses and like them are masters of the air. You can distinguish them from gulls by their ridged, flat wings as they sail the wind close to the waves with the occasional burst of fast flapping. Fulmars are incredibly tenacious at holding their nesting sites and vomit a stinking oily secretion over any intruders, including rock-climbers! The elegant **kittiwake** (*Rissa tridactyla*), the one true seagull that never feeds on land, is another cliff nester, identified by its 'dipped in ink' black wingtips.

Black above, white below, **manx shearwaters** (*Puffinus puffinus*) make globe-encircling journeys as they sail effortlessly just above even the wildest sea. Small and fast on hard-beating wings black and white **guillemots** (*Uria troile*) and **razorbills** (*Alca torda*) shoot out from their nesting ledges hidden in the cliffs. Guillemot have a long thin bill, razorbill a heavy half circle. There are

SWALLOW
L: 190mm/7½"

large colonies of auks, razorbills and guillemots around the Highveer Point to Lynmouth area. **Puffins** (*Fratercula arctica*) with their unmistakable parrot-shaped bills are a rare prize round these coasts. Lundy, once again, is the best place to see these lovely birds.

Less lovely in most people's eyes, though undeniably magnificent, the big, rapacious **great black-backed gulls** (*Larus marinus*) cruise the nesting colonies for prey. Star of the sea show, however, has to be the big, sharp-winged, Persil-white **gannets** (*Morus bassanus*) cruising slowly for fish, then suddenly plunging with folded wings into the sea. Their strengthened skulls protect them from the huge force of the impact with the water.

HOUSE MARTIN
L: 140mm/5½"

Two birds more familiar from the artificial cliffs of our cities can be seen here in their natural habitat – **house martins** (*Delichon urbica*), steely-blue backed like a **swallow** (*Hirundo rustica*), but with more V-shaped wings and a distinctive white rump, and **rock**

doves (*Columba livia*). These are so mixed with **town pigeons** (*Columba livia domest.*) it's hard to say if any 'pure' wild birds remain, but many individuals with the characteristic grey back, small white rump and two black wing bars can be seen.

Where the path drops steeply to a rocky bay, **oystercatchers** (*Haematopus ostralegus*), with their black and white plumage and spectacular carrot-coloured bill, pipe in panic when they fly off. This is also a good spot to get close to **shags** (*Phalacrocorax aristotelis*) and **cormorants** (*Phalacrocorax pygmeus*), common all round the coast, swimming low and black in the water. Shags are smaller and are always seen on the sea – cormorants are also on rivers and estuaries – and in the summer have a crest whilst cormorants have a white patch near their tail and white face. Close up, these oily birds shine iridescently; shags are green, cormorants are purple. They are a primitive species and since their feathers are not completely waterproof both have to dry their bodies after time in the sea; their heraldic pose, standing upright with half-spread wings on drying rocks is one of the special sights of the coast path.

SKYLARK
L: 185MM/7.25"

In pastures, combes and woods

The path rises up onto rich green pasture. **Skylarks** (*Alauda arvensis*) soar tunefully – almost disappearing into the spring sky, while in winter small green-brown **meadow pipits** (*Anthus pratensis*) flit weakly, giving a small high-pitched call. Spring also brings migrant **wheatears** (*Oenanthe oenanthe*): they are beautiful with their grey and black feathers above, buff and white below, and unmistakable when they fly and show their distinctive white rump. **Buzzards** (*Buteo buteo*) soar up with their tilted, broad round wings, giving their high, wild Ke-oow cry. **Ravens** (*Corvus corax*) cronk-cronk over the cliffs and are distinguished from more common **carrion crows** (*Corvus corone*) by their huge size and wedge-shaped tail. In the woods you'll find all three native species of **woodpecker – green**, **great** and **lesser spotted** (*Picus viridis* and *Dendrocopos major* and *minor* respectively); the latter two are very much wedded to the woods, while the former, with its laughing call, can often be seen on the moors looking for insects.

In spring familiar birds such as **robins** (*Erithacus rubecula*), **blackbirds** (*Turdus merula*), **blue** and **great tits**

GREEN
WOODPECKER
L: 330MM/13"

GREAT SPOTTED
WOODPECKER
L: 230MM/9"

(*Parus major* & *caeruleus*), **chaffinches** (*Fringila coelebs*) and **dunnocks** (*Prunella modularis*) are joined by the small green **chiffchaff** (*Phylloscopus collybita*); it's not much to look at but is one of the earliest returning migrants and unmistakably calls its own name in two repeated notes.

In and around estuaries

Descending to the long walk round the estuaries is moving into a different, softer world of shelter and rich farmland. Best for birds in winter, they are a welcome refuge from the ferocity of the worst weather for wildlife and people. There are large flocks of ducks – whistling **wigeon** (*Anas penelope*), a combination of grey and pinky brown, with big white wing patches in flight – and waders like the brown **curlew** (*Numenius arquata*) with its impossibly long, down-curved beak and beautiful sad fluting call, evocative of summer moors. The **redshank** (*Tringa totanus*), **greenshank** (*Tringa nebularia*), golden and grey **plover** (*Pluvialis sp.*) and black-tailed and bar-tailed **godwit** (*Limosa sp.*) can also be seen in winter.

CURLEW
L: 600MM/24"

Look out for the big black, white and chestnut **shelduck** (*Tadorna tadorna*), and for the tall grey **heron** (*Ardea cinerea*), hunched at rest or extended to its full 175cm as it slowly, patiently stalks fish in the shallows. A real rarity 10 years ago, another species of heron, the stunning white **little egret** (*Egretta garzetta*) is now unmissable on estuaries. Here the more common gull is the nimble **black-headed gull** (*Larus ridibundus*), with its elegant cap, dark in summer but pale in winter. In summer, terns come: the big **sandwich tern** (*Sterna sandvicensis*) with its shaggy black cap and loud rasping call, and the smaller sleeker aerobatic **common tern** (*Sterna hirundo*).

BUTTERFLIES AND MOTHS

Butterflies are an unexpected treat on the SWCP. Not only are they numerous, but there are several different varieties too. Braunton Burrows (see box p142) plays host to several species including marbled whites, graylings, ringlets and skippers, as well as to **moths**, including ghost, common swift, diamond-back, garden grass veneer and small China mark moths. Butterflies and moths aren't confined to the burrows, however.

The most famous butterfly in the region is the orange and brown heath fritillary, which has declined rapidly over the last 30 years in the UK, but which is thriving in the combes of Exmoor (indeed, Exmoor is one of only four places where they still live, and there are now 15 colonies in the national park).

ROUTE GUIDE & MAPS

Using this guide

The route guide has been described from east to west and divided into ten stages. Though each of these roughly corresponds to a day's walk, do not assume that this is the only way to plan your walk. There are so many places to stay en route that you can pretty much divide up the walk wherever you want. However, see the boxes on p32 and p33 for some suggested itineraries.

To provide further help, practical information is presented on the trail maps, including walking times, places to stay, camp and eat, as well as shops where you can buy supplies, and public toilets. Further service details are given in the text under the entry for each settlement.

For a condensed overview of this information see the village and town facilities table on pp30-1.

TRAIL MAPS

Scale and walking times

The trail maps are to a scale of 1:20,000 (1cm = 200m; $3^1/_8$ inches = one mile). Walking times are given along the side of each map and the arrow shows the direction to which the time refers. Black triangles indicate the points between which the times have been taken. **See note in the box on p74 on walking times**.

The time-bars are a tool and are not there to judge your walking ability. There are so many variables that affect walking speed, from the weather conditions to how many beers you drank the previous evening. After the first hour or two of walking you will be able to see how your speed relates to the timings on the maps.

Up or down?

Other than when on a track or bridleway the trail is shown as a dotted line. An arrow across the trail indicates the slope; two arrows show that it is steep. Note that the arrow points towards the higher part of the trail. If, for example, you are walking from A (at 80m) to B (at 200m) and the trail between the two is short and steep it would be shown thus: A — — — >> — — – B. Reversed arrow heads indicate downward gradient.

GPS waypoints

The numbered GPS waypoints refer to the list on pp206-7.

Accommodation

Apart from in large towns where some selection of places has been necessary, almost every place to stay that is within easy reach of the trail is marked. Details of each place are given in the accompanying text.

For **B&B-style accommodation** the number and type of rooms is given after each entry: **S** = single room (one single bed), **T** = twin room (two single beds), **D** = double room (one double bed, or two single beds pushed/joined together), **Tr** = triple room and **Qd** = quad. Note that many of the triple/quad rooms have a double bed and either one/two single beds, or bunk beds, thus in a group of three or four, two people would have to share the double bed, but it also means the room can be used as a double or twin. Many places describe these rooms as family rooms.

Rates quoted are are **per person (pp)** based on two people sharing a room for a one-night stay; rates are usually discounted for longer stays. Where a single room **(sgl)** is available the rate for that is quoted if different from the rate per person. The rate for single occupancy **(sgl occ)** of a double/twin may be higher and the per person rate for **three/four sharing** a triple/quad may be lower. Unless specified, rates are for bed and breakfast. At some places, generally chain hotels, the only option is a **room rate**; this will be the same whether one or two people (or more if permissible) use the room; this rate generally doesn't include breakfast. See p21 for more information on rates.

The text also mentions whether the rooms are en suite or whether they have private or shared facilities and also if a **bath** (🛁) is available in at least one room. Also noted is whether premises have **wi-fi** (WI-FI), packed lunches (Ⓛ) are available if requested in advance and if **dogs** (🐕) are welcome. Most places will not take more than one dog in a room and also accept them only subject to prior arrangement. Some make an additional charge (usually per night but occasionally per stay) while others may require a deposit which is refundable if the dog doesn't make a mess. See also pp20-1.

Many places do not accept advance **bookings** for a single-night stay at weekends or in peak holiday periods but they will if someone calls near the actual date or on the day. Some B&Bs don't accept credit/debit cards but guesthouses and hotels usually do. Booking is essential for all **campsites** in school holidays but is usually not necessary at other times.

Other features

Features are marked on the map when pertinent to navigation. In order to avoid cluttering the maps and making them unusable not all features have been marked each time they occur.

❑ **Important note – walking times**
Unless otherwise specified, **all times in this book refer only to the time spent walking**. You will need to add 20-30% to allow for rests, photography, checking the map, drinking water etc. When planning the day's hike count on 5-7 hours' actual walking.

The route guide

MINEHEAD   [MAP 1, p77]

Some towns inspire. They have an air of adventure and a sense of urgency. They are mysterious and just a little frightening. You know as soon as you walk into them they are special places. Minehead isn't one of them.

Mark Wallington, *500 Mile Walkies*

Minehead may not be quite as bad as Mr Wallington would have you believe but there's not much to delay you here. The town's major draw, the huge Butlin's holiday camp on Minehead's eastern fringes, will probably hold little appeal to the average walker. Indeed, Minehead doesn't even have a mine – the name actually derives from the Celtic word, Mynedd, meaning 'hill'.

Nevertheless, Minehead's location, where the flat, former marshlands of Somerset collide with the rolling hills of Exmoor, is a good one, and the town's port was once, during Elizabethan times, a thriving place, built on foundations that date back to Saxon times. Today, however, the place is much sleepier, the biggest thrill in town being the intermittent arrival of the steam trains of **West Somerset Railway** (see box p45) as they puff and chuff into Minehead's centre.

Despite its lack of thrills, as a place to begin a 124½ mile/200km adventure (630 miles if you're hoping to complete the SWCP!), Minehead is pretty good: there are reasonable transport connections (by the standards of the South-West, anyway); plenty of places to stay and eat, should you require them; and with no 'must-sees' in town that demand to be visited, there's little to delay you should you wish to push on with your walking as soon as you arrive.

Services

Minehead Information Centre (☎ 01643-702624, 🖳 www.visit-exmoor.co.uk/mine head; Apr-Oct Tue-Sat 10am-4pm, Sun 11am-4pm, Oct-Apr Sat & Sun noon-3pm) can be found where the main drag meets the

sea at The Beach Hotel (see Where to stay). The centre has a decent range of information on the SWCP including bus timetables and is staffed by knowledgeable locals who can also do accommodation booking. There is also a small **museum** (same hours).

For supplies the most central **supermarket** is the Co-op (Mon-Sat 6am-10pm, Sun 10am-4pm), on The Avenue, at the back of which you'll find the **post office** (Mon-Fri 9am-5.30pm, Sat 9am-5pm). For last-minute **camping** or **photography** requirements, opposite each other on Friday St are The Camping and Outdoor Shop (🖳 www.thecampingandoutdoorshop .co.uk; Mon-Sat 9.30am-5pm) and Priddy's Photoshop (🖳 www.priddys.co.uk; Mon-Fri 9am-5.30pm, Sat 9am-5pm).

The **library** (🖳 www.librarieswest .org.uk; Mon, Tue, Thur 9am-5.30pm, Fri to 5pm, Sat to 1pm) has a few terminals dedicated to **internet access**. Walkers can access one for free for up to an hour with a temporary membership.

If on the journey here you've already managed to acquire blisters or other ailments, Boots the **chemist** (Mon-Sat 8.30am-5.30pm, Sun 10am-4pm) has a branch on the main drag of The Parade and there are several **banks** with ATMs scattered along it, including HSBC by The Duke of Wellington.

Transport

For details on getting to Minehead, see pp44-50 and for local services see pp48-50. For destinations further along the path, Buses of Somerset's No 10 **bus** service runs between Minehead and Porlock Weir and their No 28 goes to Taunton. Filers Travel and Quantock Heritage operate the seasonal No 300 (to Lynmouth via Porlock) service. Most services stop on The Avenue.

For a **taxi** call Minehead Taxis (☎ 01643-704123, 🖳 minehead-taxis.co.uk).

ROUTE GUIDE AND MAPS

Where to stay

For **campers**, the nearest site lies about 1¼ miles from town. *Minehead Camping and Caravanning Club* (☎ 01643-704138, 🖥 www.campingandcaravanningclub.co.uk; WI-FI £3/day; late Apr to early Oct) is on Hill Rd on North Hill. It's a well-equipped place which boasts wonderful views over the town to the sea. It's good value, too, at £5.90-10.05pp; the only problem is getting to the place, which involves a 30-minute walk up a steep hill (though you can cut in from the coast path).

There's an independent hostel, *Base Lodge* (☎ 0773 165 1536, 🖥 independent hostels.co.uk/members/baselodge; 1 x 5-, 1 x 6-, 1 x 7-bed dorm/2T, shared facilities; WI-FI), at 16 The Parks, just west of the town centre. The genial host is a qualified mountain guide and a mine of information. The rooms are clean, basic and pleasant and the kitchen is well equipped. A dorm bed costs £17.50pp (twin £20pp, sgl occ £25).

YHA Minehead (☎ 0345-371 9033, 🖥 www.yha.org.uk/hostel/minehead; 2 x 3-, 4 x 4-, 1 x 5-, 1 x 6- bed dorms shared facilities; WI-FI; Ⓛ; Mar-end Oct) is actually a little way out of town at **Alcombe Combe** – and far from the coast path too – so is not really practical for most people. A dorm bed costs £12.99-24.99pp, private rooms sleeping three to six people £49.99-109.99.

One of the finest **B&Bs** in Minehead, *The Parks* (☎ 01643-703547, 🖥 www .parksguesthouse.co.uk; 4D/1T/2Qd, all en suite; WI-FI; Ⓛ; 🐾), 26 Parks Rd, is an elegant Georgian property in a leafy part of town with immaculately maintained rooms. They charge £39.50-43.50pp (sgl occ £60, three/four sharing £100-130).

Most B&Bs are at the eastern side of town. The first place to look is Tregonwell Rd, where a string of guesthouses & B&Bs stand cheek-by-jowl. *Tregonwell House* (☎ 01643-709287, 🖥 www.tregonwellhouse .co.uk; 4D/2T/1D or T, all en suite; WI-FI; Ⓛ; Mar-Oct), at No 1, is fairly typical – it's an unassuming B&B (£35-37.50pp, sgl occ £55-75) with comfy rooms and amiable owners.

Heading south along the road, next door is *Candlelight* (☎ 01643-703977, 🖥 www.candlelightbb.co.uk; 3D/1T/1Tr, all en suite; WI-FI; Ⓛ), popular with walkers, possibly as packed lunches can be made instead of breakfast; B&B costs £32.50-37.50pp (sgl occ £58-67.50, three sharing £88). Call them direct for the best rates.

Kenella House (☎ 01643-703128, 🖥 www.kenellahouse.co.uk; 4D/2T, all en suite; WI-FI; Ⓛ; Mar-Oct), at No 7, is slightly smarter than most on this street and the landlady has been a finalist in a Landlady of the Year competition; the tariff is £35pp (sgl occ from £60).

Across the road at No 14 is *Montrose Guesthouse* (☎ 01643-706473, 🖥 www .montroseminehead.co.uk; 3D/2D or T, all en suite; WI-FI; Ⓛ; Feb-Dec). B&B costs £32.50-37.50pp (sgl occ full room rate); homemade bread and jam are served at breakfast.

Tranmere Guesthouse (☎ 01643-702647, 🖥 www.tranmereguesthouse.co .uk; 3D/1T/2Tr, all en suite; WI-FI) is another smart place and good value (£32.50-36pp, sgl occ £50, three sharing £95), whilst *Lorna Doone* (☎ 01643-702540, 🖥 www.lornadooneguesthouse.co.uk; 2S/1T/ 2D, all en suite; WI-FI; Ⓛ), at No 26, was recommended by more than one coastal walker. They charge £35pp (sgl occ £45).

Finally, on this strip there's *Glendower House* (☎ 01643-707144, 🖥 www.glen

---

❏ Where to stay: the details
In the descriptions of accommodation in this book: 🛏 means at least one room has a bath; Ⓛ means a packed lunch can be prepared if arranged in advance; 🐾 signifies that dogs are welcome in at least one room but also subject to prior arrangement. Note that virtually everywhere only accepts advance bookings for a minimum stay of two nights at peak periods such as weekends, bank holidays and school holiday periods. See also p74.

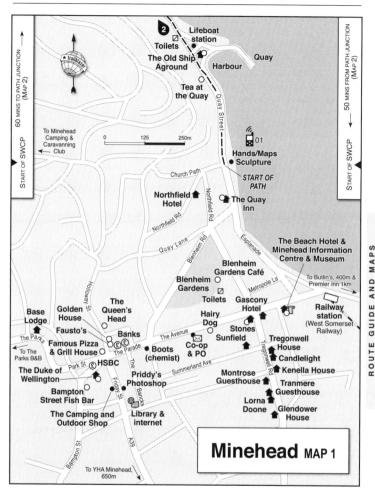

dower-house.co.uk; 3S/4D/2T/2Tr, all en suite; WI-FI), another large Edwardian place. B&B here costs £37.50-42pp (sgl/sgl occ £48/66, three sharing £102).

Sunfield (☎ 01643-703565, 🖳 www .sunfieldminehead.co.uk; 1S/3D/2T, all en suite; WI-FI; ⒧; 🐾), at 83 Summerland Ave, is also popular with walkers. The rates are £34pp (sgl occ £43).

There are some **pubs with rooms** and real character on Quay St, which conveniently is also the street where the SWCP starts. *The Quay Inn* (☎ 01643-702839, 🖳 www.thequayinnminehead.co.uk; 1D/1T/ 1Tr, all en suite, 1Qd private bathroom; ☞; WI-FI; ⒧; 🐾), the first you come to, is a smart and modern affair with a good kitchen (see Where to eat). They charge

£30-35pp (sgl occ £50-60, three/four sharing £85-140).

At the northern edge of town, and right on the trail, *The Old Ship Aground* (☎ 01643-703516, 🖳 www.theoldship aground.com; 2S/4D/6T, all en suite; WI-FI; 🐕) is not actually as old as it looks, having been built in the 1900s, though it's still got a certain charm, pleasant rooms (£34-44pp, sgl £33-37.50, sgl occ £58-78) and, best of all, the finest views in Minehead over the harbour.

Another pub, and one whose origins are significantly older, is *The Duke of Wellington* (☎ 01643-701910, 🖳 www .jdwetherspoon.co.uk; 5S/2T/13D/5Tr, all en suite; WI-FI), built in 1820 as a coaching inn but now a Wetherspoons-owned place and thus typical of the chain, being functional, central and fair value (£25.50-37.50pp, sgl/sgl occ £54-75, three sharing £59-85).

There are several **hotels** in Minehead. On The Avenue is *Stones* (☎ 01643-709717, 🖳 stonesminehead.co.uk; 1S/8D/4T/3Tr/2Qd, one room sleeping up to six, all en suite; WI-FI; Ⓛ; 🐕). If you're walking with a dog they're definitely worth a call, as they are if you're travelling in a small group as one room has a double bed and four singles. Their rates in general are: £42.50-54pp (sgl/sgl occ £55-68, three/four/six sharing from £130/140/120).

A splendid option for your first night away from home is *The Beach Hotel* (☎ 01643-704765, 🖳 www.thebeachhotel.org; 6D/8D or T, all en suite; WI-FI; Ⓛ; 🐕). Situated where The Avenue meets the Esplanade, a number of the rooms have sea views and from some you can see the start of the trail. B&B costs £42.50-55pp (sgl occ £60-80). Owned by the YMCA and a hospitality training academy for young local apprentices, attached to the hotel are a fine restaurant and café (see Where to eat).

One block back from the sea, *Gascony Hotel* (☎ 01643-705939, 🖳 www.gascony hotel.co.uk; 3S/13D or T/2Tr/2Qd, all en suite; WI-FI; Ⓛ; mid Mar to mid Dec), 50 The Avenue, is a traditional hotel with huge lounges set in an old Victorian house.

They charge from £44pp (sgl/sgl occ £56-88, three/four sharing £110/120).

Northfield Hotel (☎ 01643-705155, 🖳 www.northfield-hotel.co.uk; 3S/5D/22D or T, all en suite; 🐕; WI-FI; Ⓛ; 🐕), on Northfield Rd, has a pool, Jacuzzi and some pleasant gardens. B&B costs £59-85pp (sgl £75-85, sgl occ £110).

A new branch of *Premier Inn* (☎ 0871 622 2313, 🖳 www.premierinn.com; 100D or T, all en suite; 🐕; WI-FI) opened in March 2017. Rates start from £48.50 but in peak periods expect to pay £95.50 (flex rate £106). Up to two children aged 15 and under can also sleep in the rooms. Breakfast (continental/cooked £6.99/8.99) is available at *Brewers Fayre* (daily 6.30/7-10.30am & 6-10pm) next door.

Where to eat and drink

Blenheim Gardens Café (daily 9.30am-4.45pm), situated in the eponymous gardens, is a pleasant spot for a pre-trek brew; whilst perfectly situated a stone's throw away from the start of the path is *Tea at the Quay* (☎ 01643-704100; Mar-Nov daily 8am-5pm, winter to 4pm). Depending on what time of the day you set off for Porlock Weir they offer breakfasts (£5.25-7.95) and lunches (£6-8); everything is home-cooked.

Centrally, *The Beach Café* at **The Beach Hotel** (see Where to stay; daily 10am-4pm, lunch noon-2pm) uses local suppliers and fresh ingredients, whilst for fine dining in the evening the hotel and café's middle sibling, the *restaurant* (Tue-Sat 6.30-8.30pm), has a superb menu.

On The Avenue, at No 32, you will find *Hairy Dog* (☎ 01643-706317, 🖳 www .thehairydog.co.uk; food served daily noon-9pm). A former 'UK Family Pub of the Year' winner, it's been well run by the same family for over 30 years. The menu includes fairly standard pub fayre (eg jacket potatoes from £6.95), but the portions are large and the steaks (rump £13.95) are good. Its sister-establishment **Stones** (see Where to stay) also has a restaurant (summer daily 8.30am-9pm, winter hours variable); there's a decent and relatively imaginative menu, although it changes often:

amongst the pizza, pasta dishes and pub classics, you may find a Pad Thai with duck (£10.95).

Holloway St has a few options. *Fausto's* (☎ 01643-706372, 🖥 www.faustos.co.uk; Mon-Sat noon-2.30pm & 6.30pm to late), at No 4, is a reasonably priced Italian, with pizzas starting from £6.95; while *The Queen's Head* (☎ 01643-702940; food served Tue-Sun noon-2.30pm, Tue-Sat 6-9pm) serves real ales including their own Queen's Head Ale and has reasonably priced meals, including some Thai dishes, most for under £10; it also offers Thai takeaway now.

Between the two, *Golden House* (☎ 01643-702723, 🖥 www.goldenhouserestaurant.co.uk; Wed-Sat noon-2pm & 5-10pm, Tue & Sun 5-10pm), offers a fairly standard Chinese menu, with huge set meals (around £18) or individual mains for £6.80-8. Nearby, *The Duke of Wellington* (see Where to stay; daily 7am-11pm) boasts a typical and ever-cheap Wetherspoons' menu.

The Quay is also a good area for food, with two decent pubs. *The Quay Inn* (see Where to stay; food served Mon-Fri noon-2pm, Sat & Sun noon-3pm, daily 6-9pm), just a walking-pole's throw from the start of the coast path, is a smart, well-furnished pub with a large multi-tiered garden and skittle alley. It has a locally sourced menu all prepared by an award-winning chef and serves real ales. *The Old Ship Aground* (see Where to stay; food served daily noon-2.30pm & 6-9.30pm) also serves locally sourced and reasonably priced food.

For takeaway, *Famous Pizza & Grill House* (☎ 01643-705416; Sun-Thur 1pm-1am, Fri & Sat 1pm-3am) is a standard fast-food outlet with a cholesterol-heavy menu including kebabs, burgers, wraps and, of course … pizzas (£4.30-11); whilst *Bampton Street Fish Bar* (☎ 01643-702968; Mon 5-8pm, Thur-Sat 11.45am-1.45pm, Tue-Sat 4.45-8.15pm) is a superlative award-winning fish bar, unpretentious but very friendly and deserving of all the plaudits it has garnered.

MINEHEAD TO PORLOCK WEIR   [MAPS 1-7]

This **9-mile (14.5km; 3hrs 30 mins, 4hrs 20 mins if taking the rugged alternative route)** first stage of the SWCP offers a taster of much that is wonderful about the Exmoor coast. Beginning with a stroll through ancient, ivy-strangled woodland (Exmoor can, after all, boast some of the most extensive broadleaved coastal woods in Britain), you emerge eventually at North Hill, whereafter the route offers two choices: a gentle pastoral stroll by fields of livestock, or a more rugged alternative that offers a wilder, longer and more remote experience (and, so it is said, a greater chance of spotting native Exmoor wildlife such as red deer) as you contour the coastline on a narrow trail.

The two paths reunite just before the descent to the cream-tea cosiness of Bossington, from where a flat track takes you across farmland, via a turn-off to nearby Porlock and a submerged forest, to the village of Porlock Weir, home to a thousand-year-old port, several thatched grade-II listed cottages – and a fabulously eccentric hotel.

The route

The South-West Coast Path begins by what has become popularly known either as the '**Hands Sculpture**' or the '**Map Sculpture**', sculpted in bronze by Owen Cunningham and erected in 2001; it is, of course, pretty much obligatory to have your photo taken next to it. Photographed, fed, backpacked and booted, it's now time for you to begin. The trail initially sticks to the waterfront as it takes

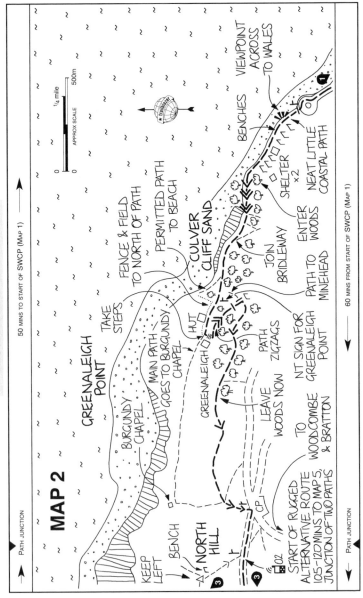

MAP 2

GREENALEIGH POINT

NORTH HILL

BURGUNDY CHAPEL

VIEWPOINT ACROSS TO WALES

BENCHES

SHELTER x2

NEAT LITTLE COASTAL PATH

CULVER CLIFF SAND

PERMITTED PATH TO BEACH

FENCE & FIELD TO NORTH OF PATH

TAKE STEPS

MAIN PATH GOES TO BURGUNDY CHAPEL

HUT

GREENALEIGH

PATH ZIGZAGS

JOIN BRIDLEWAY

ENTER WOODS

PATH TO MINEHEAD

NT SIGN FOR GREENALEIGH POINT

LEAVE WOODS NOW

TO WOODCOMBE & BRATTON

START OF RUGGED ALTERNATIVE ROUTE 105–120 MINS TO MAP 5, JUNCTION OF TWO PATHS

CP

KEEP LEFT

BENCH

APPROX SCALE

¼ mile

500m

◄ PATH JUNCTION   50 MINS TO START OF SWCP (MAP 1) ──►

60 MINS FROM START OF SWCP (MAP 1)

◄ PATH JUNCTION

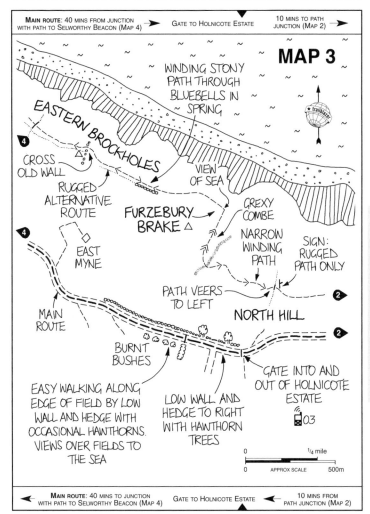

MAIN ROUTE: 40 MINS FROM JUNCTION WITH PATH TO SELWORTHY BEACON (MAP 4) → GATE TO HOLNICOTE ESTATE | 10 MINS TO PATH JUNCTION (MAP 2) →

WINDING STONY PATH THROUGH BLUEBELLS IN SPRING

MAP 3

trailblazer

EASTERN BROCKHOLES

CROSS OLD WALL

RUGGED ALTERNATIVE ROUTE

VIEW OF SEA

FURZEBURY BRAKE △

GREXY COMBE

EAST MYNE

NARROW WINDING PATH

SIGN: RUGGED PATH ONLY

PATH VEERS TO LEFT

NORTH HILL

MAIN ROUTE

BURNT BUSHES

GATE INTO AND OUT OF HOLNICOTE ESTATE

📱03

EASY WALKING ALONG EDGE OF FIELD BY LOW WALL AND HEDGE WITH OCCASIONAL HAWTHORNS. VIEWS OVER FIELDS TO THE SEA

LOW WALL AND HEDGE TO RIGHT WITH HAWTHORN TREES

0 — ¼ mile
0 — APPROX SCALE — 500m

ROUTE GUIDE AND MAPS

← **MAIN ROUTE:** 40 MINS TO JUNCTION WITH PATH TO SELWORTHY BEACON (MAP 4) | GATE TO HOLNICOTE ESTATE ← | 10 MINS FROM PATH JUNCTION (MAP 2)

you towards and beyond The Old Ship Aground (see Where to stay/Where to eat) and its neighbouring **lifeboat station**. Leaving the last vestiges of Minehead behind, the trail enters some deep, dark woods scored with numerous paths and bridleways before emerging above the trees below the summit of **North Hill**. (A diversion off the path here takes you down the steep slope to the ruined **Burgundy Chapel** and its accompanying hermitage, a medieval two-roomed construction that dates back over 600 years.) Look out for night-jars and the rare Dartford warbler flitting amongst the western gorse, which itself is a plant that's a bit of a rarity, found only in the West Country and southern Wales.

The path continues westwards a short distance before dividing; the northern path is known as 'the rugged alternative' (see p84). Meanwhile the main trail meanders gently, scarcely rising or falling, past fields and flocks, with unbroken views over the sheep to the sea. Wales winks at you across the waves to the north, while Dunkery Beacon – the highest point on Exmoor – glimpses

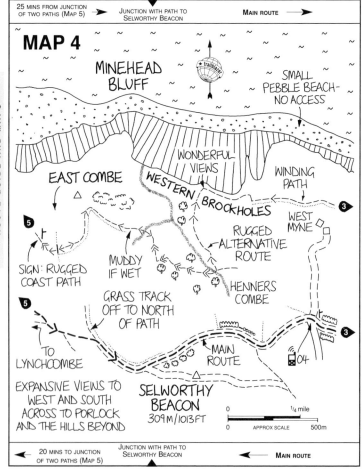

ROUTE GUIDE AND MAPS

25 MINS FROM JUNCTION OF TWO PATHS (MAP 5) → JUNCTION WITH PATH TO SELWORTHY BEACON   MAIN ROUTE ——→

MAP 4

MINEHEAD BLUFF

SMALL PEBBLE BEACH- NO ACCESS

WONDERFUL VIEWS

EAST COMBE

WESTERN BROCKHOLES

WINDING PATH

❸

WEST MYNE

RUGGED ALTERNATIVE ROUTE

SIGN: RUGGED COAST PATH

MUDDY IF WET

HENNERS COMBE

GRASS TRACK OFF TO NORTH OF PATH

❺

TO LYNCHCOMBE

MAIN ROUTE

❸

04

EXPANSIVE VIEWS TO WEST AND SOUTH ACROSS TO PORLOCK AND THE HILLS BEYOND

SELWORTHY BEACON 309M/1013FT

0   ¼ mile

0   APPROX SCALE   500m

← 20 MINS TO JUNCTION OF TWO PATHS (MAP 5)   JUNCTION WITH PATH TO SELWORTHY BEACON   ← MAIN ROUTE

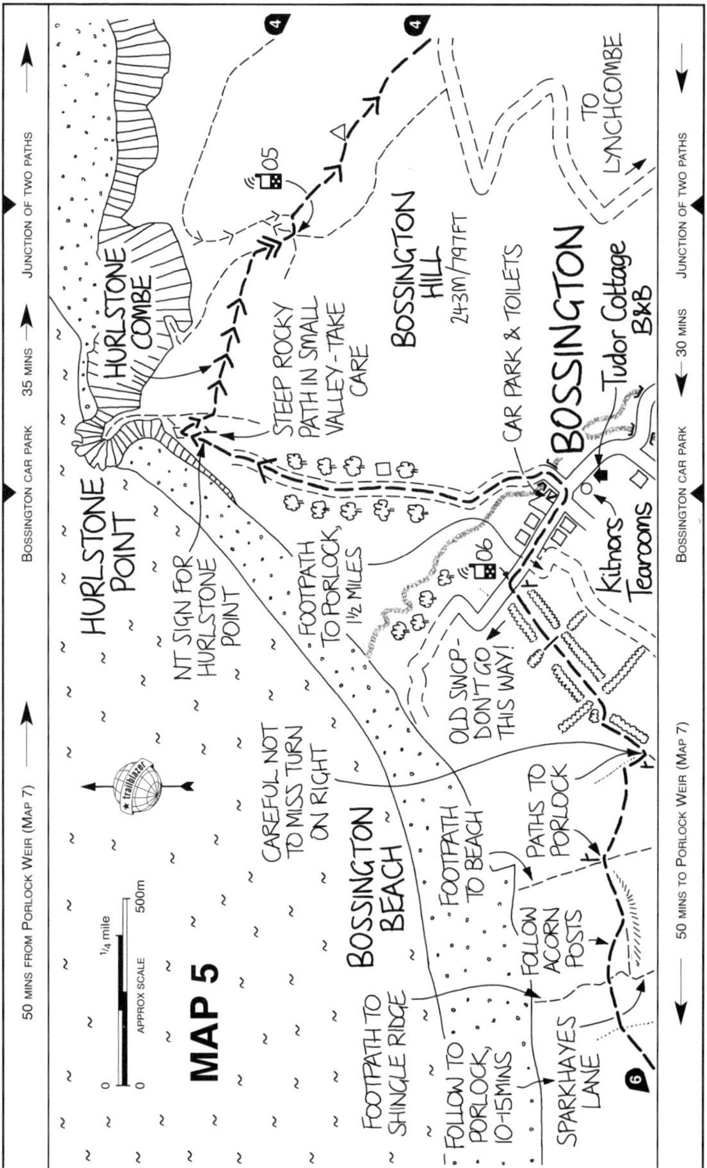

MAP 5

APPROX SCALE

0 ¼ mile

0 500m

HURLSTONE POINT

HURLSTONE COMBE

NT SIGN FOR HURLSTONE POINT

STEEP ROCKY PATH IN SMALL VALLEY - TAKE CARE

FOOTPATH TO PORLOCK 1½ MILES

BOSSINGTON HILL 243M/797FT

BOSSINGTON

CAR PARK & TOILETS

Tudor Cottage B&B

TO LYNCHCOMBE

Kitnors Tearooms

OLD SWCP - DON'T GO THIS WAY!

CAREFUL NOT TO MISS TURN ON RIGHT

BOSSINGTON BEACH

FOOTPATH TO BEACH

PATHS TO PORLOCK

FOLLOW ACORN POSTS

FOOTPATH TO SHINGLE RIDGE

FOLLOW TO PORLOCK, 10-15MINS

SPARKHAYES LANE

ROUTE GUIDE AND MAPS

your progress from the south. Passing **Selworthy Beacon** (Map 4; 309m/ 1013ft), the path descends to a reunion with the alternative trail before descending steeply through **Hurlstone Combe** and on to Bossington.

The rugged alternative route

Do not be put off by the name of this alternative trail – though more testing than the official path this route is not overly difficult and is well worth the extra 50 minutes it takes to walk it. **Note that dogs must be kept on a lead on this path**.

The trail runs along a thin and winding path, intermittently following field boundaries and keeping close to the sea, occasionally dipping into miniature combes and crossing streams. The views are tremendous, the path is wilder than the official route and you are less likely to see other people – and far more likely to see red deer. Throughout much of it you are surrounded by gorse although bluebells make for a spectacular display in spring.

Where the regular trail passes near the summit of Selworthy Beacon, the alternative path goes around its lower slopes. Having crossed the upper reaches of **Grexy Combe**, on your left but not visible is the Iron-Age hill fort of **Furzebury Brake**. Further archaeology lies ahead on the path with two medieval settlements, **East Myne** and **West Myne**, while to your right are the **Eastern Brockholes**, which along with **Western Brockholes** are considered to be the places where the stone was quarried to build the two settlements. At **East Combe** you can turn left and climb to the top of Selworthy Beacon, or you can keep on and rejoin the official path after **Hurlstone Combe**.

BOSSINGTON   [MAP 5, p83]

Bossington is the kind of blink-and-you-miss-it village that people come to Somerset specifically to see: ancient, cosy, with a gorgeous tearoom and picture-perfect cottages scattered willy-nilly along a single track lane. With its thatched roofs and lack of telegraph wires, it can feel as if you've wandered onto the set of a BBC period drama.

Kitnors Tearooms (☎ 01643-862643, 🖳 www.kitnors.com; May to Oct daily 11am-4.30pm, Oct-May Fri-Tue 11am-4pm), situated right on the path, has a splendid little garden at the rear where one can relax to a gentle cacophony of birdsong (the robins are particularly friendly). It's a lovely place to stop and they serve sandwiches, light lunches and cream teas (from £4.50). There's even handmade biscuits for dogs (£1) but your furry friend will have to indulge in such treats outside in the garden.

As for a place to stay, just up the road is *Tudor Cottage* (☎ 01643-862255, 🖳 www.tudorcottage.net; 1D/1D or T private facilities, 1D en suite; ☛; WI-FI; Ⓛ), a 15th-century cottage with a splendid garden and wonderful views across to Porlock Weir. B&B costs £40-47.50pp (£65 sgl occ).

Bossington sits at the eastern extremity of the wide **Porlock Vale**, an unusually wide, flat valley in comparison with the narrow combes typical of Exmoor. Standing between it and the sea is a natural shingle ridge – a ridge that was breached in 1996 (see box opposite), causing the farmland to turn into a salt marsh that receives a fresh inundation of salt every high tide. It also led to a rerouting of the SWCP that once followed this ridge but which now takes a more inland course, around the back of the beach. This does mean that the sea will be out of sight for the next few miles – but also that it is much less of a detour to visit the charming village of Porlock.

❏ Porlock Beach   [Map 6, p86]

The beach at Porlock Vale is a very dynamic environment. The **shingle bank** that pro-
tects the vale from flooding at high tide – and which looks for all the world like a
man-made defensive barrier – was actually established about 8000 years ago at the
end of the last Ice Age, the rising sea levels piling up the rocks and shingle that had
fallen from the nearby cliffs.

Though man may not have built it he has certainly done his best to repair it down
the centuries in order to protect the valuable farmland behind, with the last major
rebuild occurring in 1990. Man is also responsible for building the WWII **pillboxes**
(a type of defensive bunker, usually made from concrete) and the now-ruined **lime
kiln** along the beach. Yet in spite of these efforts at preservation, a further breach to
the shingle bank in 1996 forced the authorities to rethink their policy and as a result
it was decided to allow nature to take its course – meaning that, in years to come,
Porlock Vale may well become a lagoon, just as it was around 200 years ago.

The ever-changing landscape of Porlock Vale has exposed some interesting sites
and artefacts that had previously lain hidden beneath the seabed. The **submerged forest** that you walk past on the way to Porlock Weir is actually around five or six thousand years old and was first observed only in 1890. In 1998 part of a skeleton of an
auroch, a giant precursor to modern cattle that roamed these parts about 3500 years
ago, was found in the exposed blue clay of an old riverbed. The bones are now on display in Porlock Visitor Centre (see p86). A piece of worked timber from AD900 has also
been unearthed embedded in beach clay near the shingle ridge, as have numerous flints.

Perhaps unsurprisingly, the entire beach has been declared a **Site of Special
Scientific Interest** (SSSI; see box p61) as it allows scientists to study how such a
landscape will develop if left to its own devices, as well as the effect this will have
on the flora and fauna of the area, with lapwings, herons, teal, shelduck and egret regular visitors to this rare salt marsh environment.

PORLOCK   [see map p87]

Though 10-15 minutes from the path,
Porlock remains a popular stopover on the
SWCP. The plentiful accommodation,
amenities, attractions and ancient architecture are enough to tempt the tiring walker
off the trail.

Porlock was mentioned in the
Domesday Book of 1086 (as 'Portloc') and
several of the village's buildings are only
slightly younger. The oldest, **The Chantry**,
has parts dating back to the 12th century.
The truncated tower on the neighbouring
Church of St Dubricius (named after a
6th-century Welsh saint who, according to
legend, crowned King Arthur and later mar-
ried him to Guinevere) was built only a few
decades later; while, inside the church,
you'll find fragments of a cross that date
back to pre-Norman times.

The main street is also scattered with
more old thatched cottages than you can

shake a sheaf of straw at, from The Old
Rose and Crown Cottage (formerly a pub),
opposite the church, to the 13th-century
Ship Inn at the western end of the village.

For a more intimate look at one of
Porlock's hoary homes, **Dovery Manor
Museum** (🖳 www.doverymanormuseum
.org.uk; May-end Sep Mon-Fri 10am-5pm,
Sat 10.30am-4pm; free but donation welcome) is housed in a 15th-century manor
house and has a physic garden based on
designs from medieval times.

A few steps away, **Exmoor Classic
Cars Museum** (donations appreciated) has
a wonderful little collection of gleaming
vintage cars and bikes, some of which are
as old as the inhabitants of Porlock themselves. There are no set opening hours but it
is a 'working museum' so as long as there
is someone there toiling away you should
be able to pop in for a peek. At the other

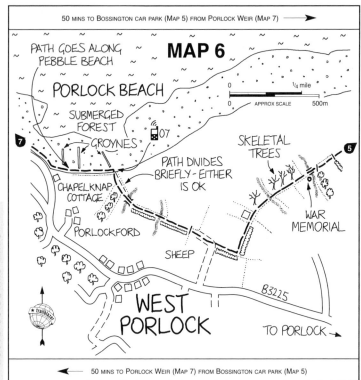

MAP 6

PATH GOES ALONG PEBBLE BEACH

PORLOCK BEACH

SUBMERGED FOREST

GROYNES

0   ¼ mile

0   500m
APPROX SCALE

7

CHAPEL KNAP COTTAGE

PATH DIVIDES BRIEFLY - EITHER IS OK

SKELETAL TREES

5

WAR MEMORIAL

PORLOCKFORD

SHEEP

★ trailblazer

B3225

WEST PORLOCK

TO PORLOCK ⟶

end of the village, the Visitor Centre (see below) boasts a small **village museum** including many of the items discovered on the beach that pre-date even Porlock (see box p85).

See p16 for details of Samphire Festival, an independent music festival.

Services

The **Visitor Centre** (TIC; ☎ 01643-863150, 🖳 www.porlock.co.uk; Easter to end Oct Mon-Fri 10am-12.30pm & 2-5pm, Sat 10am-5pm; Nov to Easter Tue-Fri 10am-12.30pm, Sat 10am-1pm) lies at the far western end of Porlock and claims to be the friendliest in the entire South-West. They are happy to do accommodation booking (see box p40).

The village is big enough for two small **supermarkets**, Costcutter (Mon-Thur 7.30am-8pm, Fri & Sat to 9pm, Sun to 6pm) towards the western end of town and One Stop Local Stores (daily 7am-10pm), which has an **ATM** (free), at the eastern end.

Opposite the Costcutter is a shop, **Exmoor Rambler** (☎ 01643-862429, 🖳 www.exmoorrambler.uk; Mon-Fri 9am-5.30pm, Sat 9am-6pm, Sun 10am-3/4pm) selling **walking gear**, and the **post office** (same hours as shop).

Nearby on the High St, **Porlock Hardware** (☎ 01643-862427; summer Mon-Sat 9am-5pm, winter Sat to 1pm) also has some camping gear. **Porlock Pharmacy** (Mon-Fri 8.30am-6pm, Sat 9am-1pm) is opposite One Stop.

Transport

[See also pp48-50] **Bus**-wise, Buses of Somerset's No 10 service call here en route between Minehead and Porlock Weir; Filers Travel and Quantock Heritage operate the seasonal No 300 service.

For a **taxi** try 1st Call Exmoor Taxis (☎ 07826-212511, 🖳 www.1stcallexmoortaxis .co.uk).

Where to stay

For **campers**, *Sparkhayes Farm Camping Site* (☎ 01643-862470, 🖳 www.sparkhayes .co.uk; Feb-Dec; 🐾) is on Sparkhayes Lane on the edge of the village. There are plenty of pitches (£8pp), laundry and hot shower facilities and a fridge freezer.

Porlock Caravan Park (☎ 01643-862269, 🖳 www.porlockcaravanpark.co .uk; WI-FI; 🐾; mid Mar to end Oct), at the High Bank end of the village, charges £8.50-12 for a hiker & tent plus £5 per additional person.

If, in this ancient place, a **night above a pub** feels appropriate *The Ship Inn* (also known as *The 'Top' Ship*; ☎ 01643-862507, 🖳 www.shipinnporlock.co.uk; 4D/1Qd, all en suite; 🛏; WI-FI; (L); 🐾) will not disappoint; B&B here costs £30-45pp (sgl occ from £40, three/four sharing from £90). A cosy, fascinating, slightly eccentric pub (check out the displays of battle helmets, gas masks and even a 'German officer's uniform', as worn by an extra in the film *The Great Escape*), they also serve up some smashing **food** (see Where to eat).

Note: you may hear The Ship Inn at Porlock referred to locally as the 'Top' Ship; this is because the establishment has a twin at Porlock Weir, also called The Ship Inn, locally referred to as The 'Bottom' Ship. It is an important distinction as the distance between the two is certainly enough to perturb a walker should you have booked a night's accommodation and end up being directed – albeit by a well-meaning local –

ROUTE GUIDE AND MAPS

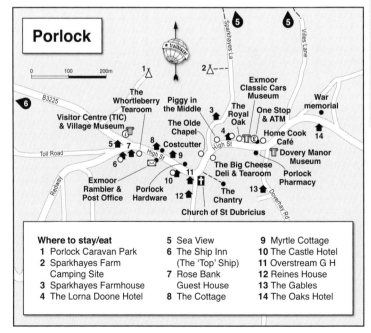

Porlock

Where to stay/eat
1 Porlock Caravan Park
2 Sparkhayes Farm
  Camping Site
3 Sparkhayes Farmhouse
4 The Lorna Doone Hotel
5 Sea View
6 The Ship Inn
  (The 'Top' Ship)
7 Rose Bank
  Guest House
8 The Cottage
9 Myrtle Cottage
10 The Castle Hotel
11 Overstream G H
12 Reines House
13 The Gables
14 The Oaks Hotel

to the wrong one: sounds unlikely – but this has happened!

B&B-wise, there are plenty of fine options. In a village with so much thatch it's possible you'll end up sleeping under a roof of straw, such as at *The Gables* (☎ 01643-863432, 🖳 www.thegablesporlock .co.uk; 2D/2Tr, all en suite; ☜; WI-FI; Ⓛ; 🐾), a gorgeous 17th-century country home on Doverhay Rd, its ancient exterior belying the modern facilities on offer including DVDs and games. They charge £35-37.50pp (sgl occ £50-70, three sharing £90-110); no one-night bookings Easter to end Sep on Fri or Sat.

A more humble, straw-topped, 17th-century dwelling, *Myrtle Cottage* (☎ 01643-862978, 🖳 www.myrtleporlock.co.uk; 2D/1Tr/1Qd, all en suite; ☜; WI-FI; Ⓛ; 🐾) has

timber-beamed rooms in a central location. B&B costs from £35pp (sgl occ £50, three/four sharing £95/120). Further ancient accommodation (though this time thatch-free) can be had at the fairly grand 17th-century *Sparkhayes Farmhouse* (☎ 01643-862765; 1D/1T, both en suite; ☜; Apr-Nov); the tariff is £35pp (sgl occ £40).

Opposite the church, *Reines House* (☎ 01643-862446, 🖳 www.reineshouse.co.uk; 2D/1Tr, all en suite; WI-FI), is one of the village's cheaper options (£32.50pp, sgl occ £45, three sharing from £85); whilst, *Overstream Guest House* (☎ 01643-862421, 🖳 www.overstream.co.uk; 4D/3D or T, all en suite; ☜; WI-FI; Ⓛ) is a sunny, pleasant and friendly place with a licensed bar. Rates here are £30-33.50pp (sgl occ £40).

❏ The poets of Porlock

Porlock has long been a favourite place of poets, romantics and dreamers. Robert Southey's friends Samuel Taylor Coleridge and William Wordsworth (who both lived nearby at Nether Stowey and Alfoxden respectively) were frequent visitors and often wandered (as lonely as clouds, presumably) the hills and beaches surrounding the village. Indeed, the regularity of their perambulations and the fact that many of them were undertaken at night aroused suspicions in the locals and rumours began to circulate that they were actually French

Porlock! thy verdant vale so fair to sight,
Thy lofty hills which fern and furze imbrown,
The waters that roll musically down
Thy woody glens, the traveller with delight
Recalls to memory, and the channel grey
Circling its surges in thy level bay.
Porlock! I shall forget thee not,
Here by the unwelcome summer rain confined;
But often shall hereafter call to mind
How here, a patient prisoner, 'twas my lot
To wear the lonely, lingering close of day,
Making my sonnet by the alehouse fire,
Whilst Idleness and Solitude inspire
Dull rhymes to pass the duller hours away.
                              Robert Southey (1774-1843)

spies. A government agent sent to investigate however, witheringly concluded that they were 'mere poets' and thus no threat to the Crown.

Today, of course, many hikers walk in the footsteps of the Romantic poets along the Coleridge Way (see box p34) which ends in the village; a walk that both celebrates the area's associations with the Romantic poets and the wonderful countryside of this part of the world. Yet, ironically, Porlock is perhaps best known not for a poem that it inspired, but one that it prevented: Samuel Coleridge was famously interrupted during the composition of his epic *Kubla Khan* by 'a person on business from Porlock', with the result that he forgot the details of the dream on which his poem was to be based and thus never completed the work! The phrase 'a person from Porlock' has since become a synonym for an unwanted visitor; characters named Porlock crop up in works by Arthur Conan Doyle and Alan Bennett amongst others – usually as somebody who arrives unannounced and interrupts the business of others.

High St has two further establishments. *The Cottage* (☎ 01643-862996, 🖳 www.cottageporlock.co.uk; 2D/1D or T/1Tr, all en suite; ♥; WI-FI; Ⓛ) is a gorgeous little place (£35pp, sgl occ £45, three sharing £105), and the large and impressive Victorian *Rose Bank Guest House* (☎ 01643-862728, 🖳 www.rosebankguesthouse.co.uk; 1S/1D/3D or T, all en suite; WI-FI; Ⓛ; 🐾) has a great reputation; £40pp (sgl £50, sgl occ £60-80).

Nearby, opposite the Visitor Centre, *Sea View* (☎ 01643-863456, 🖳 www.seaviewporlock.co.uk; 1S/2D/1T, all en suite; ♥; WI-FI; Ⓛ) lives up to its name. B&B costs £32.50-35pp (sgl £35, sgl occ £40).

Finally, there are three **hotels**. On High St are *The Castle Hotel* (☎ 01643-862504, 🖳 www.thecastleporlock.co.uk; 6D or T/2D/1Qd, all en suite; ♥; WI-FI public areas; 🐾), where rates are £37.50-47.50pp (sgl occ full room rate, three/four sharing £95) and *The Lorna Doone* (☎ 01643-862404, 🖳 lornadoonehotel.co.uk; 5D/5D or T in main building plus Courtyard rooms 1D/2Tr/1Qd, all en suite; ♥; WI-FI; Ⓛ; 🐾) which charges £32.50-47.50pp (sgl occ full room rate, three/four sharing £105/140).

The Oaks Hotel (☎ 01643-862265, 🖳 oakshotel.co.uk; 8D or T, all en suite; ♥; WI-FI; Easter to end Oct) is grander and offers dinner, bed and breakfast only (DB&B £245 for two sharing, sgl occ rates on request). It is on the edge of the village, with great views across to the sea from some rooms.

Where to eat and drink

You certainly won't starve in Porlock, with plenty of tearooms, cafés and restaurants all along the main street.

During the day the pick of the traditional tearooms are: *The Whortleberry Tearoom* (☎ 01643-862891, 🖳 www.whortleberry.co.uk; Easter to Oct Wed-Sun 9am-4pm, Oct to Easter Wed-Sat 9am-4pm), which is named after the local blueberry (see box p22); *The Olde Chapel* (☎ 01643-862241; Feb to early Dec daily 10am-8pm), a large establishment that was formerly a Methodist chapel, with tables outside on the street where you can tuck into homemade soups, freshly ground coffee and fresh crab sandwiches; and *Home Cook Café* (☎ 07790-725357; Mon-Sat 10am-4/5pm, Sun from 11am) where they also make their own soups, cakes and scones.

Even if you don't fancy eating there, do take time to visit *The Big Cheese Deli and Tearoom* (☎ 01643-862773; Mon-Sat 9am-4.30pm), the local champions of cheese (they usually have at least 50 on sale) as well as other locally produced comestibles including wines, jams and vinegars.

There's a surprisingly good choice of places to eat in the evening too. On High St, *Piggy in the Middle* (☎ 01643-862647; mid Feb-Dec Mon-Sat 5-9pm) is a fish 'n' chip restaurant which dishes up speciality pies; indeed, there are 32 on offer, including meat, vegetarian, gluten-free and vegan options. Takeaway is also an option here.

Nearby, the restaurant in *The Lorna Doone* (see Where to stay; summer daily 8-9.30am, Mon-Sat noon-2pm, Sun to 2.30pm, Mon-Sat 6-8.30pm, to 8pm in winter) is open to both residents and non-residents, and serves honest pub grub (main meals £8-16), whilst round the corner, *The Castle Hotel* (see Where to stay) also has a restaurant (food daily noon-9pm) offering a very reasonably priced standard pub-fayre menu which may include a sweet potato and chick pea curry (£7.99).

Pub-wise, *The Royal Oak* (☎ 01643-862798; food daily noon-2.30pm & 6-9pm, winter to 2pm & 8pm; WI-FI; 🐾) specialises in real ales and traditional pub grub including a great steak-and-ale pie (£10.95). Its status as the most popular place in town is rivalled only by *The Ship Inn* (see Where to stay; food daily noon-2.30pm, Sun-Thur 6.30-8.30pm, Fri-Sun 6-8.45pm), where local ales (and even local crisps) including the potent 6.6% Exmoor Beast (see box p23), braised Devon beef (£11.95) and Caribbean-style lamb curry (£12.95) are all on offer; the menu changes seasonally but could include hake fillet with sauté potatoes (£13.25) and West Country Burger (£10.50).

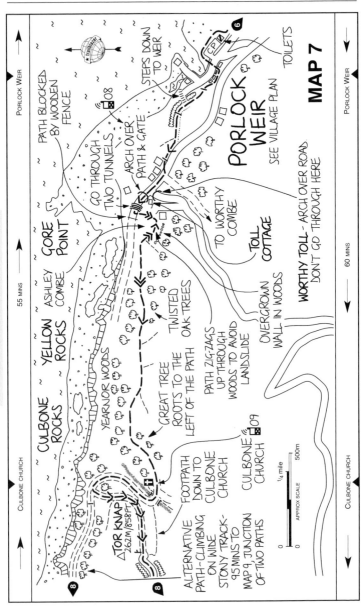

CULBONE CHURCH

55 MINS

PORLOCK WEIR

PATH BLOCKED BY WOODEN FENCE

STEPS DOWN TO WEIR

GO THROUGH TWO TUNNELS

ARCH OVER PATH & GATE

08

6

CP

TOILETS

PORLOCK WEIR

SEE VILLAGE PLAN

MAP 7

GORE POINT

ASHLEY COMBE

YELLOW ROCKS

CULBONE ROCKS

YEARNOR WOODS

TWISTED OAK TREES

TO WORTHY COMBE

TOLL COTTAGE

OVERGROWN WALL IN WOODS

WORTHY TOLL - ARCH OVER ROAD DON'T GO THROUGH HERE

60 MINS

PORLOCK WEIR

GREAT TREE ROOTS TO THE LEFT OF THE PATH

PATH ZIG-ZAGS UP THROUGH WOODS TO AVOID LANDSLIDE

CULBONE CHURCH

FOOTPATH DOWN TO CULBONE CHURCH

CULBONE CHURCH

09

TOR KNAP 262M/858FT

ALTERNATIVE PATH - CLIMBING ON WIDE STONY TRACK - 95 MINS TO MAP 9, JUNCTION OF TWO PATHS

¼ mile

500m

APPROX SCALE

0

0

8

8

Continuing on the SWCP, the path plots a flat course between the back of the beach and the farmland before turning sharp right to rejoin the shoreline to **Porlock Weir**.

PORLOCK WEIR

Peaceful Porlock Weir feels like the type of place where you could quite easily sit back and forget that you're supposed to be walking, as you opt instead to while away your time listening to the sea and staring wearily out towards Wales. The boats rock lazily in the weir's small port and the waves lap somnolently onto the pebbles and shingle of the millennia-old harbour arm.

The one-room **Boatshed Museum** (Easter-Oct daily 10am-5pm; free but donations welcome) features interesting displays about the settlement's seafaring heritage.

For supplies, **Harbour Stores** (☎ 01643-863033; summer Mon-Fri 10am-5pm, Sat & Sun 9am-5pm, winter 10am-1pm) sells essentials (including takeaway drinks).

Buses of Somerset's No 10 service operates between here and Minehead (see pp48-50 for details).

There are three **B&B** options in Porlock Weir, all with restaurants. *Millers at The Anchor* (☎ 01643-862753, ☐ www .millersuk.com/anchor; 11D/3T, all en suite; ☛; WI-FI; ⓛ; ☛) is as much a museum and gallery as it is a hotel (£45-115.50pp, sgl occ £55-144). The interior is fabulous, with paintings, busts and antiquities crammed into every spare space. The walls are lined with books, including some written by the owner himself; everywhere you look there is something to catch the eye. There's also a small **cinema** (offering a £15/20 two/three course 'Movie and Meal' deal on Sun & Wed eves, booking recommended) and even an honesty bar providing drinks on the basis of trust – definitely a novelty in this day and age! Lunch (Mon-Fri noon-3pm, Sat & Sun to 5pm; sandwiches/baguettes from £8) and cream teas (available all day; from £5.50) are served, with an

à la carte menu (Wed-Sun 7-9pm; £25-33) in the evenings. One tip: this is not a place to come with a full rucksack on your back – just turn up with an empty belly and a thirst for the obscure!

The Ship Inn (also known as *The Bottom Ship*, see p87; ☎ 01643-863288, ☐ www.shipinnporlockweir.co.uk; 2D/1T, all en suite; ☛; WI-FI; ⓛ; ☛) is a simpler place, with far fewer distractions, charging £30-37.50pp (sgl occ £40). Amongst the hearty **food** served (daily noon-2.30pm & 6-8.30pm) is an Exmoor steak and ale pie (£10.95).

The Café (☎ 01643-863300, ☐ www .thecafeporlockweir.co.uk; 4D/1D or T, all en suite; ☛; WI-FI downstairs; ⓛ sandwiches; ☛) sits in a slightly elevated position with good views across the harbour and beyond, though one room doesn't have a view. B&B costs £50-68.75pp (sgl occ £50-104) and in terms of food (Wed-Sun noon-8pm) they focus on fresh fish and main courses generally cost £10-15.50.

Lunches (£4.20-8.50) can be found at *The Harbour Gallery and Café* (☎ 01643-863514, ☐ www.harbourgalleryandcafe .co.uk; Apr-Oct daily 10am-5pm, winter Fri-Tue 10.30am-3pm but hours can vary),

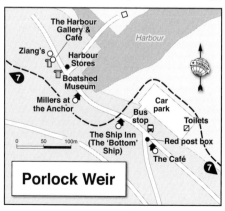

Porlock Weir

ROUTE GUIDE AND MAPS

which also has work by local artists on the walls; whilst for **takeaway**, *Ziang's* (☎ 01643-863215; summer Mon-Tue & Thur-

Sat noon-6.45pm, Wed to 2.30pm, winter closed Wed all day) deals in Far Eastern street food and fish 'n' chips.

PORLOCK WEIR TO LYNTON   [MAPS 7-12]

This **12½-mile (20.1km; 6hrs, 5¾hrs on alternative route)** stage will come as something of an unpleasant surprise for those who were hoping for a gentle few days at the start of the walk to ease themselves into the trip. While not as tough as the final two stages on this walk – nor indeed even as tough as the next one – this hike to the conjoined villages of Lynmouth and Lynton is still fairly taxing and makes for a surprisingly long day. Furthermore, with no cafés or pubs (save for The Blue Ball Inn at Countisbury, just a short distance from Lynmouth), you'll need to be self-sufficient or this long day is going to feel even longer!

Thankfully there are enough distractions on this stage – including Culbone Church – to help you ignore the quiet screaming coming from your calf muscles. There are also the rare whitebeams of Culbone Wood, dotted here and there with the remains of several humble leper huts; while a short deviation off the trail will take you to Foreland Point – Devon's most northerly extremity.

Furthermore, you can also take pride in the fact that during the day you march across the border into Devon. As such, you will have already achieved the feat of completing Somerset's entire contribution to the SWCP – and you're still only on the second day!

The route
The trail out of Porlock Weir begins between the houses behind Millers at the Anchor, climbing up behind the village and onto the thatched and rather decorative **Worthy Toll**; has a toll gate ever been so ornate? Keeping **Toll Cottage**

❏ **Ashley Combe**
Just past Worthy Toll the trail passes through a couple of tunnels which were once an integral part of the gorgeous gardens of Ashley Combe house. The **home of Ada Byron** (the only legitimate daughter of the poet, Lord Byron), later Countess Lovelace, the house was originally built in 1799 but improved significantly by Lord King, the first Lord Lovelace and Ada's husband who, influenced by the fairy-tale castles of Italy, decided in 1835 to lavish a huge sum in adapting Ashley Combe to please his wife. The tunnels from the road led to the house's tradesman's entrance and were built so that Ada and the other inhabitants didn't have their views of the ornate terraced gardens interrupted by the comings and goings of commoners. Towers, turrets, archways and other follies decorated the terraces, which were walled on three sides but opened out onto the sea, while spiral staircases led between the different levels.

A team of Swiss engineers was even brought in to lay a network of carriageways throughout the grounds. The house fell into disrepair soon after the Countess's death in 1852 and though it found a use as a home for orphans during WWII, it soon became uninhabitable and in 1974 it was pulled down for safety reasons. While its true glory has long since faded, it's still fascinating to pick out some of the original features of the gardens – the twisting paths, and the stone benches set into the garden walls – as you walk along the trail from Worthy Toll.

❏ **Culbone Church**
The small church at Culbone is one of the hidden gems of the South-West Coast Path. England's smallest complete parish church, it measures 35ft (10.66m) and seats a congregation of around 30. However, Culbone church is not just tiny – its origins are also extremely old. It is one of the few buildings that also features in the *Domesday Book*. At Culbone Stables a Bronze Age stone marker – one of many which were believed to have lined the way between Lynmouth and Porlock – was discovered in 1940. Celtic missionaries from Wales and Ireland travelled to the West Country along this path from about the late 6th century onwards, leading to a revival of the Christian faith in England. One of these missionaries was the patron saint of Culbone, **St Beuno**. Though his link with the church is unclear, it is believed that Culbone became a place of reverence in his day; and the wheeled cross on the Bronze Age standing stone marker acted as a signpost, pointing the faithful to Culbone as an important place of pilgrimage.

The Saxons are believed to have been the first to build a church here, made of wood, which in time was replaced by a stone edifice by the Normans. The oldest part of the church today is probably the sandstone window on the northern side of the chancel (the space around the altar), which is thought to be at least a thousand years old, though many other features are only slightly younger: the font, for example, is believed to be around 800 years old, as is the arch that separates the chancel from the nave (where the congregation sits). The tiny window on the north side of the nave is known as a leper squint – where lepers, who were banned from entering the church, could still watch the services.

One of the most noticeable features of the church is the number of gravestones dedicated to people with the surname 'Red'. Nicholas Red was churchwarden in 1856 (he is responsible for the Ten Commandments on one of the walls of the church) and it is his descendants who populate much of the graveyard. It is believed that the name provided the inspiration for the Ridds in the novel *Lorna Doone*. While you're in the graveyard, look at the church steeple: it was erected in around 1810, though locals swear that it is actually the missing top part of the truncated steeple of the Church of St Dubricius (see p85) in Porlock.

The church is still in use, though there is no tarmac leading to it; instead, worshippers have to take either the precarious 4WD track down to the church, or do as you have just done and walk there!

on your left, pass through the more northerly of the two arches then follow the path as it twists its way, under, over and through the overgrown terraces of **Ashley Combe** (see box opposite).

A lazy meander along a gently undulating path past the **twisted oak trees** of Yearnor Woods soon brings you out onto a better track that winds its way down to **Culbone Church** (see box above) – an essential stop on the SWCP. The path divides after Culbone Church (Map 7). The main (southern) trail from here heads up the hill, out of the trees, into farmland and from there onto a road – though we use the term loosely, for cars are something of a rarity around here and easily outnumbered by livestock to left and right. It's difficult to lose your way – just keep heading west past Silcombe Farm and Broomstreet Farm, the track eventually dwindling to a footpath. Soon after, it takes a sharp right down **Wheatham Combe** and back into the woods on the lower northern slopes of **Sugarloaf Hill**, where it is reunited with the alternative (northern) route (see overleaf).

Alternative route between Culbone Church and Sugarloaf Hill

This alternative (northern) path is at times rugged and should be trodden carefully but the woodlands it passes through make for a wonderful alternative to the fields above. The areas that you walk through have interesting histories, too.

Splendidly isolated **Culbone Wood** has throughout the ages been home to many deemed too dangerous to remain in mainstream society – from the 'mentally insane' in the 13th century to lepers in the 16th. Meanwhile, **Embelle Wood** and its stony pathways are known to have been used by smugglers carrying their ill-gotten gains away from Embelle Wood Beach. Presumably chosen for its remoteness – despite the presence of a limekiln – the beach is thought to be the most remote in Somerset. Indeed, so remote is it that David Burgess, a self-styled 21st-century Robinson Crusoe, managed to move here in 1985 and remain almost undetected until he became the focus of the national press briefly in 2011 after the park authorities finally told him to leave.

A note of caution: be wary of landslides. Although generally well signed, landslips are a common occurrence on this section and the diversions made necessary because of them can be sudden, especially around **Broomstreet Combe**. Between there and the reunion with the official path the trail is also particularly steep.

The path continues parallel to the coast now under the woodland canopy, climbing the slopes occasionally to avoid the occasional landslip, then passing through deciduous woodland and coniferous plantations before, having crossed the **Somerset–Devon border** (which isn't marked on the trail, though occurs at Coscombe Linhay, Map 9), near the signposted turn-off to Glenthorne Nature Trail. The path deviates off the large track to visit the 19th-century **stone cross** that marks the Sister's Fountain. The name comes from one of the nieces of the original owner of nearby Glenthorne House who liked to play at this spot. In local legend, the well, or spring, was created by Joseph of Arimathea by striking his staff on the ground, thus providing much-needed refreshment on his journey to Glastonbury.

Passing through the **wild boar gateposts** (the entrance to 19th-century Woodland Lodge as well as to Glenthorne House), the route follows the driveway down the hill before taking a narrow trail off to the left, the path now brightly embroidered to left and right with vivid rhododendron and gorse. The way is more exposed now too, a pleasant change after so long in the shade of trees, though patches of woodland still punctuate the trail, particularly when passing the several **combes** (Map 10) on the way: Wingate, Pudleep Gurt, Swannel and Chubhill. Eventually, with limbs wearying and feet aching, tarmac is reached before **Coddow Combe**, at which point those with enough fortitude can follow the road down to Foreland Point (see below) and the lighthouse that marks the northernmost tip of Devon, while the rest take the path off left up the slope, the reward for one's efforts being a clear view of Lynmouth.

The path to Foreland Point

For those wishing to see Devon's most northerly point, a short walk down the road on your right will take you to the **lighthouse** at Foreland Point, built in 1900. (cont'd on p98)

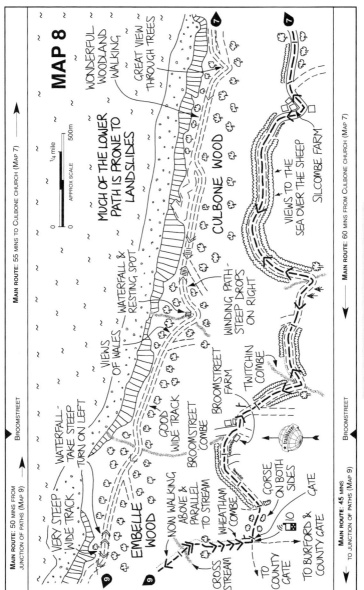

MAP 8

MAIN ROUTE: 55 MINS TO CULBONE CHURCH (MAP 7)

MAIN ROUTE: 50 MINS FROM
JUNCTION OF PATHS (MAP 9)

BROOMSTREET

WONDERFUL
WOODLAND
WALKING

GREAT VIEW
THROUGH TREES

MUCH OF THE LOWER
PATH IS PRONE TO
LANDSLIDES

CULBONE WOOD

¼ mile

500m

APPROX SCALE

VIEWS OF WALES

WATERFALL &
RESTING SPOT

WINDING PATH -
STEEP DROPS
ON RIGHT

VIEWS TO THE
SEA OVER THE SHEEP

SILCOMBE FARM

WATERFALL -
TAKE STEEP
TURN ON LEFT

GOOD WIDE TRACK

BROOMSTREET
COMBE

BROOMSTREET
FARM

TWITCHIN
COMBE

VERY STEEP
WIDE TRACK

EMBELLE WOOD

NOW WALKING
ABOVE &
PARALLEL
TO STREAM

WHEATHAM
COMBE

GORSE ON BOTH
SIDES

CROSS
STREAM

TO
COUNTY
GATE

TO BURFORD &
COUNTY GATE

GATE

MAIN ROUTE: 45 MINS
TO JUNCTION OF PATHS (MAP 9)

BROOMSTREET

MAIN ROUTE: 60 MINS FROM CULBONE CHURCH (MAP 7)

ROUTE GUIDE AND MAPS

ROUTE GUIDE AND MAPS

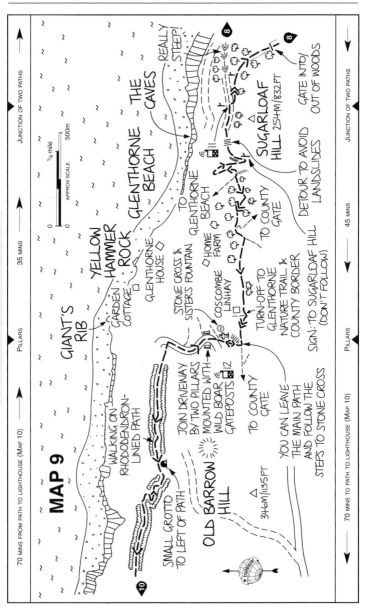

70 MINS FROM PATH TO LIGHTHOUSE (MAP 10) | PILLARS | 35 MINS | JUNCTION OF TWO PATHS

MAP 9

GIANT'S RIB

YELLOW HAMMER ROCK

GLENTHORNE BEACH

THE CAVES

REALLY STEEP!

Walking on RHODODENDRON-LINED PATH

GARDEN COTTAGE

GLENTHORNE HOUSE

STONE CROSS & SISTERS FOUNTAIN

TO GLENTHORNE BEACH

HOME FARM

SUGARLOAF HILL 254M/832FT

GATE INTO/ OUT OF WOODS

COSCOMBE LINHAY

TO COUNTY GATE

DETOUR TO AVOID LANDSLIDES

APPROX SCALE

1/4 mile

500m

SMALL GROTTO TO LEFT OF PATH

JOIN DRIVEWAY BY TWO PILLARS MOUNTED WITH WILD BOAR GATEPOSTS

12

TO COUNTY GATE

TURN-OFF TO GLENTHORNE NATURE TRAIL & COUNTY BORDER

SIGN: TO SUGARLOAF HILL (DON'T FOLLOW)

OLD BARROW HILL 346M/1135FT

YOU CAN LEAVE THE MAIN PATH AND FOLLOW THE STEPS TO STONE CROSS

10

trailblazer

70 MINS TO PATH TO LIGHTHOUSE (MAP 10) | PILLARS | 45 MINS | JUNCTION OF TWO PATHS

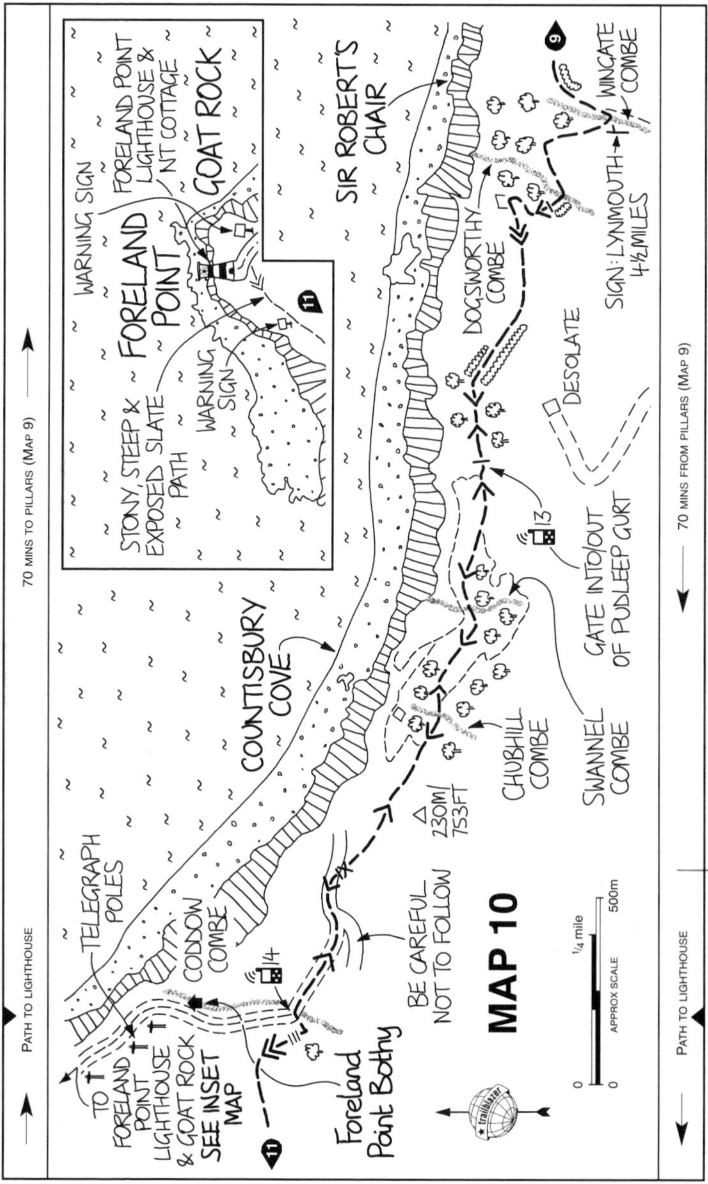

MAP 10

PATH TO LIGHTHOUSE

PATH TO LIGHTHOUSE

ROUTE GUIDE AND MAPS

Inset map:

FORELAND POINT
FORELAND POINT LIGHTHOUSE & NT COTTAGE
GOAT ROCK
WARNING SIGN
STONY, STEEP & EXPOSED SLATE PATH
WARNING SIGN

Main map labels:

SIR ROBERT'S CHAIR
DOGSWORTHY COMBE
DESOLATE
SIGN: LYNMOUTH 4½ MILES
WINCATE COMBE
GATE INTO/OUT OF PUDLEEP GURT
SWANNEL COMBE
CHUBHILL COMBE
COUNTISBURY COVE
△ 230M/753FT
BE CAREFUL NOT TO FOLLOW
CODDOW COMBE
TELEGRAPH POLES
TO FORELAND POINT LIGHTHOUSE & GOAT ROCK SEE INSET MAP
Foreland Point Bothy

¼ mile
500m
APPROX SCALE
0
0

trailblazer

(cont'd from p94) From here, you can either return on the same path or, if you would like to stick as close to the coast as possible and not retrace your steps, there is also a path that continues around The Foreland and rejoins the official coastal path. Note that much of it is exposed and it does involve walking on scree. It is a beautiful if challenging walk (especially if you are carrying a pack) but there is a need for caution. There is the option of spending a night here: ***Foreland Point Bothy*** (☎ 0344-335 1296, 💻 www.nationaltrustholidays .org.uk/bunkhouses/foreland-bothy; 🐾; open year-round) sleeps four (1D & 2S on bunk platforms; £20-25pp). Note: booking is essential and there is a sink and cold water tap and loo outside (for which you will be given a code when you book), but no cooking facilities; bedding is not provided, nor is there heating or lighting in the bothy, so you will need to be prepared for your night in the wild. To book a night here contact the National Trust.

The fairly uninteresting church of St John the Baptist at **Countisbury** marks the start of the drop down to the harbour, though at this late stage you would be forgiven for calling in first at ***The Blue Ball Inn*** (Map 11; ☎ 01598-741263, 💻 www.blueballinn.com; 11D/3Tr, all en suite; 🍺; WI-FI; Ⓛ; 🐾), called now by the original name it was given in the late 18th century. B&B costs £40-44.50pp (sgl occ £58-62, three sharing £117); each room boasts a bath (though, curiously, not all have a shower!). The **food** (summer daily noon-9pm, winter Mon-Thur noon-3pm & 6-9pm, Fri-Sun noon-9pm) is quite 'bistro-esque'; the menu changes but may include a delicious saddle of Exmoor venison (£20). Quantock Heritage's No 300 seasonal **bus** service stops outside the pub; see pp48-50.

Returning to the trail, the stagger down to Lynmouth seems long and it's a rare person who isn't exhausted by the time they've walked through the patch of woodland to emerge at the back of Lynmouth Manor House. If you, too, feel exhausted, spare a thought for the brave lifeboatmen (see below) of Lynmouth who in 1899 *carried* their craft overland all the way to Porlock Weir to rescue a nearby ship in distress – a journey that took some 10 hours in total!

LYNMOUTH   [see map p103]

'My walk to Ilfracombe led me through Lynmouth, the finest spot, except Cintra and the Arrabida, which I have ever seen.'
                                    Robert Southey

Lynmouth and its neighbour up the hill, Lynton, combine to form the biggest settlement in the whole of Exmoor National Park. Nicknamed 'Little Switzerland' by the Victorians (who popularised these twin towns as a tourist resort in the 19th century) due to the beauty, tranquillity and steep gradients of its surrounding countryside, the two villages act as a hub for a plethora of paths, with the Two Moors Way, Samaritans Way and Tarka Trail (see box p34) all joining the Coast Path in passing through or terminating here. Both have ample facilities, though note that for more than somewhere to sleep or eat you need to head up the slope to Lynton.

Two events dominate Lynmouth's history. The first is the famous **Overland Launch** of 1899, when Lynmouth's heroic lifeboat crew, wishing to rescue a boat in the Bristol Channel but unable to set sail from Lynmouth due to a force-eight gale, opted instead to drag their lifeboat *The Louisa* over Countisbury Hill and down to Porlock Weir. The second event occurred on Friday 15 August 1952 when, following almost a fortnight of torrential downpours, a cloudburst unleashed 9 inches of rain on

ROUTE GUIDE AND MAPS

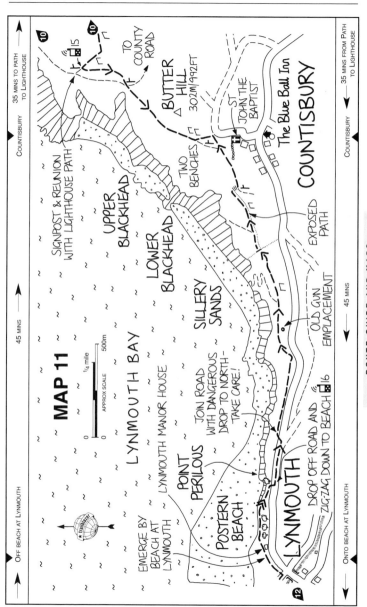

Exmoor that sent a wall of water cascading towards the unsuspecting village, dispersing boulders from the surrounding countryside onto the streets. Thirty-four people lost their lives that day and sixty buildings were destroyed entirely. **Lynmouth Flood Memorial Hall**, down near the harbour, exists as a lasting reminder of the tragedy.

Rhenish Tower, located at the end of the pier and one of only two buildings to have been reconstructed since the flood, was built in 1832 by wealthy local landowner, General Rawdon. The General returned from his grand tour of Europe in the early 19th century and had the tower built as an imitation of those that he had admired on the Rhine. Once used for pilchard spotting by the local fisherman, the tower has recovered since the flood – much like Lynmouth itself – and has become a sort of symbol of the town.

Services
Exmoor National Park Centre at **Lynmouth Pavilion** (☎ 01598-752509, 🖳 www.exmoor-nationalpark.gov.uk; daily 10am-5pm; free) has a wealth of **information** on the park. The advisors are connoisseurs of all things Exmoor and also know a thing or two about the SWCP. Inside you'll find Exmoor-related exhibitions and short informative films about the local area. For tourist information see Lynton (see p104).

There is an **ATM** (£1.75) in **Crocombes Stores** (summer daily 8.30am-7pm, winter 10am-3.30pm) on Lynmouth St, where you'll also find OS maps and stamps – there being no post office in Lynmouth. For the nearest post office, as well as free ATMs and the better supermarkets, you need to head up the hill to Lynton.

Transport
[See also pp48-50] Filers No 310 **bus** operates in the early morning and evening to Barnstaple. Quantock Heritage's & Filers Travel's No 300 only operate in the main season. Buses stop by the car park near the road bridge at the back of the village.

For a **taxi** try Riverside Taxis (☎ 01598-753442).

Where to stay
The nearest **camping** option to either Lynmouth or Lynton is *Sunny Lyn Holiday Park* (☎ 01598-753384, 🖳 www.caravan devon.co.uk; 🐕; pay as you go WI-FI; Easter-Oct) which has a **shop** (Easter-Oct daily 9am-5pm) and a *café* (Easter-Sep 8.30-10.15am) that serves breakfasts. The rate (£6.75pp) includes use of the shower facilities; laundry facilities are also available. The site can be accessed from either village. From Lynmouth walk up the very steep B3234 (Lynbridge Rd) for approximately three-quarters of a mile and it will be on your left by the river.

Lynmouth's **B&Bs** are primarily found beyond the road bridge towards the back of town (ie furthest from the sea). Along Watersmeet Rd you will find several places with many boasting lovely views over both the village and the sea. These include: *Orchard House* (☎ 01598-753247, 🖳 www.lynmouthhotel.co.uk; 1D/1T/3Tr all en suite, 1D private bathroom; 🛁; WI-FI; Ⓛ ; 🐕) which charges £30-40pp (sgl occ £48-50, three sharing £80-99) and has a free hot tub in the garden; *Hillside House* (☎ 01598-753836, 🖳 www.hillside-lynmouth .co.uk; 1S/4D/1T all with private facilities; 🛁; WI-FI; Ⓛ; 🐕), an 18th-century house though with parts that may date back to the 1400s (B&B here costs £35-36pp, sgl/sgl occ £40-45); and *East Lyn Guesthouse* (☎ 01598-752540, 🖳 www.eastlynhouse.co .uk; 7D/1T, all en suite; WI-FI; Ⓛ; 🐕) where new owners took over in April 2017 but rates are likely to be around £40-45pp (sgl occ £30-35 if booked direct).

On the other side of the East Lyn River there is *Lorna Doone House* (☎ 01598-753354, 🖳 www.lornadoonehouse.co.uk; 1S/2D/2D or T, all en suite; 🛁; WI-FI; Ⓛ; 🐕; Feb-Nov), the landlords of which have been working in the hospitality industry for over a quarter of a century. B&B costs £42pp (sgl £37, sgl occ £45); dinner, bed and breakfast rates also available.

Also by the river is *Ye Olde Sea Captain's House* (☎ 01598-753369, 🖳 www.thecaptainshouseinlynmouth.co.uk; 1S/6D or T/2Tr, most en suite, others share facilities; 🛁; WI-FI; Ⓛ; 🐕); rates here are

£30-40pp (sgl £38 sgl occ £55-75, three sharing £80-90).

Back in the heart of Lynmouth – and thus nearer the trail – *The Village Inn* (☎ 01598-752354; 4D/1Tr, en suite; ☛; WI-FI; ⓛ; 🐾), on the pedestrianised shopping street, provides B&B (£30-35pp, sgl occ £40, three sharing £70) above a 'traditional' Free House. The inn has been winner of the Lynton and Lynmouth in Bloom competition several times and, in this author's opinion, is a competitor for the friendliest place.

Riverside Cottage (☎ 01598-752390, 🖥 www.riversidecottage.co.uk; 6D/1D or T, all en suite; ☛; WI-FI; ⓛ; well-behaved 🐾), is virtually opposite and has two floors of balcony-fronted rooms overlooking the harbour and river. B&B costs £30-45pp (sgl occ rates on request).

Approximately three-quarters of a mile out of town on Lynbridge Road is *The Cottage Inn* (☎ 01598-753496, 🖥 www.the cottageinnlynton.co.uk; 4D but additional put up beds mean most rooms can sleep up to five people, all en suite; ☛; WI-FI; Feb-Dec); B&B costs £37.50-40pp (sgl occ full room rate, up to five sharing room rate plus £35pp). The breakfast here includes a full English and there's a Thai restaurant for food in the evenings (see Where to eat). The Cottage Inn also has a **micro-brewery**, which produces its own 'Fat Belly' real ales.

There are quite a few **hotels** in Lynmouth. On the harbour itself, *Rock House Hotel* (☎ 01598-753508, 🖥 www.rock-house.co.uk; 1S/5D/2D or T, all en suite; WI-FI; ⓛ; 🐾) peers out to sea and charges £55-65pp (sgl £55, sgl occ rates on request). On the opposite side of the harbour and dating back to the 14th century, *The Rising Sun* (☎ 01598-753223, 🖥 www.risingsunlynmouth.co.uk; 11D/2T, all en suite; ☛; WI-FI; ⓛ; 🐾) is an olde-worlde place with modern facilities. R D Blackmore is said to have written some of *Lorna Doone* within its walls. Rates are £85-105pp (sgl occ £105-115). They also have Shelley's Cottage (1D; ☛; WI-FI; 🐾; £105-125pp, sgl rates on request), a detached cottage where the poet, Percy Bysshe Shelley, may have stayed in 1812.

Further back from the sea is *The Bath Hotel* (☎ 01598-752238, 🖥 www.bathhotel lynmouth.co.uk; 11D/7T/3Qd, all en suite; ☛; WI-FI; ⓛ; 🐾; mid Feb to early Jan), an unpretentious place in a great location; the name comes from the fact that it is built on the site of an old inn that used to have its bathwater delivered by horse and cart from a well beneath Rhenish Tower (see opposite). B&B costs £39.50-70pp (sgl occ from £66).

By the West Lyn river is *The Lyn Valley Hotel* (☎ 01598-753300, 🖥 www .lynvalleyhotel.com; 3D/1Qd, all en suite; ☛; WI-FI; ⓛ; Mar-Dec), where the hosts are amiable and the food (see Where to eat) is good; they charge £40-55pp (sgl occ £51-70, three/four sharing £150/160).

Overlooking the West Lyn river is *Bonnicott House Hotel* (☎ 01598-753346, 🖥 www.bonnicott.com; 6D/1T, all en suite; WI-FI; ⓛ), a grade-II listed former rectory dating back to 1809. B&B costs £30-55pp (sgl occ £50-65) and they are also happy to do evening meals (Apr-Dec Mon-Tue & Thur-Sat 6.30-8.15pm) if arranged in advance; there is also a log burner in the front room should you be an intrepid winter walker.

The most famous hotel is *Shelley's* (☎ 01598-753219, 🖥 www.shelleyshotel.co .uk), a sophisticated place where the Romantic poet (see column opposite) chose to honeymoon in the summer of 1812. Closed for renovation but hopefully re-opening late 2017, the establishment is definitely worth a call to catch up with developments.

Where to eat and drink

There's a fair selection of places to eat in Lynmouth catering for all budgets. For an early breakfast head to *The Lyn Valley Hotel* (see Where to stay; food daily 7.30am-7/8pm), where a full English will cost £6.50. The food is great in the evenings (two-/three-course set menu £15/18, or their à la carte menu which may include beef fillet £18.95), and the staff certainly don't lack dedication in attempting to sell you the pictures they have displayed on the walls by local artists.

Another central option for breakfast is the café at *Riverside Cottage* (see Where to stay; daily 10am-4pm) where a locally sourced fry-up will cost £6.95. They also serve coffee potent enough to thoroughly energise you before you set off up the sharp hill to Lynton and there are splendid cakes for any early arrivals to Lynmouth.

Near the B&Bs on Watersmeet Rd are some fine places to eat: *Lyndale Tearooms* (☎ 01598-753553; summer daily 8am-4.30pm, winter hours variable) provides cheap and decent breakfasts and lunches; a cream tea is £5.95. The staff have good local knowledge, are happy to act as a kind of tourist information centre and can tell you about the bus services that run by.

Booking is advisable at *7 the Bistro* (☎ 01598-753302, 🖥 www.7thebistro.com; Tue-Sun 6.30-9pm), opposite Shelley's Hotel. The menu changes regularly but always includes a bounty of fresh local fish and amongst other meals are dishes suitable for a wheat-, gluten- or dairy-free diet.

Across the water and with wonderful views over the river, *Ye Olde Sea Captain's House* (see Where to stay; daily 10am-6pm) offers cream teas (available all day; £5.50) and light snacks.

For evening grub, *The Rising Sun* (see Where to stay; daily noon-2.30pm & 6-9pm) is one of the more sophisticated pubs on the trail serving, according to them, 'a blend of quality local produce with a European twist'. The menu changes daily, includes plentiful seafood and – considering its quality and the location – is relatively reasonably priced.

Sea-fare is also on offer at *Rock House Hotel* (see Where to stay; food served daily noon-3/4pm, restaurant 6.30-9pm), where the evening menu includes fish & chips (£11.95) and in season may include Lynmouth Bay Lobster (charges vary). Less-complicated fare is available at *The Village Inn* (see Where to stay; food served daily noon-8.45pm) which does some great, honest food (including lamb shank for £14.95) in a warm atmosphere.

Great fish dishes, such as local ale-battered sustainable fish (£12.95) can be caught at *The Bath Hotel* (see Where to stay; daily noon-3pm & 6-9pm), where there are also some mouth-watering desserts (£4.95-7.95).

For less formal fish, *Esplanade Fish Bar* (☎ 01598-753798; Feb-Easter daily noon-2.30pm, Easter to Oct noon-7/8.30pm depending also on weather and season) is one of the best chippies on the trail.

Nartnapa Thai Kitchen (☎ 01598-753496, 🖥 www.thairestaurantlynton.co.uk; food summer daily 6.30-9pm, Sun noon-3.30pm, winter Tue-Sat 6.30-9pm), where you can tuck into numerous Thai dishes. Since it is perfectly located for anyone camping at Sunny Lyn (see p100) and takeaway is available, it is a great option should you wish to enjoy your well-deserved meal sitting outside your tent (meal for one/two £12.50/22.50). Roast dinners are available on a Sunday for those whose aches and pains make the walk back to Lynmouth/Lynton undesirable.

While the sight of Lynmouth and its pubs is undoubtedly welcome, for many walkers there's one more effort required before the day is out: the zig-zag trail shadowing the direct path of the **Cliff Railway** (☎ 01598-753486, 🖥 www.cliffrailwaylynton.co.uk; mid Feb to early Nov daily 10am to between 4pm and 9pm depending on the season, check website for details; £2.80/3.80 single/return; 🐕 £1) to **Lynton**. Take it if you're early enough; after all, nobody can begrudge you this after the effort you've put in today. This railway dates back to the late 19th century; prior to its construction holidaymakers were transported between Lynmouth and Lynton by pony. The two carriages are connected by a cable that runs around pullies at each

© BT

Lynmouth & Lynton

LYNMOUTH

LYNTON

Beach

East Lyn River

Lorna Doone House

Ye Olde Sea Captain's House

East Lyn Guesthouse

Tors Rd

Hillside House

Lyndale Tearooms

7 the Bistro

Orchard House

Watersmeet Rd (A39)

Bonnicott House Hotel

Shelley's

Bus stop

CP

The Lyn Valley Hotel

Rhenish Tower

Rock House Hotel

The Rising Sun

Flood Memorial Hall & toilets

Riverside Cottage

The Village Inn

Crocombes Stores & ATM

West Lyn River

B3234

A39

Exmoor National Park Centre/ Lynmouth Pavilion/ National Park information

Lynmouth St.

The Bath Hotel

North Walk Hill

St Vincent Guest House

The Queens

Lyn & Exmoor Museum

Library & internet

Castle Hill

Lynmouth Hill

Lynbridge Rd

Lynway

Esplanade Fish Bar

North Walk

Cliff Railway

Town Hall

The Glasshouse

Lacey's

Londis & ATM

Lloyds (& ATM)

Queen St

The Nook

The Vanilla Pod

The Crown Hotel

Croft House

Bus stop

The Oak Room

Lee Rd

Post Office

Park St.

Lydiate La.

Costcutter

Lynton Pharmacy

South View Guest House

Southcliffe

Gable Lodge

Fernleigh Guest House

Cliff Top Café

To The Cottage Inn & Nartnapa Thai Kitchen, 400m & Sunny Lyn Holiday Park, 500m and very steep

Trailblazer

ROUTE GUIDE AND MAPS

0   50   100   150   200m

end. When water from the West Lyn River fills the 700-gallon tanks of the upper car – at the same time that water empties out of the tanks of the lower carriage – the heavier carriage starts to descend along the 862ft railway, pulling the bottom carriage up as it does so. Simple, but effective!

LYNTON [see map p103]

Though not as attractive, perhaps, Lynton certainly has more amenities than Lynmouth. The **tourist information centre** (TIC; ☎ 01598-752225, 💻 www.lynton-lynmouth-tourism.co.uk; WI-FI; Tue-Thur & Sat 10am-3pm but check their website) is in the Town Hall on Lee Rd; the staff offer accommodation booking (see box p20).

The **library** (☎ 01598-752505; Tue 2-4pm, Fri & Sat 10am-noon), on Market St, offers internet access (£1/15 mins).

The **post office** (Mon-Fri 9am-5.30pm, Sat to 12.30pm) is on Lee Rd, while nearby lies Lynton **pharmacy** (Mon-Fri 8am-1pm & 2-6.30pm, Sat 9am-noon) and, next door, a Costcutter **supermarket** (daily 7am-9pm). Centrally, there's also a Londis (Mon-Sat 8am-9pm, Sun 8.30am-8pm) which has a free **ATM**. There's a Lloyds **bank** (Mon, Wed & Fri 10am-3pm) with another free ATM just down the road.

Lyn and Exmoor Museum (Easter-Oct Tue-Thur & Sat 10.30am-1.30pm & 2-5pm; admission £2) has a fairly small collection of farm tools; of more interest, perhaps, is the building in which it is housed, the oldest dwelling in Lynton and perhaps the only museum in Devon which is said to be haunted!

Transport

[See also pp48-50] Filers' No 309 & 310 **bus** services stop here en route from Lynmouth to Barnstaple. To return to Lynmouth, Porlock or Minehead in the school summer holidays take Filers/Quantock Heritage's No 300 bus service. Buses stop along Lee Rd.

For a **taxi** try Riverside Taxis (☎ 01598-753442).

Where to stay

For **camping**, see Lynmouth, p100. To reach the campsite from Lynton, having arrived at the top of North Walk Hill, cross the road to descend Queen St then turn left onto Lynway and follow to the bottom of the hill.

Finding **B&B** accommodation in Lynton for a single-night stay in a peak period may be difficult (see box below). Contacting proprietors direct is generally the best way to book for one night and for single occupancy.

The main area for accommodation is Lee Rd, where an unbroken line of B&Bs border one side of the road, leading up from the TIC.

South View Guest House (☎ 01598-753728, 💻 www.southviewguesthouselynton.co.uk; 2D/1T/2Tr, all en suite; 🛁; WI-FI; Ⓛ; 🐕), at 23 Lee Rd, charges £27.50-37.50pp (sgl occ £50, three sharing £110).

Southcliffe (☎ 01598-753328, 💻 www.southcliffe.co.uk; 5D/1T, all en suite; 🛁; WI-FI; Ⓛ) is a grand Victorian property where two rooms have a balcony (rates are £36-43pp, sgl occ £48-86); and ***Gable Lodge*** (☎ 01598-752367, 💻 www.gablelodgelynton.co.uk; 5D/1Tr, all en suite; 🛁; WI-FI; Ⓛ) which charges £34-43.50pp (sgl occ £44-46, three sharing £108).

❑ Where to stay: the details

In the descriptions of accommodation in this book: 🛁 means at least one room has a bath; Ⓛ means a packed lunch can be prepared if arranged in advance; 🐕 signifies that dogs are welcome in at least one room but also subject to prior arrangement.

Note that over peak periods (such as weekends, bank holidays and school holiday periods) virtually everywhere on the Exmoor & North Devon Coast Path only accepts advance bookings for a minimum stay of two nights. See also p74.

Away from Lee Rd, on Park St is another walker-friendly option, *Fernleigh Guest House* (☎ 01598-753575, 🖳 www .fernleigh.net; 2D/1T/ 1Tr/1Qd, all en suite; 🛏; WI-FI) where rates are £30-42.50pp (sgl occ £50-65, three/four sharing £105/135).

On Lydiate Lane, *Croft House* (☎ 01598-752391, 🖳 www.lyntonbandb.co .uk; 4D/1D or T/1T, all en suite; 🛏; WI-FI) is a Georgian property, originally built in 1828 for a local sea captain but now welcoming walkers to their individually styled rooms. The house also boasts a lovely little walled garden that's a bit of a sun trap. B&B costs £39-48pp (sgl occ £55-65).

Two options on Market St are *St Vincent Guest House* (☎ 01598-752720, 🖳 www.stvincentlynton.co.uk; 1S private facilities, 5D/1T, all en suite; 🛏; WI-FI; 🅛), which charges £37.50-42.50pp (sgl £45, sgl occ £65), and *The Crown Hotel* (☎ 01598-752253, 🖳 www.thecrownlynton.co.uk; 1S/4D/1T/4Qd, all en suite; 🛏; WI-FI; 🅛; 🐾). B&B here costs £32.50-42.50pp (sgl occ £45) but walkers leaving early can have a packed lunch instead of breakfast. There's also some great food (see Where to eat).

Where to eat and drink

The choice of food is quite good. Among the different cuisines served in town, there's all-things Mediterranean at *The Oak Room* (☎ 01598-753838, 🖳 www.theoak roomlynton.co.uk; café summer daily 10.30am-2.30pm, restaurant daily 6-9pm, check website for opening hours in winter), which can be highly recommended and serves dishes such as Spanish-style meatballs (£12.50) and in the evening dinners & tapas.

Two places serving more local fare are: *Lacey's* (mid Feb-Oct daily 10am-6pm, Nov to mid Feb 11am-4.30pm), for traditional afternoon tea with over 80 teas,

and cream teas for just £3.95; and, at the top of the funicular railway, *Cliff Top Café* (☎ 01598-753486; Apr-Sep daily 9am-6pm or later, rest of year hours vary).

Several places, including The Oak Room (see column opposite), are cafés by day but become restaurants in the evening. Others include *The Glasshouse* (☎ 01598-752101, 🖳 www.theglasshouselynton.co .uk; Easter to Oct daily 10am-9pm, winter hours variable), which offers friendly service and a large menu, and, better, *The Vanilla Pod* (☎ 01598-753706, 🖳 www.thevanillapodlynton.co.uk; end Mar to end Oct café daily 10am-6pm, restaurant from 6pm; winter café 10am-4pm, restaurant Fri-Sun evenings; WI-FI; 🐾 café open only), at 10-12 Queen St, is a lovely place with great food (Middle Eastern fare and local English dishes) and they welcome walkers.

A restaurant definitely worth a visit is *The Nook* (☎ 07845-185650, 🖳 thenook lynton@gmail.com; May-end Sep daily 6-9pm or later, rest of year variable; booking advisable), 5 Queen St. With rave reviews, there's some great meat and fish dishes (main course £10-15) on the menu. Note that the restaurant is not licensed but you can take your own tipple to accompany your meal.

The best place for **pub food** is *The Crown Hotel* (see Where to stay; food Mon-Thur 11am-3pm & 4.30-9pm, Fri-Sun 11am-9pm). There's traditional pub-grub, from jacket potatoes (£4.50) to daily specials (from £9.95) as well as real ales to wash it all down.

Another place serving real ales and typical pub-fayre is *The Queens* (☎ 01598-752075; food served daily noon-9pm; 🐾), an old pub but one with a modern 'bistro' feel and some huge portions of grub including home-made lamb curry (£8.50).

LYNTON TO COMBE MARTIN [MAPS 12-17]

This **13½-mile (21.7km; 6¼hrs)** stage is the longest of the three spent within Exmoor and as your last day in the park it certainly does not disappoint. Including both the weird and mysterious landscape of the Valley of Rocks and the SWCP's highest point, Great Hangman, it is a day of both varied terrain and

❏ The Valley of Rocks

'...covered with huge stones ... the very bones and skeletons of the earth; rock reeling upon rock, stone piled upon stone, a huge terrific mass.'   **Robert Southey**

The Valley of Rocks is a group of peculiarly weathered rock formations, most with equally unusual names, that was formed by the last Ice Age. Unlike other combes in Exmoor and North Devon, the Valley of Rocks runs parallel with the sea instead of towards it. As a result, this valley is unlike any other in the South-West and, possibly as a result, many myths and legends have grown up around the area.

The names given to many of the rock formations hint at some of these myths. The formations known as **Devil's Cheesewring** and **Ragged Jack**, for example, could refer to a local legend that suggests that the Devil (also known as 'Jack' in local mythology) built a castle here for some of his wives. On returning to the castle one day, the Devil was enraged to discover that they had been indulging in a drunken orgy with a neighbour, an act of betrayal that compelled the Devil, in a fit of temper, to destroy the castle and turn the women into rock – which is the scene that confronts us today.

Since the Devil's residency there have been several other inhabitants in the valley. Evidence of both Iron and Bronze Age settlements have been discovered and amongst the bracken there are the faint remains of stone circles, possibly once used by Druids. Probably the best-known tenant, however, is a fictional one: Mother Melldrum, the soothsayer in RD Blackmore's *Lorna Doone*, who 'kept her winter' here.

Today, the most famous residents are the huge birds of prey that soar and swoop above the valley, along with the Exmoor ponies that graze in the area and the feral goats who clip-clop amongst the rocky outcrops. The current curly-horned inhabitants have occupied the valley since the 1970s, though there are thought to have been goats living here as far back as Neolithic times, making them almost as much a part of the valley as the rocks themselves.

The path through the valley passes between Castle Rock and Ragged Jack. Having joined the road to Lee Abbey, Devil's Cheesewring will be on your left. If, when you're tackling this section, you suddenly become surrounded by crowds of exhausted runners, you will have unwittingly become a part of **The Doone Run** (see p16), an annual long-distance race that takes place each September in the valley.

spectacular scenery: superlatives include Great Hangman itself (see p114) and one of Britain's biggest waterfalls, Hollow Brook, as well as one of its steepest valleys, Heddon. Then, finally, having conquered all that the path can throw at you, you end the day with a slow descent to the village that, purportedly, has the longest high street in England: Combe Martin. But even without these record breakers this stage would still make for a fascinating day's walking, with ancient abbeys, wild woodland and grazing goats to occupy your attention.

Being the longest stage in Exmoor, and one of the more remote sections of the SWCP, you won't be surprised to find that we recommend you plan your day carefully. There are, after all, only two places where you can get food – one on the path (the tearooms at Lee Abbey), and one a short walk off it (The Hunters Inn at Heddon) – so if you don't intend to stop at either of these you must **carry your own refreshments**; Heddon Valley is a fine and timely place to stop and see if you can spot any of the local wildlife while scoffing your sandwiches, or watching the waves from the shelter of the reconstructed lime kiln.

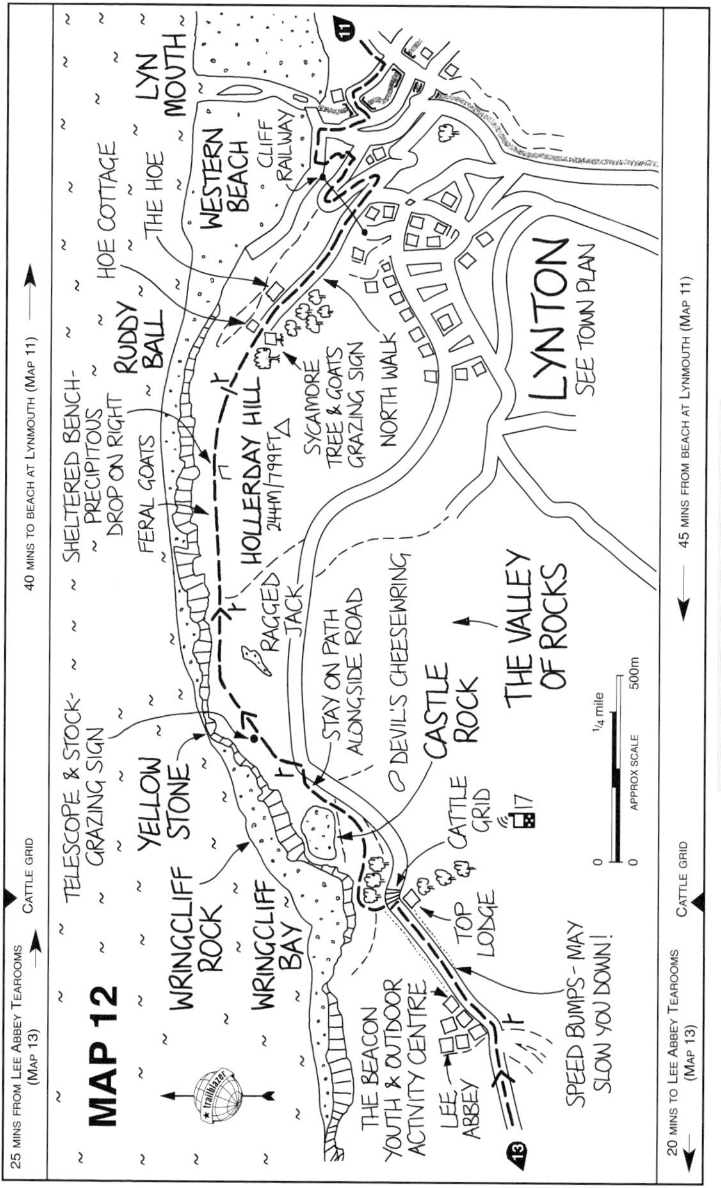

CATTLE GRID

TELESCOPE & STOCK-GRAZING SIGN

SHELTERED BENCH- ~ PRECIPITOUS DROP ON RIGHT

HOE COTTAGE

THE HOE

WESTERN BEACH

LYN MOUTH

CLIFF RAILWAY

RUDDY BALL

FERAL GOATS

HOLLERDAY HILL 244M/799FT △

SYCAMORE TREE & GOATS GRAZING SIGN

NORTH WALK

LYNTON SEE TOWN PLAN

RAGGED JACK

STAY ON PATH ALONGSIDE ROAD

DEVIL'S CHEESEWRING

WRINGCLIFF ROCK

YELLOW STONE

WRINGCLIFF BAY

CASTLE ROCK

THE VALLEY OF ROCKS

CATTLE GRID

17

TOP LODGE

MAP 12

THE BEACON YOUTH & OUTDOOR ACTIVITY CENTRE

LEE ABBEY

SPEED BUMPS- MAY SLOW YOU DOWN!

¼ mile

500m

APPROX SCALE

CATTLE GRID

* Trailblazer

ROUTE GUIDE AND MAPS

The route

The day begins simply enough by following **North Walk** across the cliff railway and out of town along a path skirting **Hollerday Hill**. There are tremendous views out to sea and along the shoreline. Indeed, so distracting can this
prove that it usually comes as something of a surprise when you round a corner
and are confronted by the **Valley of Rocks** (see box p106) with the appropriately named **Castle Rock** ahead of you, its silhouette like a hilltop fortress overlooking the sea. There now follows a short but pleasant-enough road walk with
Lee Abbey on your right. Built in 1850, and an evacuated boys' school during
the Second World War, the abbey is now a Christian conference centre. There
are some tearooms a little further down the road from the abbey itself. *Lee
Abbey Tea Cottage* (summer Tue-Sat 10.30am-5pm) serves a lot of homemade
and Fairtrade produce including some delicious cakes and, of course, cream teas
(£3.75 for one scone, £4.50 for two).

Shortly after the tearooms you have the option of continuing up the steep
and wooded road route, or you can choose the more off-piste **Woody Bay
Alternative Route** (see below) around Crock Point.

The Woody Bay alternative route

This route is a delight for those who believe that the Coast Path should stick
as close to the shoreline as possible; others, however, will wonder exactly what
the point of this short diversion is. There's nothing wrong with it, of course,
though on first viewing it doesn't seem to add much to the overall experience,
being a simple ramble along field edges bookended by a stroll through woodland. Nor do you even get a good view of the bay after which it is named due
to the thick vegetation you pass through (a clear case of not being able to see
the Woody for the trees).

Less than 30 minutes after setting off, you are reunited with the main trail.

The two paths do not stay apart for too long and, having reconnected on the
road, the SWCP continues through attractive woodland. **Hollow Brook
Waterfall** (Map 14) presents an impressive distraction, though perhaps not as
impressive as you were hoping if it hasn't rained recently: while it is one of the
biggest waterfalls in the UK, dropping 200m (656ft) in total, it does so over a
total horizontal distance of 400m. That said, there are some 50m drops (off the
path) which will have you reaching for your camera.

The path leaves the woods and takes to the cliffs again, with the views back
along the coast little short of extraordinary. **Beacon Roman Fortlet**, excavated
in the 1960s and capable of holding around 80 soldiers, still watches the Welsh
tribes from the hill above you but the path remains virtually horizontal as far as
rocky **Highveer Point**, from where the descent to **Heddon's Mouth** begins.

(cont'd on p114)

ROUTE GUIDE AND MAPS

❏ **Important note – walking times**
All times in this book refer only to the time spent walking. You will need to add
20-30% to allow for rests, photography, checking the map, drinking water etc.

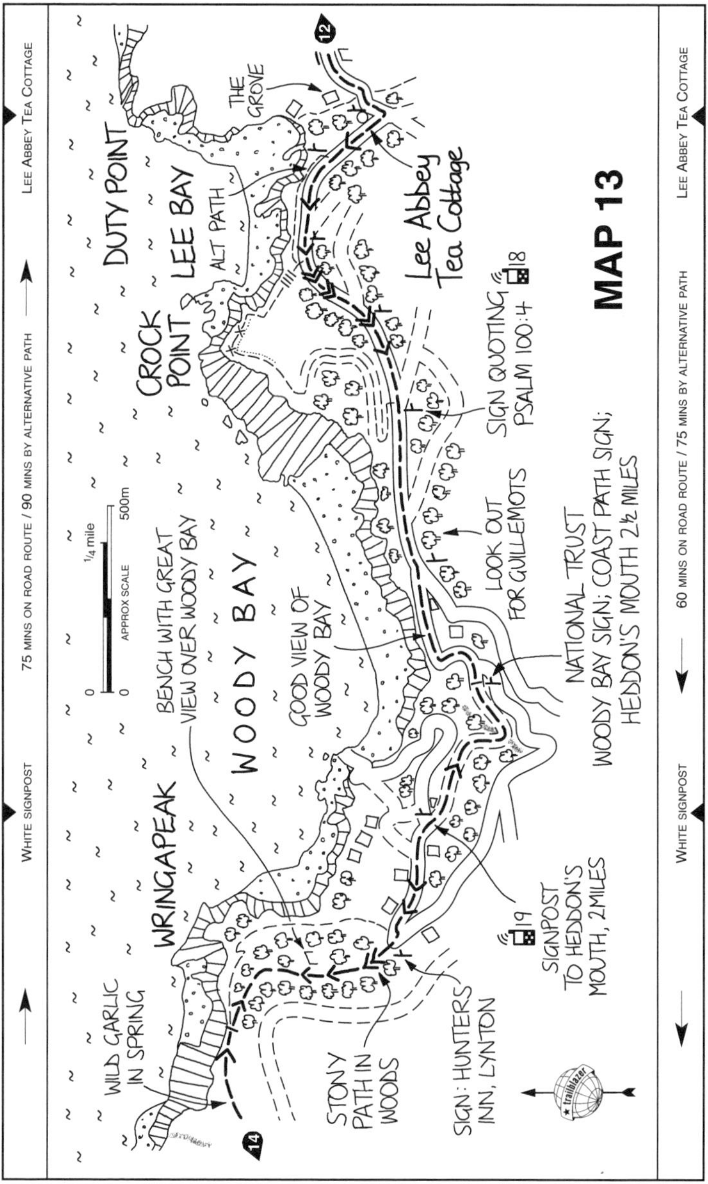

WHITE SIGNPOST → 75 MINS ON ROAD ROUTE / 90 MINS BY ALTERNATIVE PATH → LEE ABBEY TEA COTTAGE

DUTY POINT

CROCK POINT

LEE BAY

THE GROVE

ALT PATH

Lee Abbey Tea Cottage

12

WRINGAPEAK

WOODY BAY

BENCH WITH GREAT VIEW OVER WOODY BAY

GOOD VIEW OF WOODY BAY

WILD GARLIC IN SPRING

14

STONY PATH IN WOODS

SIGN: HUNTERS INN, LYNTON

SIGNPOST TO HEDDON'S MOUTH, 2 MILES

19

NATIONAL TRUST WOODY BAY SIGN; COAST PATH SIGN; HEDDON'S MOUTH 2½ MILES

LOOK OUT FOR GUILLEMOTS

SIGN QUOTING PSALM 100:4

18

MAP 13

¼ mile

500m

0   APPROX SCALE

WHITE SIGNPOST → 60 MINS ON ROAD ROUTE / 75 MINS BY ALTERNATIVE PATH → LEE ABBEY TEA COTTAGE

ROUTE GUIDE AND MAPS

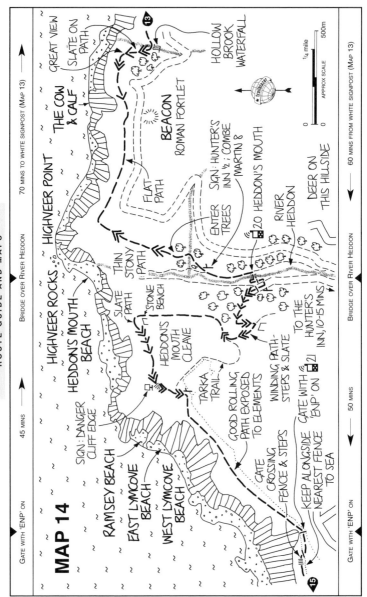

MAP 14

GATE WITH 'ENP' ON ◄ ─────── 45 MINS ─────── ► BRIDGE OVER RIVER HEDDON ◄ ─────── 70 MINS TO WHITE SIGNPOST (MAP 13) ───────

GATE WITH 'ENP' ON ◄ ─────── 50 MINS ─────── ► BRIDGE OVER RIVER HEDDON ◄ ─────── 60 MINS FROM WHITE SIGNPOST (MAP 13) ───────

GREAT VIEW
SLATE ON PATH
13
THE COW & CALF
HIGHVEER POINT
HOLLOW BROOK WATERFALL
BEACON
ROMAN FORTLET
FLAT PATH
SIGN: HUNTER'S INN ½; COMBE MARTIN 8
ENTER TREES
20 HEDDON'S MOUTH
RIVER HEDDON
DEER ON THIS HILLSIDE
THIN STONY PATH
HIGHVEER ROCKS
HEDDON'S MOUTH BEACH
SLATE PATH
STONE BENCH
HEDDON'S MOUTH CLEAVE
TARKA TRAIL
TO THE HUNTER'S INN, 10-15 MINS
WINDING PATH - STEPS & SLATE
GATE WITH 'ENP' ON 21
SIGN: DANGER CLIFF EDGE
RAMSEY BEACH
EAST LYMCOVE BEACH
WEST LYMCOVE BEACH
GOOD ROLLING PATH EXPOSED TO ELEMENTS
GATE CROSSING FENCE & STEPS
KEEP ALONGSIDE NEAREST FENCE TO SEA
15

¼ mile
APPROX SCALE
0   500m
0

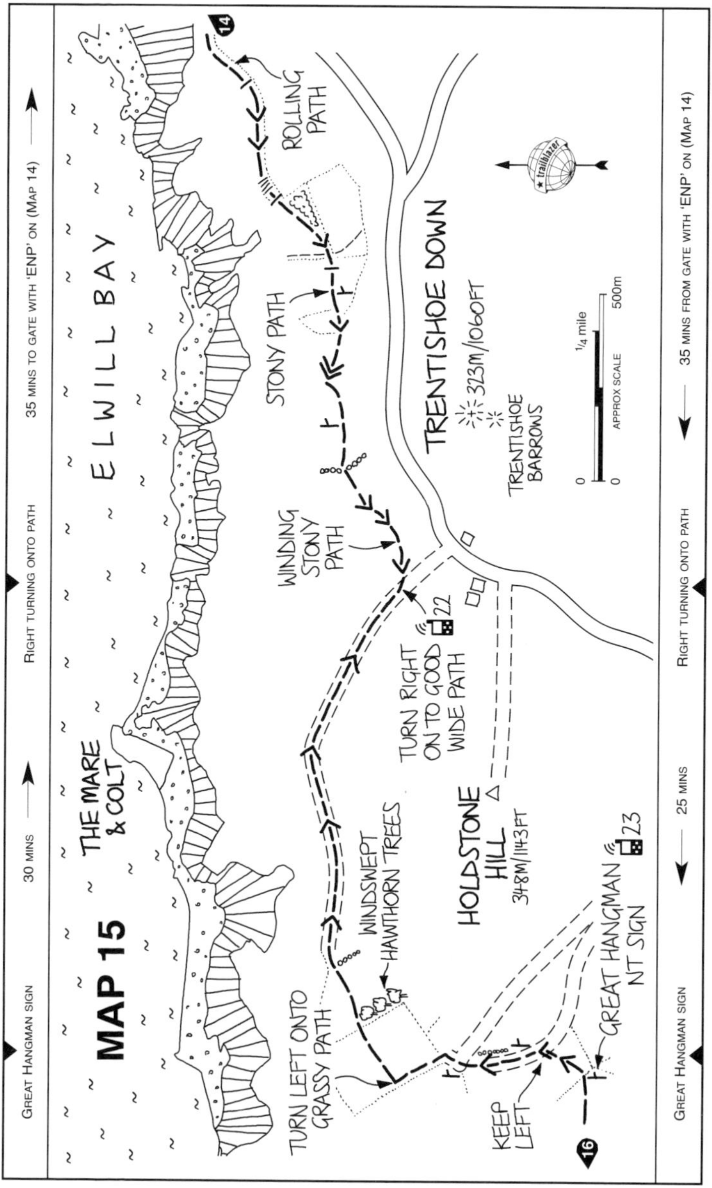
MAP 15
GREAT HANGMAN SIGN
30 MINS
RIGHT TURNING ONTO PATH
35 MINS TO GATE WITH 'ENP' ON (MAP 14)
ELWILL BAY
THE MARE & COLT
14
ROLLING PATH
STONY PATH
WINDING STONY PATH
TURN RIGHT ON TO GOOD WIDE PATH
22
TRENTISHOE DOWN
323M/1060FT
TRENTISHOE BARROWS
0
1/4 mile
0
APPROX SCALE
500m
trailblazer
WINDSWEPT HAWTHORN TREES
HOLDSTONE HILL
348M/1143FT
23
TURN LEFT ONTO GRASSY PATH
KEEP LEFT
GREAT HANGMAN NT SIGN
16
GREAT HANGMAN SIGN
25 MINS
RIGHT TURNING ONTO PATH
35 MINS FROM GATE WITH 'ENP' ON (MAP 14)

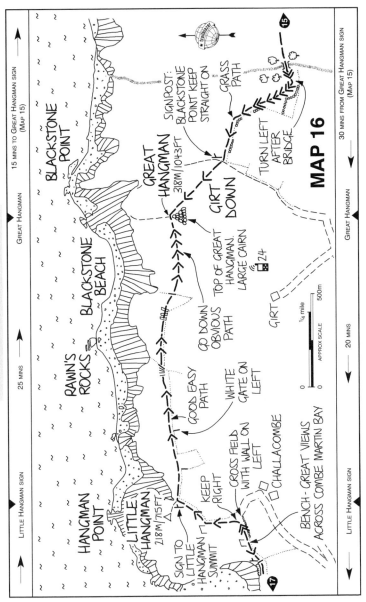

MAP 16

15 MINS TO GREAT HANGMAN SIGN (MAP 15)

GREAT HANGMAN

25 MINS

LITTLE HANGMAN SIGN

30 MINS FROM GREAT HANGMAN SIGN (MAP 15)

GREAT HANGMAN

20 MINS

LITTLE HANGMAN SIGN

BLACKSTONE POINT

BLACKSTONE BEACH

RAWN'S ROCKS

HANGMAN POINT

LITTLE HANGMAN 218M/715FT

GREAT HANGMAN 318M/1043FT

GIRT DOWN

SIGNPOST: BLACKSTONE POINT KEEP STRAIGHT ON

GRASS PATH

TURN LEFT AFTER BRIDGE

TOP OF GREAT HANGMAN. LARGE CAIRN

GIRT

GO DOWN OBVIOUS PATH

GOOD EASY PATH

WHITE GATE ON LEFT

CROSS FIELD WITH WALL ON LEFT

CHALLACOMBE

KEEP RIGHT

SIGN TO LITTLE HANGMAN SUMMIT

BENCH - GREAT VIEWS ACROSS COMBE MARTIN BAY

24

¼ mile

APPROX SCALE

0   500m

15

17

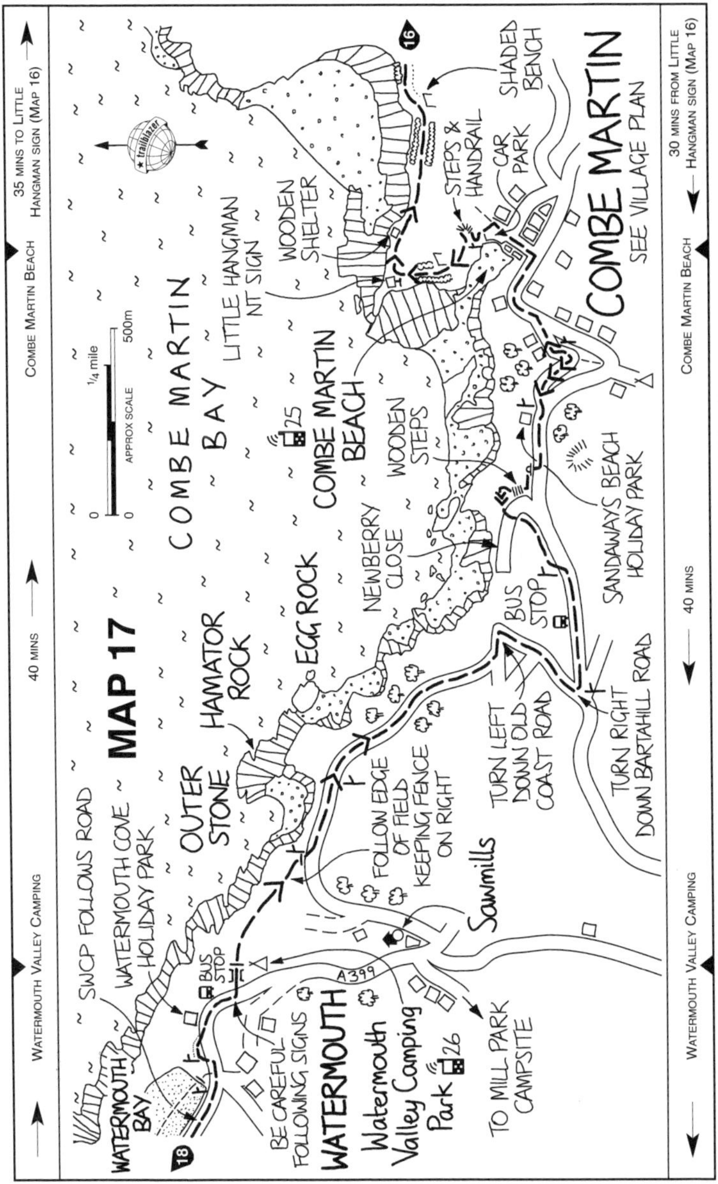

MAP 17

COMBE MARTIN

SEE VILLAGE PLAN

COMBE MARTIN BAY

COMBE MARTIN BEACH

WATERMOUTH BAY

WATERMOUTH

Watermouth Valley Camping Park 📠26

WATERMOUTH COVE ~ HOLIDAY PARK

SWCP FOLLOWS ROAD

OUTER STONE

HAMATOR ROCK

EGG ROCK

NEWBERRY CLOSE

WOODEN STEPS

📠25

LITTLE HANGMAN NT SIGN

WOODEN SHELTER

STEPS & HANDRAIL

SHADED BENCH

CAR PARK

SANDAWAYS BEACH HOLIDAY PARK

BUS STOP

TURN LEFT DOWN OLD COAST ROAD

TURN RIGHT DOWN BARTAHILL ROAD

FOLLOW EDGE OF FIELD KEEPING FENCE ON RIGHT

Sawmills

A399

BE CAREFUL FOLLOWING SIGNS

BUS STOP

TO MILL PARK CAMPSITE

trailblazer

¼ mile

APPROX SCALE

0   500m

35 MINS TO LITTLE HANGMAN SIGN (MAP 16)

30 MINS FROM LITTLE HANGMAN SIGN (MAP 16)

COMBE MARTIN BEACH

COMBE MARTIN BEACH

40 MINS

40 MINS

WATERMOUTH VALLEY CAMPING

WATERMOUTH VALLEY CAMPING

(cont'd from p108) Despite feeling far from civilisation, it's only a short jaunt (10-15 mins) from the path to **The Hunters Inn** (off Map 14; ☎ 01598-763230, 🖳 www.thehuntersinnexmoor.co.uk; 7D/1T/2Qd, all en suite; 🛥; WI-FI; Ⓛ; 🐾), full of charm (some rooms have a four-poster bed) and a good place to stay – if only to delay your exit from Exmoor! B&B costs £50-70pp (sgl occ £70-100, three/four sharing £105-150). They also have a self-contained apartment (2D; £105-150pp, sgl occ £150). The **food** (daily noon-3pm & 6-9pm) is good too, with baguettes and filling cream teas (3-6pm) in the afternoon and hearty meals – hot crust beef and ale pie (£12), for example – served in the evenings; just watch out for the peacocks!

Heddon Valley is actually one of the steepest in England, a fact you'll realise soon enough as the path continues by climbing sharply up a wooded hillside, from where deer can often be seen on the hills opposite while birds of prey circle above. There are good views back down the combe with the roof of the inn emerging through the trees. Continuing on the path, magnificent cliff-top walking leads you onto bare, scrubby **Trentishoe Down** (Map 15), before a slow descent brings you to the foot of Great Hangman. **Great Hangman** is the highest point on the SWCP at 318m or 1043ft (though bear in mind, of course, that you won't be starting your ascent from sea-level but a point approximately 140m above sea level at Sherrycombe – which is a small mercy). On its northern side it also happens to be mainland Britain's highest sea cliff, with a vertical face of around 250m (around 800ft).

The initial climb will certainly get the heart pounding but you'll also be pleasantly surprised at how brief (hopefully!) the assault is; what's more, the huge **cairn** at the top of Great Hangman is a great spot to survey the land, take photos and enjoy a rest – safe in the knowledge that your day's walking is almost at an end.

The path now has only one way to go and the long, slow walk downwards begins. The path passes by **Little Hangman** (218m/715ft), visitable off to the right of the trail; non-masochists, however, should continue downwards where, shortly afterwards, there are splendid views down to your destination for this stage: **Combe Martin Bay**.

COMBE MARTIN

Combe Martin, anciently Marhuscombe, which lieth low as the name implies, and near the sea, having a cove for boats to land, a place noted for yielding the best hemp in all the County of Devon, and that in great abundance, but in former times famous for mines of tin, and, that which is better merchandise, silver, though Cicero denieth that there is any in Britain.

Tristram Risdon, 1640

Today the hemp fields and mines of tin and silver have all disappeared and if Combe Martin is known for anything now, it is its

high street which, so it is said, is the longest in England. (It's a claim that is dubious at best, especially given that much of the street is residential rather than commercial; though it is true that they once featured in *Guinness World Records* for holding the longest street party.)

The town is perhaps not as attractive as some on the route though it's not without some points of interest including the small **Combe Martin Museum** (☎ 01271-889031, 🖳 combemartinmuseum.co.uk; Apr to Oct Mon-Sat 10.30am-5pm, Sun

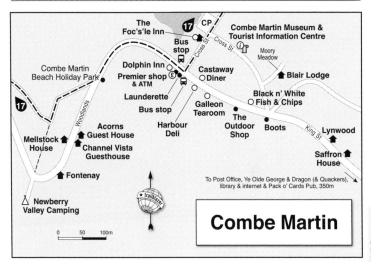

The Foc'sle Inn

CP

Combe Martin Museum & Tourist Information Centre

Bus stop

Moory Meadow

Combe Martin Beach Holiday Park

Dolphin Inn
Premier shop & ATM

Castaway Diner

Blair Lodge

Launderette

Black n' White Fish & Chips

Bus stop

Galleon Tearoom

Acorns Guest House

Harbour Deli

The Outdoor Shop

Boots

Lynwood

Mellstock House

Channel Vista Guesthouse

Saffron House

Fontenay

To Post Office, Ye Olde George & Dragon (& Quackers), library & internet & Pack o' Cards Pub, 350m

Newberry Valley Camping

0   50   100m

trailster

Combe Martin

11.30am-2pm, Nov-Mar Tue-Thur 10.30am-3pm; £2.50) on Cross St. With displays on the industrial, maritime and natural history of the village a visit is worthwhile. There's also the **Pack o' Cards** pub (see Where to stay), built in 1690 by a local dignitary following a particularly large win whilst gambling, an event that led to his decision to construct the inn with 52 stairs and 52 windows (52 being the number of cards in a pack), 4 floors (ie the number of suits in a pack), and with 13 doors on every floor and 13 fireplaces throughout (representing the number of cards in a suit)!

See p16 for details of festivals and events here.

Services

The museum is home to the **tourist information centre** (same details as museum); the staff have information about accommodation but can't do bookings; there is free WI-FI as well as **internet access** (donations welcome).

The village also boasts a **post office** (Mon-Fri 9am-5pm, Sat 9am-noon); Premier **shop** (Mon-Sat 7.30am-10pm) which has a free **ATM**; **launderette** (daily 8am-8pm); Boots **pharmacy** (Mon-Wed

9am-6pm, Thur & Fri to 5.30pm, Sat to 1pm) and a **walking/camping outlet**, The Outdoor Shop (daily 10am-5pm).

Transport

[See also pp48-50] Filer's 301 **bus** service to Barnstaple via Ilfracombe calls here as does their No 300, but the latter only in the school summer holidays. Buses run along the main street and stop at several places including by the beach.

For a **taxi**, try Andy's (☎ 01271-889200).

Where to stay

By the standards of this path there's not a great choice of places to stay in Combe Martin, though most are OK and two are positively quirky.

There are two large holiday parks on the outskirts of Combe Martin but the best option for **campers** is *Newberry Valley Camping and Caravanning Park* (☎ 01271-882334, ☐ www.newberryvalleypark.co.uk; £8-15 per hiker & one-man tent; WI-FI; 🐾; Mar-Oct). The facilities are excellent and there's a little **shop** (daily 8.30am-6.30pm in high season, limited hours in low season) that sells basics only.

The site is abundant in wildlife and has won the David Bellamy Conservation & Nature Gold Award numerous times! It is located a short distance out of the town on the bend a little way up Newberry Hill.

If you feel you have a few more miles in you it is also well worth considering continuing to Watermouth (see p118) where there are some campsites, including a couple that are better value for hikers.

There is a huddle of **B&Bs** on Woodlands, up the hill on the way out of town. The best, perhaps, is *Mellstock House* (☎ 01271-882592, 🖳 www.mell stockhouse.co.uk; 2D/1D or T/1T/1Tr, all en suite; WI-FI; Ⓛ) with a licensed bar and the offer of evening meals. There's a decent breakfast menu including smoked salmon and eggs, and a drying room too – little wonder that this place is perhaps the most popular with walkers. They also offer a pick-up and drop-off service from/to Lynton/Lynmouth and Woolacombe should you book for two nights. B&B costs £35-40pp (sgl occ from £45, three sharing £100).

Providing close competition is *Fontenay* (☎ 01271-889368, 🖳 www.visit fontenay.co.uk; 1S/1D/1T shared bathroom; 🐾; WI-FI; Ⓛ; 🐴), just before the bend in the road near the top of the hill; it's a large family house with a nice sideline in selling crafts made from locally sourced driftwood. The bread and other food at breakfast is home cooked and organic where possible; the eggs are from their chickens. They charge £27pp (sgl/sgl occ £27).

Back down the hill, *Acorns Guest House* (☎ 01271-882769, 🖳 www.acorns guesthouse.co.uk; 6D en suite/1T private facilities; WI-FI; Ⓛ; 🐴) is a huge late-Victorian terrace with friendly owners who charge £36.50-40pp (£55 sgl occ), while *Channel Vista* (☎ 01271-883514, 🖳 www .channelvista.co.uk; 1S/1T/4D/1Tr, all en suite; 🐾; WI-FI; Ⓛ; 🐴) has a licensed honesty bar in their pleasant Victorian conservatory. B&B costs £40pp (sgl £40, sgl occ £55 three sharing £100).

There are also some B&Bs in the centre of town. *Blair Lodge* (☎ 01271-882294, 🖳 www.blairlodge.co.uk; 1S private bathroom, 2T/5D/1Qd, all en suite; 🐾; WI-FI;

Feb-Oct), at the top of Moory Meadow, just off the main street, is licensed to sell alcohol and provides evening meals. They charge £33-39pp (sgl £39, sgl occ £51, three/four sharing £99/110).

On King St, *Lynwood* (☎ 01271-882013, 🖳 wendyadruce@gmail.com; 2D en suite/1T private facilities; 🐾; WI-FI; Ⓛ), is a small, good-value place. Rates are from £35pp (sgl occ from £37.50).

Much grander, *Saffron House* (☎ 01271-883521; 3D/2Tr/1Qd, all en suite; 🐾; WI-FI; Ⓛ; 🐴; mid Feb-end Oct) is a large former farmhouse with its own outdoor swimming pool (May-Sep). Saffron House lies away from the traffic, up the steps on King St. Expect to pay £37.50-42.50pp (£50 sgl occ, three/four sharing £90/95).

Combe Martin also has two **pubs** in which you could spend the night: *The Fo'c's'le Inn* (☎ 01271-883354, 🖳 www .focsleinn.co.uk; 5D/1Qd, all en suite; 🐾; WI-FI; 🐴; Easter-Nov) is perfectly located for walkers where the path enters Combe Martin and charges from £37.50pp (sgl occ from £45, three/four sharing £90).

Pack o' Cards (☎ 01271-882300, 🖳 www.packocards.co.uk; 2D/4Tr, all en suite; WI-FI intermittent in rooms; Ⓛ) is a listed building (see p115) but still takes guests. Their rooms are amongst the smartest in town, with one featuring a four-poster bed. Rates are £42.50-47.50pp (sgl occ/three sharing full room rate).

Where to eat and drink

There are a few splendid options for breakfast. *Harbour Deli* (☎ 01271-883688; Apr-Nov Mon-Sat 9am-5pm, winter hours variable), where you'll get a large full English for £6.95 – there's lunches and great cakes too The other place is *The Castaways Diner* (☎ 01271-882918; late Mar to late Oct daily 9am-5pm, rest of year closed Mon; WI-FI; 🐴), which charges £6-8 for breakfasts; vegetarian/gluten-free options, and even sausages for dogs!

Also on Borough Rd is *Galleon Tearoom* (☎ 01271-883732; Mar-Oct daily 10am-5pm, WI-FI; 🐴), which has a great little terrace: a delight on a sunny day.

Dogs are also welcome in this family-run establishment with breakfasts and cream teas a speciality.

By the beach, **pub food** can be found at *The Fo'c's'le Inn* (see Where to stay; food served Easter-Nov daily noon-3pm & 6-8.30pm) – where you'll get a decent meal for £10-17 – and also at *The Dolphin Inn* (☎ 01271-883424; food Easter-Sep daily noon-3pm & 5-9pm but may differ out of season) which serves bar-meals and a carvery on a Sunday (£8.50). Further out of town, *Pack o' Cards* (see Where to stay) also serves food (summer holidays daily noon-9pm, rest of year Mon-Sat noon-3pm & 5.30-9pm, Sun noon-8pm). You'll get a carvery dinner for £10.95.

The place with the best reputation in Combe Martin is *Quackers* restaurant (Mar-Aug Mon-Fri 6-9pm, winter Wed-Fri 6-9pm, year-round Sat noon-3pm & 6-10pm, Sun noon-3pm & 5-8pm) at *Ye Olde George and Dragon* (☎ 01271-882282, 🖳 www.georgeanddragon.uk.com; food Mar-end Aug Mon-Fri 6-9pm, Sat noon-3pm & 6-10pm, Sun noon-3pm & 5-8pm, Sep-Feb Wed-Sun only), around 2km back from the sea on the main street, a 400-year-old tavern with a restaurant that has daily specials as well as a fixed menu including fillet of sea bass for £14.95. They also do a takeaway service.

For more traditional **takeaway** look no further than *Black & White Fish 'n' Chips* (☎ 01271-883548; Mon-Wed, Fri & Sat noon-2pm, Mon-Sat 5-8.30pm) on Borough Rd.

COMBE MARTIN TO WOOLACOMBE   [MAPS 17-22]

For this **14¼-mile (23km; 6hrs 35 mins)** stage, and the one after it, the landscape is no longer dominated by the high rolling hills, hanging woodlands, steep-sided canyons and soaring cliffs prevalent in Exmoor. The scenery instead is one of sand and seals, smugglers' coves and surfers, broad beige beaches and bleach-blonde hair. This stage still provides a fairly strenuous workout for your calf muscles, with some stiff climbs, though generally the gradients are kind. That said, the start of the walk is punctuated by some fairly mundane road walking, but this is more than made up for by some great cliff-top walking and some wonderful views of Lundy Island and Ilfracombe – a tourist hot-spot with plenty of amenities. Refreshments are also available at several spots along the way.

After Ilfracombe the path meanders through the greenery of Torrs Park before following a wonderfully undulating route around Morte Point from where you will be treated to your first views of Woolacombe and its long, gorgeous expanse of sand. Seals, dolphins and basking sharks are frequently spotted from the cliffs around Morte Point (with Rockham Bay being an especially good spot for seals). Whether you'll see one of those exotic British creatures is largely a matter of luck, of course – though one mammal you definitely will see bobbing up and down in Morte Bay as you stroll/stagger into Woolacombe are the local surfers, a largely migratory creature that populates the coastline from Woolacombe to Saunton in huge numbers, particularly in summertime.

The route

There is a need for caution when leaving Combe Martin: both that you take great care whilst walking along the road and that you do not miss the sign that directs you off it. Accompanied by some rather pleasant woodland the path initially takes a rather haphazard route before arriving at **Watermouth Bay**.

WATERMOUTH   [MAP 17, p113]

There's not much to Watermouth other than a small, pretty harbour, the old Victorian **Watermouth Castle**, now a theme park (⌨ www.watermouthcastle.com) and several decent **campsites**.

In the school summer holidays Filers Travel's No 300 **bus** service stops here en route between Minehead/Lynmouth and Ilfracombe; see pp48-50.

Watermouth Valley Camping Park (☎ 01271-862282, ⌨ www.watermouthpark .co.uk; WI-FI; ✾; May-Sep) is a cheap and lovely campsite, perfectly situated on the path and near the pub. The rate for hikers (£5pp) is for a one-night stay only. (Please note: don't get confused between this campsite and Watermouth Cove Holiday Park next-door.)

Across the road and up the hill from the pub, *Mill Park* (☎ 01271-882647, ⌨ www .millparklimited.co.uk; WI-FI main bldg; ✾; Mar-Oct) is a smarter affair whose chief recommendation for hikers may be their '**tent cocoon**' (£25-50) – a two-person wooden hut with electricity that makes a great alter-native to sleeping in a tent, particularly if the weather doesn't look too friendly. However, you need to bring a sleeping mat & bag. Alternatively they have three **bell tents** and three '**glampods**' each of which costs £30-60; however, there is a minimum two-night stay for these. For a normal **tent** and up to two people they charge £10-23.

The pub, by the way, is *Sawmills* (☎ 01271-883388, ⌨ www.sawmillsfree house.co.uk; WI-FI; ✾), which was being renovated at the time of research and should be offering accommodation by the time you read this so it's certainly worth contacting them. They already serve **food** all day (daily 8/9am till 10pm); the extensive menu includes pub grub such as whole-tail scampi (£10.95), burgers (from £9.25) and tapas (from £3.95).

About 500m west of Watermouth and on the left up the hill is *Little Meadow Campsite* (**Map 18, p119**; ☎ 01271-866862, ⌨ www.littlemeadow.co.uk; ✾; Mar-Sep), part of Lydford Farm. The rate for a hiker and a tent is £5.

A brief dalliance with Watermouth Harbour follows. Tranquil and sleepy it may seem now, but this harbour played an integral part in the allies' Operation Pluto (an acronym for Pipelines Under The Ocean) during WWII. The idea was to lay pipes under the Channel to supply fuel to allied forces, and to test the plan a 51½-mile (83km) pipe was laid between Watermouth and Swansea across the Bristol Channel. It proved a success and the first pipe was laid under the English Channel to France in 1944 – with further pipes installed for the remainder of the war as the fighting moved closer to Germany.

Some woodland cliff-side walking to **Widmouth Head** follows, from where, sadly, you will get your last good views of Great Hangman. Your eyes will not remain unoccupied for long, however, as from **Rillage Point** another magical spectre arrives on the horizon – that of Lundy Island (see box p122).

Having passed the edge of **Hele** ...

HELE   [MAP 18]

The beach here has been a popular bathing spot since Victorian times but whether stopping for a paddle or you just need a quick snack to spur you on to Ilfracombe, you may be glad to see the Premier **shop** (daily 7am-9pm).

In the school summer holidays Filers Travel's No 300 **bus** service calls here; see pp48-50.

If you'd rather sit down for your lunch, there are two options for **food** before you navigate Beacon Point to Ilfracombe. *Hele Bay Pub* (☎ 01271-867795; WI-FI; ✾; food Apr-Oct Mon-Sat noon-3pm & 5-9pm, Sun noon-8pm, Oct-Apr closed Mon, Sun noon-5pm), 39 Beach Rd, produces award-winning traditional homemade pub grub; as well as a

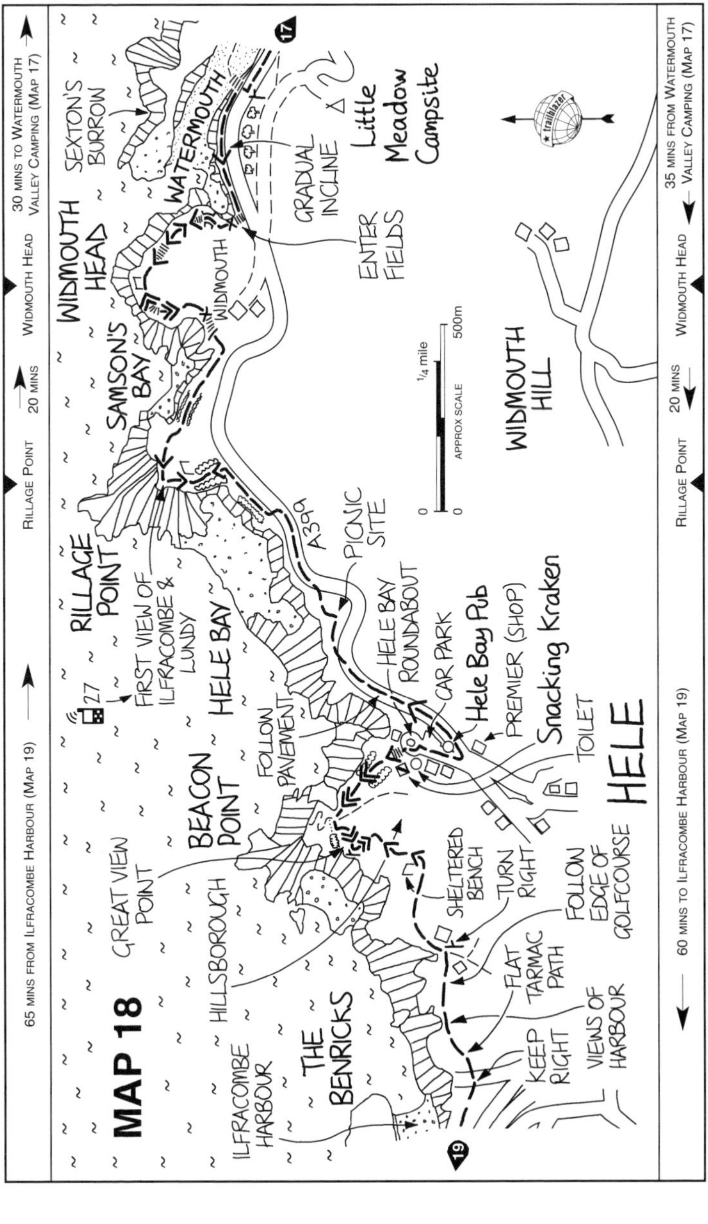
MAP 18
65 mins from Ilfracombe Harbour (Map 19)
Rillage Point
20 mins
Widmouth Head
30 mins to Watermouth Valley Camping (Map 17)
60 mins to Ilfracombe Harbour (Map 19)
Rillage Point
20 mins
Widmouth Head
35 mins from Watermouth Valley Camping (Map 17)
19
17
ILFRACOMBE HARBOUR
THE BENRICKS
HILLSBOROUGH
GREAT VIEW POINT
BEACON POINT
27
FIRST VIEW OF ILFRACOMBE & LUNDY
HELE BAY
RILLAGE POINT
SAMSON'S BAY
WIDMOUTH HEAD
WIDMOUTH
WATERMOUTH
SEXTON'S BURROW
KEEP RIGHT
VIEWS OF HARBOUR
FLAT TARMAC PATH
FOLLOW EDGE OF GOLFCOURSE
TURN RIGHT
SHELTERED BENCH
FOLLOW PAVEMENT
HELE BAY ROUNDABOUT
CAR PARK
Hele Bay Pub
PREMIER (SHOP)
Snacking Kraken
TOILET
HELE
PICNIC SITE
A399
0
0
1/4 mile
500m
APPROX SCALE
WIDMOUTH HILL
ENTER FIELDS
GRADUAL INCLINE
Little Meadow Campsite
trailblazer

ROUTE GUIDE AND MAPS

specials' board there are some mighty fine pie meals (from £10) and real ales.

By the roundabout and beach, **Snacking Kraken** (☎ 01271-863911, 💻 www.snackingkraken.com; late Mar-June & Sep daily 9am-5pm, July & Aug Sun-Thur 9am-6pm, Fri-Sun to 9pm) serves breakfasts (£3.95-8.45), light bites and lunches. Their regular specials' board features locally sourced fish tacos and there is pizza to have-in or takeaway.

... the path navigates the wooded slopes and fields of **Hillsborough**, from where fabulous views of Ilfracombe and its harbour (since 2012 featuring Damien Hirst's *Verity* statue; see box below and map p125) greet you.

ILFRACOMBE   [see map p125]

'The situation of Ilfracombe is by nature lovely'   **S Baring-Gould** *Devon* (1907)
The first part of Ilfracombe that's visible as you stroll around Beacon Point is the town's harbour.

Whether *MS Oldenburg*, the boat to Lundy (see box p122), is in dock or not, it's difficult not to be struck by the natural beauty of this little haven. Sheltered between the hills of Capstone and Hillsborough, it's little wonder there's been a harbour here since the 12th century, though, as with just about every resort on the North Devon coastline, the town owes its prosperity largely to the Victorians, whose decision to route the steamships and railways here bought the crowds to Ilfracombe en masse.

Today, the town can be divided into four distinct areas. The **harbour** is the largest in North Devon and, somewhat surprisingly given its rather homely aspect, experiences the world's second highest tidal rise and fall. It is also the place from which to embark on a coastal cruise or sea-

---

❏ *Verity*

Mention Ilfracombe's controversial steel and bronze resident to a local and many will proudly inform you that British artist Damien Hirst's *Verity* is the tallest statue in the United Kingdom, standing 25cm (10") taller than Antony Gormley's *Angel of the North* (which peers down over the A1 near Gateshead).

When approaching Ilfracombe (from Hillsborough) *Verity* can be difficult to spot in the harbour, which can lead one to question this claim regarding the statue's stature. It is, however, true. Unless directly beneath *Verity* you generally don't appreciate the sculpture's scale. (*Angel of the North* you always gaze up at.) A great deal of *Verity*'s height of 20.25 metres (66.43ft) is made up of her sword but it won't be this aspect of the sculpture that makes you wonder what it's all about. The torso and head of the 25-tonne statue have been truly controversial as they depict half of *Verity*'s body skinless with her skull and womb (including a developing foetus) revealed. Standing on a pile of legal books, in her sword-free hand you'll also spot a set of scales. So ... what is it all about? Well, a verity (*Veritas*), is 'the quality or state of being true' and Hirst describes the statue as a 'modern allegory of truth and justice.' Whilst the sword and scales represent the traditional symbols of Justice, *Verity*'s stance is based on the sculpture *Little Dancer of Fourteen Years* (c.1881) by French artist Edgar Degas (1834-1917).

Verity took two years to plan and produce, and was erected over a week in October 2012. Weather and lightning proof, it appears she'll be splitting opinion in the town for at least the next two decades: that being the span of time that Hirst has kindly (depending on your opinion on it) loaned the sculpture to Ilfracombe for.

More information on Damien Hirst can be found at 💻 www.damienhirst.com.

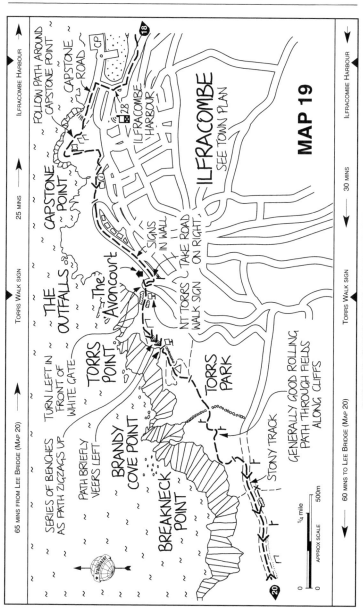

ILFRACOMBE HARBOUR

FOLLOW PATH AROUND CAPSTONE POINT

CAPSTONE POINT

CAPSTONE ROAD

CP

18

ILFRACOMBE HARBOUR

ILFRACOMBE

SEE TOWN PLAN

MAP 19

ILFRACOMBE HARBOUR

25 MINS

30 MINS

SIGNS IN WALL

The 'Avoncourt'

THE OUTFALLS

TAKE ROAD ON RIGHT,

TORRS POINT

NT TORRS WALK SIGN

TORRS WALK SIGN

TORRS PARK

TORRS WALK SIGN

65 MINS FROM LEE BRIDGE (MAP 20)

TURN LEFT IN FRONT OF WHITE GATE

SERIES OF BENCHES AS PATH ZIGZAGS UP

PATH BRIEFLY VEERS LEFT

BRANDY COVE POINT

BREAKNECK POINT

GENERALLY GOOD ROLLING PATH THROUGH FIELDS ALONG CLIFFS

STONY TRACK

60 MINS TO LEE BRIDGE (MAP 20)

ROUTE GUIDE AND MAPS

¼ mile

APPROX SCALE

500m

20

❑ Lundy Island

Lying 11 miles off the coast of North Devon, where the Bristol Channel meets the Atlantic Ocean, Lundy Island is an extraordinary place in a wonderful location. It is also one that, with careful planning, can be reached by the intrepid pedestrian – and its coastline walked – in just one day.

Measuring 3½ miles long and just a mile wide, the island is renowned for its **wildlife**: approximately 35 species of bird breed on the island annually including puffins ('Lund-ey' means Puffin Island in Norse) and many other seabirds such as razorbills and guillemots. Amongst the landlubbers there are Sika deer and Lundy ponies, while out at sea you may glimpse basking sharks and dolphins.

Standing on the clifftops amongst wildflowers – possibly even next to a famous Lundy cabbage – the walker can stare out across the water and easily imagine why for many centuries Lundy was a favoured hiding place for **pirates**, its remoteness and proximity to both two coastlines and Bristol Channel's bustling shipping lane making it the perfect hideout. **Marisco Castle** is named after a famous family of swashbuckling criminals including William de Marisco, who met a most unfortunate end – in 1242 he was charged with conspiring to kill King Henry III and it is thought that he was the first man to have been hung, drawn and quartered.

Taking less than two hours, *MS Oldenburg* (late Mar to late Oct; 3-5 sailings per week; day return £37/19 adults/children, open return £65/33) carries passengers to the car-free island from Ilfracombe and Bideford. Alternatively, in winter a helicopter service (return fare £116/62 adult/child) runs on Mondays and Fridays from Hartland Point (see p188).

If a single day on Lundy seems inadequate – which it will if you wish both to walk the whole coastline and have time to investigate all its other attractions – there are 23 restored historic buildings on the island in which you can stay, including the castle and a **lighthouse**. The cost varies greatly depending on the size of the property and the season in which you visit, and be aware that some can be rented only on a weekly basis over the school summer holidays. **Camping** (£16pp; late Mar to early Oct) is also an option in a field near the island's public house and **shop** (hours vary but generally 9am-4.30pm). All accommodation booking must be done in advance as even the campsite is very popular in the summer months. *Marisco Tavern* (food served daily 8.30-10am, noon-2/3pm & 6-8.30/9pm) serves food to suit all budgets.

For more information in regards to sailings, helicopter flights and the island in general you should contact Lundy Booking Office (☎ 01271-863636) in Ilfracombe or, for accommodation, The Landmark Trust (🖳 www.landmarktrust.org.uk). For Lundy Island itself call ☎ 01237-431831.

---

life safari. **Fore St** is the oldest part of Ilfracombe and used to be the town's social and business hub. It is still home to many of the town's better eateries and whilst strolling up or down the steep cobbled street it is easy to envisage the seafaring residents of old staggering out of the George and Dragon, the town's oldest pub, dating from 1360.

The third area is **High St**, the continuation of Fore St (there's a large metal arch separating the two) and a town-centre of

sorts. Just after the divide you will find **Ilfracombe Chocolate Emporium** (☎ 01271-867193 or ☎ 07774-411954, 🖳 www.chocolate-emporium.co.uk; Easter-Oct Mon-Sat 10am-5pm, Aug Sun 10am-4pm, Oct-Easter Tue-Sat 10am-4pm; free), a museum dedicated to the humble cocoa bean and all its derivatives; with luck you will be here on a day when they are making chocolate so you can watch it.

The fourth and final area, the **seafront and The Promenade**, is pretty enough, and the large conical buildings that greet you as you circle Capstone Hill are certainly striking. This is the home of the TIC, a gallery and Landmark Theatre (though the theatre went into liquidation in January 2017). Nearby is **Ilfracombe Museum** (☎ 01271-863541, 🖥 www.ilfracombemuseum.co .uk; late Mar/Easter-late Oct Mon-Sat 10am-5pm, Nov-late Mar/Easter Tue-Fri 10am-1pm; £5, £4 concs); it has five rooms, with sections dedicated to sailing, Lundy and the harbour, and makes for a diverting half-hour or so.

St Nicholas Chapel, on Lantern Hill, guards the harbour's entrance. Built in 1321, the chapel's use has changed down the centuries from place of worship to lighthouse to family home; currently it's maintained by Ilfracombe Rotary Club and you can look around (free, although donations are welcome).

See p16 for details of festivals and events held here.

Services
The **tourist information centre** (☎ 01271-863001; Easter to Oct Mon-Fri 9.30am-4.30pm, Sat & Sun 10.30am-4.30pm, Nov to Easter Mon-Fri 10am-4pm, Sat to 4.30pm) shares one of the conical buildings with the theatre; they do accommodation booking (see box p40).

Internet access can be found at **Ilfracombe Library** (☎ 01271-862388; Mon & Sat 9am-1pm, Tue & Fri to 5pm, Thur to 6pm; £2/hr, free if you join the library), on Sommers Crescent between The Promenade and Fore St.

Also on the High St there is: the **post office** (Mon-Fri 9am-5.30pm, Sat to 12.30pm), part of the **general store** McColls (daily 7am-11pm); the **Co-op** (Mon-Sat 7am-9pm, Sun 10am-4pm), which is the best place for food supplies in the centre; the **chemists** Superdrug (Mon-Sat 8.30am-5.30pm, Sun 10am-4pm) and **banks** with **ATMs** including Barclays, NatWest and Lloyds.

Ilfracombe **Laundrette** (daily 8am-7.30pm, manned 9.30am-4pm) is at 15 Wilder Rd. Another shop selling general necessities, though nearer the harbour on St James Place, is St James **Newsagents** & Minimarket (daily 8.30am-9pm).

Transport
[See also pp48-50] Ilfracombe is well-served with **bus** services (Filers Travel's No 31 and their seasonal 300 & 302; Stagecoach's No 21 & 21A) to and from most other destinations along the path.

For a **taxi** try A Taxis (☎ 01271-865321), or Ilfracombe Taxis (☎ 01271-440258).

Where to stay
Campers will need to continue onto Woolacombe for the nearest campsite. However, there is a **hostel** here: *Ocean Backpackers* (☎ 01271-867835, 🖥 www .oceanbackpackers.co.uk; 5 x 6-, 1 x 8-dorm beds, 1S/2D/3Qd, most en suite, rest share facilities; ▼; WI-FI; 🐾 but in private room only; Mar-Nov), at 29 St James Place. It is a comfortable place (dorm beds £16-19pp, sgl £20-25, two/three/four sharing a room £21-24/19-21/17-19pp, sgl occ £30-35) right in the centre of town and it even provides free tea and coffee for its guests. It also has self-catering facilities and a drying room.

There are plenty of **B&Bs** in town. In terms of location, it's hard to beat *Slipway Cottage* (☎ 01271-863035; 4D/1T, most rooms have en suite toilet and basin but separate bath/shower; ▼; Ⓛ), right on both the harbour and the trail at 2 Hierns Lane. They charge £28-30pp (sgl occ also £28-30).

Also a short stroll from the SWCP are *Acorn Lodge* (☎ 01271-862505, 🖥 www .theacornlodge.co.uk; 2S share facilities, 4D/1D or T/1Tr, all en suite; WI-FI; Ⓛ), at 4 St James Place, which charges £30-35pp (sgl £35, sgl occ from £55), but they only accept bookings for a minimum of two nights in July and August, and *The Olive Branch* (☎ 01271-879005, 🖥 www.olive branchguesthouse.co.uk; 1S/3D/1T, all en suite; ▼; WI-FI; Ⓛ), a Georgian Grade-II listed building on Fore St, where rates are £39-52.50pp (sgl £50, sgl occ £68). There is also the chance to fine dine in the restaurant below (see Where to eat).

A little out of town there is a whole
stretch of B&Bs. Along St Brannock's Rd
are: the particularly pleasant *Coastal
Fringes* (☎ 01271-865096, 🖳 www.coas
talfringes.com; 3D, all en suite; 🐾), No 76,
with its 1930s/'40s film-themed rooms
(B&B costs £35-38pp, sgl occ £43);
Burnside (☎ 01271-863097, 🖳 www.burn
side-ilfracombe.co.uk; 2D/1D or T, all en
suite; WI-FI), No 34, which charges £30-
37.50pp (sgl occ £55) and has a room with
a four-poster bed; *The Dorchester* (☎
01271-865472, 🖳 www.the-dorchester.co
.uk; 6D/1Tr, all en suite; WI-FI; Ⓛ; Mar-
Nov), No 59, which charges £31.50-40pp
(sgl occ £45-55, three sharing £90) and is
licensed; and *Strathmore* (☎ 01271-
862248, 🖳 www.the-strathmore.co.uk; 2S/
4D/1T/1Tr, all en suite; 🐾; WI-FI; Ⓛ; 🐾
half of the charge goes to a charity, the
Dogs Trust), No 57, which is also licensed
and charges £37.50-40pp (sgl £42, sgl occ
£45-50, three sharing £110).

At No 56 *Lyncott House* (☎ 01271-
862425, 🖳 www.lyncotthouse.co.uk; 4D/
1Tr, all en suite; 🐾; WI-F) claims to be
Ilfracombe's premier guest house; rates
here are £37.50-45pp (sgl occ £50, three
sharing £120).

Close to where the path leaves the
town, at 6 Torrs Walk Ave, *The Avoncourt*
(Map 19; ☎ 01271-862543, 🖳 www.avon
courtilfracombe.co.uk; 2S/4D/1T/1Tr, all
en suite; 🐾; Ⓛ; 🐾) is a fairly standard
guesthouse charging £38-42pp (sgl £48, sgl
occ £48-54) but has its own bar.

In addition to the B&Bs there are plenty of **hotels**. On Wilder Rd, close to the
Promenade, is *The Imperial* (☎ 01271-
862536, 🖳 www.leisureplex.co.uk; 16S/
37D/37T/7Tr, all en suite; 🐾; WI-FI in public areas) which charges £29-45pp (sgl £36-
51, sgl occ/three sharing rates on request).
Note that in the winter months (end
Oct/early Nov to Mar) accommodation is
only available Monday to Friday.

The Royal Britannia (☎ 01271-
862939, 🖳 www.royalbritannia.co.uk;
10D/2T/2Tr/6Qd, all en suite; 🐾; WI-FI;
🐾) is well sited, actually overlooking the
boats from its location on Broad St. Rates
here are £25-52.50pp (sgl occ from £46,

three/four sharing from £75/80). Back on
Fore St there is *Harcourt Hotel* (☎ 01271-
862931, 🖳 www.harcourt hotel.co.uk;
2S/3D/1T/2D or T, all en suite; 🐾 WI-FI; Ⓛ
; 🐾); expect to pay £36-37pp (sgl occ
£50). They have drying facilities.

Where to eat and drink
Tearooms and cafés A short stroll
along Wilder Rd, will present you with
numerous tearooms and cafés, most of
which also provide breakfasts and lunches.
Particularly good are *Dolly's Café* (daily
9am-5pm, summer to late; 🐾 outside only)
and *The Naked Cake* (☎ 01271-864641;
WI-FI; 🐾 outside only; Mar-Oct 10am-
4pm). There's plenty of types of food
including – at the latter – a range of toast
with different toppings (from £6.25) as well
as cakes (!).

Also worth a look on St James Place is
Curiosity Cottage (☎ 01271-863510; 🐾
garden only; Easter-Oct daily 9.30am-
4.30pm) which does cream teas (£5.50,
mini for £3.50); whilst centrally, if you're
looking for a typical English tea room,
Swiss Cottage Café (☎ 01271-864433;
Mon-Sat 9am-4pm, summer later if busy),
on High St, is your best bet.

Vegetarian and gluten-free options are
available close to the path on the corner of
Hiern's Lane and Broad St at *Adele's Café*
(☎ 01271-863268; Mar-Dec daily 7.30am-
4pm; 🐾).

Pubs Good pub-grub can be found at
Prince of Wales (☎ 01271-866391; food
served Wed-Sun noon-9pm & bank hol
Mons; WI-FI; 🐾) on Fore St. An old-fashioned boozer and the menu includes homemade curries (£6.95).

Also on Fore St, Ilfracombe's oldest
pub, *George & Dragon* (☎ 01271-863851,
🖳 www.georgeanddragonilfracombe.co.uk;
food served daily noon-3pm & 6.30-9pm)
has a selection of real ales, a no mobile
phones policy and the menu may include
boozy beef braised in real ale for £8.95.

The Smugglers (☎ 01271-863620;
food served Easter to Nov daily 10am-late,
winter hours variable), on The Quay, is a
quirky place with red leather alcoves, fish

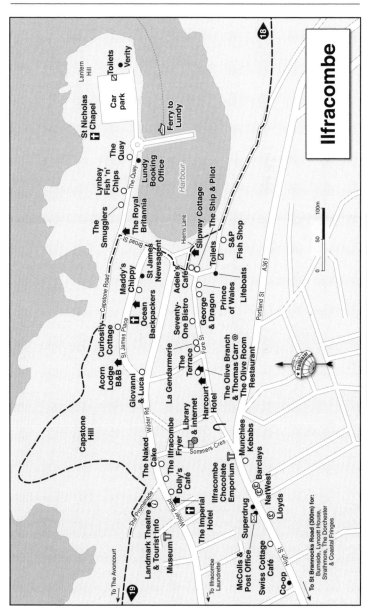

tanks set in the wall and seafaring antiquities hanging from the ceiling. The menu is huge and includes steaks and fish.

The Ship and Pilot (☎ 01271-863562; Mon-Sat 11am-midnight, Sun 11.30am-11.30pm) may interest those with a thirst for cider: there's up to 40 different types here as well as real ales, the majority of which are local. However, at the time of research food was not served.

Restaurants For smarter dining there are several places on Fore St.

Highly recommended, *Seventy-one Bistro* (☎ 01271-863632, 🖥 www.seventy one.biz; school summer holidays Mon-Sat 6.30pm to late; mid Mar/Easter to July Tue-Sat 6.30pm to late, rest of year Fri & Sat 6.30pm to late, Thur if enough bookings) is great; a mouth-watering 71 surf 'n' turf (west country rump steak and local lobster) costs £17.95; while at *La Gendarmerie* (☎ 01271-865984, 🖥 lagendarmerie.co.uk; Easter to Oct Tue-Thur 7-10.30pm, Fri & Sat to 11.30pm; limited days/hours in the winter) you can get two/three courses for £24.90/29.90.

Thomas Carr @ The Olive Room Restaurant (below The Olive Branch; see Where to stay; ☎ 01271-867831, 🖥 www .thomascarrchef.co.uk; Tue-Sat 6.30-9pm) was awarded a Michelin Star in the 2017 guide. It serves 'ultra-fresh seafood' and menu-wise is hard to beat, although the prices (mains from £20) may put some walkers off; that said, if you're already in the mood for splashing out, this is definitely the place to do so! Booking is essential.

The Quay (☎ 01271-868090, 🖥 11the quay.co.uk; food served Apr-Sep daily noon-2.30pm & 6-9pm, Oct-Mar Wed-Sat noon-2.30pm & 6-9pm, Sun noon-3pm), on the road of the same name, is another highly respected restaurant. A whole Lundy lobster will set you back £45, but they also offer salads, pasta dishes and risottos (£9.25-15).

Spanish food is available at *The Terrace* (☎ 01271-863482, 🖥 www.terrace tapasbar.co.uk; summer daily from 6pm; winter Tue-Sat only), a tapas and wine bar which was voted one of the top five restaurants in North Devon in 2016. There is a gin menu to supplement the tapas (£2.95-6.25 per dish).

For authentic Italian at reasonable prices you should head to Wilder Rd and *Giovanni & Luca* (☎ 01271-879394; Mar-Oct Tue-Sun noon-2.30pm & 6-9.30pm, winter to 9pm).

Takeaways For fish 'n' chips, there is *The Ilfracombe Fryer* (☎ 01271-865003, 🖥 www.ilfracombefryer.co.uk; Tue-Sat noon-2pm & 5-7pm) on Wilder Rd; *Maddy's Chippy* (☎ 01271-863351; daily noon-9pm), 25 St James Place; or, on The Quay, *Lynbay Fish 'n' Chips* (☎ 01271-866850, 🖥 www.lynbayfishandchipsilfra combe.co.uk; daily 11.30am-9pm).

If you fancy your fish straight off the trawler *S & P Fish Shop* (☎ 01271-865923, 🖥 www.sandpfish.co.uk; Tue-Sat 10am-3pm or later depending on demand, winter opening hours may vary) is on the harbour itself and as well as supplying takeaway, the café is well worth a visit! High St favourite *Munchies Kebabs* (☎ 01271-855666; Sun-Thur 4pm to midnight, Fri & Sat 4pm-3.30am) is your best option if you're all fish 'n' chipped-out!

Leaving Ilfracombe the path ventures along the hills and cliffs of **Torrs Park** before passing via *The Blue Mushroom* (Map 20; ☎ 01271-862947, 🖥 www.leebay.co.uk/the_blue_mushroom.htm; 1D or T en suite facilities), a delightful self-contained place (room only £55 for two sharing; light/cooked breakfast £5/7pp; bring a torch for the lane at night) with sea views as well as a sun lounge leading to a private garden, before heading down to **Lee Bay**. The vale in which the nearby village of **Lee** sits is known locally as 'Fuchsia Valley' due to the abundance of the scarlet flower blossoming in the area's hedgerows at certain times of year.

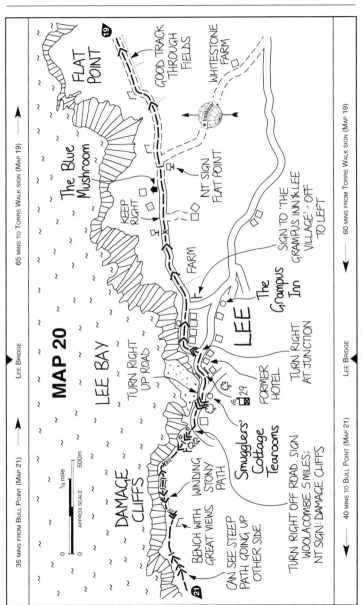

MAP 20

35 MINS FROM BULL POINT (MAP 21)

LEE BRIDGE

65 MINS TO TORRS WALK SIGN (MAP 19)

FLAT POINT

19

GOOD TRACK THROUGH FIELDS

WHITESTONE FARM

Trailblazer

The Blue Mushroom

KEEP RIGHT

NT SIGN: FLAT POINT

FARM

SIGN TO 'THE GRAMPUS INN & LEE VILLAGE' - OFF TO LEFT

LEE BAY

TURN RIGHT UP ROAD

LEE

The Grampus Inn

TURN RIGHT AT JUNCTION

FORMER HOTEL

29

Smugglers' Cottage Tearooms

DAMACE CLIFFS

WINDING STONY PATH

BENCH WITH GREAT VIEWS

TURN RIGHT OFF ROAD. SIGN: WOOLACOMBE 5 MILES; NT SIGN: DAMACE CLIFFS

CAN SEE STEEP PATH GOING UP OTHER SIDE

21

¼ mile

500m

0

0

APPROX SCALE

LEE BRIDGE

60 MINS FROM TORRS WALK SIGN (MAP 19)

40 MINS TO BULL POINT (MAP 21)

ROUTE GUIDE AND MAPS

LEE AND LEE BAY [MAP 20, p127]
On your left before you leave Lee Bay is *Smuggler's Cottage Tearooms* (☎ 01271-864897; Easter-Oct daily 10.15am-5/5.30pm but weather/business dependent; WI-FI; 🐾). Evidence exists of a tea garden being here for 150 years – although not consistently – and the current incarnation has been in the same family for 40 years. Breakfasts and lunches (£4.50-9) are on offer as are snacks and homemade cakes; hot food is available all day and is freshly cooked. There are vegetarian and gluten-free options and the tearoom is licensed.

In the village itself, *The Grampus Inn* (☎ 01271-862906, 🖥 www.thegrampus-inn.co.uk; **food** served daily noon-3pm, Mon-Sat 7-9pm) serves real ales and reasonably priced sandwiches/ploughmans (£5-7.50) as well as a more hearty menu including bangers & mash (£9) and venison steak & chips (£18). They also do cream teas (Easter-Oct daily 3-6pm) for £4.80.

Ilfracombe & District's No 35 **bus** service calls here on a Tuesday and Friday; see pp48-50.

Becoming a little more testing, the path now makes its way along **Damage Cliffs**, a National Trust site. The trail then passes by 19th-century **Bull Point Lighthouse** (Map 21) housed in its own secure compound (the Bull Point Pen?), before following the cliff-tops to **Morte Point**, a place so wild it was once referred to locally as 'the place God made last and the Devil will take first'.

Notice that despite all this natural splendour many of the cliffs and peninsulas have such morbid names: Damage Cliffs, Breakneck Point, 'Morte' (French for 'Death') Point; shipwrecks were common here in the 19th century and many of the geological culprits were named appropriately. Indeed, Morte Point was said to be responsible for five shipwrecks in 1852 alone, while **Grunta Beach** is so named because after one unlucky ship ran aground the cargo of pigs she was carrying ran into the cove – grunting.

As you coax and tease your legs into the final stretch around Morte Point, take time to admire Baggy Point across the bay and stare in awe at the golden sands of Woolacombe's blue-flag beach: surf's up!

WOOLACOMBE [see map p131]
Nestling at the eastern end of Morte Bay, the village of Woolacombe has a friendly and pleasant atmosphere. Stretching out to the south, its vast and wonderful beach, which accompanies the path for approximately two miles (3.2km), is often granted the title of 'Britain's best beach' by traveller surveys and magazines. The view of

the golden expanse as you enter the village certainly acts as a fine welcome.

The village remained pretty much untouched until a fashion for sea bathing took the country by storm in the early 19th century, leading to the village's slow conversion into a resort. Bustling now with surfers in summer, it also has all the amenities a coastal-path walker needs.

❏ **Dogs on Woolacombe Beach**
Dogs are allowed on the beach but only to the south of the stream which lies a couple of hundred metres south of town (ie the main entrance to the beach) – and even then only on a lead. You can release them, however, beyond the large Mill Rock that lies at the back of the beach. There are no restrictions between December and March.

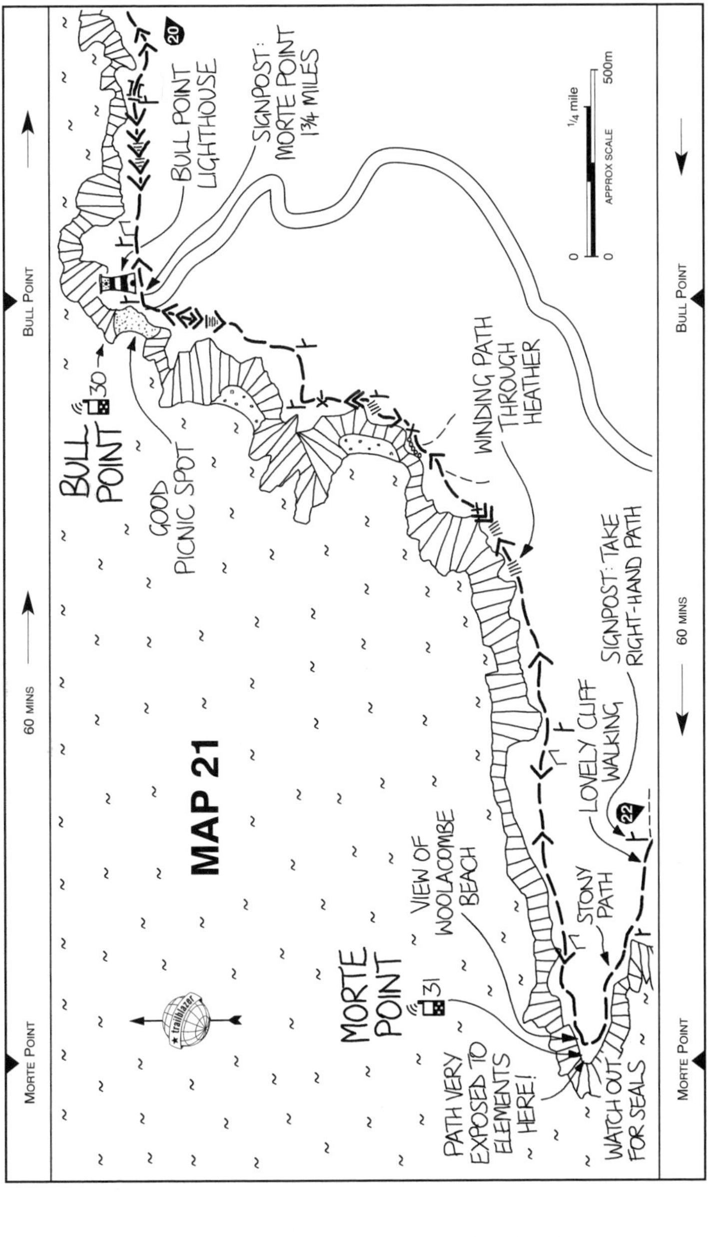

MORTE POINT

BULL POINT

60 MINS

MAP 21

20

BULL POINT LIGHTHOUSE

SIGNPOST: MORTE POINT 1¾ MILES

500m

¼ mile

0

0

APPROX SCALE

BULL POINT

BULL POINT 30

GOOD PICNIC SPOT

WINDING PATH THROUGH HEATHER

60 MINS

SIGNPOST: TAKE RIGHT-HAND PATH

LOVELY CLIFF WALKING

22

STONY PATH

VIEW OF WOOLACOMBE BEACH

MORTE POINT 31

PATH VERY EXPOSED TO ELEMENTS HERE!

WATCH OUT FOR SEALS

MORTE POINT

* trailblazer

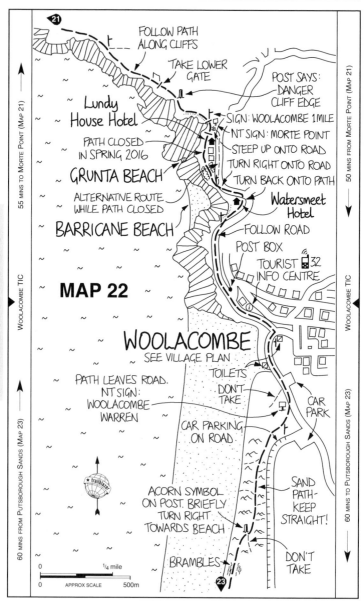

55 MINS TO MORTE POINT (MAP 21)

WOOLACOMBE TIC

60 MINS FROM PUTSBOROUGH SANDS (MAP 23)

ROUTE GUIDE AND MAPS

FOLLOW PATH ALONG CLIFFS

TAKE LOWER GATE

POST SAYS: DANGER CLIFF EDGE

Lundy House Hotel

SIGN: WOOLACOMBE 1 MILE
NT SIGN: MORTE POINT
STEEP UP ONTO ROAD
TURN RIGHT ONTO ROAD
TURN BACK ONTO PATH

PATH CLOSED IN SPRING 2016

GRUNTA BEACH

ALTERNATIVE ROUTE WHILE PATH CLOSED

BARRICANE BEACH

Watersmeet Hotel

FOLLOW ROAD

POST BOX

TOURIST INFO CENTRE 32

MAP 22

WOOLACOMBE

SEE VILLAGE PLAN

TOILETS
DON'T TAKE

CAR PARK

PATH LEAVES ROAD.
NT SIGN: WOOLACOMBE WARREN

CAR PARKING ON ROAD

SAND PATH - KEEP STRAIGHT!

ACORN SYMBOL ON POST. BRIEFLY TURN RIGHT TOWARDS BEACH

DON'T TAKE

BRAMBLES

trailblazer

0   ¼ mile
0   APPROX SCALE   500m

50 MINS FROM MORTE POINT (MAP 21)

WOOLACOMBE TIC

60 MINS TO PUTSBOROUGH SANDS (MAP 23)

21

23

Oddly, the name 'Woolacombe' is said to have nothing to do with the large sheep population that lives hereabouts, but actually comes from Wolmecoma, or 'Wolves Valley', referring to the large wolf population that presumably lived in the woods that existed around here at one time!

Services
The helpful and well-stocked **tourist information centre** (☎ 01271-870553, 🖳 www .woolacombetourism.co.uk; Easter-Oct daily 10am-5pm, Oct to Easter Mon-Sat 10am-1/4pm weather dependent) also boasts free **internet access** and **wi-fi**: they've even got iPads for customers to use They are also happy to book accommodation (see box p40) and sell tickets for Lundy (see box p122).

You can take money out for free at the **ATM** on South St (with others that charge for withdrawals at Red Barn, see p133, and by the post office): money that you can then spend at the Londis **supermarket** (daily 8.30am-8pm) on West Rd or at Barton **Pharmacy** (Mon-Fri 9am-1pm & 2-6pm, Sat 9am-4pm) opposite. Also on West Rd is the **post office** (Mon-Fri 9am-5.30pm, Sat 9am-12.30pm) at the back of a newsagent. Another **newsagent**, Shirley's (Mon & Tue 6.45am-7pm, Wed-Fri 6.45am-7.30pm, Sat

7am-7.30pm, Sun 7am-6.30pm), near Puffin Café, is well stocked and sells OS maps.

Back up on South St is a **launderette**; and for tent pegs, also on South St, is **Devon Camping Equipment** (☎ 01271-871551, 🖳 loveyourcampervan.com; Easter-Oct daily 10am-5pm but hours may vary depending on business).

Transport
[See also pp48-50] As is usual for this path, Woolacombe is once again poorly served by public transport. Filers Travel's No 31 **bus** operates to Ilfracombe, as does their No 302, but on Sunday (May-Sep) only. Their No 303 goes to Braunton and Barnstaple. There are bus stops on Barton Rd and The Esplanade.

The local **taxi** firm is E Zee cabs (☎ 07966 548303).

Where to stay
Campers should head straight for *Woolacombe Sands Holiday Park* (☎ 01271-870569, 🖳 www.woolacombe-sands .co.uk; £5-20pp; WI-FI free in the club house; 🐾; late Mar to Oct) on Beach Rd. Though it's about 15 minutes' walk from the village centre it's a nice place with exceptional facilities and even has its own restaurant and bar.

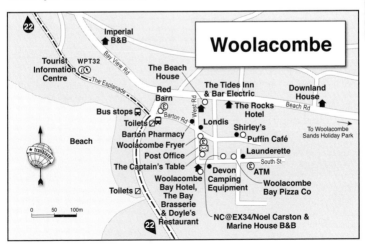

Woolacombe

There's no shortage of **B&B-style accommodation** in Woolacombe, though once again finding places suitable for walkers – ie that don't mind muddy boots and, most importantly, are willing to accept one-night bookings (see box below) – is surprisingly difficult.

Before you even reach the town, with private steps leading up from the path, there's *Lundy House Hotel* (Map 22; ☎ 01271-870372, 🖳 www.lundyhousehotel .co.uk; 6D/2D or T, all en suite; ☛; WI-FI; 🐾; Mar/Easter to end Oct). They charge £40-62.50pp (sgl occ full room rate), but only accept advance bookings for a minimum of two nights.

Entering the village you also pass the large *Watersmeet Hotel* (Map 22; ☎ 01271-870333, 🖳 www.watersmeethotel.co.uk; 1S/13D/9D or T/1T/4Tr, all en suite; ☛; WI-FI), originally built in 1907 as an Edwardian 'Gentleman's residence' and now charging £80-150pp (sgl £98-133, sgl occ £130-200, three sharing room rate plus £75-100).

Centrally, at 3 West Rd, *The Beach House* (☎ 01271-871727, 🖳 www.thebeach housedevon.co.uk; 1D or T/1Tr/4 'pods' sleeping up to four people, share facilities; WI-FI; ℚ; Mar-Dec) is more '**boutique hostel**' than B&B; although there's not a kitchen, as you would expect in a more traditional hostel. The 'pods' have curtained-off bunk beds for privacy. For a clearer idea of what their 'pods' are it is worth looking at the pictures on their website before you book yourself in. The breakfast is continental and there's a café/restaurant attached (see Where to eat). Rates are £35-38pp (sgl occ room rate).

More typical B&B accommodation can be found tucked away on South St:

sharing an entrance with NC@EX34 (see Where to eat) is *Marine House* (☎ 01271-870972, 🖳 www.marinehouse.co.uk; 1D/1D or T, both en suite; WI-FI) which charges £42.50pp with breakfast (sgl occ £85) and £36pp (sgl occ £72) for room only; while on Bay View Rd, *Imperial B&B* (☎ 01271-870594, 🖳 www.theimperialwoolacombe .co.uk; 1D/1D or T/1Tr/annexe double bed plus bunk beds, all en suite, 1T private facilities; ☛; small 🐾; Mar-early July & Sep-end Oct) is a decent place. Rates here are £35-42.50pp (£60-85 sgl occ, three sharing £90), though do note that they do not offer B&B at all during the school summer holidays. They have a hot tub which is free for guests to use and faces the sea.

Chic and friendly *The Rocks Hotel* (☎ 01271-870361, 🖳 www.therockshotel.co .uk; 7D/3T, all en suite; WI-FI; ℚ; Mar-Dec) is the first place offering B&B on Beach Rd. Rates are £39.50-49.50pp (sgl occ from £69). There's a minimum two-night stay in July and August but subject to prior arrangement they will pick up and drop anyone staying two nights. Further along Beach Rd is *Downland House* (☎ 01271-870426, 🖳 www.downlandhouse.co.uk; 2D both en suite/1D private bathroom; ☛; WI-FI; late Mar-end Oct); all three rooms face south and have private balconies from which you can see Baggy Point and Lundy; rates are £37.50-42.50pp (sgl occ room rate). As well as the typical full English breakfast there is the option of scrambled eggs and salmon before you trek off in the morning.

By far the grandest place in the village is *Woolacombe Bay Hotel* (☎ 01271-870388, 🖳 www.woolacombe-bay-hotel .co.uk; 64 rooms inc 26D/4T, rest can be

---

❏ **Where to stay: the details**
In the descriptions of accommodation in this book: ☛ means at least one room has a bath; ℚ means a packed lunch can be prepared if arranged in advance; 🐾 signifies that dogs are welcome in at least one room but also subject to prior arrangement. Note that virtually everywhere only accepts advance bookings for a minimum stay of two nights at peak periods such as weekends, bank holidays and school holiday periods. See also p74.

adapted for three/four sharing, all en suite; ▼; WI-FI; Feb-Dec), where all the rooms are stylish and some are nothing short of huge. They charge £80-150pp (sgl occ £90-200, three/four sharing £80-150pp) but note that one-night bookings are not accepted for the May/June half-term, school summer holidays or at weekends.

Where to eat and drink

There is a decent range of places to eat in Woolacombe. Campers searching for an early morning fry-up should head to *The Captain's Table* (☎ 01271-870618; food Mar-Oct daily 8.30am-6pm, summer up to 9pm but weather/business dependant; well-behaved 🐾). The menu includes a number of breakfasts (£4.90-9.50) as well as fine food (their speciality being seafood) throughout the rest of the day.

The Beach House (see Where to stay; main meals Feb-Dec daily noon-2.30pm & 5.30-9pm) has a seafood restaurant and café/bistro. Voted in Devon's top ten coastal restaurants there's a great menu to choose from which includes: tapas (£3.50-5 per item), tasting boards (£10-12), steaks (£19-25), gourmet burgers (£9-10.50) and daily specials. Coffee, teas and cakes can be had throughout the day (from 11am).

At the time of writing new owners were about to take over *Puffin Café* (☎ 01271-870807; Mon-Thur 9am-3pm, Fri-Sun 9am-5pm, season dependent; WI-FI; 🐾), on Barton Rd, but the details were expected to stay the same; we hope so as it was a pleasant and laidback place with reasonable prices (full English breakfast £5, cream tea £4).

By the main junction in town and with perhaps the best views of the sea, family friendly *Red Barn* (☎ 01271-870264, 🖳 www.redbarnwoolacombe.co.uk; food served summer daily 9am-9.30pm, winter Mon-Thur 10am-9pm, Fri to 9.30pm, Sat & Sun 9am-9.30pm; WI-FI; well-behaved 🐾) is one of Woolacombe's livelier places, complemented by surfers watching for waves and live music on Fridays (Mar-Dec), the menu includes steaks (£11.25-18.95) and a daily specials' board which may include a mixed grill (£19.95), or smoked salmon and crayfish tagliatelle (£10.95) as well as breakfasts (Sat & Sun 9-11.30am).

On Beach Rd, *The Tides Inn* (☎ 01271-871420; food served daily summer holidays noon-2.30pm & 6-9pm, winter evenings only; WI-FI; 🐾) overlooks the Crazy Golf course from its veranda and has a decent and imaginative menu; however, their most popular dish is their steak & kidney pie (£10.95). Below it and part of the same building, *Bar Electric* (☎ 01271-870429, 🖳 www.barelectric.co.uk; food summer daily 9am-9pm, rest of year Fri-Sun 9am-9pm; WI-FI; 🐾) produces gastropub style food including stone-baked pizzas (£10-15).

Possibly the most renowned – and most expensive – restaurant on the entire SWCP is *NC@EX34* (☎ 01271-871187, 🖳 www.noelcorston.com; Easter to end Oct Wed-Sat from 7pm), on South St, though by the time you are here the name may be *Noel Corston*. Chef Noel Corston's multi-award-winning establishment now has a chef's table and offers a tasting menu (7-/9-courses £75/95), sourced, designed and prepared to reflect the season. Recommended in the 2017 Michelin guide, reservations are essential.

Cheaper – but still of a high standard – is *The Bay Brasserie* in Woolacombe Bay Hotel (see Where to stay; Easter to Oct food daily noon-9pm, Nov-Dec hours variable), where the menu includes pizza and pasta (from £10.50) as well as a fish of the day. *Doyle's Restaurant* here also has a fish of the day and, from the shore, braised shank of lamb (£15), though the menu does change.

Takeaway can be found at *Woolacombe Bay Pizza Company* (☎ 01271-871222, 🖳 woolacombepizza.co.uk; Apr-Sep daily noon-11pm, Oct-Mar hours variable), which serves pizzas with standard toppings from £6.50, and at *Woolacombe Fryer* (☎ 01271-870752, 🖳 www.woolacombefryer.com; summer daily noon-9pm, out of season Thur-Sat noon-2.30pm & 5-8pm, Sun noon-5pm), 1 Barton Rd, where you'll discover fabulous fish 'n' chips.

WOOLACOMBE TO BRAUNTON [MAPS 22-28]

This **14¾-mile (23.8km; 6½hrs inc 10 mins from Velator Bridge to Braunton)** stage is the most diverse in this book. From the cliffs and beaches surrounding Woolacombe and Croyde to the more easygoing terrain through Braunton Burrows – the focal point of the North Devon UNESCO Biosphere Reserve (see box p142) – this is a fulfilling although physically undemanding day's walk.

Magnificent, sweeping views from Baggy Point across the busy sands of Woolacombe and Croyde contrast sharply with the bleaker beauty of Braunton Burrows and the lonely Taw Estuary, where the only sounds are the slap of rope against mast or the shrill whistle of an oystercatcher on the wing.

Diverse though the landscape may be on this stage, there can be no doubt that the predominant features are the beaches. There are in fact three vast stretches of golden sand, each separated by a single grassy promontory. The first, Woolacombe, has of course been visible since you rounded Morte Point on the previous stage and is one of the bigger beaches on the entire path – a vast flat bronze plain that stretches for almost two miles from the village to Baggy Point. Take a stroll around this promontory and you'll then be greeted by the sight of Croyde, Woolacombe's trendier, more glamorous neighbour and rival and a favourite with surfers and families, even though the beach is considerably smaller. While less than an hour's walk from the end of Croyde beach lies the even vaster sands at Saunton.

Indeed, the only disappointment with these beaches is that the SWCP doesn't officially cross any of them, preferring instead to pick its way between the sand dunes at the back of the beach – though only the most pedantic of coastal walkers will choose to stick to the path rather than kick their boots off and stroll along the flats. The exception to this is Saunton Sands, parts of which are used by the army for training practice and thus access is limited. But even here the coastal walker is well compensated as the dunes at the back of Saunton form Braunton Burrows Nature Reserve, the largest sand dune system in England and home to rare lizards and snails.

There are numerous places to stop for refreshments along the way including both Croyde and Saunton, though Saunton itself can be bypassed via an alternative path which, if taken, will be the last gradient of any description you'll encounter until Westward Ho!, over two days away. Stick to the main trail, however, and you'll be forced instead to walk along the busy, pavement-less Saunton Rd – the worst bit of walking on this path. Continuing on through the Burrows, and along the banks of the Taw – the favoured home of egrets, godwits, herons and oystercatchers – you pass Horsey Island and follow the

---

❏ **Important note – walking times**
All times in this book refer only to the time spent walking. You will need to add 20-30% to allow for rests, photography, checking the map, drinking water etc.

River Caen, eventually finding yourself on the outskirts of Braunton and the end of this stage.

The route

The day starts simply enough with a walk through the sand dunes of **Woolacombe Warren** (Map 23) and neighbouring **Putsborough Sands**, from where you start the haul to Baggy Point; alternatively, if the tide allows, you can just walk straight along the beach cutting through the car park at the beach's southern end to rejoin the main trail.

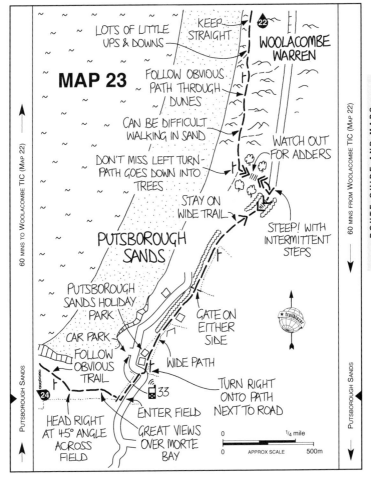

MAP 23

LOTS OF LITTLE UPS & DOWNS

KEEP STRAIGHT

WOOLACOMBE WARREN

FOLLOW OBVIOUS PATH THROUGH DUNES

CAN BE DIFFICULT WALKING IN SAND

DON'T MISS LEFT TURN – PATH GOES DOWN INTO TREES

STAY ON WIDE TRAIL

PUTSBOROUGH SANDS

WATCH OUT FOR ADDERS

STEEP! WITH INTERMITTENT STEPS

PUTSBOROUGH SANDS HOLIDAY PARK

CAR PARK

FOLLOW OBVIOUS TRAIL

GATE ON EITHER SIDE

WIDE PATH

TURN RIGHT ONTO PATH NEXT TO ROAD

ENTER FIELD

HEAD RIGHT AT 45° ANGLE ACROSS FIELD

GREAT VIEWS OVER MORTE BAY

★ trailblazer

60 MINS TO WOOLACOMBE TIC (MAP 22)

60 MINS FROM WOOLACOMBE TIC (MAP 22)

PUTSBOROUGH SANDS

PUTSBOROUGH SANDS

ROUTE GUIDE AND MAPS

0   ¼ mile
0   APPROX SCALE   500m

A splendid stroll leads to **Baggy Point**. Owned by the National Trust and a popular spot with climbers, it is also part of an SSSI (see p61) – of scientific interest due to its mixture of Devonian Age (417-354 million years ago) stone. The **white mast** is a 'wreck post' – a spot where, if the sea was too rough to launch a lifeboat but a shipwreck was close enough to the shore, a pulley system would be set up (using a cannon to fire one end of the rope out to the ship) between the point and the ship's mast in order to rescue the stranded sailors. There are tremendous views of Lundy and along the coast to Croyde Bay and Saunton Sands from here.

The clusters of buildings that you can see in the far distance are Westward Ho!, Clovelly and Hartland Point. As you walk around the point admire the views south and imagine the American troops practising for D-day on the sands below you as you stroll into Croyde. General Eisenhower and the Allied leaders decided that the beaches of Woolacombe, Croyde and Saunton most closely resembled those on France's Normandy coast, thus they were used for rehearsing for the big day. WWII pillboxes on Croydehoe Farm can still be seen.

On your way into Croyde and slightly before the National Trust car park for Baggy Point is ***Baggy Lodge and Café*** (see Map 24; ☎ 01271-890078, 🖳 baggys.co.uk; 2 x 3-, 1 x 6-bed dorm/4D; WI-FI; 🐾). It has magnificent views over Croyde beach and offers – surprisingly, given it's such a surfer town – the only **hostel** accommodation (dorm bed £33pp) as well as B&B accommodation (£55pp, sgl occ £110); all rates include a continental breakfast. It also has its own *café* (daily 9am-6pm, summer also 6-10pm, closed Dec), which serves a Full Baggy's Breakfast for £4.95. ***Sandleigh Tea Room and Gardens*** (☎ 01271-890930, 🖳 www.sandleighcroyde.com; Feb-Oct daily 10am-4pm, main season to 5pm), just beyond the car park, is a truly glorious place. Run by the National Trust, amongst other comestibles, homity pie (£7.95), crab sandwiches (£8.90) and cream teas with strawberries (£5.95) are on offer as are cakes.

CROYDE   [see map p139]

Croyde can feel as if its sole purpose is to serve its beach and its world-class surf. However, people were aware of the bay way before surfing took off in Cornwall in the 1960s. The village actually has an ancient heart which you can see if you look amongst the noisy bars of the village centre (which is about 15 minutes back from the beach that has earned Croyde its popularity). Indeed, some of the B&Bs and pubs are housed in buildings that are over 300 years old. But if you're not planning on staying in Croyde, you can forego them altogether, for the coast path continues to hug the beach.

The **post office** (Mon, Tue, Thur & Fri 8am-5.30pm, Wed & Sat 8am-12.30pm) has a **shop** (Mon-Sat 8am-5.30pm, Sun 8am-1pm). If you need money the post

office has an **ATM** (£1.75), as does Billy Budd's (£1.95; see Where to eat). Debit/credit cards are readily accepted throughout the village but if you're desperate for money free of charge you will have to go to Braunton. **The Stores Croyde** (🖳 www.thestorescroyde.co.uk; summer Mon-Sat 8am-6pm, Sun 8am-4pm; winter Mon-Thur 8.45am-4pm, Fri-Sun to 4.30pm) is more *café/deli* (see Where to eat) than stores although it does still sell some basic goods.

See p16 for details of the GoldCoast Oceanfest.

Transport

[See also pp48-50] Stagecoach's 21 **bus** runs regularly to Westward Ho! via Barnstaple.

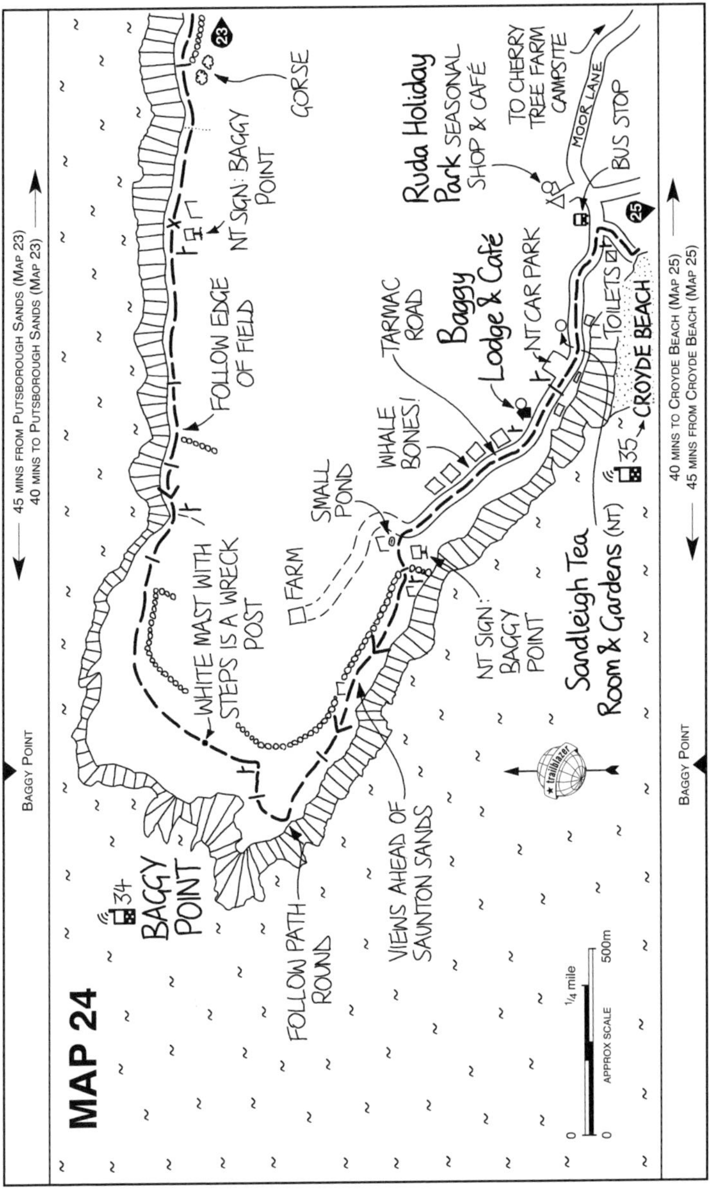

MAP 24

BAGGY POINT

◀ 45 MINS FROM PUTSBOROUGH SANDS (MAP 23)
40 MINS TO PUTSBOROUGH SANDS (MAP 23) ▶

GORSE

NT SIGN: BAGGY POINT

FOLLOW EDGE OF FIELD

WHITE MAST WITH STEPS IS A WRECK POST

FARM

SMALL POND

WHALE BONES!

TARMAC ROAD

Baggy Lodge & Café

NT CAR PARK

Ruda Holiday Park SEASONAL SHOP & CAFÉ

TO CHERRY TREE FARM CAMPSITE

MOOR LANE

BUS STOP

TOILETS

CROYDE BEACH

35

40 MINS TO CROYDE BEACH (MAP 25)
45 MINS FROM CROYDE BEACH (MAP 25) ▶

Sandleigh Tea Room & Gardens (NT)

NT SIGN: BAGGY POINT

VIEWS AHEAD OF SAUNTON SANDS

BAGGY POINT

34

BAGGY POINT

FOLLOW PATH ROUND

trailblazer

¼ mile

APPROX SCALE

0   500m

ROUTE GUIDE AND MAPS

If you wish to go north to Woolacombe or Ilfracombe you will need to change in either Braunton or Barnstaple.

There are **bus stops** near Billy Budd's in the centre of the village as well as nearer the beach close to Ruda Holiday Park.

For a **taxi** try Croyde Coastal (☎ 07788-703188, 🖳 www.croydecoastal.co.uk).

Where to stay

Croyde has a number of **campsites**. *Ruda Holiday Park* (Map 24; ☎ 0844-335 3677, 🖳 www.parkdeantouring.com; £14-50 per pitch; mid Mar to end Oct) is a behemoth with its own Costcutter **supermarket** (daily 8am-6pm) and *café* (daily 10am-6pm, later if resident), both of which are open when the park is open.

Smaller and cheaper than Ruda are *Bay View Farm Caravan & Camping Park* (☎ 01271-890501, 🖳 www.bayviewfarm .co.uk; WI-FI; Easter to end Sep; approx £23pp) and *Cherry Tree Farm Campsite* (☎ 01271-890495, 🖳 www.cherrytree croyde.co.uk; £13pp plus a £5-10 bond, see website for details; May half-term & mid July to late Aug); the latter, despite advertising a minimum three-night stay policy, will often allow walkers to stay for only one night. To reach the campsite go to the end of Moor Lane then left up Stentaway Lane.

In central Croyde, *The Orchard* (☎ 07779-371195, 🖳 www.theorchardcamp sitecroyde.co.uk; £12pp; WI-FI; 🐕) is the only site in Croyde to allow dogs. They

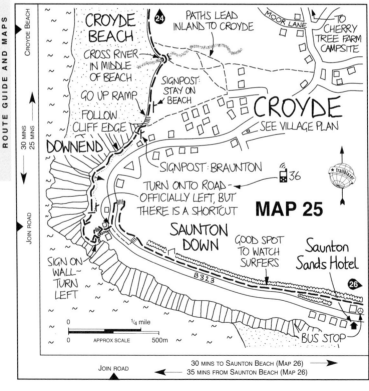

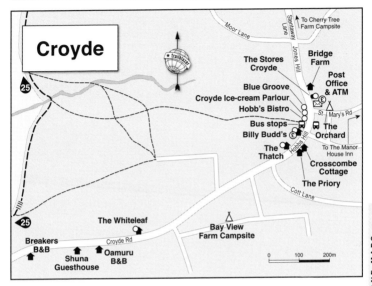

always try to squeeze hikers in but booking is recommended, particularly for Bank holiday weekends.

For **B&Bs** look on Croyde Rd which runs into Hobbs Hill – the centre of the village – at its southern end. Close to both the beach and the path you will find *Breakers* (☎ 01271-890101, 💻 www.croydebreaks .co.uk; 2D or T/1Tr, all en suite; WI-FI; Ⓛ; Easter to end Oct), which charges from £45pp (sgl occ £60, three sharing £135), but does not take one-night bookings on Friday or Saturday nights; the small and family-run *Shuna Guesthouse* (☎ 01271-890537, 💻 www.shunaguesthouse.co.uk; 5D, all en suite; WI-FI) which charges £45-50pp (sgl occ £85), and *Oamaru* (☎ 01271-890765, 💻 www.oamarucroyde.co.uk; 1D/1Tr both en suite; ✔; WI-FI; Ⓛ), where B&B costs £35pp (sgl occ £52.50).

A little closer to town and with its own restaurant you will find *The Whiteleaf* (☎ 01271-890266, 💻 www.thewhiteleaf.co .uk; 3D/1T/1Qd, all en suite; ✔; WI-FI; Ⓛ); the tariff here is £41-49pp (sgl occ £68-74, three sharing £115-140, rates on request for four sharing).

More central still is *The Thatch* (☎ 01271-890349, 💻 www.thethatchcroyde .com; 10D/5T/2Tr, bunk-bed room, most en suite but three rooms share facilities; ✔; WI-FI; Ⓛ; 🐾), whose rooms are in four different buildings, including some at *Billy Budd's* (see Where to eat), *Crosscombe Cottage* and *The Priory*. B&B costs £30-50pp (sgl occ rates available on request, three sharing room rate plus £10).

The most charming place to stay is right in the noisy centre. The pretty, thatched *Bridge Farm* (☎ 01271-890422; 2D en suite/1Tr private facilities; ✔; WI-FI; 🐾; Easter to end Oct/Nov), 8 Jones Hill, is, according to the owner, at least 400 years old. The place is quirky and full of character – as you'd expect from a house this old – and the owners are pleasant too. It also provides a lovely contrast to the brash and noisy street outside. The tariff is £35-37.50pp (sgl occ room rate, three sharing £85).

Where to eat and drink

Croyde Ice Cream Parlour, in the centre on Hobb's Hill, is famed in the village because of its use of clotted cream as one of its toppings! *The Stores Croyde* (see Services) has some splendid breakfast and lunch options!

For a pub meal try *Billy Budd's* (☎ 01271-890606, 🖥 www.billybudds.co.uk; daily noon-10pm; WI-FI) which has Sky TV and does pizzas (from £8.95) to eat-in or take away and burgers (£11.95-14.95) as well as nachos (£6.95-11.95), paninis (£6.95) and fish 'n' chips (£11.95).

Pretty much next door, *The Thatch* (see Where to stay; daily 8am-10pm) is known for its beef nachos (£9.95-11.95). It's a large pub with surfboards hanging off the walls and daily surf reports adorning them as well as real ales such as Proper Job and Tribute.

At *The Manor House Inn* (☎ 01271-890241, 🖥 www.themanorcroyde.co.uk; food served daily noon-10pm), a little out of town at 39 St Mary's Rd, the menu is extensive and varies but may include pan-fried

tiger prawns and chorizo linguine for £14.95. They also serve real ales.

For an à la carte menu made up of local produce there is the restaurant at *The Whiteleaf* (see Where to stay; Mon-Sat 7-8.30pm; booking essential); a roast loin fillet of venison is just one of the mouth-watering meals that may be on offer (all the produce is seasonal and prices can vary). *Hobb's Bistro* (☎ 01271-890256, 🖥 www.hobbsbistrocroyde.co.uk; daily 6.30-9pm, school hols Tue-Sat 9am-2pm) is the smartest place in town and has some great dishes such as seafood paella (£16.95) whilst just a few yards down the hill, *Blue Groove* (☎ 01271-890111, 🖥 www.blue-groove.co.uk; mid Mar to Oct daily 9am to late, Nov & Dec Fri & Sat 10am-late, Sun & Mon 10am-4pm, closed Jan-mid Mar) serves breakfasts, lunches and evening meals, though it's best known for its *moules frites* (£13.95).

Having navigated **Croyde Sands** a small headland – **Downend** – separates you from Saunton. Round this and the path drops down to the busy B3231 before running around the side of Saunton Sands Hotel (see p142).

From the car park below the hotel the path heads up the slope on the tarmac, turning off right halfway up (unmarked) to walk around the back of houses before rejoining the B3231 for an unpleasant stretch of pavement-less road walking. Thankfully, there is an alternative.

The alternative route begins after you reach Saunton Sands Hotel, though the price you pay is to climb instead the biggest gradient between Woolacombe and Westward Ho!. This route then passes through a couple of fields before dropping down via elegant Saunton Court to a crossroads, where you rejoin the main trail. Turn left at the crossroads if going to Lobbs Field Caravan and Camping Park (see p142).

SAUNTON   [MAP 26]
Despite Saunton's far larger beach there are fewer amenities than in Croyde, with scant options for food and accommodation.

The beach is renowned for its wildlife, with the possibility of spying oystercatchers, cormorants, and numerous other birds. From the shore you might see porpoise, seals and possibly dolphins in summer. Fishermen have reported foxes and even otters sneaking up behind them in attempts to steal their catch!

If wishing to get a **bus** (see pp48-50), Stagecoach's 21 service stops by Saunton Sands Hotel.

The nearest **campsite** is approximately two miles along the road (B3231) although there is an alternative way, leading via a series of footpaths, to the top of the campsite; this is worth doing as the road is very busy. From the road by Saunton Court, turn left up unmade Hannaburrow Lane to Long Lane (first turning on the right). Follow this

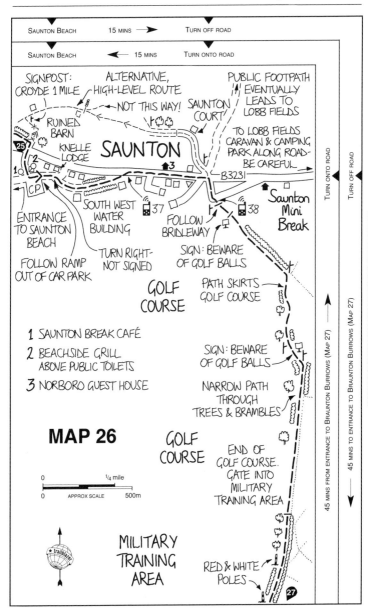

SAUNTON BEACH   15 MINS ⟶   TURN OFF ROAD

SAUNTON BEACH   ⟵ 15 MINS   TURN ONTO ROAD

SIGNPOST: CROYDE 1 MILE

ALTERNATIVE, HIGH-LEVEL ROUTE

←— NOT THIS WAY!

PUBLIC FOOTPATH EVENTUALLY LEADS TO LOBB FIELDS

SAUNTON COURT

RUINED BARN

KNELLE LODGE

SAUNTON

25

2

1

TO LOBB FIELDS CARAVAN & CAMPING PARK ALONG ROAD- BE CAREFUL

3

B3231

CP

ENTRANCE TO SAUNTON BEACH

FOLLOW RAMP OUT OF CAR PARK

SOUTH WEST WATER BUILDING

TURN RIGHT- NOT SIGNED

37

FOLLOW BRIDLEWAY

SIGN: BEWARE OF GOLF BALLS

38

Saunton Mini Break

TURN ONTO ROAD

TURN OFF ROAD

GOLF COURSE

PATH SKIRTS GOLF COURSE →

1 SAUNTON BREAK CAFÉ

2 BEACHSIDE GRILL ABOVE PUBLIC TOILETS

3 NORBORO GUEST HOUSE

SIGN: BEWARE OF GOLF BALLS

NARROW PATH THROUGH TREES & BRAMBLES

MAP 26

GOLF COURSE

END OF GOLF COURSE. GATE INTO MILITARY TRAINING AREA

0   ¼ mile

0   APPROX SCALE   500m

MILITARY TRAINING AREA

RED & WHITE POLES

27

45 MINS FROM ENTRANCE TO BRAUNTON BURROWS (MAP 27)

45 MINS TO ENTRANCE TO BRAUNTON BURROWS (MAP 27)

ROUTE GUIDE AND MAPS

to the road junction, then take a right down Lobthorn Lane, following it down the hill until you can see Lobb Fields campsite. *Lobb Fields Caravan and Camping Park* (☎ 01271-812090, 🖥 www.lobbfields.com; WI-FI; 🐾; walkers £7-16 tent plus up to two people; mid Mar-late Oct) has its own snack bar and a laundry room.

There are two **B&Bs**, both a short jaunt inland from the beach and close to where the path leaves the road. *Norboro Guest House* (☎ 01271-816210, 🖥 www .norboroguesthouse.co.uk; 2D/2T, all en suite or private facilities; 🛁; WI-FI) is an Edwardian house that has views across the Burrows and charges £35-37.50pp (sgl occ £40-55); at *Saunton Minibreak* (☎ 01271-813672, 🖥 sauntonminibreak@hotmail .com; 1T, en suite; WI-FI; 🐾), 1 Warren Cottages, one-night stops are not available at the weekend from July to September and the breakfast is continental. The tariff is £32.50-37.50pp (sgl occ £45-55).

Saunton Sands Hotel (Map 25; ☎ 01271-890212, 🖥 sauntonsands.co.uk; 11S/79D or T, all en suite; 🛁; WI-FI; Ⓛ) is owned by the local Brend chain. This whitewashed colossus is something of a landmark; indeed, you will see this hotel from as far away as Westward Ho!. Rates are £101-205pp (sgl occ/three sharing rates on request), but they also have special offers so it is worth contacting them to check). The rooms are comfortable without being remarkable – but, given the views along the three-mile beach from most of them, who cares! – and some can have additional beds. Note that in the summer school holidays it's week-long stays only, and at Easter guests are required to stay for a minimum of three nights. **Food** is served daily from 7.30am till about 9.30pm).

There are two other options for **food** by the sand. *Saunton Break Cafe* (☎ 01271-890077; July-Aug daily 8am-7pm, Feb half-term daily 9am-4pm, Mar-July & Sep-Oct Mon-Fri 10am-4pm, Sat & Sun 9am-5pm, rest of year Fri 10.30am-3pm, Sat & Sun 10am-4pm) is a takeaway which sells pasties and sandwiches. Note that their opening hours do also depend on the weather. *Beachside Grill* (☎ 01271-891288, 🖥 www.beachsidegrill.co.uk; food Mar-Dec Wed-Mon noon-7pm, Jan-Mar Wed-Sun) is owned by the hotel and has a sizeable balcony with magnificent views. The menu's impressive too, including open grilled sandwiches (£8-10), steaks (£19-24) and Lundy lobster (£19/31 half/whole).

The path then heads off along the edge of a **golf course** and through a **military training area** to **Braunton Burrows** (see box below). *(cont'd on p146)*

❏ Braunton Burrows and The North Devon UNESCO Biosphere Reserve

Braunton Burrows is the centre of The North Devon UNESCO Biosphere Reserve (🖥 www.northdevonbiosphere.org.uk), an area of 3300 sq km that, according to the United Nations, encompasses a 'world-class environment' rich in wildlife and containing a mix of extraordinary landscapes. As well as the Burrows, the Biosphere Reserve includes **Braunton Marsh and Great Field**, the **Taw and Torridge Estuary**, **Fremington Quay** and **Northam Burrows Country Park**. No wonder, therefore, that there are over 60 SSSIs (see p61) within the area's boundaries.

The Burrows themselves are home to a wide variety of flora and fauna, as well as the largest sand dune system in England. There are nearly 500 recorded species of **flowering plants** on the site, including such rarities as the sand toadflax, which is unique to the Burrows, the water germander and the round-headed club-rush. There are also 33 species of **butterfly**, over half of Great Britain's regularly recorded species. For enthusiasts, resident is the small blue butterfly (*Cupido minimus*), although you are far more likely to spot a dark green fritillary (*Argynnis aglaja*) or marbled white (*Melanargia galathea*). **Guided tours** of the Burrows run regularly throughout the summer. Details can be found at 🖥 www.brauntoncountrysidecentre.org.

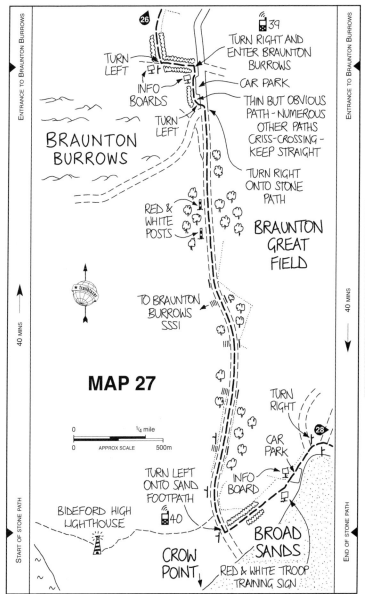

26

39

TURN RIGHT AND
ENTER BRAUNTON
BURROWS

TURN LEFT

CAR PARK

INFO BOARDS

THIN BUT OBVIOUS
PATH – NUMEROUS
OTHER PATHS
CRISS-CROSSING –
KEEP STRAIGHT

TURN LEFT

BRAUNTON BURROWS

TURN RIGHT ONTO STONE PATH

RED & WHITE POSTS

BRAUNTON GREAT FIELD

40 MINS

TO BRAUNTON BURROWS SSSI

MAP 27

0   1/4 mile
0   APPROX SCALE   500m

TURN RIGHT

28

CAR PARK

INFO BOARD

40 MINS

TURN LEFT ONTO SAND FOOTPATH

40

BIDEFORD HIGH LIGHTHOUSE

BROAD SANDS

CROW POINT

RED & WHITE TROOP TRAINING SIGN

START OF STONE PATH

END OF STONE PATH

ROUTE GUIDE AND MAPS

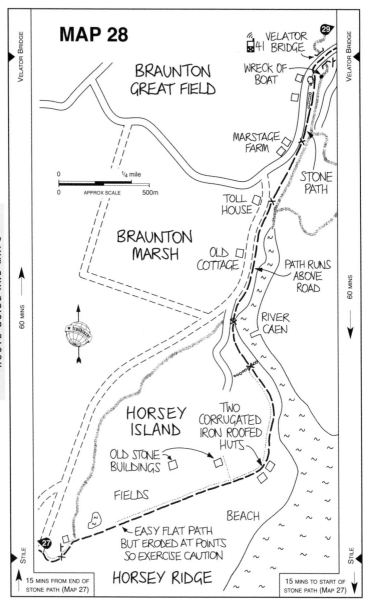

MAP 28

BRAUNTON
GREAT FIELD

VELATOR BRIDGE

VELATOR BRIDGE

📶 41 VELATOR
BRIDGE

29

WRECK OF
BOAT

MARSTAGE
FARM

STONE
PATH

0   ¼ mile
0   500m
APPROX SCALE

TOLL
HOUSE

BRAUNTON
MARSH

OLD
COTTAGE

PATH RUNS
ABOVE
ROAD

★ trailblazer

RIVER
CAEN

60 MINS

60 MINS

ROUTE GUIDE AND MAPS

TWO
CORRUGATED
IRON ROOFED
HUTS

HORSEY
ISLAND

OLD STONE
BUILDINGS

FIELDS

BEACH

EASY FLAT PATH
BUT ERODED AT POINTS
SO EXERCISE CAUTION

HORSEY RIDGE

27

STILE

STILE

15 MINS FROM END OF
STONE PATH (MAP 27)

15 MINS TO START OF
STONE PATH (MAP 27)

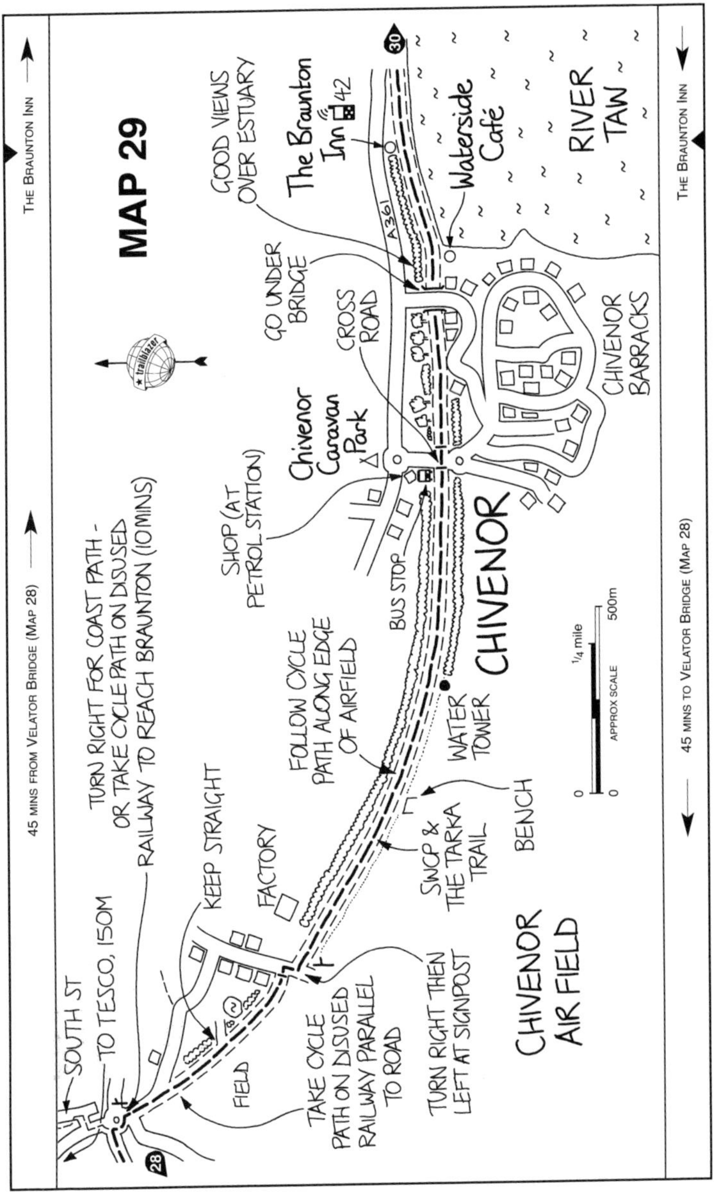

MAP 29

THE BRAUNTON INN →

← 45 MINS FROM VELATOR BRIDGE (MAP 28) —

45 MINS TO VELATOR BRIDGE (MAP 28) →

THE BRAUNTON INN →

TRAILBLAZER

N

SOUTH ST

TO TESCO, 150M

KEEP STRAIGHT

FIELD

FACTORY

TAKE CYCLE PATH ON DISUSED RAILWAY PARALLEL TO ROAD

TURN RIGHT THEN LEFT AT SIGNPOST

FOLLOW CYCLE PATH ALONG EDGE OF AIRFIELD

WATER TOWER

SWCP & THE TARKA TRAIL

BENCH

CHIVENOR AIR FIELD

BUS STOP

CHIVENOR

SHOP (AT PETROL STATION)

Chivenor Caravan Park

CROSS ROAD

GO UNDER BRIDGE

CHIVENOR BARRACKS

GOOD VIEWS OVER ESTUARY

The Braunton Inn 42

Waterside Café

RIVER TAW

TURN RIGHT FOR COAST PATH - OR TAKE CYCLE PATH ON DISUSED RAILWAY TO REACH BRAUNTON (10MINS)

A361

30

28

¼ mile

APPROX SCALE

0   500m
0

(cont'd from p142) Leaving the Burrows you take a sharp left-turn before **Crow Point**, a spit of land popular with fishermen, before taking a path atop an embankment that was built in 1857 to keep marsh, estuary and river apart. During WWII the marshes were turned into a dummy airfield in the hope of distracting the enemy's attention away from the nearby Chivenor Airbase.

On the other side of the estuary you can see the villages of Appledore and Instow, possibly still a day's walk away. Wrecked boats and small fishing craft are dotted about in the sand as you stroll on along the riverside. Between Braunton and the Burrows lie the 350 acres of **Braunton Great Field** – a famous archaeological site and one of only two medieval field systems to survive in England. Some of the 'strip' system which parcelled this land up is still visible.

Eventually you arrive at **Velator Bridge** and, a few hundred metres further on, a roundabout where you have a choice: turn right and continue along the Coast Path, which here, together with the Tarka Trail (see box p34), makes its merry way along a disused rail-track. Or you can turn left, cross the roundabout to South St and head along the disused railway line in the other direction on the marked footpath to Braunton. **Braunton** has several services and is a pleasant-enough village but if you feel up to walking a further 5½ miles there is more to distract you in Barnstaple. If you need a loo-stop or wish to pick up supplies there is a **Tesco Superstore** (Mon-Sat 6am-midnight, Sun 10am-4pm) approximately 200 metres from the roundabout (see Map 29; p145).

BRAUNTON

Recorded as Brantona in the Domesday Book, some claim Braunton to be the largest village in England and, as a result, it's more like a small town. Settlement is reputed to have begun in earnest around **St Brannock's Church**, originally founded by the eponymous saint in c550AD as part of his campaign to convert the Celts. His remains are said to be buried there. Braunton's debt to the saint is celebrated with a three-day festival of music, dance and literature around 26 June, St Brannock's Day.

Braunton and District Museum (☎ 01271-816688, 🖥 www.devonmuseums .netbraunton; Feb-Dec Mon-Fri 10am-3/4pm, Sat to 1pm; free but donations appreciated) has several interesting displays on the local area spread over two floors. **Braunton Countryside Centre** (☎ 01271-817171, 🖥 www.brauntoncountrysidecen tre.org; Apr-Oct Mon-Sat 10am-4pm; donations also appreciated) has displays about the local nature and also offers 'Braunton Explorers' – personal GPS systems (£5 per day) that guide you via a set of headphones

around different areas of interest in the area including the Burrows. Also available are tours of Braunton's industrial past and another entitled 'D-day and the dunes.'

For anyone interested in a point break (get it?) from walking, the **Museum of British Surfing** (☎ 01271-815155, 🖥 www .museumofbritishsurfing.org.uk; Easter-Dec Tue-Sat 10am-3pm; £2) is next door.

Services
Braunton Information Centre (🖥 www .visitbraunton.co.uk) shares both its walls, phone number and opening hours with the town's museum and is staffed by exceedingly helpful local volunteers. They have information about accommodation but can't book it.

For **food** there is a Co-op (Mon-Sat 7am-9pm, Sun 9am-6pm) on Exeter Rd and if you wish to send any postcards from your trip so far there is a **post office** (Mon-Fri 9am-5.30pm, Sat 9am-12.30pm) on the same road. For a **chemist** there's a Lloyds Pharmacy (Mon-Fri 8.30am-6pm, Sat to 5pm) on Caen St. Nearby, there is an **ATM** outside the Lloyds bank on Caen St. Finally, Braunton **launderette** (daily 6am-9pm) is on South St.

Transport
[See also pp48-50] For **buses**, Stagecoach's No 21 & 21A and Filers' No 303 services pass through regularly whilst travelling to and from the surrounding towns and villages.

For a **taxi** try Shoreline Taxi (☎ 07812-104034, 🖳 www.shorelinetaxi.co.uk).

Where to stay
Campers should head for Chivenor Caravan Park (see p149), 1¼ miles (2km) further along the trail.

Centrally, *The George Hotel* (also known as *The George Inn* ☎ 01271-

814903, 🖳 www.ohhpubs.co.uk/the-george-inn; 5D, all en suite; WI-FI; Ⓛ) is a large establishment in the heart of Braunton; as well as 'boutique' rooms (£42.50-70pp, sgl occ £65-140) it has a thriving bar and an à la carte restaurant (see Where to eat).

There are several **B&Bs** on quiet South St: *The Brookfield* (☎ 01271-812382, 🖳 www.thebrookfield.co.uk; 4D or T/1Tr, all en suite; ✎; WI-FI; Ⓛ; Apr-Dec) is a large and luxurious place which charges £40-50pp, sgl occ £60-65, three sharing £116-21; whilst comfortable *Stockwell Lodge* (☎ 01271-817128, 🖳 www.stockwell-lodge.co.uk; 2S shared bathroom/2D or T/1Tr, all en suite; ✎; WI-FI; Ⓛ), offers one-night stops diary-allowing but this is unlikely in the summer months; £37.50pp (sgl £35, sgl occ £50, three sharing £105).

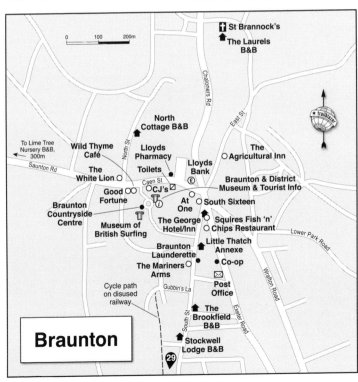

ROUTE GUIDE AND MAPS

Closer to the village centre is the cute, thatched *Little Thatch Annexe* (☎ 01271-815328, 🖳 www.thatchbandbbraunton.co.uk; 1D, en suite; WI-FI). B&B here costs £35pp (sgl occ £45). The accommodation is in a self-contained annexe.

The other options are scattered around town. On Saunton Rd there is the smart, homely *Lime Tree Nursery* (☎ 01271-593696, 🖳 www.limetreenursery.co.uk; 1D private facilities, 1Tr en suite; WI-FI); the tariff (£32.50pp, sgl occ £65, three sharing £85) does not include breakfast and – unfortunately – there is a minimum two-night stay policy throughout the year; whilst on North St you will find sweet little *North Cottage* (☎ 01271-812703, 🖳 www.northcottagebraunton.co.uk; 2S share bathroom, 1Tr/1D, both en suite; ✒; WI-FI; 🐾) where B&B costs £35pp (sgl/sgl occ/three sharing also £35pp).

Finally, right at the northern end of town, near St Brannock's Church, is the 300-year-old cottage, *The Laurels* (☎ 01271-812872, 🖳 www.thelaurelsbraunton.co.uk; 1S/1D/1T, all share bathroom; ✒; WI-FI; 🐾); which, having been running for over 40 years, is the oldest B&B in the village. They charge £35pp.

Where to eat and drink

Several pubs here serve good food. At *The Agricultural Inn* (☎ 01271-817980, 🖳 www.theaggibraunton.co.uk; food served summer daily 10.30am-9pm, winter Mon-Fri noon-2.30pm & 5-9pm, Sat 10.30am-9pm, Sun noon-8.30pm; WI-FI; 🐾), or 'The Aggie' as it is known locally, fresh local produce is used and you can get a 10oz rump steak for £14.95.

If you fancy watching some sport or spending more time outside, *The Mariners Arms* (☎ 01271-813160; food served end May-Sep daily noon-2pm & 6.30-9.30pm, Oct-May Thur & Fri 6.30-9pm, Sat/Sun noon-2pm & 6-8pm; WI-FI; 🐾) has a big enclosed beer garden & Sky TV. All the food is home-cooked and you'll get a main meal for £5-12.

Opening earlier, cooked breakfasts (£7.75) can be salivated over at *The George Hotel* (see Where to stay; food served daily 8am-9.30pm) and main courses cost £10-30.

On Caen St numerous dishes from pub classics to nachos (and all for less than £10) can be found at *The White Lion* (☎ 01271-813085, 🖳 www.thewhitelionbraunton.co.uk; food Mon-Sat noon-9pm, Sun to 8pm; WI-FI). On the opposite side of Caen St there is *Good Fortune* (☎ 01271-817889; Mon & Wed-Sat 5-10.30pm, Sun 6-10.30pm), a fairly standard Chinese take-away.

A few metres further on *Wild Thyme Café* (☎ 01271-815191, 🖳 www.wildthymecafe.co.uk; daily 9am-4pm) is a popular and award-winning café specialising in homemade pizzas (from £6.25) and 'rustic baguettes' (from £5.50). Further along, *CJ's* (☎ 01271-812007; Feb-Dec daily 8.30am-4pm) is a sandwich bar which is good for those who aren't planning on stopping for too long.

For an à la carte menu there is *At One* (☎ 01271-814444, 🖳 atonedining.co.uk; Wed-Sat 10am-2.30pm & from 6pm, Sun 9.30am-4pm) where there are also breakfast, lunch and tapas menus. There are many wonderful dishes and the menu may include mushroom and mango stroganoff (£12).

For **fish 'n' chips** you could try *South Sixteen* (☎ 01271-816445, 🖳 southsixteenfishandchips.com; Mon-Thur 11.30am-2pm & 5-9pm, Fri & Sat to 9.30pm) which is a restaurant (the menu may include poached salmon in a white wine and chive sauce £8) and takeaway.

The best-known eatery in town, however, is the renowned *Squires Fish 'n' Chips Restaurant* (☎ 01271-815533, 🖳 www.squiresfishrestaurant.co.uk; Mon-Sat 11.45am-9.45pm, Sun noon-8.30pm, hours may change in winter) where they raise the frying of our humble national dish to an art form; again **takeaway** is available.

BRAUNTON TO INSTOW   [MAPS 29-34]

After the delights of the previous stages, this **12½-mile (20km; 5hrs inc 10 mins Braunton to Velator Bridge)** leg is distinctly more low key. The path continues with the Tarka Trail out of Braunton, hugging the banks of the Taw as it takes a riparian ramble into Barnstaple – the biggest town on this trail. It then continues along the tarmac until approximately two miles (45 mins) before Instow, where it suddenly deviates to follow a dyke around the marshes of East Yelland and Instow Barton. (You could, however, stay on the tarmac Tarka Trail which remains straight, providing an alternative to the SWCP.)

Scenically, this day is few people's favourite; but, while the terrain will not supply you with much to talk about, the day's walk does pass through some interesting areas. Bird-spotters will find much to enjoy with the views across the estuary where egret, curlew and oystercatchers stalk, as well as on Home Farm Marsh, a habitat for all sorts of wildlife.

Railway historians might also find something to titillate their senses during the long plod from Chivenor to Fremington, the path being decorated with various bits of ironmongery from its days as part of the long-defunct London and South Western Railway. Gourmands will tuck in to the heavenly cream teas at Fremington Quay; while historians will enjoy the architecture of Barnstaple, which also offers numerous options for refreshment.

Even if none of the above particularly appeals there is always the consolation that both this walk and the next to Westward Ho! are, on the whole, pancake flat. As such, it's possible to count off the miles rapidly and indeed it's not unusual for walkers to notch up a mightily impressive 24 miles and combine the two stages in one long day. So, if disused railways, military airfields and mudflats aren't your thing, prepare to get your marching boots on, clock up the miles and look forward to the more spectacular sights on the path ahead.

The route

The day begins by following the edge of **Chivenor Airfield**. Currently a base for the Royal Marines, the airfield also has two RAF search-and-rescue helicopters stationed there. Just before coming to a roundabout a right turn leads to the barracks, while turning left leads onto the A361, on the other side of which is *Chivenor Caravan Park* (Map 29; ☎ 01271-812217; £10 per pitch; 🐾; Mar to end Oct). The site has free showers and will charge mobile phones for a small fee. For basic **supplies** there is a **shop** (daily 7am-10pm) at the petrol station across the road.

Ideal for campers in need of a hearty breakfast, perfectly perched above the Taw Estuary is *Waterside Café* (☎ 01271-814086, 🖥 www.watersidediner.com; Tue-Sun 10am-5pm, summer from 9am; WI-FI; 🐾). You'll find a wide range of breakfasts (served until 11am; from £6) as well as lunches (until 4pm; £6-12) including paninis, salads, burgers, pizzas and their popular poached-egg range. For campers – or indeed, any evening amblers – the café is hoping to be licensed in 2017 and will then open in the evenings in the summer.

(cont'd on p152)

ROUTE GUIDE AND MAPS

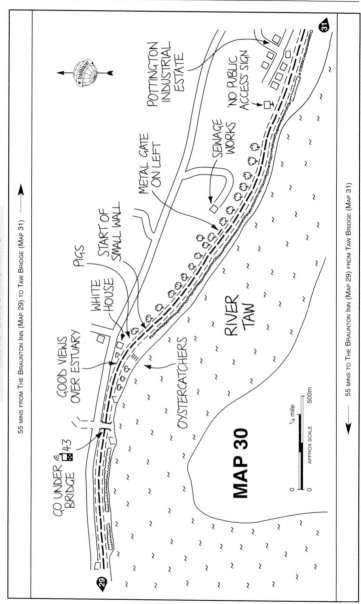

55 MINS FROM THE BRAUNTON INN (MAP 29) TO TAW BRIDGE (MAP 31) →

31

POTTINGTON INDUSTRIAL ESTATE

'NO PUBLIC ACCESS' SIGN

SEWAGE WORKS

METAL GATE ON LEFT

START OF SMALL WALL

PIGS

WHITE HOUSE

GOOD VIEWS OVER ESTUARY

43

GO UNDER BRIDGE

OYSTERCATCHERS

RIVER TAW

MAP 30

APPROX SCALE

¼ mile

500m

0   0

29

← 55 MINS TO THE BRAUNTON INN (MAP 29) FROM TAW BRIDGE (MAP 31) →

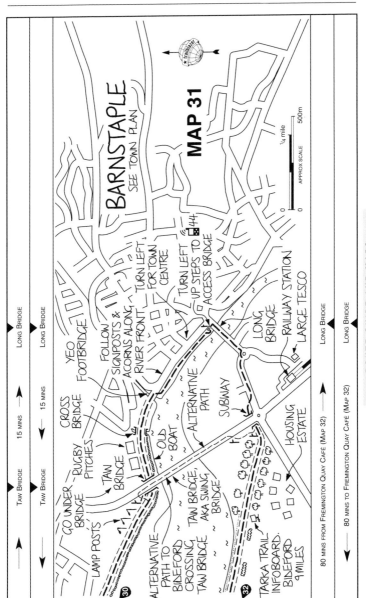

MAP 31

BARNSTAPLE
SEE TOWN PLAN

TAW BRIDGE → 15 MINS → CROSS BRIDGE → 15 MINS → LONG BRIDGE →
TAW BRIDGE ← 15 MINS ← ← 15 MINS ← LONG BRIDGE ←

YEO FOOTBRIDGE

FOLLOW SIGNPOSTS & ACORNS ALONG RIVER FRONT

TURN LEFT FOR TOWN CENTRE

TURN LEFT UP STEPS TO ACCESS BRIDGE

GO UNDER BRIDGE — RUGBY PITCHES

LAMP POSTS

TAW BRIDGE

OLD BOAT

ALTERNATIVE PATH

SUBWAY

ALTERNATIVE PATH TO BIDEFORD CROSSING TAW BRIDGE

TAW BRIDGE, AKA SWING BRIDGE

HOUSING ESTATE

TARKA TRAIL INFOBOARD. BIDEFORD 9 MILES

LONG BRIDGE

RAILWAY STATION

LARGE TESCO

ROUTE GUIDE AND MAPS

80 MINS FROM FREMINGTON QUAY CAFÉ (MAP 32) →

← 80 MINS TO FREMINGTON QUAY CAFÉ (MAP 32)

LONG BRIDGE

APPROX SCALE
0   ¼ mile
0   500m

30   32

(cont'd from p149) Shortly after joining the estuary you come to ***The Braunton Inn*** (Map 29; ☎ 01271-816547, 🖳 www.vintageinn.co.uk/thebrauntoninnbarn staple; food served daily noon-10pm), a huge crenelated place that used to be a manor house called Heanton Court. It has wonderful views straight over the estuary from its patio, guest ales are served and much of the menu is reasonably priced (2-/3-course menu Mon-Fri noon-5pm £11.95/14.95, 5-10pm £14.95/18.95; Sun lunch costs from £10.50).

The route continues along the River Taw to Barnstaple. If you don't wish to visit the town there is an alternative route over the busy new **Taw Bridge**. But if you've got the time, Barnstaple is worth a look.

BARNSTAPLE   [see map p155]

Barnstaple acts as a centre of sorts for North Devon. Historically one of the first four boroughs in England, by the advent of the Norman period the town was already busy and prosperous. Having originally been granted the right to mint coins during the reign of King Athelstan, it had long been a centre of commerce. Indeed, Athelstan also granted the town a charter to hold a market and a fair – both of which remain major cultural and financial contributors to the town today.

Barnstaple Fair is held each September and **Pannier Market** (☎ 01271-379084, 🖳 www.barnstaplepanniermarket.co.uk; Mon-Sat) operates for most of the year. (*Pannier*, incidentally, are the wicker baskets that were once used by traders to bring their goods to the market.) Stalls differ daily but are usually a real smörgåsbord, varying from antiques and jewellery to pet supplies and home-made preserves. The market building was constructed in 1855 but plans for the area's development had already begun following the completion of the **Guildhall** in 1827. A remarkably impressive building, the Guildhall includes portraits of – amongst previous councillors – the poet John Gay, who was born in the town. A contemporary of both Samuel Johnson and Alexander Pope, Gay is best known for his satire *The Beggar's Opera*.

On the other side of Butcher's Row from the market and Guildhall are the **parish church** (St Peter's), in existence since 1107, and the Grade-I listed **St Anne's Chapel**. Dating from the early 14th century, the chapel has some splendid features including what some consider to have been

a 'charnel house' – a place for storing bones. There are also some wonderfully gruesome gargoyles dotted around the place. Other historical sites which may be of interest include the **Castle Mound**, across the bridge over the Yeo, which was originally the base of a wooden Norman castle; and, if you have the time to inspecting the doors of almshouses, you'll find bullet holes from the Civil War in one of the doors at **Penrose Almshouses** in Litchdon St.

The **Museum of Barnstaple & North Devon** (☎ 01271-346747, 🖳 www.barnstaplemuseum.org.uk; late Mar/Easter to Oct Mon-Sat 10am-5pm, Oct to Easter to 4pm; free) has permanent exhibitions including The Tarka Gallery, which deals with the local wildlife, and North Devon at War.

See p16 for details of festivals and events in Barnstaple.

Services

Barnstaple is not short of services and anything you need should be easy to source. In the same building as the museum, the **tourist information centre** (☎ 01271-346747, 🖳 www.staynorthdevon.co.uk; Mon-Sat 10am-4pm) is staffed by very helpful and knowledgeable locals and is worth a visit; they have information on accommodation but can't make bookings. The **post office** (Mon-Fri 9am-5.30pm, Sat 9am-12.30pm) is on the corner of Boutport and Queen Sts but still only a brief stroll from the river. The large number of computers in the town's **library** (☎ 01271-318780; Mon, Tue, Thur & Fri 9.30am-6pm, Wed 10am-5.30pm, Sat 9.30am-4pm;

WI-FI) on Tuly St, means getting **internet access** (£1/30 mins) shouldn't be a problem but they also offer free wi-fi. There is also a **local studies section** (Wed-Fri 10am-5pm) that is well worth a perusal.

If you're in need of **walking gear** there's a Mountain Warehouse (☎ 01271-372253; Mon-Fri 9am-5.30pm, Sat to 6pm, Sun 10am-5pm) and a Millets (Mon-Sat 9am-5.30pm, Sun 10am-4pm) on the High St, while for **cameras and repairs** J & A Cameras (☎ 01271-375037; Mon-Sat 9am-5.30pm) is on Gammon Walk.

Back on the High St there's also a Boots the **Chemist** (Mon-Sat 8.30am-6pm, Sun 10.30am-4pm) and a Superdrug (Mon-Sat 9am-5.30pm, Sun 10am-4pm), a Waterstone's **bookshop** (Mon-Sat 9am-5.30pm, Sun 10.30am-4.30pm), and a small Co-op **supermarket** (daily 7am-7pm). Out near the railway station there is also a large Tesco.

There are several **ATMs** in the centre including at both HSBC and NatWest.

Transport
[See also pp44-50] Barnstaple is the only place on the path to be connected with the national **rail** network. Great Western Railway runs regular services to Exeter, from where you can connect with other services.

Barnstaple is also very well served by **buses**, with regular services (Filers' Nos 301, 303 309 & 310; Stagecoach's Nos 5B, 21/21A, 85, 155, & 319) to and from surrounding towns and villages. Bude can be accessed by connecting with Stagecoach's 219 service from Hartland. The bus station is on Belle Meadow Rd.

Where to stay
For a town this size there is scant accommodation. However, there are places for those with a good budget.

One of the more central options, *The Old Vicarage* (☎ 01271-328504, 🖥 www .oldvicaragebarnstaple.co.uk; 1S/1D/1D or T/1Tr/1Qd, all en suite; ✿; WI-FI), was once upon a time home to the vicar for the nearby Holy Trinity Church but now finds a purpose by providing accommodation for tired walkers. The owners have walked the path so they have maps and are happy to help people plan itineraries; their website also includes a very useful guide describing how you could stay here for as long as you need to complete the stretch of SWCP between Lynmouth and Hartland using public transport. They charge £45-50pp (sgl £48, sgl occ £79-89, three/four sharing £125-140).

For a **room above a pub** (£30-37.50pp, sgl occ £40-45; no breakfast), *The Olive Branch* (☎ 01271-370784, 🖥 www .olivebranchdevon.co.uk; 1S/1D shared bathroom/1Tr en suite; WI-FI) is opposite the post office. It's rather basic but is very close to the action. Note, that there is karaoke on a Wednesday night and live bands on a Friday night so it can be rather noisy.

Regarding **hotels**, the local Brend chain has three fine representatives in Barnstaple. Right in the centre, there is the elegant Georgian *Royal & Fortescue* (☎ 01271-342289, 🖥 royalfortescue.co.uk; 4S/44D or T, all en suite; ✿; WI-FI; 🐾); room only costs £45-60pp (sgl/sgl occ £70-85) and they charge £10/12.50pp for a continental/cooked breakfast.

The second, *Park Hotel* (☎ 01271-372166, 🖥 parkhotel.co.uk; 2S/17D/15D or T/4T, all en suite; ✿; WI-FI), is only a 5-minute walk away on quieter Taw Vale; it overlooks Rock Park and the Taw beyond. Room only costs £45-90pp (sgl £57-75, sgl occ £65-110); a continental/cooked breakfast here is £8/10pp.

Surpassing both in terms of style, however, *The Imperial* (☎ 01271-345861, 🖥 brend-imperial.co.uk; 10S/63D or T/2Tr, all en suite; ✿; WI-FI; 🐾 annexe only) has rooms (£60-80pp, sgl £87-112, sgl occ full room rate, three sharing rates on request) whose prices reflect the extra sumptuousness and luxury on offer. A continental/ cooked breakfast here costs £10/15pp.

Where to eat and drink
There are quite a few options for food in Barnstaple. Not far from the path – if you're willing to take a small diversion after crossing Yeo Footbridge – *Corner*

Café (☎ 01271-859555; Tue-Sat 7.45am-3pm; WI-FI; 🐕 outside) is a homely little place that does daily specials such as vegetable curry, or cauliflower cheese, for only £4, and a daily special pudding for £1.20.

Slightly further along the trail and actually on the river (and path), *Tea by the Taw* (☎ 01271-370032; summer Mon-Sat 10am-5pm, Sun to 4pm, winter Tue-Sat to 4pm; WI-FI; 🐕 outside) sells sandwiches/paninis, jacket potatoes and cream teas and also has outdoor seating; the homemade soup of the day costs £5.95.

Heading into town, by far the best option is on Tuly St. *Boston Tea Party* (☎ 01271-329070, 🖥 www.bostonteaparty.co.uk/our_cafes/barnstaple; Mon-Sat 7am-6pm, Sun 9.30am-5pm; WI-FI; 🐕) is a spacious and modern café that serves a great and varied menu. A West Country breakfast costs £8.15 whilst a burger will set you back only £9.25. There's a great range of brunches and such lighter delights as a goats' cheese and beetroot salad (£8). There is also a fine selection of homemade cakes and pastries.

Close by, on Holland Walk, *Sheppard's Sandwich Bar* (☎ 01271-375383; Mon-Sat 8.30am-3pm, summer to 4pm; WI-FI; 🐕 outside) sells sandwiches and coffee to both eat-in and takeaway; and if you're truly determined to get a card stamped or a strawberry-flavoured latte there are also representatives of the national chains in Barnstaple including a *Caffè Nero* (☎ 01271-379247; Mon-Sat 7.30am-5.30pm, Sun 9.30am-5pm; WI-FI) on the High St.

There are a few **pubs** that serve food. For a modern pub/restaurant wander along to Boutport St and *Alfie Browns* (☎ 01271-344477, 🖥 www.alfiebrowns.co.uk; food Mon-Thur 11.30am-2.30pm & 5.30-9pm, Fri & Sat to 10pm, Sun to 8.30pm; WI-FI). Traditional pub food is on offer (main meal £10.95-19.95) as are sandwiches (£6.25-8.25) and on the seventh day Alfie's Sunday roast (£10.50). There's local ales and ciders to wash it all down with.

If sports channels and Americana attract you then at the other end of Boutport St is *Bull & Bear* (☎ 01271-323238, 🖥

www.ilovebullandbear.com; food Mon-Sat 11am-9pm, Sun to 6pm; WI-FI). With buffalo wings (£4.95-14.95), nachos (£8.95-9.95) and burgers (£9.95-14.95) all on the food menu it's hardly a surprise to find an American-style whiskey menu too.

Traditional home-made pub-grub including cottage pie (£5.95) and tempura-battered cod (£8.95) is available at *The Olive Branch* (see Where to stay; food Mon-Sat noon-9pm, Sun to 7pm; WI-FI; 🐕); and Wetherspoons has its representative – *The Water Gate* (☎ 01271-335410, 🖥 www.jdwetherspoon.com; food served daily 8am-11pm; WI-FI) – which faces towards the river on The Strand and serves the standard Wetherspoons' menu.

With a great decorative ceiling, finer dining can be found at *62 The Bank* (☎ 01271-324446, 🖥 www.62thebank.co.uk; Mon-Fri 11am-3pm & 6-10pm, Sat 10am-5pm & 6-10pm), adjoining Royal & Fortescue Hotel, which started life as a merchant's house some 300 years ago. The menu is imaginative and varied and includes such unusual items as tortilla pancakes filled with seafood in a white-wine sauce (£14.50).

For Mexican, *Jalapenos* (☎ 01271-327122, 🖥 jalapenosmexican.co.uk; food served Mon-Thur noon-3pm & 5.30-9pm, Fri & Sat same but to 10pm) has friendly staff and offers a decent selection of food; while for something equally Hispanic, near Long Bridge there's *Lilico's* (☎ 01271-372933, 🖥 www.lilicos.co.uk; food served Mon-Sat 10am-5pm & 5.30-9.30pm), a Tapas Lounge & Bar; delicious deep-fried calamari with sweet chilli and honey costs £5.75 (tapas).

At 35 Boutport St, *Giovanni's* (☎ 01271-321274, 🖥 www.giovannisdevon.co.uk; Mon-Fri noon-2.30pm & 5.30-10pm, Sat noon-10.30pm, Sun noon-9pm) is, as you may have already guessed, an Italian restaurant with spaghetti bolognaise for £9.75. Takeaway is also available.

Tucked away between Boutport St and the Pannier Market, Nepalese cuisine can be found at *Gurkha* (☎ 01271-377665; daily noon-2pm & 5.30-11pm, Sun to 10pm). The interesting menu includes such

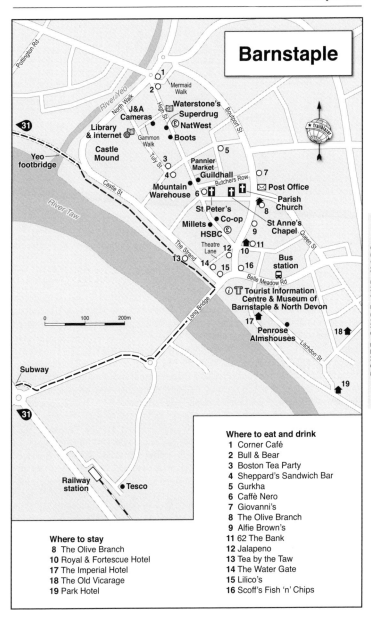

Barnstaple

ROUTE GUIDE AND MAPS

Where to stay
- 8 The Olive Branch
- 10 Royal & Fortescue Hotel
- 17 The Imperial Hotel
- 18 The Old Vicarage
- 19 Park Hotel

Where to eat and drink
- 1 Corner Café
- 2 Bull & Bear
- 3 Boston Tea Party
- 4 Sheppard's Sandwich Bar
- 5 Gurkha
- 6 Caffè Nero
- 7 Giovanni's
- 8 The Olive Branch
- 9 Alfie Brown's
- 11 62 The Bank
- 12 Jalapeno
- 13 Tea by the Taw
- 14 The Water Gate
- 15 Lilico's
- 16 Scoff's Fish 'n' Chips

dishes as *lasun chicken* (cooked with garlic, onion, capsicum and spices) for £8.95.

For **takeaway**, at 1 The Square, *Scoff's Fish 'n' Chips* (☎ 01271-346671;

Mon-Sat 11am-8pm, closed Bank Hol Mons) won't disappoint. A portion of fish 'n' their signature lightly battered chips costs £6.

From Barnstaple the route follows a long straight path – decorated with benches and shelters – along the disused Barnstaple to Torrington railway line with mud and sand to one side and fields, in the main, on the other – eventually turning in just before **Penhill Point** and arriving at **Fremington Quay**.

FREMINGTON QUAY   [MAP 32]

A tranquil spot and a lovely place for a rest, Fremington Quay used to be the busiest port between Bristol and Land's End. The import of coal and the export of, amongst other things, local clay and pottery led to the area thriving throughout the first half of the 20th century. The railway finally closed in 1982; a replica railway station (the old one is on the other side of the trail) houses **Fremington Quay Heritage Centre**.

The centre shares a building and space with *Fremington Quay Café* (☎ 01271-268720, 🖳 www.fremingtonquay.co.uk;

Mar-Oct Mon-Fri 9am-5pm, Sat & Sun to 5.30pm, Oct-Mar Mon-Fri 10am-4pm, Sat & Sun 9am-5pm; 🐾 outside), a popular place with walkers, cyclists and locals. Serving breakfast until 11am, plus lunches, drinks and snacks, their cream teas (£4.45) are, to put it simply, divine. There are toilets but you have to pay to use them. Doggy biscuits for four-legged friends are baked on the premiss.

Stagecoach's No 5B, 21 & 21A **bus** services call at the New Inn in Fremington; see pp48-50 for details.

Leaving the quay behind, the path crosses the small **bridge** to some disused **lime kilns** on your right. Fields continue to accompany the path on the one side, marshes on the other. **Home Farm Marsh** used to be the site of a dairy farm but since 2002 has been owned by the Gaia Trust, a charity that aims to protect the countryside by promoting sustainable farming and wildlife conservation. Due to the trust's work in returning much of the marsh to its original state as a wetland, wild flowers and birds are once again flourishing – look out for little egret, skylark and bittern. There is a 2km walking route that you can follow around the marsh with information boards helping you to ascertain what wildlife to look out for. Stray off the path towards the water and you may come across a **granite cross**, erected in memory of Lady Hilda McNeill who drowned there whilst trying to rescue a child in 1904. Be warned that **the waters of the estuary are very fast-running – do not go in**! Note also, that **dogs** are not allowed within the marsh.

The path then runs between **Isley Marsh Nature Reserve** and **East Yelland Marsh** (Map 34), both of which form part of the estuary's SSSI. Isley Marsh, whilst owned by the RSPB, is mostly consumed by the sea at high-tide so has no breeding birds nesting on it. It is, however, an important habitat for resting birds and between there and the other marshes there is a chance of seeing anything from barn owls to kingfishers. Less spectacular but every bit as fascinating as the kingfisher, East Yelland Marsh is also known to be home to greater horseshoe bats. *(cont'd on p160)*

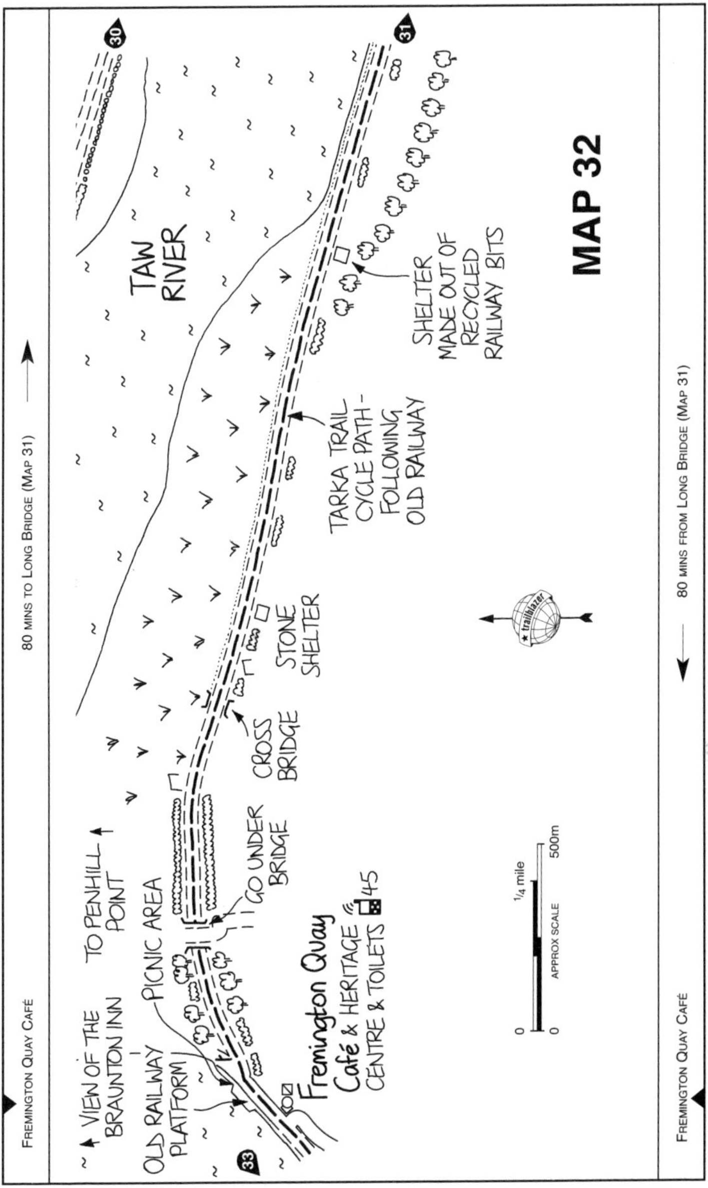

80 MINS TO LONG BRIDGE (MAP 31)
FREMINGTON QUAY CAFÉ
30
31
TAW RIVER
SHELTER MADE OUT OF RECYCLED RAILWAY BITS
MAP 32
TARKA TRAIL CYCLE PATH - FOLLOWING OLD RAILWAY
STONE SHELTER
CROSS BRIDGE
GO UNDER BRIDGE
TO PENHILL POINT
PICNIC AREA
VIEW OF THE BRAUNTON INN
OLD RAILWAY PLATFORM
33
Fremington Quay Café & HERITAGE CENTRE & TOILETS
45
trailblazer
0
1/4 mile
APPROX SCALE
0
500m
80 MINS FROM LONG BRIDGE (MAP 31)
FREMINGTON QUAY CAFÉ

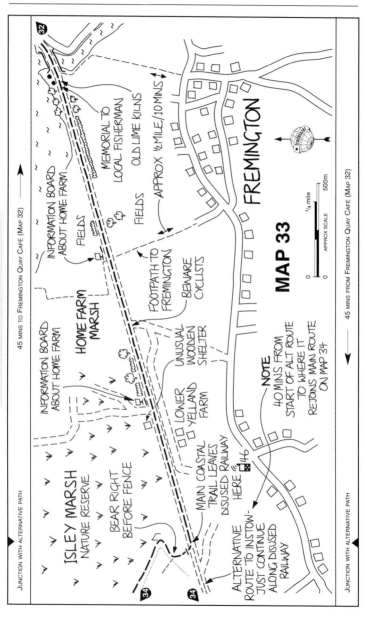

JUNCTION WITH ALTERNATIVE PATH

45 MINS TO FREMINGTON QUAY CAFÉ (MAP 32) →

ISLEY MARSH
NATURE RESERVE

BEAR RIGHT
BEFORE FENCE

INFORMATION BOARD
ABOUT HOME FARM

HOME FARM
MARSH

INFORMATION BOARD
ABOUT HOME FARM

FIELDS

MEMORIAL TO
LOCAL FISHERMAN

OLD LIME KILNS

APPROX ½ MILE /10 MINS

FIELDS

FOOTPATH TO
FREMINGTON

BEWARE
CYCLISTS

UNUSUAL
WOODEN
SHELTER

LOWER
YELLAND
FARM

MAIN COASTAL
TRAIL LEAVES
DISUSED RAILWAY
HERE

ALTERNATIVE
ROUTE TO INSTOW-
JUST CONTINUE
ALONG DISUSED
RAILWAY

FREMINGTON

MAP 33

NOTE
40 MINS FROM
START OF ALT ROUTE
TO WHERE IT
REJOINS MAIN ROUTE
ON MAP 34

0   ¼ mile
APPROX SCALE
0   500m

32

34

34

JUNCTION WITH ALTERNATIVE PATH

← 45 MINS FROM FREMINGTON QUAY CAFÉ (MAP 32)

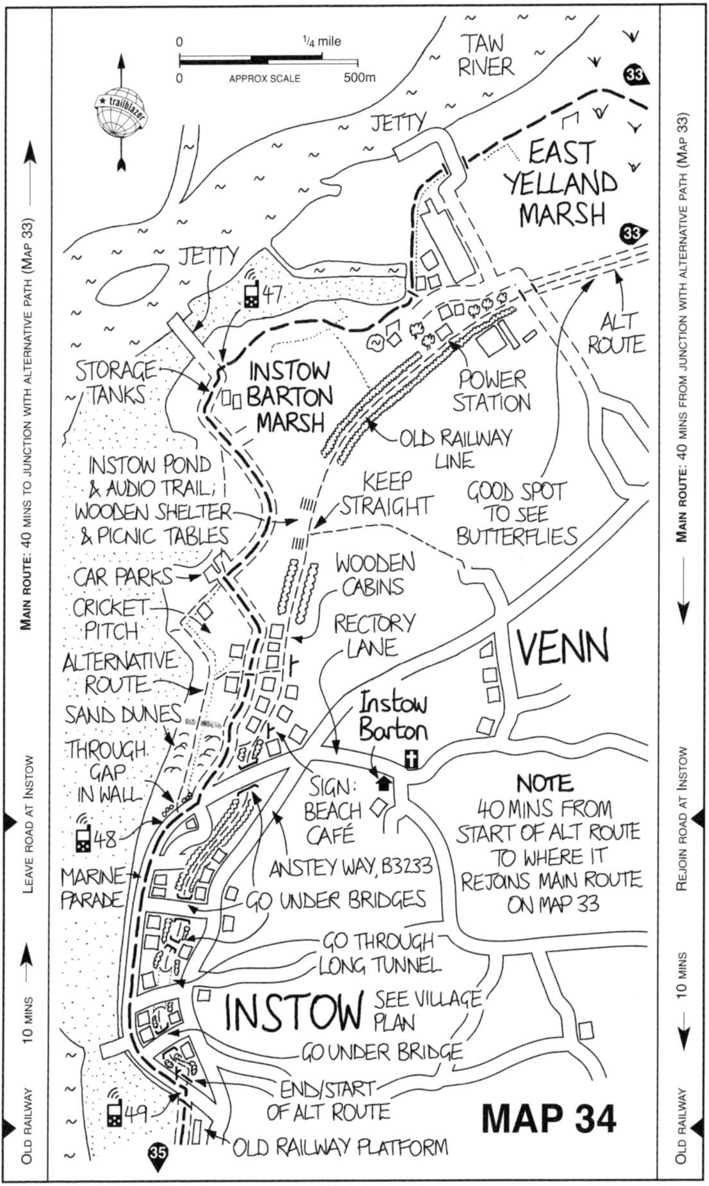

MAP 34

TAW RIVER

JETTY

EAST YELLAND MARSH

33

33

MAIN ROUTE: 40 MINS TO JUNCTION WITH ALTERNATIVE PATH (MAP 33)

MAIN ROUTE: 40 MINS FROM JUNCTION WITH ALTERNATIVE PATH (MAP 33)

JETTY

47

STORAGE TANKS

INSTOW BARTON MARSH

ALT ROUTE

POWER STATION

OLD RAILWAY LINE

INSTOW POND & AUDIO TRAIL; WOODEN SHELTER & PICNIC TABLES

KEEP STRAIGHT

GOOD SPOT TO SEE BUTTERFLIES

CAR PARKS

WOODEN CABINS

CRICKET PITCH

RECTORY LANE

VENN

ALTERNATIVE ROUTE

SAND DUNES

Instow Barton

THROUGH GAP IN WALL

48

SIGN: BEACH CAFÉ

NOTE
40 MINS FROM START OF ALT ROUTE TO WHERE IT REJOINS MAIN ROUTE ON MAP 33

MARINE PARADE

ANSTEY WAY, B3233

GO UNDER BRIDGES

GO THROUGH LONG TUNNEL

INSTOW SEE VILLAGE PLAN

GO UNDER BRIDGE

END/START OF ALT ROUTE

49

OLD RAILWAY PLATFORM

35

0   1/4 mile

0   APPROX SCALE   500m

trailblazer

LEAVE ROAD AT INSTOW

REJOIN ROAD AT INSTOW

10 MINS

10 MINS

OLD RAILWAY

OLD RAILWAY

(cont'd from p156) The path ambles around Instow Barton Marsh before following the sands of the estuary into Instow. (Note: if walking around windswept marshes doesn't appeal, you can continue along the disused railway track all the way into Instow).

INSTOW

Instow is a pretty little village, the main highlight of which is its beach and the views it commands across the confluence of the Taw and Torridge rivers. It is a pleasant place to relax in at the end of a day's walk and contrasts splendidly with the hustle and bustle of Barnstaple.

For railway enthusiasts, where the North Devon Yacht Club (Map 35) now stands used to be Instow Railway Station and for those with a nose for trivia, Instow **signal box** (bank holidays and some Sundays Easter-Oct 2-5pm, Nov-Easter 2-4pm; free, donation appreciated) was the UK's first Grade-II listed signal box.

On the other side of the estuary, through the sails and seagulls, Appledore glistens on a summer's day and if you are willing to bypass Bideford there is a **ferry** (www.appledoreinstowferry.com) that will take you directly there. Weather permitting, it runs (Apr-Oct daily; adults £1.50 one way; charged at the skipper's discretion) for two hours either side of high tide; the service operates between Instow ferry slip, opposite Johns of Instow, and Appledore Quay. You should always check notices in the villages themselves for the actual operating times.

The village feels a little like Porlock Weir in that it has an air of serenity about it, although, also similarly, there are amenities here. For **general supplies** there is *Johns* (see also Where to eat; ☎ 01271-860310, www.johnsofinstow.co.uk; generally daily 8am-6pm but check their website as the hours can vary), which also includes the **post office** (Mon-Fri 9am-5.30pm, Sat 9am-12.30pm) and a café (see Where to eat). **Cashback** is available (£3 minimum spend or 50p charge).

Instow is well served by public transport. In addition to the **ferry** service (see above) Stagecoach's Nos 5B, 21 & 21A **buses** call here (see pp48-50).

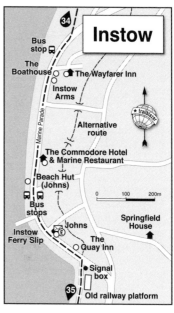

For **accommodation** close to the path try *The Wayfarer Inn* (☎ 01271-860342, www.thewayfarerinn.co.uk; 2D/2T/2Tr, one room sleeps up to six, all en suite; ; WI-FI; ;). It is the first place you come to as you head into Instow along the beach and is also signed from the Tarka Trail. The rooms (£35-42.50pp, sgl occ £55-65, three-six sharing £100-150) are simple but smart and the whole place is very welcoming. Note that some rooms have bunk beds.

Other possibilities in Instow include the rather austere-looking *Springfield House* (☎ 01271-860895, www.springfield-instow.co.uk; 2D both private bathroom; ; WI-FI; ;), up the hill on New Rd, which charges £47.50-50pp (sgl occ £75). There's drying facilities for walkers and a wood-burner and afternoon tea is served on arrival. They don't take single-night bookings on Friday or Saturday (Apr-Nov) but, subject to prior arrangement, for a two-night stay they will do pick up and drop off and also your laundry.

More established, *The Commodore Hotel* (☎ 01271-860347, ⬚ www.commo dore-instow.co.uk; 24D or T, all en suite; ☛; WI-FI; (Ⓛ) is the largest place on the front and is a grand and sophisticated whitewashed affair. B&B (£37.50-64pp, sgl occ from £75) is available in side and rear rooms only. Rates for rooms with a view are Dinner B&B only (£80-115pp).

A 5-minute amble away from the SWCP (see Map 34; p159) is *Instow Barton* (☎ 01271-860845, ⬚ www.instow barton.co.uk; 4D or T/1Tr, all en suite; ☛; WI-FI; (Ⓛ); well-behaved 🐾), where B&B is available in a farmhouse near to the church. The tariff (£55pp, sgl occ £95, three sharing £130) not only includes breakfast but also afternoon tea.

For **food** and refreshments there are several good options. Johns (see opposite) incorporates an award-winning *café* and deli (daily 8am-4.30pm, sometimes also open in the evening in summer) and also runs the **beach hut** (seasonal) which you pass as you follow the path through Instow. The menu in the café is splendid.

Overlooking the harbour and estuary, *The Quay Inn* (☎ 01271-860624, ⬚ www .thequayinninstow.co.uk; food Mon-Sat 10am-9pm, Sun to 8pm; WI-FI; 🐾) serves real ales and food; the menu changes regu-larly but includes a pasta/pie of the day

£10.95/12.50. Note that between 3pm and 6pm only sandwiches are available.

Make sure you look up and check out the wonderful painting on the ceiling by a local artist if you choose to eat in *Instow Arms* (☎ 01271-860608, ⬚ www.instow arms.com; food Mon-Fri 11am-9pm, Sat & Sun 10am-9pm, limited menu 3-6pm; WI-FI; 🐾 in the bar). There is a strong focus on locally sourced seafood; the *moules marinière* costs £15.95.

The Boathouse (☎ 01271-861292, ⬚ theboathouseinstow.wordpress.com; food daily noon-2pm, Mon-Sat 6-9.30pm, Sun to 9pm, Nov-Feb Tue-Sun noon-2pm, Tue-Sat 6-9pm) is also decorated splendidly, with surfboards hanging off the ceiling and mopeds displayed on the walls. Much of its seafood is served straight off the beach and it has an extensive fish-themed specials' menu. Clovelly lobster and crab salad may be available. There are also always non fish options. If you're after a beer garden *The Wayfarer Inn* (see opposite; daily noon-2/3pm & 6-8.30/9.30pm) serves a full menu as well as daily specials in the main season– you can even eat your fish dinner whilst the man who caught it sups at the bar.

Finally, *Marine Restaurant* at The Commodore Hotel (see column opposite; Mon-Sat 7-8.45pm Sun noon-1.15pm & 7-8pm – booking essential in the evening) adjusts its menu daily with a strong focus on local and seasonal food. Food is also avail-able in the *bar* (daily 10am-noon morning coffee, noon-2pm light lunches, 3-5.30pm cream teas, 6.30-8.45pm light meals).

INSTOW TO WESTWARD HO! [MAPS 34-39]

This **11-mile (17.6km; 4hrs 50 mins)** stage is where the coastal path and the Tarka Trail shake hands, embrace and bid a final, fond farewell to each other. Nevertheless, though you finally leave the otter and its old railway line behind at Bideford by crossing the Torridge River, the path still remains flat and easy all the way to Westward Ho!.

From Bideford it follows a slightly incoherent path that twists and turns its way between estuary-edge, road and woodland all the way to Appledore. Leaving this pretty village behind, the route meanders through Northam Burrows Country Park before finally arriving in Westward Ho!, which is not as bad as some will have you believe (though the exclamation mark at the end of the name does tend to raise expectations that the town struggles to satisfy). There are plenty of options for refreshment on this straightforward stage and you would be well advised to enjoy them as tomorrow the easy walking ends. So, get a good night's sleep in Westward Ho! and prepare yourself to re-embrace the sharp ups and nigh-on-vertical downs of the jagged North Devon coast!

The route

From Instow continue along the tracks to **East-the-Water** (see below) where you cross the Torridge via the historic Long Bridge to **Bideford**. Looking across the river you can see the route you will follow when leaving the town, as well as the one you've just finished.

EAST-THE-WATER   [Map 36]

Blink and you could miss East-the-Water as you march on towards Long Bridge and Bideford.

There's little here to distract you but English history buffs may wish to visit **Chudleigh Fort**. Located above the path, the fort was erected between 1642 and 1643, during the Civil War, to defend Bideford. It was rebuilt in the 19th century and it is now an ornamental garden.

Stagecoach's Nos 15A & 15C **bus** services call here; see pp48-50.

Just before you cross Long Bridge, is **The Royal Hotel** (☎ 01237-472005, 🖳 royalbideford.co.uk; 4S/12D/4T/7D or T/2Tr, all en suite; ☕; WI-FI; Ⓛ; 🐾). The prices (B&B £64pp, sgl £79, sgl occ £94, three sharing £142) are fair and The Kingsley Bedroom is gorgeous, with an ornate, plastered ceiling and original panelling.

By the roundabout at the foot of the steps, **Riverbank Bistro** (☎ 01237-473399, 🖳 www.theriverbankbistro.co.uk; Apr-Nov Mon & Tue 5-9pm, Wed-Fri noon-3pm &

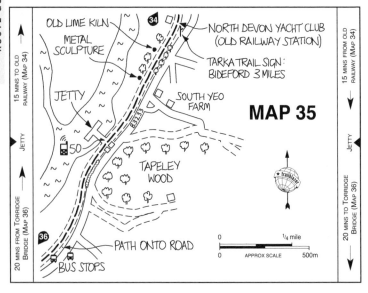

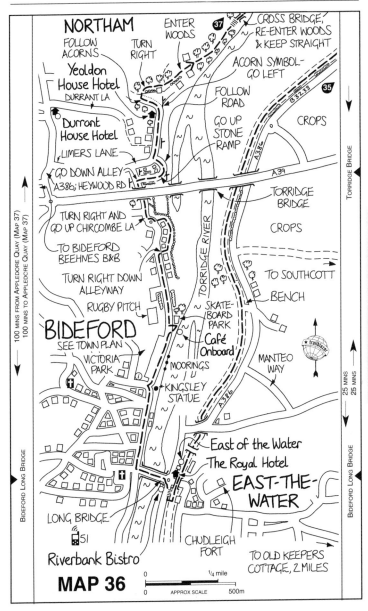

NORTHAM

FOLLOW ACORNS

TURN RIGHT

ENTER WOODS

CROSS BRIDGE, RE-ENTER WOODS & KEEP STRAIGHT

Yeoldon House Hotel

DURRANT LA

ACORN SYMBOL- GO LEFT

FOLLOW ROAD

GO UP STONE RAMP

CROPS

Durrant House Hotel

LIMERS LANE

GO DOWN ALLEY

A386; HEYWOOD RD

TORRIDGE BRIDGE

A39

TORRIDGE BRIDGE

TURN RIGHT AND GO UP CHIRCOMBE LA

CROPS

TO BIDEFORD BEEHNES B&B

TURN RIGHT DOWN ALLEYWAY

TO SOUTHCOTT

BENCH

RUGBY PITCH

BIDEFORD

SEE TOWN PLAN

SKATE-BOARD PARK

Café Onboard

VICTORIA PARK

MANTEO WAY

MOORINGS

KINGSLEY STATUE

East of the Water
The Royal Hotel

EAST-THE-WATER

LONG BRIDGE

51

Riverbank Bistro

CHUDLEIGH FORT

TO OLD KEEPERS COTTAGE, 2 MILES

MAP 36

0   ¼ mile
0   APPROX SCALE   500m

TORRIDGE RIVER

trailblazer

100 MINS FROM APPLEDORE QUAY (MAP 37)
100 MINS TO APPLEDORE QUAY (MAP 37)

BIDEFORD LONG BRIDGE

25 MINS
25 MINS

BIDEFORD LONG BRIDGE

TORRIDGE BRIDGE

ROUTE GUIDE AND MAPS

6-9pm, Sat noon-9pm, Sun noon-5pm, rest of year Mon-Sat 5-9pm, Sat noon-9pm, Sun noon-5pm), is a modern bar and restaurant with a great menu, including such treats as king prawn linguine (£13.95); mixed grill (£18.95) and a Sunday carvery (£9.95); they also have gluten-free options.

East of the Water (☎ 01237-425329; Tue-Fri & Sun 5-10.30pm, Sat to 11pm) is a notch above most Chinese restaurants, with an imaginative menu including a starter of Indonesian chicken satay, and mains including Peking-style lamb (strips of lamb stir-fried in wine, chilli, beans, hoi sin & soy sauce) served with vegetables and rice. Ordering both – or two similar dishes – will cost approximately £15.

BIDEFORD

'All who have travelled through the delicious scenery of North Devon must needs know the little white town of Bideford, which slopes upwards from its broad tide-river paved with yellow sands, towards the pleasant upland in the west.'
      Charles Kingsley, *Westward Ho!*
The 'little white town' of Bideford has a long and rich history spanning from Roman times. Pivotal to the town's existence is its position on the Torridge and since the 16th century onwards its primary function has been as a port and place of trade. One of the town's most famous residents, Sir Richard Grenville, set sail from Bideford on several expeditions to the New World. He is also, famously, the subject of Tennyson's poem, *Revenge*, following his death fighting the Spanish during the Battle of Flores in 1591.

There is evidence of **The Quay** having been here in some form since 1619 and it was refurbished in 2006, a project that included the construction of the **Quay Fountain**, which at high tide shoots 24 jets of water up into the air and out over the river. The 24 jets are supposed to mirror the 24 arches that hold up **Long Bridge**. First constructed from oak in 1280 as a pack-horse bridge, it replaced what was a dangerous ford – the name Bideford is derived from 'By the ford'. Originally the bridge had a chapel at either end. The Quay is also a departure point for ferries to Lundy Island (see box p122).

The current church, **St Mary's**, is actually the third to have been built on the site, having been constructed in 1865 around the original Norman tower. Inside, the font is thought to be from 1080 and is thus the oldest relic in town.

Other sites in Bideford include the **Pannier Market** – held in Bideford since 1272, when the town was granted charter to hold a market by Henry III, and located on the same site since 1675, though the current building dates 'only' from 1884. Today, as ever, there is as rich a variety of stalls, with trading taking place on Tuesdays and Saturdays year-round. The area is now slightly rundown in parts, though it is also the most interesting of quarters to browse around. Should you have the time **Bideford Heritage Trail** takes you on a tour around the town's most historically significant areas. Information about the tour can be found at the tourist office.

If more walking isn't your idea of fun **Burton Art Gallery & Museum** (☎ 01237-471455, 🖳 www.burtonartgallery.co .uk; Mon-Sat 10am-4pm, Aug to 5pm, Sun 11am-4pm; free) boasts a number of interesting artefacts and houses a scale replica of Long Bridge, displaying its various forms down the ages. There is also information on many of the town's most famous residents including Edward Capern (1819-94), aka the Postman Poet, a man who could obviously multitask; and the story of the trial of the Bideford witches – who in 1682 became the last women in England to be hanged for witchcraft.

Services
Bideford has a good selection of services. The **tourist information centre** (☎ 01237-477676; opening hours same as for Gallery) is in Burton Art Gallery; the staff can do accommodation booking (see box p40) over the counter but not over the phone. The **post office** (Mon-Fri 9am-5.30pm, Sat

9am-12.30pm) is nearby on The Quay. For **internet access** (£1/30 mins), or free WI-FI, try Bideford **Library** (☎ 01237-476075; Mon, Tue, Thur & Fri 9.30am-6pm, Sat 9.30am-1.30pm) near Long Bridge. There are several **ATM**s dotted along The Quay.

For **food** there is a Co-op (Mon-Sat 6am-11pm, Sun 10am-4pm), on Mill St in the centre, and a Boots (Mon-Sat 8.30am-5.30pm), on High St, should you need a **chemist**.

Transport

[See also pp48-50] Stagecoach's 5B, 15A, 15C, 21, 21A, 85 & 319 **bus** services connect Bideford with most surrounding towns and villages. Buses stop on The Quay.

For a **taxi** try A1-Taxis (☎ 01237-666060).

Where to stay

Campers looking to pitch their tents in the area should continue walking to Northam

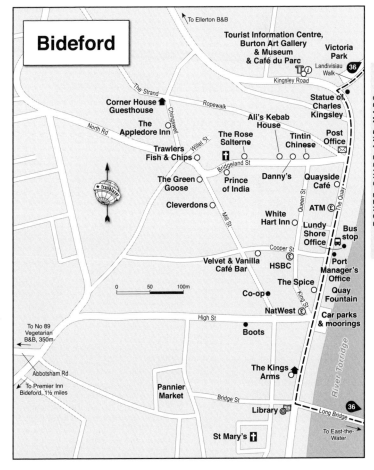

(see p168). Indeed, there is a distinct lack of accommodation in Bideford, which may make the extra 3½ miles to Appledore – or stopping at one of the B&B options en route (see Northam p168; Map 36) – seem rather appealing to everyone.

Rooms (only) above a pub are available on The Quay – and so the SWCP – at *The Kings Arms* (☎ 01237-475196; 1S/1T/1Tr, all en suite; ✆; WI-FI; 🐾), an old-fashioned pub which is over 400 years old. Rooms cost £30pp (sgl/sgl occ £45, three sharing £60). There may not be a breakfast – or at least until 11am when the kitchen opens and by which point your average walker will be well on their way – there are some decent cafés in Bideford in which to start your day (see Where to eat).

Centrally, **B&B** accommodation can be found on The Strand at *Corner House Guesthouse* (☎ 01237-473722, 🖳 www.cornerhouseguesthouse.co.uk; 2S/2D/2T shared facilities; ✆; WI-FI; 🐾), where you can sleep and devour breakfast in a pretty 18th-century merchant seaman's house. They charge £35pp (sgl £37, sgl occ £45).

Less than half-a-mile from the town centre on Glenburnie Rd is *Ellerton B&B* (☎ 01237-470393, 🖳 www.ellertonbedandbreakfast.co.uk; 2D both en suite, 1S/1D both with private bathroom; ✆; WI-FI). Rates are from £35pp (sgl/sgl occ £45).

At the other end of town, approximately a mile from the trail, is the fabulous *No 89 Vegetarian B&B* (☎ 01237-472975, 🖳 www.bandbno89.co.uk; 1S shared facilities, 1D/1D or T both en suite; WI-FI; Ⓛ), which is – you've guessed it! – at No 89 (Abbotsham Rd). The single room shares a bathroom with the owners and the cooked breakfast is – yes, you've guessed it, again! – vegetarian. They charge £32.50-35pp (sgl £35, sgl occ £45).

Recommended by coastal path walkers, approximately two miles from Bideford Quay (and once you've left the road, 1½ miles down a single track lane), is *Old Keepers Cottage* (☎ 01237-479113, 🖳 www.oldkeeperscottage.net; 1Qd en suite, 1D/1T private bathroom; ✆; WI-FI; Ⓛ; Feb-Oct); so named as the main building is an old game keepers' cottage built in 1835. Set

in 35 acres of field, garden and woodland, subject to prior arrangement free pick up/drop offs from the path are available. There's a Tesco one mile away for any urgent purchases. B&B costs £35-45pp (sgl occ £40-60, three/four sharing £125). Note the bathroom for the double and twin rooms is downstairs and the quad consists of two connecting rooms and people staying in one room have to walk through the other to reach the en suite facilities.

Hotel-wise, there is an option in East-the-Water (see p162) and also *Premier Inn Bideford* (☎ 0871 527 9564, 🖳 www.premierinn.com; 70D or T, all en suite; ✆; WI-FI), which is on Clovelly Rd, opposite Atlantic Village, a couple of miles from the centre of town. Room rates start from £47.50 but expect to pay double that in peak periods. Breakfast (daily 6.30/7-10.30am & 6-10pm; continental/cooked £6.99/8.99) is available at the Brewers Fayre next door. This hotel is also near Abbotsham and approximately 3½ miles from Westward Ho!

Where to eat and drink

There are numerous cafés in Bideford, although most involve a short diversion away from The Quay and the path. Having said that, *Quayside Café* (Mon-Sat 9am-5pm, Sun 10am-4pm) is where its name suggests and is a pleasant spot for a morning tea or for lunch. Just off the path and attached to the museum and tourist information is *Café du Parc* (☎ 01237-429317; Mon-Sat 10am-4pm, Aug to 5pm, Sun 11am-4pm), selling soups and sandwiches amongst other items; and as you leave Bideford you pass the floating *Café Onboard* (Map 36; ☎ 07403 194194; Easter-Nov daily 10am-5pm, rest of year Tue-Sun to 4pm; 🐾), where you have the option of a brew and a butty on a boat.

Off the path on Mill St are *Cleverdons* (☎ 01237-472179; Mon-Sat 9am-4pm; WI-FI; 🐾 at other customers' discretion) which provides cream teas (£3.20/4.25 one/two scones) and lunches; and *The Green Goose* (☎ 01237-459599, 🖳 www.thegreengoosecafe.co.uk; Mon-Sat 9am-4pm, Fri & Sat 6-8.45pm; WI-FI; 🐾), a family-run café/

bistro. The evening menu here (booking essential) may include a whole rack of pork ribs (£11.95) and vegetarian options are available.

Not far away on Cooper St, a Mediterranean-style menu is on offer at **Velvet & Vanilla Café Bar** (☎ 01237-420444; food served Mon-Sat 10am-4pm, Fri & Sat 7-11pm in summer but by booking only out of season); they are also licensed, so you can drink without eating.

For decent **pub food** the SWCP passes by **The Kings Arms** (see Where to stay). The food here (Mar-Dec daily 11am-3pm, Jan-Feb Sat & Sun 11am-3pm) is homemade, locally sourced, and includes their gigantic 'stacked' burger (£9.95) as well as a huge bowl of mussels cooked in a cider broth (£7.95).

On Queen St, **White Hart Inn** (☎ 01237-473203, 🖳 www.whitehartbideford .co.uk; daily 11am-11pm, Sun to 10.30pm, food daily noon-3pm; WI-FI; 🐾) serves local real ales. A Sunday roast costs £6 (bookings only); all the meats used for the roast dinners are locally sourced.

Thai cuisine to eat in or takeaway is available at **The Appledore Inn** (☎ 01237-476956, 🖳 www.appledoreinnbideford.co .uk; food daily noon-9.30pm; WI-FI; 🐾 bar area only), 18 Chingswell St: set menus for two/three people cost £31.50/47.40.

Complementing the spicy food are local real ales including Grenvilles from Jolly Boats and Doom Bar from Cornwall.

The Rose Salterne (☎ 01237-426110, 🖳 www.jdwetherspoon.com; food served daily 8am-11pm; WI-FI), on Bridgeland St, is Bideford's Wetherspoons' offering, serving their normal and reliably cheap fare.

Bideford has numerous **takeaways**. For Chinese food there is **Tintin Chinese** (☎ 01237-429633; Sun, Mon, Tue & Thur 5-10.30pm, Fri & Sat to 11pm), and for Indian, **Prince of India** (☎ 01237-424295; Wed-Mon 5-11pm); both are on Bridgeland St.

Indian food can also be found at **The Spice** (☎ 01237-471133, 🖳 www.thespice bideford.co.uk; daily noon-2.30pm & 5.30-11.30pm), on The Quay, where you can also eat in. They also sometimes serve Thai food here but you need to check this in advance.

For pizzas, kebabs and burgers try **Danny's** (☎ 01237-474555, 🖳 www.dan nysbideford.co.uk; Sun-Thur 4pm to midnight, Fri & Sat to 2am) or **Ali's Kebab House** (☎ 01237-474621; daily 4-11.30pm); both are on Bridgeland St.

For more standard waterside fare there's **Trawlers Fish & Chips** (Mon-Sat noon-9pm, Sun 4-9pm), at No 38, which has a restaurant as well as a takeaway.

From Bideford the path takes a slightly convoluted route to Appledore. It initially follows the river. Where the road turns away from the water as you leave town you'll find a **statue of Charles Kingsley** (Kingsley is said to have written much of *Westward Ho!* in Bideford). Beyond this, for about 275 metres, the tarmac path is known as **Landivisiau Walk** – named after the town's French twin. The park to your left is **Victoria Park**. Hidden amongst the flowerbeds and playing children are a couple of old cannons, thought to have been captured from the Spanish Armada in 1588. There is also a tree in the park planted in 1944 by American Lt Col F Holmes to commemorate the good relations the US army had with the people of Bideford whilst stationed there between 1940 and 1944.

As the ugly but necessary new **Torridge Bridge** looms ever closer, the path seems to lose its sense of direction somewhat. The bridge was built in 1987 due to the long-existing problems with the sheer weight of traffic crossing Bideford Long Bridge; indeed, in 1968 some of the bridge had even collapsed.

The path meanders between river and farmland and passes by the turning for **Northam** (see p168), emerging, after a short road-walk, at **Appledore**.

NORTHAM [Map 36, p163]

The village of Northam provides some B&B options as well as a campsite.

Follow Limers Lane up to the A386 Heywood Rd for *Bideford Beehives B&B* (☎ 01237-421139, 🖥 www.bidefordbee hivesbb.co.uk; 1D/1T private facilities if only one room booked; WI-FI; 🐾) charges £30-40pp (sgl occ £50). By the time you read this they should also have an en suite double.

The tariff at the plush *Durrant House Hotel* (☎ 01237-472361, 🖥 www.durrant househotel.com; 5S/50D/50T/8Tr, all en suite; ✆; WI-FI most rooms; 🐾) is £35-65pp (sgl occ £45-75; Jacuzzi room and suite £160-250 per night); both of these accept one-night bookings from walkers. The path passes alongside the walls of the friendly

Victorian *Yeoldon House Hotel* (☎ 01237-474400, 🖥 www.yeoldonhousehotel.co.uk; 7D/3D or T, all en suite; ✆; WI-FI; 🐾); they charge £62.50-72.50pp (sgl occ £125-135).

Marshford Camping and Caravan Site (Map 37; ☎ 01237-477160, 🖥 www .marshfordcamping.co.uk; hiker & tent £8, pitch fee for two people £12-15; WI-FI variable; 🐾; Apr-end Oct) is approximately a kilometre to the south of Appledore. They also run the organic food **shop** (🖥 www .marshford.co.uk; Mon & Sat 10am-6pm, Tue, Wed & Fri 9am-6pm, Thur 9am-7pm) at the same site. There is a short-cut to the site from the SWCP before you reach Appledore (see Map 37).

Stagecoach's No 21 **bus** service calls here (see pp48-50).

APPLEDORE

Quaint and quirky, Appledore is a lovely little place that, though its location between Bideford and Westward Ho! probably means you won't stay here (unless camping) for the night, really deserves as much of your time as you can give it.

At heart it's a typical old West Country fishing village, but one onto which a vivid coat of creativity and craftsmanship has been painted, its centre a jumble of tiny cottages connected by narrow cobbled alleyways in which one finds galleries and workshops, studios and showrooms.

There's an interesting museum at the top of town. **North Devon Maritime Museum** (☎ 01237-422064, 🖥 www.north devonmaritimemuseum.co.uk; Apr-Oct daily 10.30am-5pm; £3) contains exhibitions on Appledore's seafaring history, including displays on shipbuilding, fishing and shipwrecks. The house in which it is contained, by the way, was once owned by the father of Jerome K Jerome, author of *Three Men in a Boat*.

See p16 for details of festivals and events in Appledore.

Services

There are some **tourist information** leaflets in the **library** (☎ 01237-477442;

Tue 10am-1pm, Wed 2-5pm, Thur & Sat 10am-noon) on the front, but possibly a better source of information is 🖥 www .appledore.org. The library also has **internet access** (£1/30 mins) but wi-fi is free.

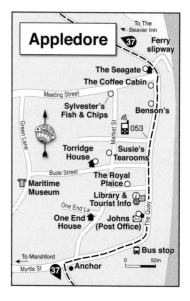

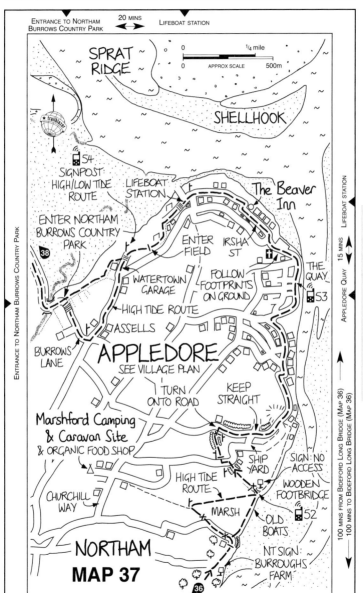

Close by is the **post office** (Mon-Fri 9am-5.30pm, Sat 9am-12.30pm) in Johns – twin to the branch of Johns in Instow (see p160) – similarly it is a **general store** (Mon-Sat 8am-7.30pm, Sun 8am-7pm; deli to 6.30pm/6pm) and café (see Where to eat). **Cashback** is available (minimum spend £3 or 50p charge).

In the summer months for those who want to return to Instow (or are heading in the other direction and are happy to miss Bideford) a **ferry** (see p160) runs daily, weather and tide permitting, from The Quay.

Transport
[See also pp48-50]   Appledore is on Stagecoach's 15 & 15A **bus** services to East-the-Water via Bideford as well as their Sunday No 21A service to Ilfracombe. Buses stop on The Quay.

Where to stay
Regarding **camping** see Northam (p168); for **B&B accommodation** there are three options. *One End House* (☎ 01237-473846, ✉ ejanemhayman@gmail.com; 1D en suite, 1S/1T share facilities if both rooms booked; ☛; WI-FI; ✗) is on the lane of the same name and is one of the charming little 18th-century terraced cottages that make up the centre of the village. Rates here are from £50pp.

Up the hill at 19 Bude St, *Torridge House* (☎ 01237-477127, ✉ www.torridgehouseappledore.com; 2D/1T, all en suite; ☛; WI-FI; ⓛ; ✗) is a lovely Georgian place, tastefully furnished and with its own chickens; it charges £42.50pp (sgl occ £60). They are happy to pick up drop off for guests who stay two nights.

Completing the lonely trilogy is *The Seagate* (☎ 01237-472589, ✉ theseagate.co.uk; 1S/8D/1T, all en suite; ☛; WI-FI; ✗), a 17th-century building at the end of The Quay, where the tariff is £49.50-62.50pp (sgl £60, sgl occ £80).

Where to eat and drink
Food-wise, during the day there are several options. Hiding away on narrow Market St, at No 25, *Susie's Tearooms* (☎ 01237-

474168, ✉ www.appledoretearooms.co.uk; daily 10am-4pm) sells homemade cakes, sandwiches, cream teas and light lunches (£3.50-10.90).

Along The Quay – and so remaining on the SWCP – there are two other fine places to eat. The first you come to is *Johns* (☎ 01237-425870, ✉ www.johnsofinstow.co.uk; café Mon-Sat 8am-5pm, Sun to 4.30pm but hours can vary so check their website), part of the chain of delicatessens, where there are breakfast, brunch, lunch, and 'deli platters' (Devon smoked fish platter £9.95); whilst further along The Quay is *The Coffee Cabin* (☎ 01237-475843; daily 9am-5pm): the staff are friendly, the sandwiches magnificent.

In the evening, *The Royal Plaice* (☎ 01237-478673; Mon-Sat noon-2pm & 5-9pm, summer Sun 5-9pm) is an unpretentious fish restaurant and takeaway, with a rival takeaway, *Sylvester's Fish & Chips* (☎ 01237-423548; school summer holidays daily noon-9pm, Mar-mid July & Sep-Oct Mon 5-9pm, Tue-Sat noon-2pm & 5-9pm, Nov-mid Mar Tue-Sat noon-2pm & 5-8pm), at the other end of Market St.

There's some smashing food at *The Seagate* (see Where to stay; food served daily noon-2.30pm & 6-9pm) including braised pork belly (£15) and tempura-battered lemon sole fillet (£15.75). For slightly finer dining, 'marine cuisine' – the menu depends upon the day's catch – can be found at *Benson's* (☎ 01237-424093, www.bensononthequay.com; summer Tue-Sat from 7pm, winter hours variable), 20 The Quay, which describes itself as an 'adult sanctuary' with no-one under 12 allowed. Reserving a table is essential.

At the northern end of town (see Map 37), at No 85 Irsha St, is *The Beaver Inn* (Map 37; ☎ 01237-474822, ✉ www.beaverinn.co.uk; food Mon-Fri noon-2.30pm & 6-9pm, Sat to 9pm, Sun to 8.30pm; WI-FI; ✗ bar area), a popular place with the locals: always a good measure of an establishment's pedigree. The food is standard pub grub with dishes such as Traditional Appledore fish pie (£9.95) and many other fine choices available; bar snacks are served in the afternoon during the week.

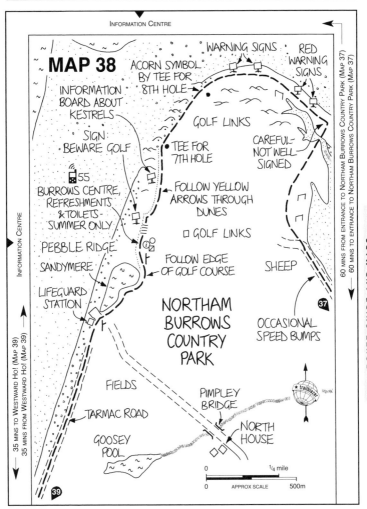

Leaving Appledore you have a choice between two routes – although as one of them is only accessible at low tide, nature may well make your decision for you. The two paths soon reunite at the entrance to **Northam Burrows Country Park**. Consisting of 253 hectares of coastal plain and sand dunes the Burrows are an SSSI, due partly to the pebble ridge that separates the Burrows from the sea. The golf course you skirt is The Royal North Devon – the oldest links course in England. Be warned: it's not unknown for half-blind amateur golfers to send a wayward shot too close! The main route passes via the **Burrows Centre** (Map 38; ☎ 01237-479708; Easter/May-Sep daily 11am-5pm, toilets open 9.30am-5pm), an information centre and small souvenir shop; and from there heads along a long, straight, wide path along the back of the pebble ridge. If you find walking with golfers not to your taste – tide permitting – you can cross the ridge and stroll along the beach all the way to **Westward Ho!**. If walking with a dog note that they have to be on a lead here.

WESTWARD HO!   [see map p174]

The town of Westward Ho! may come as something of a disappointment to those for whom the name (the only one in England with an exclamation mark and, as far as we know, the only one named after a novel as opposed to the other way round) conjures up images of seafarers, buccaneers and adventure on the high seas.

It's true that this once ramshackle but now much rejuvenated conglomeration of residential care homes and static caravan sites may not be challenging Clovelly or Appledore for any beauty awards in the near future. It also lacks the history of other towns around here, having been built as a holiday resort (the first hotel, The Westward Ho!, was built in 1864, when it was decided that there was money to be made in a tourist development overlooking the Pebbleridge described in the book).

But having said that, those who bother to spend some time in the town often find that they actually grow to really like it. The warmth and openness of the locals is undoubtedly one of the reasons why this is so – and the fact that they all seem so proud of the place is quite infectious after a while. So, while you may not take too many photos as you pass through (though the view over the town's massive beach from the top of town is quite magnificent), don't dismiss Westward Ho! out of hand, despite what other walkers may tell you. The SWCP is all about variety, and whatever else you may think of it, there's nowhere else quite like Westward Ho! on the entire path.

Services

The Co-op **supermarket** (daily 7am-10pm) boasts the usual lengthy opening hours and has a free **ATM**; its rival round

the corner, Nisa Local (also called Village Stores; Mon-Sat 8am-8pm, Sun 8am-4pm), also has an ATM (£1.50) as well as the **post office** (Mon-Fri 9.30am-5.30pm, Sat to 12.30pm).

Another free ATM can be found on the corner of Golf Links Rd and Nelson Rd next to the **pharmacy** (Mon-Fri 9am-5.30pm, Sat 9am-1pm). These are the last ATMs on the path before Bude, though the hotel at Hartland Quay does cashback.

Transport

[See also pp48-50] Westward Ho! is fairly well served by **buses**. Stagecoach's No 21 operates to Ilfracombe, Croyde and Braunton as well as other towns and villages in the area.

Some National Express **coach** services also call here (see box p46). The bus stop is on Nelson Rd.

For a **taxi** call A1 Taxis (☎ 01237-666060).

Where to stay

Campers need to either return (by bus) to Northam (see p168) or walk approximately 3½ miles further to Abbotsham (see p175 and Map 40).

There are four **B&B** options in Westward Ho!. The views from the premier rooms at the Victorian *Culloden House* (☎ 01237-479421, 🖥 www.culloden-house .co.uk; 6D/3T, all en suite; WI-FI reception area; Mar to end Oct), Fosketh Hill, are hard to surpass, looking out directly along the main swathe of sand. With its huge rooms the inside of this guest house is a joy too. The tariff is £37.50-42.50pp (sgl occ from £55). Note, you need to book direct and preferably via their website.

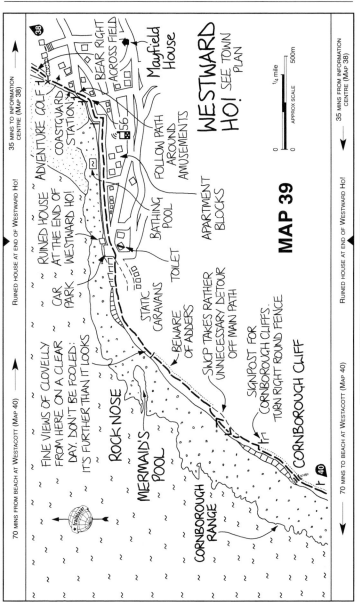

35 MINS TO INFORMATION CENTRE (MAP 38)

35 MINS FROM INFORMATION CENTRE (MAP 38)

70 MINS FROM BEACH AT WESTACOTT (MAP 40)

RUINED HOUSE AT END OF WESTWARD HO!

RUINED HOUSE AT END OF WESTWARD HO!

70 MINS TO BEACH AT WESTACOTT (MAP 40)

38

BEAR RIGHT ACROSS FIELD

Mayfield House

WESTWARD HO! SEE TOWN PLAN

COASTGUARD STATION

ADVENTURE GOLF

FOLLOW PATH AROUND AMUSEMENTS

APPROX SCALE

¼ mile

0   500m

MAP 39

RUINED HOUSE AT THE END OF WESTWARD HO!

CAR PARK

BATHING POOL

APARTMENT BLOCKS

TOILET

STATIC CARAVANS

BEWARE OF ADDERS

ROCK NOSE

SHORTCUT TAKES RATHER UNNECESSARY DETOUR OFF MAIN PATH

SIGNPOST FOR CORNBOROUGH CLIFFS. TURN RIGHT ROUND FENCE

CORNBOROUGH CLIFF

40

FINE VIEWS OF CLOVELLY FROM HERE ON A CLEAR DAY. DON'T BE FOOLED: IT'S FURTHER THAN IT LOOKS

MERMAID'S POOL

CORNBOROUGH RANGE

ROUTE GUIDE AND MAPS

Your second option is *Mayfield House*
(Map 39; ☎ 01237-477128, 🖳 www.may
fieldbandb.co.uk; 2D/2T, all en suite; WI-FI;
(L)) on Avon Lane. B&B here costs £35pp.

The pub, *The Village Inn* (☎ 01237-
477331, 🖳 www.villageinndevon.co.uk;
2D/1Qd, all en suite; ☛; WI-FI; (L); 🐾 bar
only) provides B&B and has fine rooms but
the warmth of the owners and the food (see
Where to eat) make this place truly special!
They charge £45pp (£55 sgl occ, three/four
people sharing £150).

Your fourth option is on Golf Links Rd.
The Waterfront Inn (☎ 01237-474737, 🖳
waterfrontinn.co.uk; 4D/1T/2Qd, all en
suite; ☛; WI-FI; (L); 🐾) is fairly character-
less but is comfy enough and good value
(£35-40pp, sgl occ rates on request; three to
four sharing £90-106). If requested they can
offer a packed lunch instead of breakfast.

Where to eat and drink

For a café/tea-room the following two –
both on Golf Links Rd – can be recommended. *The Rock Pool Café* (☎ 01237-
477763; daily 9am-5pm; WI-FI; 🐾 outside)
produces breakfasts (£4.25-6.25) as well as
sandwiches and jacket potatoes within the
same price range; it's a friendly and
bustling establishment and has outside seating on which to peruse the photos of your
day's walk.

For cream teas and lunches (£5-10),
Tea on the Green (☎ 01237-429406, 🖳
www.teaonthegreen.net; Wed-Sun 11am-
5pm; 🐾 outside) is hard to beat. There are
six different cream teas, three are savoury,
and the other three are sweet (including
gluten free; £4.60-7.50). The homemade
cake cabinet (again with gluten-free
options) is always kept full and there is the
option of High Tea (booking at least three
days in advance is essential; £12pp).

Pub food can be found in a number of
places; your first port of call, however,
should be at the top of the hill on Youngaton
Rd. At *The Village Inn* (see Where to stay)
food is served daily (noon-2pm & 6-9pm)
and can include special offers such as two
courses for £7.50 (during the day). A free
house, there are real ales and banter on offer
to complement the food. It's the type of
place you'll be reluctant to leave!

Back down at the bottom of Golf Links
Rd, *The Waterfront Inn* (see Where to
stay; food served daily noon-9pm) has a
menu that may include jacket spuds from
£7 and seabream with stir-fry vegetables
and noodles for £11.25.

There's a Chinese restaurant with a
takeaway section: *Hong Kong Diner* (☎
01237-477661; summer daily 5-10.30pm,
winter Tue-Sun and they may close earlier),
on Nelson Rd; whilst opposite *Venners*

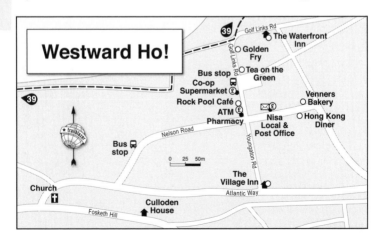

Bakery (☎ 01237-474378; Mon-Sat 8.30am-5pm, school summer hols Sun 10am-4pm) serves sarnis and baguettes. On Golf Links Rd, *Golden Fry* (☎ 01237-470815; summer Mon-Sat 11.45am-10pm, Sun noon-7pm, winter Mon-Sat 11.45am-2pm & 5-9pm) is a decent chippy with some covered seating outside.

WESTWARD HO! TO CLOVELLY [MAPS 39-43]

This **11-mile (17.7km; 4hrs 35 mins)** section is very much a tale of two terrains. Leaving Westward Ho!, the path assumes a southerly direction along exposed and open cliffs, lacerated, once again, by several deep and fairly testing combes. On reaching Peppercombe, however, the path not only takes a more westerly direction but also changes in nature from clifftop clamber to woodland walk. Aside from a visit to the small huddle of houses that is Buck's Mills, as well as the occasional field, you remain under the forest canopy for pretty much the rest of the stage as the trail leads you towards and then onto Hobby Drive – a wide and gentle tree-shaded track coaxing you to lovely Clovelly.

Note that (except for Buck's Mills, see p179) there is nowhere to get any refreshments on the way nor is there anywhere to stay on the path (though there are several places a short walk inland). As such, do remember to bring supplies and plan your day properly.

The route
Though the first half of this walk is undoubtedly more testing than the second, it begins in a fairly gentle manner as you escape from Westward Ho! along the path of a disused railway that used to run inland to Bideford. Soon the trail leaves the tarmac to head towards **Abbotsham Cliff** and then **Green Cliff**, both owned by the National Trust. Pause at the top of either and you should, weather permitting, make out Saunton Sands and even Baggy Point, which you probably walked around about four days ago! Look south, on the other hand, and the keen-eyed may just be able to make out Clovelly in the cliffs ahead.

Campers have the option here of a short diversion inland (approximately half a mile; 10-15 mins) to **Abbotsham** for either *Greencliff Farm* (☎ 01237-424674, 💻 www.greencliff-farm.co.uk; 🐾; £14 per pitch, £7 for a hiker & tent; Easter-Oct), or *Westacott Farm* (☎ 01237-472351, 💻 www.westacottfarm.co.uk; WI-FI; 🐾; hiker £5pp; open year-round). Both have toilets and showers and at the latter there is a kitchen, a laundry, a **shop** (Easter-end Oct) which sells basic provisions, and you can sit outside the farmhouse and connect to the owner's wi-fi if needed.

The nearest option to the campsites for **food** is a 25-minute stroll away but, be reassured, the food at *The Thatched Inn* (☎ 01237-471321, 💻 www.the thatchedinn.com; food served daily 11am-2.30pm & 5-9pm; WI-FI temperamental; 🐾 in the bar area) is certainly worth the trek! There's a large and varied menu which includes Penang fish curry (£11.95) and 'The Blackened Pig' (slow-roasted pork belly stuffed with sausage meat and black pudding; £14.95). It's the kind of place where you could easily forget that you're camping and not notice it getting dark … and then end up leaving far too late! See Map 40 (p176) for directions from the SWCP. *(cont'd on p179)*

ROUTE GUIDE AND MAPS

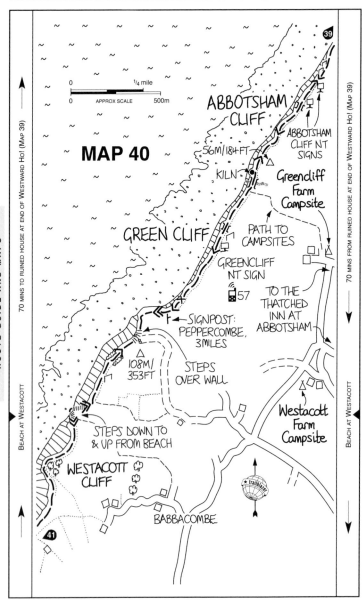

70 MINS TO RUINED HOUSE AT END OF WESTWARD HO! (MAP 39)

70 MINS FROM RUINED HOUSE AT END OF WESTWARD HO! (MAP 39)

ROUTE GUIDE AND MAPS

BEACH AT WESTACOTT

BEACH AT WESTACOTT

MAP 40

0   ¼ mile
0   APPROX SCALE   500m

39

ABBOTSHAM CLIFF

ABBOTSHAM CLIFF NT SIGNS

56M/184FT

KILN

Greencliff Farm Campsite

GREEN CLIFF

PATH TO CAMPSITES

GREENCLIFF NT SIGN

57

TO THE THATCHED INN AT ABBOTSHAM

SIGNPOST: PEPPERCOMBE, 3 MILES

108M/353FT

STEPS OVER WALL

STEPS DOWN TO & UP FROM BEACH

Westacott Farm Campsite

WESTACOTT CLIFF

★ trailblazer

BABBACOMBE

41

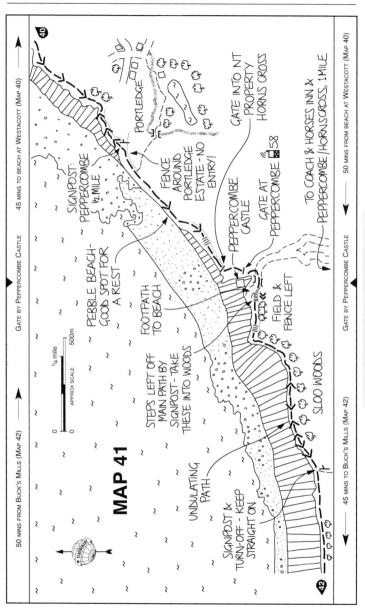

ROUTE GUIDE AND MAPS

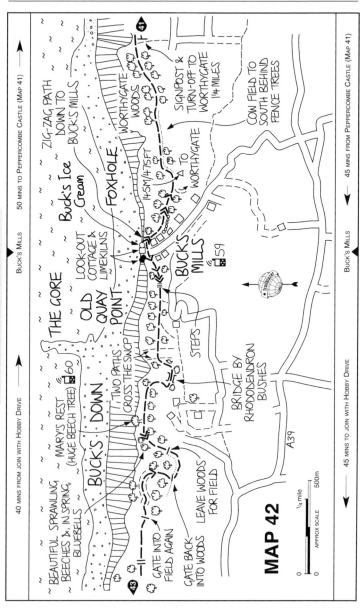

MAP 42

40 MINS FROM JOIN WITH HOBBY DRIVE →

BUCK'S MILLS

50 MINS TO PEPPERCOMBE CASTLE (MAP 41) →

45 MINS FROM PEPPERCOMBE CASTLE (MAP 41) →

BUCK'S MILLS

← 45 MINS TO JOIN WITH HOBBY DRIVE

47

BEAUTIFUL SPRAWLING BEECHES &, IN SPRING, BLUEBELLS

MARY'S REST (HUGE BEECH TREE) 🏠60

ZIG-ZAG PATH DOWN TO BUCK'S MILLS

WORTHYGATE WOODS

SIGNPOST & TURN-OFF TO WORTHYGATE ¼ MILES

COW FIELD TO SOUTH BEHIND FENCE TREES

THE GORE

FOXHOLE

Buck's Ice Cream

14-SM/475FT

↑ TO WORTHYGATE

OLD QUAY POINT

LOOK-OUT COTTAGE & LIMEKILNS

BUCK'S MILLS

59

BUCK'S DOWN

↑ TWO PATHS CROSS THE SWCP

STEPS

BRIDGE BY RHODODENDRON BUSHES

A39

LEAVE WOODS FOR FIELD

GATE INTO FIELD AGAIN

GATE BACK INTO WOODS

43

¼ mile

500m

APPROX SCALE

0

0

★trailblazer

(cont'd from p175) For those not camping there's plenty of walking still to be done. The gradients increase as you drop to the beach, briefly, at **Westacott**, and again by the private **Portledge Estate**, before you reach Peppercombe, another National Trust property. **Peppercombe Castle**, labelled on OS maps, is actually an Iron-Age fort though little remains today. Inland along the valley from here, about three-quarters of a mile from the path, is *Coach & Horses Inn* (off Map 41; ☎ 01237-451214, 🖳 www.thebestpubindevon.co.uk; 1D/1T/1Tr, all en suite; WI-FI; Ⓛ), which charges £32.50-37.50pp (£55-70 sgl occ, three sharing room rate plus £15) for B&B and serves **food** (daily noon-2pm & 6-9pm, winter closed Wed lunch).

The path now meanders along the slopes through **Sloo** and **Worthygate woods** (the border between the two being unmarked) before dropping down to the hamlet of **Buck's Mills**. Unless you require a refreshment from *Buck's Ice Cream* (Mar-Oct daily 10am-5.30pm; hot drinks, snacks … ice-cream) there's little to detain you here, though there's a couple of old **limekilns** down at the bottom of the road by the beach and on the way is **Look-out Cottage**, a tiny studio used from the 1920s to the 1970s by artists Mary Stella Edwards and Judith Ackland, who renamed it The Cabin and whose work now hangs in Burton Art Gallery (see p164) at Bideford. It has barely been touched in the 40 years since the artists left it.

The woods on the other side of the hamlet are, if anything, even more beautiful than those you've just left, with some huge beech trees and gigantic rhododendron bushes shading the way. Emerging briefly into meadows above the trees, the path plunges into the shade again to reach **Hobby Drive**, a 19th-century 'bridleway' that provides an easy and picturesque stroll into Clovelly, leisurely snaking its way along the cliffside, with benches placed here and there to the right of the trail to encourage wayfarers to tarry a while and appreciate the views down onto the rooftops of Clovelly. Hard to believe in such a tranquil place that, according to legend, in a giant cave below the trail lived a certain John Gregg and his family, who made their living robbing, murdering and eating passers-by around 250 years ago. These days, the most dangerous creature you're likely to encounter is the occasional pheasant strutting along the path or scampering through the undergrowth. Just over an hour after joining the Drive you reach its end and arrive at one of the more unique and individual settlements on the entire South-West Coast Path …

CLOVELLY & HIGHER CLOVELLY
[MAP 43, p181]

Clovelly is one of the loveliest villages on the entire SWCP. Four-hundred feet of cobbled street rolling down a narrow cleft in the coastline of North Devon, lined on either side by wonderfully preserved cottages which, viewed from the sea, appear to have been stacked on each other's shoulders. It really is the most photogenic of places.

The gradient of the main street – which bears the names Up-a-Long and Down-a-Long – is enough to prevent traffic from driving down it (though there is a road linking the harbour with the top of the village which is used by Land Rovers to shuttle the elderly and the lazy to the harbour). Instead, goods are brought in by sled from the top of the village, while rubbish is taken to the bottom where it is removed by boat.

In between are some gorgeous little cottages, each full of character and entirely individual. Much of the credit for the place's wonderful state of preservation is down to the fact that Clovelly is actually privately owned, the Hamlyn family acquiring the fishing village as part of their purchase of the entire Clovelly Estate in 1738. One of the family, Christine Hamlyn, spent years restoring many of the cottages on the main street; her initials and a date can be seen carved into many of the structures.

For such a small village (the estimated population for the entire ward of Clovelly Bay is about 1600), Clovelly has a surprising number of claims to fame: the village was a boyhood home of Charles Kingsley, who returned here years later to write some of his best work, including *The Water Babies*; Charles Dickens also wrote about it (though he calls it, appropriately enough, 'Steepways'); Rex Whistler painted it, as did JMW Turner; and Wedgewood used cameos of the village on their china service. It is also mentioned in the Domesday Book.

The opening of the huge **visitor centre** above the village – and the subsequent charging of an **entrance fee** (£7.25) to visit the village – are controversies over which coast-path walkers can remain in blissful ignorance, for the entrance into Clovelly along The Hobby bypasses the entrance gates altogether, thus allowing walkers (at least at the time of research) to enter the village without paying. There are two small museums (daily approx 9am-5pm; entry charge inc in village fee): **Kingsley Museum** celebrates the life and work of the author, but perhaps more interesting is the **Fisherman's Cottage**, across the courtyard, where the cob-and-stone dwelling has been preserved in a 1930s' style with a sail loft

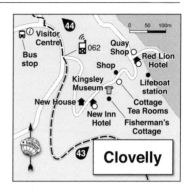

Clovelly

and even a covered well. At the foot of the village, beyond the 19th-century **Lifeboat Station**, is a **waterfall**, behind which you'll find a cave where the Arthurian magician Merlin was supposedly born.

Services

The **Visitor Centre** (☎ 01237-431781, 🖳 www.clovelly.co.uk; daily school summer holidays 9am-6.30pm, Easter to mid July & Sep to end Oct 9.30am-5.30pm Nov to Easter 10am-4pm) is very much concerned with Clovelly and information about other parts of Devon is slight. In the village itself you'll find a fairly poorly stocked **shop** (daily 9.30am-5 or 6pm but one reader told us it was closed at 4pm on a Friday).

Transport

[See also pp48-50] Stagecoach's No 319 **bus** leaves from the visitor centre and connects Clovelly with Barnstaple and Hartland.

Where to stay, eat and drink

Regarding **accommodation**, *Red Lion Hotel* (☎ 01237-431237, 🖳 www.stayatclo

---

❏ **'Steepways'**
The village was built sheer up the face of a steep and lofty cliff. There was no road in it, there was no wheeled vehicle in it, there was no level yard in it. From the sea-beach to the cliff-top two irregular rows of white houses, placed opposite to one another, and twisting here and there, and there and here, rose, like the sides of a long succession of stages of crooked ladders, and you climbed up the village or you climbed down the village by the staves between, some six feet wide or so, and made of sharp irregular stones. **Charles Dickens**, *Message from The Sea*

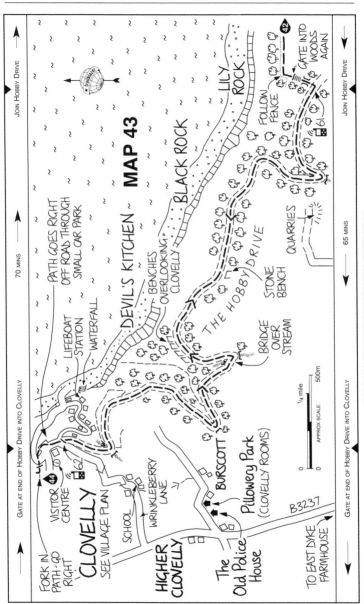

MAP 43

JOIN HOBBY DRIVE

JOIN HOBBY DRIVE

PATH GOES RIGHT OFF ROAD THROUGH SMALL CAR PARK

LIFEBOAT STATION

WATERFALL

DEVIL'S KITCHEN

BENCHES OVERLOOKING CLOVELLY

BLACK ROCK

LILY ROCK

42

GATE INTO WOODS AGAIN

FOLLOW FENCE

61

QUARRIES

STONE BENCH

THE HOBBY DRIVE

BRIDGE OVER STREAM

65 MINS

70 MINS

FORK IN PATH - GO RIGHT

CLOVELLY SEE VILLAGE PLAN

VISITOR CENTRE 44 62

SCHOOL

WRINKLEBERRY LANE

HIGHER CLOVELLY

The Old Police House

BURSCOTT

PILLOWERY PARK (CLOVELLY ROOMS)

B3237

TO EAST DYKE FARMHOUSE

GATE AT END OF HOBBY DRIVE INTO CLOVELLY

GATE AT END OF HOBBY DRIVE INTO CLOVELLY

1/4 mile

0   500m

APPROX SCALE

velly.co.uk/the-red-lion; 16D/2D or T, all
en suite; ☛; WI-FI; (L); ☺) is a bit of a landmark in the village and is situated right by
the harbour, and it's a lovely old place too.
B&B costs £39-47.50pp (sgl occ £70-90).
Some rooms can also sleep up two children.

Bookending Clovelly at the top end of
the village and owned by the same company, *New Inn Hotel* (☎ 01237-431303, 💻
www.stayatclovelly.co.uk/new-inn; 1S/6D/
1Tr, all en suite; ☛; WI-FI; (L); ☺) is perhaps the most elegant place in Clovelly; the
smart rooms have a sea view or, in one
case, a balcony overlooking part of the
street. B&B costs £30-60pp, sgl/sgl occ
£60-80). New Inn also own *New House*
(*Hamlyn's B&B*); contact details as above)
across the road, with slightly inferior rooms
(5T/6D/1Qd, all en suite rest shared facilities; ☛; WI-FI; (L); ☺) which charges from
£35pp (from £41pp for en suite room; sgl
occ £50-70). Patrons are allowed to use all
the facilities available over the road.

When it comes to **food**, there are a few
choices in the village – *Cottage Tearooms*
are open during the day (Easter-Oct) and
boast a lovely outside eating area. The two
hotels also serve food: *Red Lion Hotel* (see
p180; daily noon-2.30pm & 6.30-8.30pm,
restaurant 7-8.30pm) unsurprisingly boasts
some fine fresh dishes, available both in the
bar and its restaurant area. Two/three/four
courses, including such treats as Clovelly
lobster for mains and local crab mousse to
start are £26/30/35. The menu at *New Inn
Hotel* (see above; daily noon-2.30pm &
6.30-8.30pm, winter hours variable)
includes burgers (from £7.25) and scampi
& chips (£8.50).

A simple pasty or ice-cream can be
found by the harbour at *Quay Shop* (Easter-
Oct daily 10am-5pm weather/business
dependent).

Higher Clovelly

There are more options further up the hill,
beginning about 1km from the top of the
main village; sometimes these B&Bs offer
a pick-up/drop-off service from/to the path.
If no lift is available, to reach them from the
end of Hobby Drive take the path signposted towards Wrinkleberry. Once you reach
this tiny hamlet, walk past the school and on
your left is another footpath clearly signed
through the fields that takes you to the foot
of Burscott on the edge of the hamlet.

East Dyke Farmhouse (☎ 01237-
431216, 💻 www.bedbreakfastclovelly.co
.uk; 1D/1Tr both en suite, 1T private bathroom; ☛; WI-FI; (L); ☺) is a lovely friendly place, a grand 19th-century building with
exposed beams and flagstone floors. B&B
costs £32.50-37.50pp (£45-55 sgl occ). You
are free to explore Clovelly Dykes, a 200-
year-old Iron Age hill fort, lying just
beyond their back garden. They even have
bedding and bowls for dogs!

There are two smaller places in
Burscott. The first you reach from the
coast path is tidy, efficient, walker-friendly,
Clovelly Rooms (☎ 01237-431668, 💻
www.clovellyrooms.co.uk; 1D en suite/2T
with private facilities; WI-FI; (L)) at
Pillowery Park. There are drying facilities
for sodden walkers and the proprietors are
happy to offer use of their washing machine
if required; indeed, they've been taking
great care of coastal path pilgrims here for
over 16 years. They charge £30-35pp (sgl
occ £40-70). Two-night stays are preferred.

Around 10 metres further on is *The
Old Police House* (☎ 01237-431256, 💻
www.clovellybandb.co.uk; 1D private
bathroom/1T en suite; ☛; WI-FI; (L); ☺).
Their rates are £30pp (sgl occ £40). If
booked in advance the owner can cook an
evening meal.

CLOVELLY TO HARTLAND QUAY   [MAPS 43-48]

The final two stages of this walk are renowned for being amongst the wildest,
most remote and most spectacular on the entire SWCP. The paucity of amenities
and accommodation on the trail also mean that walkers really need to plan their
walk on this stretch thoroughly. True, when it comes to **accommodation** there
are several B&Bs, a (YHA) hostel and a campsite, but these are sometimes a fair

hike away and should definitely be booked in advance. Similarly, for **food** you need to plan well: the first stage is fairly straightforward, with a small, albeit seasonal, tearoom right on the trail and a fabulous hotel with food and ale at the end. But the second stage has nothing actually on the path save for an outdoor (seasonal) café which is just a mile or two before Bude. Otherwise, the only options are a great tearoom and pub at Morwenstow that are both about a third of a mile (500 metres) off the trail; which, on a day that's already 16 miles long, is quite a demanding diversion!

One way round this, of course, is to ask your accommodation to make a packed lunch for you; or, of course, you could make it yourself – though as the poorly stocked shop in Clovelly is the only place selling provisions on these last two stages, the chances are you won't be eating that well.

However, assuming you *have* planned properly, there is much to look forward to on both these stages. The reputation of the second stage for being the toughest and amongst the most awe-inspiring on the entire path is well known but there's plenty to appreciate on this first stage to Hartland Quay too.

The first part of this **10½-mile (16.9km; 5hrs 5mins)** walk is gentle enough, beginning with a stroll through the woods of Gallantry Bower and Snaxland before you indulge in a meadowside meander along the clifftops of Brownsham and Beckland. So far, so familiar. But when you round Hartland Point, the path takes an abrupt turn to the south ... and things get a little more dramatic. Wild seas crash against rocks carved by time and tide into alcoves and archways, canyons and caves, tunnels and towers, where grey seals slumber and seagulls soar. It's a land of rock and reef, storm and shipwreck, lonely, baleful shorelines and looming, brooding skies; while, above it all, a 19th-century lighthouse and the enigmatic ruins of a much older tower sit in stoical silence – untouched and untroubled by the chaos below.

The route

Your first task on this stage is to avoid the scary-looking (but presumably benign) steers of the Clovelly Court estate as you skip through fields and forest, passing on your way two curious man-made structures tucked away among the trees. The first, just 10 minutes from Clovelly itself, is **The Cabin**, built in the 19th century by Sir James Hamlyn Williams (a former owner of Clovelly Estate) and now used, bizarrely, as a venue for weddings. The second, reached via a tunnel of rhododendrons, is an ornate wooden pagoda-style structure known as **Angel's Wings**, which was carved by a former butler of the estate.

More woodland wandering ensues as you make your way to **Mouthmill Beach**, once the haunt of smugglers but now the home to a ruined limekiln and, more famously, **Blackchurch Rock** with its two sea-sculpted 'windows'.

Climbing out of the valley you now follow an endless series of fields towards Hartland Point, the only features of note being **Windbury Castle**, an Iron Age fort that has largely disappeared due to erosion, though the keen-eyed expert can still make out parts of the southern ramparts amongst the undergrowth; and, just a short walk further on, a **memorial to a Wellington bomber** that crashed at the foot of Beckland Cliff in 1942. *(cont'd on p188)*

ROUTE GUIDE AND MAPS

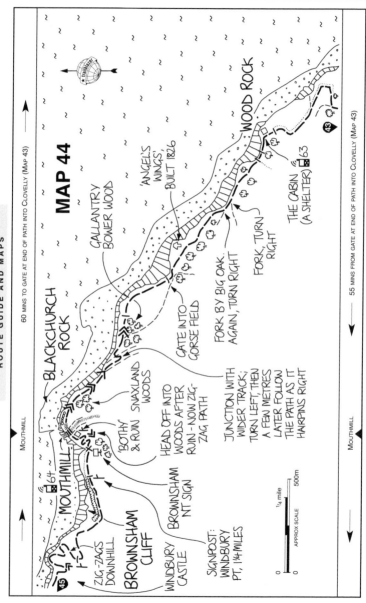

MAP 44

60 MINS TO GATE AT END OF PATH INTO CLOVELLY (MAP 43)

55 MINS FROM GATE AT END OF PATH INTO CLOVELLY (MAP 43)

MOUTHMILL

MOUTHMILL

WOOD ROCK

'ANGEL'S WINGS', BUILT 1826

GALLANTRY BOWER WOODS

THE CABIN (A SHELTER)

FORK, TURN RIGHT

FORK BY BIG OAK, AGAIN, TURN RIGHT

GATE INTO GORSE FIELD

BLACKCHURCH ROCK

SNAXLAND WOODS

'BOTHY' & RUIN

HEAD OFF INTO WOODS AFTER RUIN - NOW ZIG-ZAG PATH

JUNCTION WITH WIDER TRACK; TURN LEFT, THEN A FEW METRES LATER FOLLOW THE PATH AS IT HAIRPINS RIGHT

BROWNSHAM NT SIGN

MOUTHMILL

BROWNSHAM CLIFF

ZIG-ZAGS DOWNHILL

WINDBURY CASTLE

SIGNPOST: WINDBURY PT, 1¼ MILES

¼ mile
500m
APPROX SCALE
0
0

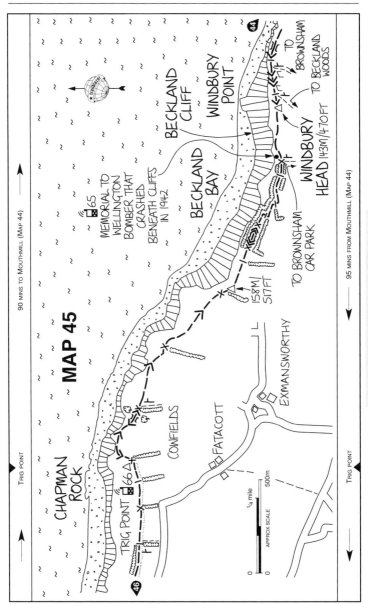

MAP 45

90 MINS TO MOUTHMILL (MAP 44)

CHAPMAN ROCK

TRIG POINT

66

CORNFIELDS

FATACOTT

EXMANSWORTHY

158M 517FT

MEMORIAL TO WELLINGTON BOMBER THAT CRASHED BENEATH CLIFFS IN 1942

65

BECKLAND BAY

BECKLAND CLIFF

WINDBURY POINT

44

TO BROWNSHAM

TO BECKLAND WOODS

WINDBURY HEAD 143M 470FT

TO BROWNSHAM CAR PARK

95 MINS FROM MOUTHMILL (MAP 44)

46

TRIG POINT

TRIG POINT

¼ mile

500m

APPROX SCALE

0

0

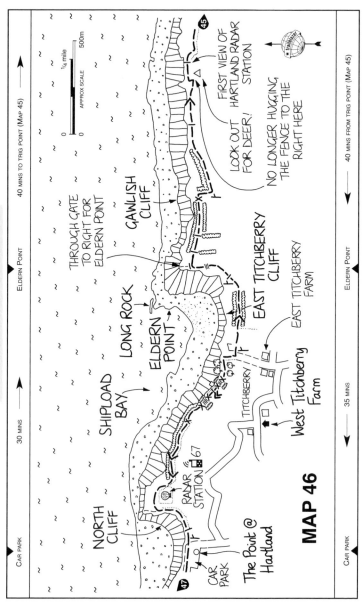

CAR PARK ▶   30 MINS ──▶   ◀── 40 MINS TO TRIG POINT (MAP 45)

▶ ELDERN POINT

¼ mile
500m
APPROX SCALE
0   0

45

FIRST VIEW OF
HARTLAND RADAR
STATION

LOOK OUT
FOR DEER!

NO LONGER HUGGING
THE FENCE TO THE
RIGHT HERE

THROUGH GATE
TO RIGHT FOR
ELDERN POINT

GAWLISH
CLIFF

LONG ROCK

ELDERN
POINT

EAST TITCHBERRY
CLIFF

EAST TITCHBERRY
FARM

SHIPLOAD
BAY

NORTH
CLIFF

RADAR
STATION ⌂ 67

TITCHBERRY

West Titchberry
Farm

The Point @ Hartland

CAR
PARK

47

MAP 46

CAR PARK ▶   ◀── 35 MINS ──▶ ◀── ELDERN POINT   ◀── 40 MINS FROM TRIG POINT (MAP 45)

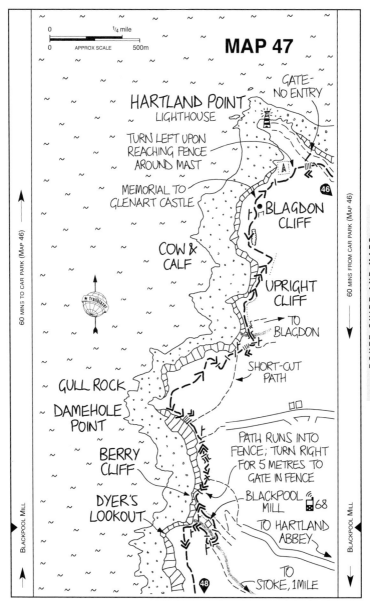

MAP 47

GATE-
NO ENTRY

HARTLAND POINT
LIGHTHOUSE

TURN LEFT UPON
REACHING FENCE
AROUND MAST

MEMORIAL TO
GLENART CASTLE

COW &
CALF

BLAGDON
CLIFF

UPRIGHT
CLIFF

TO
BLAGDON

SHORT-CUT
PATH

GULL ROCK

DAMEHOLE
POINT

BERRY
CLIFF

PATH RUNS INTO
FENCE; TURN RIGHT
FOR 5 METRES TO
GATE IN FENCE

DYER'S
LOOKOUT

BLACKPOOL
MILL 68

TO HARTLAND
ABBEY

TO
STOKE, 1 MILE

0   ¼ mile
0   APPROX SCALE   500m

trailblazer

46

48

A

60 MINS TO CAR PARK (MAP 46)

60 MINS FROM CAR PARK (MAP 46)

BLACKPOOL MILL

BLACKPOOL MILL

ROUTE GUIDE AND MAPS

(cont'd from p183) Eventually, around four hours after setting off, you pass the turn-off to *West Titchberry Farm* (Map 46; ☎ 01237-441287, 🖳 westtitcher ryfarm.co.uk; 1Qd en suite, 1D/1T private facilities if only one room booked; ☞; WI-FI; Ⓛ), a typical Devon longhouse and B&B that charges £30-35pp (sgl occ £35-37, three/four sharing £90/120), and offers evening meals (£13/15 two/three courses if requested in advance) as well as a pick-up/drop-off facility (subject to a small charge) for walkers. (Its neighbour, by the way, **East Titchberry Farm**, is a 17th-century National Trust property with its own malt-house that's unfortunately closed to the public.)

Shortly afterwards – though it's been visible a long way beforehand – is the giant white golf-ball-on-a-tee that is the **radar station**. At its foot is *The Point @ Hartland* (☎ 07977-010463, 🖳 www.thepointhartland.co.uk; Easter-Oct daily 10am-5pm); a rest stop is hard to resist at this stage, though note that they do not have a toilet. Lunches, hot drinks and cream teas are available, as are OS maps, sun-cream and Compeeds (£1.50) should you have developed any blisters.

From here, it's but a short skip to **Hartland Point** (Map 47), where the Bristol Channel meets the Atlantic and the SWCP begins to head in a more southerly direction after so long heading west. The point is marked by the **lighthouse**, built in 1874 and said to be visible up to 25 miles away.

Though you're on the homeward stretch, there's still plenty to be done on this leg before you can finally call it a day. Passing a **memorial** to *Glenart Castle* (a hospital ship that was torpedoed by a German U-boat in 1918 with the loss of 153 men and women out of a total of 186 on board), the path takes you on several steep descents, the second leading towards **Gull Rock**, the third towards the isolated valley of **Blackpool Mill**. Heading up and out of here, the path finally flattens as it crosses **The Warren**, decorated by the ruins of a **tower** – once a folly, so it is believed, but which now makes a nice frame for your photo of the village church in the distance. From here, the way is straightforward to **Hartland Quay**, turning right down the hill by Rocket House.

HARTLAND QUAY, STOKE & HARTLAND

Hartland Quay   [Map 48]

There's little to Hartland Quay other than the hotel. This hotel, converted from what were once stables and customs houses, hints at the importance of this spot as a major port in Tudor times. A storm in 1887 destroyed the quay, and these days there's only a small modern slipway. Nevertheless, the past can still be glimpsed in the hotel's very own museum, with photos and mementoes of various shipwrecks that have occurred on this stretch of shoreline over four centuries. (They've plenty of raw material to choose from, for it's said that

this coastline has approximately ten ship-wrecks per mile!)

As for the accommodation, *Hartland Quay Hotel* (☎ 01237-441218, 🖳 hartland quayhotel.co.uk;   1S/1T/5D/3Tr/2Qd/ annexe sleeps up to 6; all en suite; ☞; WI-FI; 🐾 stay in annexe only) offers rooms (from £50pp, sgl/sgl occ from £65, three-six sharing £50pp) that are the perfect place to nurse sore feet while gazing out over the crashing surf.

The hotel's bar, *The Wreckers' Retreat* (food served daily noon-2.30pm & 6-9pm plus 3-5.30pm at weekends and in summer) is also decorated with photos and souvenirs

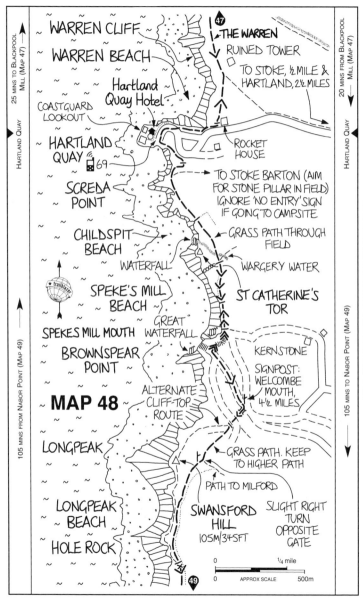

WARREN CLIFF

WARREN BEACH

Hartland Quay Hotel

COASTGUARD LOOKOUT

HARTLAND QUAY 📶 69

SCREDA POINT

CHILDSPIT BEACH

WATERFALL

SPEKE'S MILL BEACH

SPEKES MILL MOUTH

BROWNSPEAR POINT

MAP 48

GREAT WATERFALL

ALTERNATE CLIFF-TOP ROUTE

LONGPEAK

LONGPEAK BEACH

HOLE ROCK

THE WARREN

RUINED TOWER

TO STOKE, ½ MILE & HARTLAND, 2½ MILES

ROCKET HOUSE

TO STOKE BARTON (AIM FOR STONE PILLAR IN FIELD) IGNORE 'NO ENTRY' SIGN IF GOING TO CAMPSITE

GRASS PATH THROUGH FIELD

WARGERY WATER

ST CATHERINE'S TOR

KERNSTONE

SIGNPOST: WELCOMBE MOUTH, 4½ MILES

GRASS PATH. KEEP TO HIGHER PATH

PATH TO MILFORD

SWANSFORD HILL 105M/345FT

SLIGHT RIGHT TURN OPPOSITE GATE

25 MINS TO BLACKPOOL MILL (MAP 47)

HARTLAND QUAY

105 MINS FROM NABOR POINT (MAP 49)

20 MINS FROM BLACKPOOL MILL (MAP 47)

HARTLAND QUAY

105 MINS TO NABOR POINT (MAP 49)

ROUTE GUIDE AND MAPS

trailblazer

0   ¼ mile
0   APPROX SCALE   500m

of local shipwrecks. The bar serves local ales (including many from St Austell brewery) and does a nice line in healthy portions of resuscitating food.

Stoke

If you can't get a room at Hartland Quay Hotel, you'll have to head half a mile inland to this tiny settlement, centred around the 14th-century **Church of St Nectan**, known and famed for its soaring tower, said to be the highest in Devon and for centuries a vital landmark to sailors at sea.

Nearby is an excellent **campsite**. *Stoke Barton Farm* (☎ 01237-441238, 💻 www.westcountry-camping.co.uk; £7.50-9pp; WI-FI shop only; 🐾; end Mar to end Oct) is a great place with hot showers and owners who are helpful and they have a small camp **shop** (8.30-10.30am) with the main essentials and may even be able to sell you a tin of dog food if you're desperate. Booking is recommended and is essential for peak periods. They even have their own short-cut from the path (see Map 48). **B&B** (1D en suite; WI-FI; ©; £32.50-35pp, sgl occ £45) is available at the farm as is the opportunity to stay in a 'pixie hut' (2D inc bedding; £27.50pp, sgl occ £45, £5 less without bedding) – essentially a tiny log cabin – although you'll need to bring a torch and your own cooking equipment and be prepared to stay for two nights.

There are two other **B&Bs** in Stoke. *One Coastguard Cottages* (☎ 01237-441011, 💻 www.coastguardcottagestoke .com; 1D, en suite; 🖥; WI-FI; ©; 🐾) is a friendly and welcoming B&B that, thanks to its fine reputation and relative proximity to the path, is more than used to seeing walkers. A good service they provide too, with comfortable rooms costing £35pp (sgl occ £50), as well as evening meals (subject to prior arrangement). They provide luggage transfer (for a fee) and lifts to/from the path or other villages. They also provide their grid reference: SS2340324784.

Clouds (☎ 01237-440236, 💻 www .cloudsatstoke.com; 2D or T, both en suite; 🖥; WI-FI; ©), a 'luxury' B&B, has a suite in the house and a studio (detached from the house) with a kitchenette and its own

wood-burner. They charge £37.50-40pp (sgl occ £65-70); minimum two-night stay on Friday & Saturday nights. Breakfast (which includes kippers as an option) can be eaten on the patio.

Hartland

Though around 2½ miles (3.75km) from the path, coastal walkers may find themselves in Hartland as it's the nearest village to this section of the path with shops and facilities, as well as a few places providing B&B, some of which offer packed lunches and a pick-up/drop-off service if arranged in advance.

The **post office** (Mon-Fri 9am-5.30pm & Sat 9am-12.30pm) is in the well-stocked general **shop** Christmas Stores (Mon-Sat 8am-9pm, Sun 8am-1pm & 4.30-7.30pm). You can withdraw cash from the post office if it is open and you have a suitable account (see p26); if not there is an **ATM** that charges £1.85. Nearby, *The Pop-in* (☎ 01237-441488; daily 8am-7.30pm) sells hot drinks, hot pasties and sandwiches to take away and offers **cashback** (subject to a minimum spend).

Hartland is the only place on the peninsula connected by a **bus service**. Stagecoach's 319 runs via Bideford and Clovelly to Barnstaple, connecting with their 219 service between Hartland & Bude; see pp48-50.

B&B is available at *Two Harton Manor* (☎ 01237-441670, 💻 www.twoharton manor.co.uk; 1S/1T shared facilities/1D en suite; 🖥; WI-FI; 🐾), next to The Hart Inn (see opposite), which is actually the west wing of a 400-year-old manor house. In addition to B&B (£36-50pp) they offer woodblock-printing lessons.

Alternatively try *Home from Home B&B* (☎ 01237-441652, 💻 john.sheppard 12@gmail.com; 2D, both en suite; 🖥; WI-FI; ©; 🐾), which charges £32.50pp (sgl occ £65). The breakfast is splendid and there's a garden to relax in.

The Granary at Leigh Farm (☎ 01237-441918; 💻 andrew.heard47@gmail .com; 1D self-contained, en suite; WI-FI; © ; 🐾) is about a mile inland from the coast to the south-west of Hartland village. B&B

here costs £35pp (sgl occ £50).

The Acorns (☎ 01237-441543; 1D/1Tr, both en suite; ☞; WI-FI) is a 5-minute walk from the centre of Hartland at 19 Pengilly Way. They charge £35pp (sgl occ £35).

For accommodation above a pub, *The Anchor Inn* (☎ 01237-441414, 💻 www .theanchorinnhartland.co.uk; 4D/2T/3Tr/ 1Qd, most en suite; ☞; WI-FI; ⓛ; 🐾 bar only) sits in the centre of the village and is one of two decent pubs here. It is a traditional boozer with real ale (they are in the CAMRA guide), pool and darts and the occasional live music or karaoke evening. Rates (£27.50-32.50pp, sgl occ from £45, three/four sharing from £95/110) do not include breakfast although this is available for an extra £6pp. The pub recently featured in the BBC's adaptation of John Le Carre's *The Night Manager*. The Anchor is also one of your three options for **food** (served daily 6-9pm; Sun lunch noon-2pm), with good grub (mains £8.45-15.50) made from local produce and a Sunday carvery.

There is another pub in the village whose reputation for food is also good. *The Hart Inn* (☎ 01237-441474; food Tue-Sat 6-9pm, Thur-Sun noon-3pm; WI-FI; 🐾) is the heart of the village, an old place with roots going back to the 14th century. The menu may include rump steaks (£16.95), and local pork sausages with bubble and squeak (£11.95); sandwiches are available at lunch time.

Your third choice of eatery in Hartland – although with no booze involved – is *The Old Bakery Coffee Shop* (☎ 01237-440283, 💻 www.theoldbakery.co.uk; Easter-Oct Mon-Sat 9am-5pm, Sun 11am-5pm, rest of year to 4pm; WI-FI; 🐾 outside), The Square, where options include coffee, cake, cream teas and light lunches (£4-6.50); it is also a good place to get things for a packed lunch.

Other accommodation around Hartland

For those who think they'll find this last stretch a tad too demanding there are several B&Bs in the area. Many of these offer evening meals, packed lunches and most

will, if arranged in advance and for a fee (or even free), offer lifts from and to the path. Note that though they may say that they are only a short distance from the trail, there is often no path between the two so walking to them may take much longer than you'd anticipated.

Further information on the peninsula and other accommodation options can be found at 💻 www.hartlandpeninsula.co.uk.

The Old Farmhouse Hescott (☎ 01237-441709, 💻 www.oldhescottfarm house.co.uk; 1D/1T both en suite, 1Tr private bathroom; ☞; WI-FI; ⓛ) lies 1½ miles from the path and around two miles west of Clovelly. An evening meal is possible if requested at the time of booking (£15 for two courses with a vegetarian option). B&B costs £40pp (sgl occ £40).

Situated just two miles from Higher Clovelly and a similar distance from Hartland, *Southdown B&B* (☎ 01237-431504, 💻 maryfmcoll@hotmail.com; 1D/ 1Tr, both en suite; ☞; WI-FI; ⓛ; 🐾) charges £32.50pp (sgl occ £40, three sharing £80). Note that the 'triple' consists of twin beds and a bed which would only be suitable for a small adult.

Two miles north of Hartland, *Gawlish Farm* (☎ 01237-441320; 2D/2T, all en suite; ☞; WI-FI; ⓛ) is less than a mile from the path. If arranged in advance they can provide an evening meal (£14 for two courses), or they can drop you off at a local pub in Hartland. B&B costs £35pp (sgl occ £40).

Finally, approximately eight miles from Hartland and seven miles from Clovelly, in the tiny hamlet of **Bradworthy**, *Lake Villa Holiday Cottages* (☎ 01409-241962, 💻 www.lakevilla.co.uk; three self-catering cottages sleeping 2/5/7; ☞; WI-FI; 🐾) offers a pick-up and drop-off service for a fee from anywhere between Westward Ho! and Crackington Haven (Cornwall). Note that there is a minimum stay of three nights and they are nowhere near the actual path; the rates, however, are reasonable so if you like the idea of basing yourself somewhere and catering for yourselves for a few nights you should contact them for further details. For an evening meal, there is a pub a 10-minute stroll away.

HARTLAND QUAY TO BUDE   [MAPS 48-55]

By the time you reach this stage you should be well on your way to becoming acclimatised to your new, itinerant way of life; your feet hardened, your back strong, and your legs like two solid tubes of reinforced steel emanating from the bottom of your shorts.

You are now, in short, a walker.

Which is just as well, for this stage is said to be the most taxing in the entire book; indeed, by common consent it's actually the hardest on the entire South-West Coast Path! It's a **15½-mile (24.9km; 8¾hrs)** slog across soaring summit and plunging combe that includes, by our reckoning, ten *major* ascents and descents as you scramble across valley after valley, with no refreshments along the way until right near the end (though it's possible to divert off the path to Morwenstow where there is both a wonderful tea room and a marvellous pub).

Thankfully, the rewards are manifold: the views along the way, especially the panorama at Higher Sharpnose Point, the vista south from Steeple Point and the aspect from Yeolmouth Cliff back to Devil's Hole, are little short of magnificent. If surveying the scenery is difficult due to inclement conditions you can find shelter in the huts of writers Robert Hawker, near Morwenstow, and Ronald Duncan, above the border with Cornwall. While if the weather is good, it seems churlish not to pay a visit to the endless stretch of sand before Bude, the perfect place to cool one's corns and paddle in the sea. All this, and we haven't even mentioned the waterfalls (with a particularly fine example at Speke's Mill Mouth), Iron Age forts, Roman sites, radio stations ... and the sheer joy of being on one of the remotest and most beautiful stretches of coastline this country can offer. Plus of course, nothing can beat the feeling that, at the end of this day, you will have completed the walk described in this book – which is no small achievement. While for those who are walking the entire trail – and thus for whom this book was little more than an *hors d'oeuvre* – you too can celebrate the fact that you've finished your time in North Devon, and you won't be seeing this county again for another 300 miles!

The route

Despite the fearsome reputation of this stage, the beginning of the walk is rather gentle as you leave Hartland Point to head towards the triangular promontory of **St Catherine's Tor**. The path ignores the scramble up the Tor (which is believed to have had a Roman villa on its summit), preferring instead to follow **Wargery Water** upstream, a waterway that ends its journey in impressive fashion by plummeting over the cliffs to the north of the Tor. Those who miss this waterfall (which, after all, is not actually on the path) needn't be too concerned, for the next valley, **Speke's Mill Mouth**, has, if anything, an even more spectacular version, and one that is easily visible just a few metres from the path.

Climbing out of the combe – the first of many calf-popping ascents – up **Swansford Hill** and past the turn-off to Elmscott (see p194).

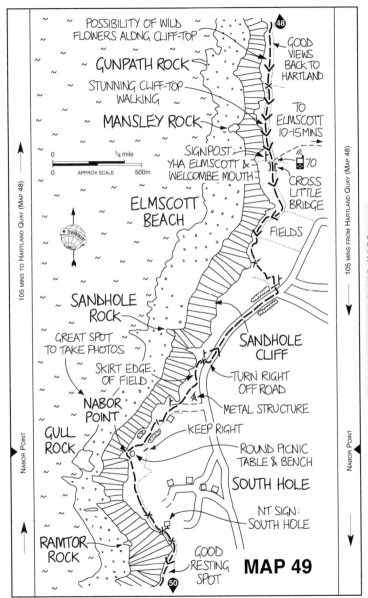

POSSIBILITY OF WILD FLOWERS ALONG CLIFF-TOP

48

GOOD VIEWS BACK TO HARTLAND

GUNPATH ROCK

STUNNING CLIFF-TOP WALKING

TO ELMSCOTT 10-15 MINS

MANSLEY ROCK

SIGNPOST: YHA ELMSCOTT & WELCOMBE MOUTH

70

CROSS LITTLE BRIDGE

0   ¼ mile
APPROX SCALE
0   500m

ELMSCOTT BEACH

FIELDS

trailblazer

SANDHOLE ROCK

GREAT SPOT TO TAKE PHOTOS

SKIRT EDGE OF FIELD

SANDHOLE CLIFF

TURN RIGHT OFF ROAD

METAL STRUCTURE

NABOR POINT

KEEP RIGHT

ROUND PICNIC TABLE & BENCH

GULL ROCK

SOUTH HOLE

NT SIGN: SOUTH HOLE

RAMTOR ROCK

GOOD RESTING SPOT

MAP 49

50

105 MINS TO HARTLAND QUAY (MAP 48)

NABOR POINT

105 MINS FROM HARTLAND QUAY (MAP 48)

NABOR POINT

ROUTE GUIDE AND MAPS

ELMSCOTT [off MAP 49]

Elmscott is an easy, short walk from the path (10-15 mins) and the accommodation is rather pleasant. ***YHA Elmscott*** (☎ 01237-441367, 💻 www.yha.org.uk/hostel/elmscott-bunkhouse; 1T/3 x 4- & 3 x 6-bed dorms, shared facilities; Mar-Oct), originally built as a school in Victorian times, is now a cosy hostel (from £20/23pp members/non-members) with a small **shop** (8-10am & 5-10pm), good kitchen facilities (which is just as well as meals aren't provided and there's nowhere to eat around here) and a drying room. **Camping** is available (two-/four-person tent £10/20) although for three tents only; booking is therefore recommended.

Elmscott Farm, on which it is set, is also a **B&B** (☎ 01237-441276, 💻 elmscott.org.uk/bed-and-breakfast.asp; 2D en suite/1T private bathroom; ♥; Ⓛ) charging £35pp (sgl occ £35). They don't do evening meals but will direct you to the local pub.

The path is rather uneventful to **Nabor Point**, even joining a road at one point, and only gets exciting again at **Embury Beacon** (Map 50), where the path runs alongside the defensive earthwork of an Iron Age fort. Yet another vertiginous descent follows, this time at **Welcombe Mouth**, where the path crosses the stream on stepping stones. It's a beautiful spot surpassed in its noteworthiness for walkers only, perhaps, by the next laceration in the surface of the land: **Marsland Valley**. Another steep combe, it is here on its northern slopes that you'll find the **Ronald Duncan's hut**. Author, poet, playwright and pacifist, Duncan is perhaps best known for writing the libretto of Benjamin's Britten's opera *The Rape of Lucretia*; but also for this lovely hut that he constructed so he could have views over the sea while writing. You can often pick up free copies of his work in the hut.

Struggle down the steps to the floor of the valley and you cross the **border into Cornwall**, the exact boundary marked by a bridge and a signpost welcoming you to '**Kernow**' (as they call it round here). But while the county might have changed, the path remains as challenging as ever as you traverse yet more stamina-sapping undulations at **Litter Mouth** and **Yeol Mouth** (Map 51) and around **St Morwenna's Well** – so easy to write, so exhausting to complete.

Thankfully, soon after the latter, it's possible to get off the rollercoaster for a while by taking the short diversion to the hamlet of **Morwenstow**.

MORWENSTOW [MAP 51, p197]

There's little more to this ancient settlement than a church, a tearoom, a pub and a B&B. All four, however, are full of character. The church is dedicated to St Morwenna and St John the Baptist, and while the earliest part of the current church is Norman, there is believed to have been a church on this site since Anglo-Saxon times. The Rev Hawker, of Hawker's Hut fame (see box p196), was one of the vicars here.

Stagecoach's No 216/217 **bus** services connect Morwenstow with Bude; see pp48-50 for details.

Opposite the church sits the award-winning ***Rectory Farm Tearoom*** (☎ 01288-331251, 💻 www.rectory-tearooms.co.uk; late Mar/Easter-end Oct daily 11am-5pm, winter hours variable; 🐕 outside area), part of a charming 13th-century farm that's been serving cream-topped scones to hungry walkers for over 50 years. Gluten-, wheat-, and dairy-free options are available and their field mushrooms stuffed with Cornish blue cheese wrapped in bacon (£9.95) are scrumptious: a fine meal indeed to see you on your way to Bude – and they

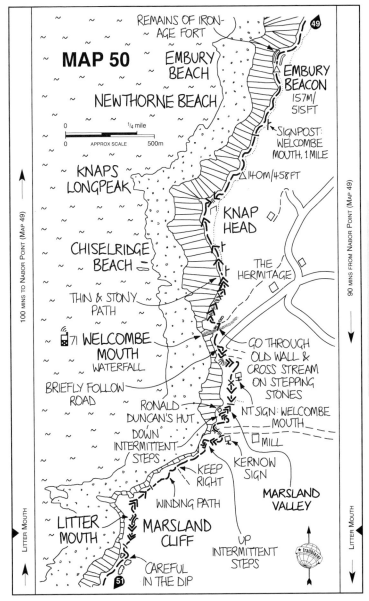

MAP 50

REMAINS OF IRON-AGE FORT

EMBURY BEACH

NEWTHORNE BEACH

EMBURY BEACON
157M/
515FT

SIGNPOST:
WELCOMBE
MOUTH, 1 MILE

KNAPS
LONGPEAK

△140M/458FT

KNAP
HEAD

CHISELRIDGE
BEACH

THE
HERMITAGE

THIN & STONY
PATH

71 WELCOMBE
MOUTH
WATERFALL

GO THROUGH
OLD WALL &
CROSS STREAM
ON STEPPING
STONES

BRIEFLY FOLLOW
ROAD

RONALD
DUNCAN'S HUT

NT SIGN: WELCOMBE
MOUTH

DOWN
INTERMITTENT
STEPS

MILL

KEEP
RIGHT

KERNOW
SIGN

MARSLAND
VALLEY

WINDING PATH

LITTER
MOUTH

MARSLAND
CLIFF

UP
INTERMITTENT
STEPS

CAREFUL
IN THE DIP

0   ¼ mile
APPROX SCALE
0   500m

100 MINS TO NABOR POINT (MAP 49)

LITTER MOUTH

90 MINS FROM NABOR POINT (MAP 49)

LITTER MOUTH

ROUTE GUIDE AND MAPS

trailblazer

are now licensed so will be selling cider and wine. Dogs are welcome in the outside area and may be allowed indoors weather and business depending.

To the south, the 13th-century **Bush Inn** (☎ 01288-331242, 🖳 www.thebushinn morwenstow.com; 2D/2T, all en suite; ☛; WI-FI; ⒧; 🐾) provides B&B (£45pp, sgl occ £65-80) and serves **food** (daily noon-9pm, may close earlier in winter). The menu changes seasonally but may include Mediterranean lamb (£14.95), mussels (small/large £8.95/12.95) and grilled rump

steak (£15.95). Ask the owners to point out some of the ancient features of the inn, including the lepers' squint, through which the diseased of the parish were fed scraps, and a monastic cross carved into a flagstone in the floor. Note: there is a minimum two-night stay in high season.

Although **Old Vicarage** (☎ 01288-331369, 🖳 rshawker.co.uk; 1S/1D/1T, all en suite/private facilities; ☛; WI-FI; ⒧; Feb-Nov) is a wonderful place to stay, there's also generally a two-night minimum stay here. They charge £48pp.

Those who forego the delights of Morwenstow will continue along **Vicarage Cliff**, in time coming to the cliff-face path to **Hawker's Hut** (see box below), built by a local vicar from the timbers of shipwrecked craft. *(cont'd on p200)*

(cont'd on p200)

❏ Hawker and his hut

Writer, maverick and saviour of shipwrecked sailors, Robert Stephen Hawker was born in 1803 and became vicar of St Morwenna and St John the Baptist Church at Morwenstow in 1834. Prior to his arrival the church had had no serving clergy for well over a century and, lacking any guiding moral influence, the coastline in this region had instead become a base for smugglers and wreckers (who used to lure passing ships onto the rocks, regardless of the safety of those onboard, so they could then loot the wreck of its cargo).

Hawker, horrified at the behaviour of many of his parishioners, went out of his way to both ameliorate their behaviour and educate them in the errors of their ways. The hut that he built out of driftwood into the cliff-face, and which still carries his name, was originally designed as a lookout, so Hawker could warn any ships of the dangers of navigation. He also used the hut as his study, from where he could compose such works as '*Footprints of Former Men in Far Cornwall*', which included an account of the wrecking of the *Caledonia* in 1842, and where he also received friends such as Charles Kingsley and Alfred, Lord Tennyson.

Contemporary sources describe Hawker as a bit of an eccentric, given to wearing colourful clothes, dressing up as a mermaid, and excommunicating his cat for mousing on a Sunday. But he was also extremely compassionate and introduced the practice of giving the bodies of shipwrecked sailors a Christian burial (where previously they had been allowed to bob in the ocean for days). The **figurehead of** *Caledonia* marks the spot in Morwenstow Church where the crew are buried. Nearby is a granite cross into which the words 'Unknown Yet Well Known' are carved, a tribute to the thirty or so bodies of seafarers that he buried nearby. He is most remembered, however, as the man who introduced the Harvest Festival into the Christian calendar, having invited his congregation to a service in October 1841 to give thanks to God for his bounty; and as the composer of '*The Song of the Western Men*', which has become something of a 'national' anthem for Cornwall.

Hawker died in 1875, the mourners at his funeral wearing purple rather than the traditional black. He was survived by his wife, who was forty years his junior – plus, of course, by his small driftwood hut, today the smallest building in the entire portfolio of the National Trust.

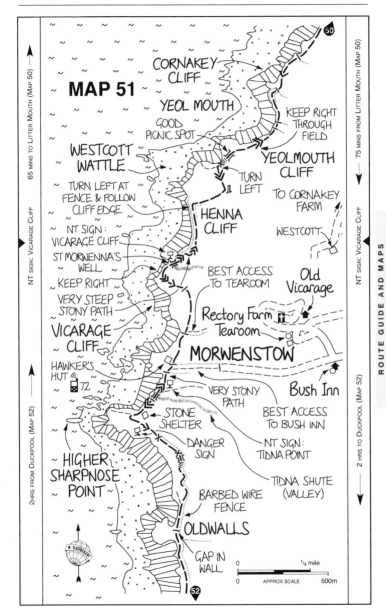

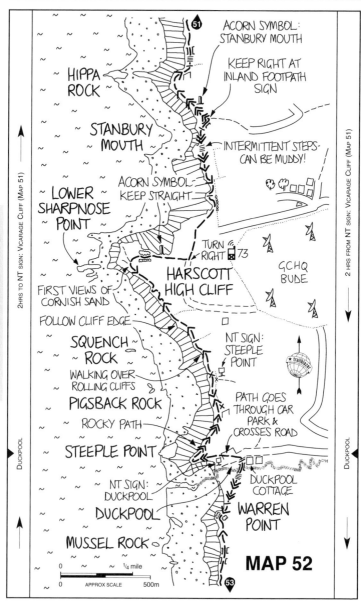

ACORN SYMBOL:
STANBURY MOUTH

KEEP RIGHT AT
INLAND FOOTPATH
SIGN

HIPPA
ROCK

STANBURY
MOUTH

INTERMITTENT STEPS-
CAN BE MUDDY!

ACORN SYMBOL-
KEEP STRAIGHT

LOWER
SHARPNOSE
POINT

TURN
RIGHT 🚌 73

HARSCOTT
HIGH CLIFF

GCHQ
BUDE

FIRST VIEWS OF
CORNISH SAND

FOLLOW CLIFF EDGE

NT SIGN:
STEEPLE
POINT

SQUENCH
ROCK

WALKING OVER
ROLLING CLIFFS

PATH GOES
THROUGH CAR
PARK &
CROSSES ROAD

PIGSBACK ROCK

ROCKY PATH

STEEPLE POINT

NT SIGN:
DUCKPOOL

DUCKPOOL
COTTAGE

DUCKPOOL

WARREN
POINT

MUSSEL ROCK

MAP 52

0   ¼ mile
0   APPROX SCALE   500m

ROUTE GUIDE AND MAPS

2 HRS TO NT SIGN: VICARAGE CLIFF (MAP 51)

DUCKPOOL

2 HRS FROM NT SIGN: VICARAGE CLIFF (MAP 51)

DUCKPOOL

★ trailblazer

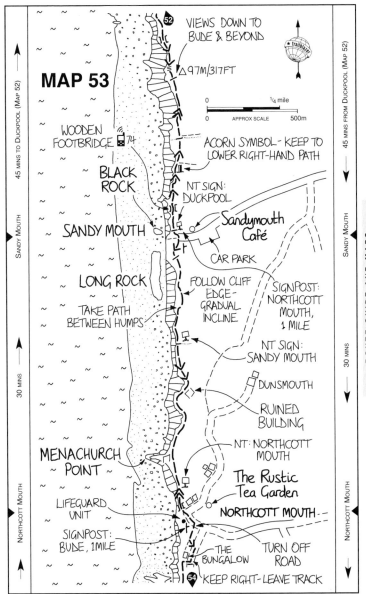

MAP 53

52

VIEWS DOWN TO
BUDE & BEYOND

△97M/317FT

0   ¼ mile
0   500m
APPROX SCALE

WOODEN
FOOTBRIDGE 74

ACORN SYMBOL- KEEP TO
LOWER RIGHT-HAND PATH

BLACK
ROCK

NT SIGN:
DUCKPOOL

SANDY MOUTH

Sandymouth
Café

CAR PARK

LONG ROCK

FOLLOW CLIFF
EDGE-
GRADUAL
INCLINE

SIGNPOST:
NORTHCOTT
MOUTH,
1 MILE

TAKE PATH
BETWEEN HUMPS

NT SIGN:
SANDY MOUTH

DUNSMOUTH

RUINED
BUILDING

NT: NORTHCOTT
MOUTH

MENACHURCH
~ POINT ~

The Rustic
Tea Garden

NORTHCOTT MOUTH

LIFEGUARD
UNIT

SIGNPOST:
BUDE, 1MILE

THE
BUNGALOW

TURN OFF
ROAD

54 KEEP RIGHT- LEAVE TRACK

45 MINS TO DUCKPOOL (MAP 52)

SANDY MOUTH

30 MINS

NORTHCOTT MOUTH

45 MINS FROM DUCKPOOL (MAP 52)

SANDY MOUTH

30 MINS

NORTHCOTT MOUTH

ROUTE GUIDE AND MAPS

(cont'd from p196) Still the relentless gradients of the path continue as you clamber in and out of the valleys of **Tidna Shute** and **Stanbury Mouth**, the latter, in this author's reckoning, the steepest of all today's climbs. Your reward at the top is the enormous **GCHQ Bude** site from where, at its southern end, the first views of Bude can be glimpsed. Another steep valley, **Duckpool**, follows, where in July at dusk you can see the rare spectacle of glow worms. Along this coast, over 150 ships have been wrecked between Morwenstow and Bude. No wonder Alfred, Lord Tennyson, described this stretch thus:

> *But after tempest, when the long wave broke*
> *All down the thundering shores of Bude and Bos.*
> **Alfred, Lord Tennyson**, *The Birth of King Arthur*

Duckpool is also the last serious challenge on this stage. The gradients finally relent now and the path, though still long and undulating, is more merciful than it has been previously on this stage.

Cafés start to appear on the route too, including ***Sandymouth Café*** (Map 53; ☎ 01288-354286, 🖥 www.sandymouth.com; daily 10am-4pm, later in summer) and the lovely eatery, ***The Rustic Tea Garden*** (Map 53; Easter-early Oct daily 10am-5.30pm), by the stream at **Northcott Mouth**. Margaret provides wonderful cream teas, served from an old green caravan. But by now even this idyllic place may not be enough to halt your determined march to Bude ... which

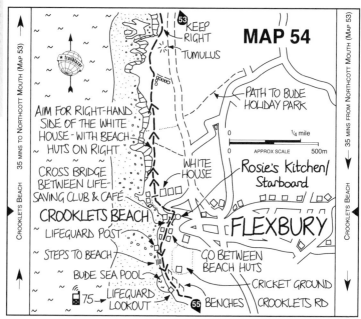

ROUTE GUIDE AND MAPS

35 MINS TO NORTHCOTT MOUTH (MAP 53)

CROOKLETS BEACH

MAP 54

KEEP RIGHT
TUMULUS
PATH TO BUDE HOLIDAY PARK

AIM FOR RIGHT-HAND SIDE OF THE WHITE HOUSE - WITH BEACH HUTS ON RIGHT

CROSS BRIDGE BETWEEN LIFE-SAVING CLUB & CAFÉ

CROOKLETS BEACH

LIFEGUARD POST

STEPS TO BEACH

BUDE SEA POOL

75 → LIFEGUARD LOOKOUT

WHITE HOUSE

Rosie's Kitchen/ Starboard

FLEXBURY

GO BETWEEN BEACH HUTS

CRICKET GROUND

BENCHES   CROOKLETS RD

¼ mile
APPROX SCALE   500m

35 MINS FROM NORTHCOTT MOUTH (MAP 53)

CROOKLETS BEACH

you should reach, weary, exhausted and happy, about 2-2½ hours after leaving Duckpool.

Should you begin to wane just before Bude, however, there is one final option for a rest-stop: *Rosie's Kitchen* (Map 54; ☎ 01288-354238, 🖳 www. rosieskitchen.co.uk; Mar-Oct daily 10am-4pm, can be up to 9pm in summer, Nov-Feb Tue-Sun 10am-4pm but daily in Feb half-term; sandwiches from £5.50) is at **Crooklets Beach**. Also now here, and serving wood-fired pizzas, is *Starboard* (same contact details; late Mar-Oct Fri and Sat from 5pm).

BUDE [Map 55 p203]

Bude is a small, compact seaside town with plenty of charm and character that sprawls out from its famous beach, Summerleaze.

Summer and bank holidays are when this normally sleepy little town springs into life and it can become quite hectic. However, arrive at any other time and you shouldn't have any trouble booking accommodation and making your way around town.

Built in 1830, the town's small **castle** (🖳 www.thecastlebude.org.uk; daily 10am-4/5pm winter/summer; free) is worth exploring. Its **heritage centre** contains exhibitions on shipwrecks and lifeboats as well as displays on the Bude Canal and the geology of the Cornish coast. Inside too is **Willoughby Gallery**, which holds local art

exhibitions, a gift shop and the pleasant Limelight Café (see Where to eat).

Pretty **Bude Canal** (see box below) runs from the beach past the castle and can be followed for a mile or so along the towpath or in boats. Also nearby is **Bude Light**, a Millennium project built to commemorate the life of Sir Goldsworthy Gurney, a Cornish scientist and inventor for whom the castle was originally built.

Bude Sea Pool (Map 54; 🖳 www .budeseapool.org; open year-round; free) is a man-made tidal swimming pool, built in 1930 to provide a safe place for people to go sea swimming.

Bude is also known for its **Jazz Festival** (see p16).

❏ Bude Canal

Bude Canal (🖳 www.bude-canal.co.uk) was dug to transport mainly sand inland from the seashore so that it could be spread on the fields to improve the soil which was rather poor in parts of north Cornwall. The Canal was the brainchild of one John Endyvean, the intention being to link up with the River Tamar at Calstock, thus providing a waterway between the Bristol Channel and the English Channel, 90 miles of canal to span just 28 miles as the crow flies.

The full scheme was never realised although by 1823 some 35 miles of canal were in operation. Once the railways were built the use of the canal began to decline and by the Second World War it became ineffective as a waterway. Today only a short stretch remains between Bude and Helebridge.

A project to restore the canal with the aid of a £45m grant from the Heritage Lottery Fund was completed in 2009. Whilst the lock-gates giving access to the open sea suffered damage in the early part of 2008 during some huge storms, the canal itself is currently in good working order. At the Helebridge end, **Weir Nature Centre** at Whalesborough Farm opened in 2011. It is a 40-minute walk along a flat tarmac path by the side of the canal.

You can also hire rowing boats and pedalos to take out on the canal from **Bude Rowing Boats** (☎ 0796-868 8782, 🖳 www.budeboathire.co.uk; Good Fri to end Sep daily 10am to late).

ROUTE GUIDE AND MAPS

Services

Bude Tourist Information and Canal Centre (☎ 01288-354240, 💻 www.visit bude.info; Easter-Oct Mon-Sat 10am-5pm, Sun 10am-4pm, Oct-Easter daily to 4pm; WI-FI) has a comprehensive listing of accommodation in the area (you can book accommodation in the centre and through its website too) and the enthusiastic staff are willing to help. Wi-fi is free if you log in through Facebook but if not you can buy a voucher for £1 which is valid for three hours. They are happy to store luggage for the day (£1.50).

There is **internet access** (free for 30 mins) at **Bude Library** (Mon, Wed & Fri 9.30am-5pm, Sat 10am-1pm; WI-FI), which has a good Cornish reference section, and at The Coffee Pot (see Where to eat; £1/20 mins). Most cafés, restaurants and pubs here have free wi-fi.

Bude's main **post office** (Mon-Fri 9am-5pm, Sat 9am-12.30pm) is at the top of Belle Vue, the main shopping street. There's also a **sub-post office** which is part of a newsagent (daily 7am-5.30pm) almost directly opposite the tourist office.

For **food** shopping, there is a Sainsbury's (Mon-Sat 8am-8pm, Sun 10am-4pm), and a Co-op (Mon-Sat 7am-10pm, Sun 10am-4pm). There is a Boots **pharmacy** (Mon-Sat 9am-5.30pm, Sun 10am-4pm) while, for **walking and camping gear**, there is a Mountain Warehouse (Mon-Fri 9am-5.30pm, Sat 9am-6pm, Sun 10am-5pm) and a good camping section in Wroes (Mon-Sat 9.30am-5pm).

Spencer Thorn Bookshop (☎ 01288-352518; Mon-Sat 9am-5pm, summer school hols Sun 10am-4pm) has a good selection of books on Cornwall.

There are several **banks** including a NatWest (Mon-Fri 9am-4.30pm), a TSB (Mon-Fri 9am-5pm, Sat 9am-1pm) and a Barclays (Mon-Fri 9.30am-4.30pm, Sat 9.30am-noon); all have **ATMs**. You will also find ATMs at the town's supermarkets and convenience stores.

There's a **launderette** (Mon-Thur 8.30am-5pm, Fri to 8pm, Sat 9am-5pm, Sun 10am-5pm) tucked away off Lansdown Rd.

Transport

[See also pp48-50] **Bus**-wise, for destinations north, some of Stagecoach's No 85 services go from here to Barnstaple, where you'll find the nearest railway station. Alternatively, their Nos 6 & 6A run to the main rail hub at Exeter. Their Nos 216/217 operate to Morwenstow and their 219 service travels to Hartland from where you can connect with their 319 to Bideford and Barnstaple. Plymouth Citybus's 12B service heads to Launceston, while First's 95 runs to Wadebridge. Buses stop on The Strand.

For a **taxi**, call: Bea-line (☎ 07747-196090, 💻 www.bea-line.co.uk); Trev's Taxi (☎ 07799-663217, 💻 www.trevs taxi.co.uk); or Bayside Taxis (☎ 01288-358076, 💻 www.baysidetaxis.co.uk).

Where to stay

Campsites and hostels For **campers**, the 10-minute stroll out of town to *Upper Lynstone Caravan & Camping Park* (☎ 01288-352017, 💻 upperlynstone.co.uk; WI-FI; 🐾 on lead; Apr to end Sep; walker & small tent £8-10, 2 people & tent £15.50-22) is well worth the effort. The quiet location is perfect for those continuing on the trail as it backs on to the cliffs and the coastal path to Upton and Widemouth Bay. There is a well-stocked **shop** and **laundry** facilities; the free showers are roomy and spotlessly clean.

Another option is the fabulous *Cerenety Eco Campsite* (☎ 01288-356778, 💻 www.cerenetycampsite.co.uk; WI-FI; 🐾; Mar-Oct). It's in **Upton**, just off the coast path toward Crackington Haven, so not really in Bude itself, although not much further away than Upper Lynstone. It's basic (solar-heated showers, compost toilets) but friendly, well organised and genuinely eco-conscious; a tent pitch costs £4-5 plus £2pp. There's a **caravan café** (peak season & weekends 8-11am) serving breakfast. There are also open fires for self-caterers and marshmallow-toasters.

NorthShore Bude Backpackers (☎ 01288-354256, 💻 www.northshorebude .com; one 3-, 4 x 4- & 2 x 6-bed dorms, 2D/1T share facilities, 1D or T en suite; 🛏;

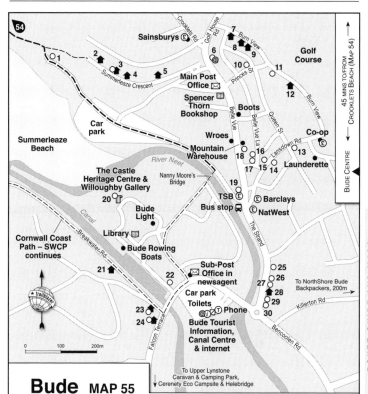

Bude MAP 55

Where to stay
2 The Beach
3 The Edgcumbe
4 Atlantic House
5 The Grosvenor
7 Tee-Side Guest House
8 Sunrise
9 Links Side Guest House
12 Sea Jade Guest House
21 Breakwater House
23 Falcon Hotel
24 Brendon Arms
28 Premier Inn

Where to eat and drink
1 Life's a Beach
3 The Deck (at The Edgcumbe)
6 Coffee Pot Café (& internet access)
10 Sizzlers (Fish & Chips)
11 Bude Tandoori
13 The Coffee Shop
14 Lansdowne Bakery
15 Scrummies
16 KJ's
17 Pengenna's Pasties
18 Costa Coffee
19 Atlantic Diner
20 Limelight Café
22 Olive Tree Coffee House & Bistro
23 Falcon Hotel
24 Brendon Arms
25 Tiandi
26 Silver River Chinese Takeaway
27 Carriers Inn
29 La Bocca Pizza Kitchen
30 The Shack

WI-FI), 57 Killerton Rd, has everything a walker needs: internet access, a drying room and a laundry. It also benefits from a big and clean living area, kitchen (meals are not provided) and garden, and has Sky TV. They charge £20-22pp for a dorm bed (£25-27.50pp for two sharing, sgl occ £50-55). Booking is recommended.

B&Bs, guesthouses and pubs B&B-style accommodation is scattered about the town. Pretty much on the SWCP is the lovely *Breakwater House* (☎ 01288-353137, 🖳 www.breakwaterhouse.co.uk; 3D, all en suite; ✆; WI-FI; Apr-Oct) which is at the luxury end of the scale. Whilst they usually take only two-night bookings (May-Sep) they will consider one-night stays should you call requiring accommodation that night. They charge £45-50pp (sgl occ £63-70).

On Burn View you will find: *Links Side Guest House* (☎ 01288-352410, 🖳 www.linkssidebude.co.uk; 1S/4D/1T all en suite, 1D private facilities; WI-FI) where B&B costs £32.50-42.50pp (sgl £36-50, sgl occ £36-60); *Sea Jade Guest House* (☎ 01288-353404, 🖳 www.seajadeguesthouse.co.uk; 2D/4Tr all en suite, 1D private bathroom; WI-FI) where the tariff is £34-38pp (sgl occ £35-55, three sharing from £35pp); *Sunrise* (☎ 01288-353214, 🖳 www.sunrise-bude.co.uk; 2S/1T/3D/1D or T, all en suite; ✆; WI-FI; 🐾), which charges £40-45pp (sgl £40-45, sgl occ £60); and *Tee-Side Guest House* (☎ 01288-352351, 🖳 www.tee-side.co.uk; 1S private facilities, 4D or T, all en suite; WI-FI), from where, as its name suggests, you can enjoy views overlooking the golf course while eating your breakfast. Rates here are £37.50-47.50pp (sgl/sgl occ £45-65).

Brendon Arms (☎ 01288-354542, 🖳 www.brendonarms.co.uk; 1S/5D/3T, all en suite; ✆; WI-FI) is a popular **pub** which also has rooms (£39-45pp, sgl occ £49-55).

Hotels Overlooking the beach from a great vantage point on the edge of Summerleaze Down, *The Beach* (☎ 01288-389800, 🖳 www.thebeachatbude.co.uk; 2T/14D, all en suite; ✆; WI-FI) is Bude's most boutique-like hotel, with heated floors

and very smart, modern rooms, half of which have sea views. The terraces from the bar and restaurant have sea views too. B&B costs £75-125pp (sgl occ £137.50-237.50); room only and bed, breakfast and dinner rates are also available.

On the same road, *The Edgcumbe* (☎ 01288-353846, 🖳 www.edgcumbe-hotel .co.uk; 6D/5D or T/1Tr, all en suite; ✆; WI-FI; Feb-Dec) is a friendly place, with a young vibe to it. Rates are £44-53pp (sgl occ £53-64, three sharing £44pp). There's a small bar-restaurant with excellent meals, and a drying room too; handy for wet tents and soggy walking boots.

Atlantic House (☎ 01288-352451, 🖳 www.atlantichousehotel.com; 1S private bathroom, 12D/3D or T, all en suite; ✆; WI-FI) has some nice sea-view rooms, although some of the rear rooms are a bit poky. Rates are £45-75pp (sgl from £45, sgl occ £70-150). Next door is *The Grosvenor* (☎ 01288-352062, 🖳 www.thegrosvenor-bude .co.uk; 1S/3D/1D or T/1T/1Tr, all en suite; WI-FI; late Mar-end Nov), which has two rooms with sea views and one en suite room can connect with a bunk bed room for children aged 7-14 (£115 for a family). They charge £29.50-49pp (sgl occ £52-81, three sharing £110) but they have a two-night minimum stay at weekends (mid July to mid Sep).

On the other side of the canal, *Falcon Hotel* (☎ 01288-352005, 🖳 www.falcon hotel.com; 4S/7T/18D, all en suite; ✆; WI-FI) is an impressive place, and a more traditional, classier alternative to its main top-end rival, The Beach. B&B costs approximately £70-80pp but rates vary depending on demand so contact them for details.

There is – as seems to be the case in numerous locations along this trail – a *Premier Inn* (consult 🖳 www.premier inn.com for details) being built on the site of the old Strand Hotel. It is scheduled to open in November 2017 and will have an on-site restaurant.

Where to eat and drink
There are numerous options for food in Bude. Inside the castle is *Limelight Café* (daily 10am-4pm), which does sandwiches,

cream teas and coffee. *The Coffee Shop* (☎ 01288-355973; Mar-Nov daily 10am-6.30pm, Dec-Feb 10.30am-4pm), on Lansdown Rd, sells freshly baked goods (from *Lansdowne Bakery*), while nearby *Pengenna Pasties* (daily 9am-5pm) does excellent pasties, scones and other baked goods.

On the outskirts of town, *Coffee Pot Café* (☎ 01288-356142; daily June-Sep 8am-7pm, winter 8.30am-3pm; WI-FI; 🐾) is a down-to-earth, friendly café with cream teas, full English breakfasts, some roadside patio seating and internet access. On Belle Vue, *Costa Coffee* (Mon-Sat 7am-6.30pm, Sun 9am-5pm) is the first place to open in the middle of town.

Café by day, bistro by night, *Olive Tree Coffee House and Bistro* (☎ 01288-359577, 🖳 www.olivetreebude.co.uk; daily 10am-4pm, summer Mon-Sat 5-9pm; WI-FI) serves a good variety of gluten-free and vegetarian dishes. It's a lovely spot beside the canal, but prices aren't cheap.

More affordable, *Scrummies* (summer Mon-Sat 8am-9pm, Sun 9am-9pm, winter days/hours variable) is owned by local fisherman Cliff Bowden who catches, prepares and cooks 60-70% of the fish himself and offers a gigantic cod 'n' chips.

Close to where Belle Vue meets The Strand, *Atlantic Diner* (☎ 01288-354167, 🖳 www.atlanticdiner.co.uk; summer daily 10am-9pm, rest of year hours may vary, closed Nov-Feb; WI-FI; 🐾) serves a splendid breakfast (until noon; £5.50-8); their specials, such as their 6oz burger topped with halloumi and chorizo (£8.50) certainly hit the spot, and their homemade lemon cake (£2) is divine!

Just before The Strand arrives at the road bridge *The Shack* (☎ 01288-350850, 🖳 www.theshackbude.co.uk; summer daily 8am-2pm & 4.30-8/9pm, rest of year Sun-Wed 8am-2pm, Thur-Sat 8am-2pm & 4.30-8/9pm; WI-FI; 🐾) is the place to head for an early breakfast (£4-5). There's food served throughout the day including gluten-free and vegan options, and treats for dogs.

There are a few decent **pubs**. Next to the canal, *Brendon Arms* (see Where to stay; food daily noon-2pm & 6-9pm, school

summer hols noon-9pm) is a 150-year-old pub with plenty of garden seating out front. Meanwhile, at the bottom of The Strand, *Carriers Inn* (☎ 01288-352459; food Mon-Sat noon-3pm & 6-9pm, Sun noon-5.30pm; WI-FI; 🐾 on a lead in the bar) is even older, although less cheery.

Falcon Hotel (see Where to stay) has a bar (food served daily 10am-9pm; 🐾) and a restaurant (daily 6.30-9pm, Sun noon-2.30pm; booking preferred) but the menu is fairly standard pub grub. The recently opened bar-restaurant *The Deck* (🖳 www.thedeckbude.co.uk; May-Sep daily 4-8.30pm, Apr & Oct Tue-Sat, Nov-Mar Thur-Sat), at The Edgcumbe (see Where to stay), can also be recommended.

In terms of restaurants, *Life's a Beach* (☎ 01288-355222, 🖳 lifesabeach.info; mid Feb-Dec café daily 10.30am-3.30pm, bistro Mon-Sat 7-8.30pm, Jan to mid Feb Fri-Sun 11am-3pm) has the pick of locations, with fabulous beach views from its terrace. The lunchtime menu is good value (baguettes/burgers from £5.50/6.25). Evening is for fine dining, including good seafood (mains £16.50-22.50, two/three courses £25.50/29.50), and is indoors only.

The best Indian restaurant, *Bude Tandoori* (☎ 01288-359994, 🖳 www.bude tandoori.co.uk; Sat-Thur noon-2pm, daily 5-11.30pm), has some Bangladeshi dishes too, plus some outdoor seating by the roadside. *Tiandi* (☎ 01288-359686, 🖳 www.tian di.co.uk; Wed-Sat 11.30am-2.30pm, Mon-Sat 5.30-10.30pm, Sun 5-10pm) advertises itself as East-Asian Fine Dining, and does a mix of mostly Chinese and Thai food.

For **takeaway** you have plentiful options. For kebabs, burgers and pizzas, on Belle Vue Lane is *KJ's* (☎ 01288-355879; daily 4pm-midnight), whilst on The Strand you'll discover *Silver River Chinese Takeaway* (☎ 01288-352028; mid Feb to mid Jan Tue-Sun 5-10.30pm) and *La Boca Pizza Kitchen* (☎ 01288-255855, 🖳 www .labocabude.co.uk; daily 5-7pm, Sat & Sun noon-2.30pm, hours may vary depending on season), where you can also eat in.

For classic British seaside fish 'n' chips look no further than *Sizzlers* (daily noon-3pm & 4.30-10pm).

ROUTE GUIDE AND MAPS

APPENDIX A: GPS WAYPOINTS

Each GPS waypoint listed was taken on the route at the reference number marked on the map as below. This list of GPS waypoints as well as instructions on how to interpret an OS grid reference can be found on the Trailblazer website: ⬛ www.trailblazer-guides.com (click on GPS waypoints).

MAP	REF	GPS WAYPOINTS	DESCRIPTION
Map 1	01	N51 12.636 W3 28.345	Hands Sculpture – start of SWCP
Map 2	02	N51 13.113 W3 30.671	Start of rugged alternative route
Map 3	03	N51 13.059 W3 31.125	Gate into and out of Holnicote Estate
Map 4	04	N51 13.383 W3 32.352	Cross metalled road
Map 5	05	N51 13.578 W3 34.057	Reunion of two trails
Map 5	06	N51 13.263 W3 34.928	Turn-off left outside Bossington
Map 6	07	N51 12.967 W3 36.986	Rejoin beach
Map 7	08	N51 13.249 W3 38.086	Arch over path and gate
Map 7	09	N51 13.263 W3 39.490	Culbone Church
Map 8	10	N51 13.325 W3 42.176	Paths to Burford and County Gate
Map 9	11	N51 13.749 W3 42.610	Reunion of two paths
Map 9	12	N51 13.806 W3 43.679	Wild Boar gateposts
Map 10	13	N51 14.096 W3 45.677	Gate into/out of Pudleep Gurt
Map 10	14	N51 14.354 W3 46.949	Turn off road
Map 11	15	N51 14.304 W3 47.445	Reunion with path from lighthouse
Map 11	16	N51 13.837 W3 49.303	Drop off road and zig-zag down to Lynmouth beach
Map 12	17	N51 13.755 W3 51.558	Cattle grid and gate
Map 13	18	N51 13.474 W3 52.942	Sign quoting Psalm 100:4
Map 13	19	N51 13.398 W3 53.844	Signpost to Heddon's Mouth
Map 14	20	N51 13.324 W3 55.618	Heddon's Mouth
Map 14	21	N51 13.138 W3 56.751	Gate with 'ENP' on
Map 15	22	N51 12.857 W3 58.228	Turn right onto good, wide path
Map 15	23	N51 12.538 W3 59.238	Great Hangman National Trust sign
Map 16	24	N51 12.855 W4 00.209	Top of Great Hangman, large cairn
Map 17	25	N51 12.375 W4 02.185	Combe Martin Beach
Map 17	26	N51 12.723 W4 03.838	Watermouth Valley Camping Park
Map 18	27	N51 12.966 W4 05.208	First view of Ilfracombe and Lundy
Map 19	28	N51 12.548 W4 06.853	Ilfracombe Harbour
Map 20	29	N51 11.829 W4 10.539	Lee Bridge
Map 21	30	N51 11.899 W4 11.993	Bull Point
Map 21	31	N51 11.241 W4 13.738	Morte Point
Map 22	32	N51 10.351 W4 12.448	Tourist information Centre, Woolacombe
Map 23	33	N51 08.543 W4 13.148	Entrance to Putsborough Sands car park
Map 24	34	N51 08.529 W4 15.510	Baggy Point
Map 24	35	N51 07.985 W4 14.163	Croyde Beach
Map 25	36	N51 07.336 W4 14.376	Turn onto road, officially left but is a shortcut
Map 26	37	N51 07.082 W4 13.086	Join road
Map 26	38	N51 07.013 W4 12.229	Leave road at gate
Map 27	39	N51 05.622 W4 11.719	Turn right and enter Braunton Burrows
Map 27	40	N51 04.309 W4 11.496	Turn left onto sand footpath
Map 28	41	N51 06.019 W4 09.788	Velator Bridge

MAP	REF	GPS WAYPOINTS	DESCRIPTION
Map 29	42	N51 05.624 W4 07.393	The Braunton Inn
Map 30	43	N51 05.650 W4 06.663	Path goes under bridge
Map 31	44	N51 04.660 W4 03.499	Turn left up steps to access bridge
Map 32	45	N51 04.744 W4 07.168	Fremington Quay Café
Map 33	46	N51 04.237 W4 09.603	Main trail leaves disused railway here
Map 34	47	N51 04.318 W4 10.113	Start of jetty
Map 34	48	N51 03.384 W4 10.726	Join road after gap in wall
Map 34	49	N51 02.987 W4 10.680	Turning off road at gate (Instow)
Map 35	50	N51 02.515 W4 11.041	Pass jetty
Map 36	51	N51 00.935 W4 12.002	Bideford Long Bridge
Map 37	52	N51 02.550 W4 11.540	Wooden footbridge
Map 37	53	N51 03.125 W4 11.371	The Quay, Appledore
Map 37	54	N51 03.203 W4 12.201	Signpost high/low tide route
Map 38	55	N51 03.338 W4 13.543	Burrows Centre
Map 39	56	N51 02.451 W4 14.208	Westward Ho! (Leave Golf Links Rd)
Map 40	57	N51 01.139 W4 16.446	Green Cliff National Trust sign
Map 41	58	N50 59.605 W4 18.327	Gate at Peppercombe
Map 42	59	N50 59.266 W4 20.635	Buck's Mills
Map 42	60	N50 59.288 W4 21.426	Mary's Rest (huge beech tree)
Map 43	61	N50 59.171 W4 22.286	Join The Hobby Drive
Map 43	62	N50 59.895 W4 23.980	Gate into Clovelly
Map 44	63	N51 00.213 W4 24.235	The Cabin
Map 44	64	N51 00.621 W4 25.261	Mouthmill
Map 45	65	N51 00.759 W4 26.710	Memorial to Wellington Bomber
Map 45	66	N51 01.153 W4 28.168	Trig Point
Map 46	67	N51 01.235 W4 30.745	Radar station
Map 47	68	N51 00.154 W4 31.648	Blackpool Mill
Map 48	69	N50 59.631 W4 31.968	Hartland Quay
Map 49	70	N50 58.069 W4 31.795	Turn-off to Elmscott
Map 50	71	N50 55.988 W4 32.624	Welcombe Mouth
Map 51	72	N50 54.389 W4 33.720	Hawker's Hut
Map 52	73	N50 53.129 W4 33.531	Right turn by radio station
Map 53	74	N50 51.659 W4 33.224	Wooden footbridge at Sandy Mouth
Map 54	75	N50 50.121 W4 33.129	Lifeguard lookout

APPENDIX B: TAKING A DOG

The South-West Coast Path is a dog-friendly path and many are the rewards that await those prepared to make the extra effort required to bring their best friend along with them. However, don't underestimate the amount of work involved in bringing your pooch to the path. Indeed, just about every decision you make will be influenced by the fact that you've got a dog: how you plan to travel to the start of the trail, where you're going to stay, how far you're going to walk each day, where you're going to eat in the evening etc, etc. The decision-making begins before you've set foot on the trail. For starters, you have to ask – and be honest with – yourself: can your dog really cope with walking 10+ miles a day, day after day, for up to a fortnight, or weeks if walking the whole path. And just as importantly, will he or she actually enjoy it? If you think the answer is yes to both, the best starting point is the village & town facilities table on pp30-1 (and the advice below), and plan where to stop, where to eat, where to buy food for your mutt.

Looking after your dog
To begin with, you need to make sure that your own dog is fully **inoculated** against the usual doggy illnesses, and also up to date with regard to **worm pills** (eg Drontal) and **flea preventatives** such as Frontline – they are, after all, following in the pawprints of many a dog before them, some of whom may well have left fleas or other parasites on the trail that now lie in wait for their next meal to arrive. **Pet insurance** is also a very good idea for a trip such as this; if you've already got insurance, do check that it will cover the kind of walk you are planning.

Perhaps the most important implement you can take with you is the **plastic tick remover**, available from vets for a couple of quid. Ticks are a real problem on the SWCP. These removers, while fiddly, help you to get rid of the tick safely (ie without leaving its head behind buried under the dog's skin).

Being in unfamiliar territory also makes it more likely that you and your dog could become separated. For this reason, make sure your dog has a **tag with your contact details on it** (a mobile phone number would be best if you are carrying one with you).

Dogs on beaches There is no general rule regarding whether dogs are allowed on beaches or not. Some of the beaches on the SWCP are open to dogs all year; some allow them on the beach only outside the summer season (1 May to 30 Sep); while a few beaches don't allow dogs at all. (Guide dogs, by the way, are usually excluded from any bans.) If in doubt, look for the noticeboards that will tell you the exact rules. On the beaches, the rules vary: at Woolacombe (see box p128), they have an area where dogs are forbidden, another where they need to be on a lead, and a third area where they can run free. At Croyde you will have to walk across a part where dogs are banned – keep the dog on a tight lead here.

For more information about which beaches allow dogs and which don't look at: 🖳 www.northdevon.com/inspire-me/four-legged-friends and 🖳 www.n-somerset.gov.uk/my-services/leisure/coast/animals-on-the-beach.

Where dogs are banned from a beach there will usually be an alternative path that you can take that avoids the sands. If there isn't, and you have no choice but to cross the beach even though dogs are officially banned, you are permitted to do so as long as you cross as speedily as possible, follow the line of the path (which is usually well above the high-water mark) and keep your dog tightly under control.

Whatever the rules of access are for the beach, remember that your dog shouldn't disturb other beach-users – and you must always **clean up after your dog**.

Finally, remember to bring drinking water with you as dogs can over-heat with the lack of shade.

When to keep your dog on a lead
● **On cliff tops** It's a sad fact that, every year, a few dogs lose their lives falling over the edge of the cliffs. It usually occurs when they are chasing rabbits (which know where the cliff-edge is and are able, unlike your poor pooch, to stop in time).
● **When crossing farmland**, particularly in the lambing season (around May) when your dog can scare the sheep, causing them to lose their young. Farmers are allowed by law to shoot at and kill any dogs that they consider are worrying their sheep. During lambing, most farmers would prefer it if you didn't bring your dog at all. The exception is if your dog is being attacked by cows. Some years ago there were three deaths in the UK caused by walkers being trampled as they tried to rescue their dogs from the attentions of cattle. The advice in this instance is to **let go of the lead**, head speedily to a position of safety (usually the other side of the field gate or stile) and call your dog to you.
● **On National Trust land**, where it is **compulsory** to keep your dog on a lead.
● **Around ground-nesting birds** It's important to keep your dog under control when crossing an area where certain species of birds nest on the ground. Most dogs love foraging around in the woods but make sure it's allowed; some woods are used as 'nurseries' for game birds and dogs are only allowed through them on a lead.

What to pack
You've probably already got a good idea of what to bring to keep your dog alive and happy, but the following is a checklist:
● **Food/water bowl** Foldable cloth bowls are popular with walkers, being light and compact in your rucksack. You can get also get a water-bottle-and-bowl combination, where the bottle folds into a 'trough' from which the dog can drink.
● **Lead and collar** An extendable one is probably preferable for this sort of trip. Make sure both lead and collar are in good condition – you don't want either to snap on the trail, or you may end up carrying your dog through sheep fields until a replacement can be found. It is worth taking a spare.
● **Medication** You'll know if you need to bring any lotions or potions.
● **Tick remover** See opposite.
● **Bedding** A simple blanket may suffice, or you can opt for something more elaborate if you aren't carrying your own luggage.
● **Poo bags** Essential (see below).
● **Hygiene wipes** For cleaning your dog after it's rolled in stuff.
● **A favourite toy** Helps prevent your dog from pining for the entire walk.
● **Corkscrew stake** Available from camping or pet shops, this will help you to keep your dog secure in one place while you set up camp/doze.

What to pack
● **Food/water** Remember to bring treats as well as regular food to keep up the mutt's morale. That said, if your dog is anything like mine the chances are they'll spend most of the walk dining on rabbit droppings and sheep poo anyway.
● **Raingear** It can rain a lot!
● **Old towels** For drying your dog after the deluge.

When it comes to packing, I always leave an exterior pocket of my rucksack empty so I can put used poo bags in there (for deposit at the first bin we come to). I always like to keep all the dog's kit together and separate from the other luggage (usually inside a plastic bag inside my rucksack). I have also seen several dogs sporting their own 'doggy rucksack', so they can carry their own food, water, poo etc – which certainly reduces the burden on their owner!

Cleaning up after your dog
It is extremely important that dog owners behave in a responsible way when walking the path. Dog excrement should be cleaned up. In towns, villages and fields where animals graze

or which will be cut for silage, hay etc, you need to pick up and bag the excrement. In other places you can possibly get away with merely flicking it with a nearby stick into the undergrowth, thus ensuring there is none left on the path to decorate the boots of others.

Staying with your dog

In this guide we have used a symbol 🐾 to denote where a hotel, pub or B&B welcomes dogs; however, this always needs to be arranged in advance and some places may charge extra. Hostels (both YHA and independent) do not permit them unless they are an assistance (guide) dog; smaller campsites tend to accept them, but some of the larger holiday parks do not. Before you turn up always double check whether the place you would like to stay accepts dogs and whether there is space for them; many places have only one or two rooms suitable for people with dogs.

When it comes to **eating**, most landlords allow dogs in at least a section of their pubs, though few restaurants do. Make sure you always ask first and ensure your dog doesn't run around the pub but is secured to your table or a radiator.

Map key

🏠	Where to stay	📖 Library/bookstore
○	Where to eat and drink	@ Internet
⟁	Campsite	🏛 Museum/gallery
✉	Post Office	✝ Church/cathedral
ⓔ	Bank/ATM	☎ Telephone
ⓘ	Tourist Information	☒ Public toilet
		▢ Building

• Other
CP Car park
🚌 Bus station/stop
═▭═ Rail line & station
Park
📱082 GPS waypoint

South West Coast Path	Sand dunes
Other path	Cliffs
4 x 4 track	Cornish hedge
Tarmac road	Bridge
Steps	Fence
Slope	Wall
Steep slope	Hedge
Stile	Water
Gate	Stream/river

Trees/woodland
Bog or marsh
Sand
Stones
🗼 Lighthouse
Lifeguard cover
◎ Rescue equipment
⟨ Golf course
㉜ Map continuation

INDEX

Page references in **bold** type refer to maps

TRAILBLAZER'S LONG-DISTANCE PATH (LDP) WALKING GUIDES

We've applied to destinations which are closer to home Trailblazer's proven formula for publishing definitive practical route guides for adventurous travellers. Britain's network of long-distance trails enables the walker to explore some of the finest landscapes in the country's best walking areas. These are guides that are user-friendly, practical, informative and environmentally sensitive.

● **Unique mapping features** In many walking guidebooks the reader has to read a route description then try to relate it to the map. Our guides are much easier to use because walking directions, tricky junctions, places to stay and eat, points of interest and walking times are all written onto the maps themselves in the places to which they apply. With their uncluttered clarity, these are not general-purpose maps but fully edited maps drawn by walkers for walkers.

● **Largest-scale walking maps** At a scale of just under 1:20,000 (8cm or 3¹/₈ inches to one mile) the maps in these guides are bigger than even the most detailed British walking maps currently available in the shops.

● **Not just a trail guide – includes where to stay, where to eat and public transport** Our guidebooks cover the complete walking experience, not just the route. Accommodation options for all budgets are provided (pubs, hotels, B&Bs, campsites, bunkhouses, hostels) as well as places to eat. Detailed public transport information for all access points to each trail means that there are itineraries for all walkers, for hiking the entire route as well as for day or weekend walks.

Coast to Coast *Henry Stedman*, 7th edition, £11.99
ISBN 978-1-905864-74-4, 268pp, 110 maps, 40 colour photos

Cornwall Coast Path (SW Coast Path Pt 2) *Stedman & Newton*, 5th edition, £11.99
ISBN 978-1-905864-71-3, 3526pp, 142 maps, 40 colour photos

Cotswold Way *Tricia & Bob Hayne* 3rd edition, £11.99
ISBN 978-1-905864-70-6, 204pp, 53 maps, 40 colour photos

Dales Way *Henry Stedman* 1st edition, £11.99
ISBN 978-1-905864-78-2, 176pp, 45 maps, 40 colour photos

Dorset & South Devon (SW Coast Path Pt 3) *Stedman & Newton*, 1st edition, £11.99
ISBN 978-1-905864-45-4, 336pp, 88 maps, 40 colour photos

Exmoor & North Devon (SW Coast Path Pt I) *Stedman & Newton*, 2nd edition, £11.99
ISBN 978-1-905864-86-7, 224pp, 68 maps, 40 colour photos

Great Glen Way *Jim Manthorpe*, 1st edition, £11.99
ISBN 978-1-905864-80-5, 192pp, 55 maps, 40 colour photos

Hadrian's Wall Path *Henry Stedman*, 5th edition, £11.99
ISBN 978-1-905864-85-0, 224pp, 60 maps, 40 colour photos

Offa's Dyke Path *Keith Carter*, 4th edition, £11.99
ISBN 978-1-905864-65-2, 240pp, 98 maps, 40 colour photos

Peddars Way & Norfolk Coast Path *Alexander Stewart*, £11.99
ISBN 978-1-905864-28-7, 192pp, 54 maps, 40 colour photos

Pembrokeshire Coast Path *Jim Manthorpe*, 5th edition, £11.99
ISBN 978-1-905864-84-3, 236pp, 96 maps, 40 colour photos

Pennine Way *Stuart Greig*, 4th edition, £11.99
ISBN 978-1-905864-61-4, 272pp, 138 maps, 40 colour photos

The Ridgeway *Nick Hill*, 4th edition, £11.99
ISBN 978-1-905864-79-9, 208pp, 53 maps, 40 colour photos

South Downs Way *Jim Manthorpe*, 5th edition, £11.99
ISBN 978-1-905864-66-9, 192pp, 60 maps, 40 colour photos

Thames Path *Joel Newton*, 1st edition, £11.99
ISBN 978-1-905864-64-5, 256pp, 99 maps, 40 colour photos

West Highland Way *Charlie Loram*, 6th edition, £11.99
ISBN 978-1-905864-76-8, 208pp, 60 maps, 40 colour photos

'The same attention to detail that distinguishes its other guides has been brought to bear here'.

THE
SUNDAY TIMES

IN PREPARATION
FOR PUBLICATION IN
2018
Cleveland Way
ISBN 978-1-905864-91-1

North Downs Way
ISBN 978-1-905864-90-4

TRAILBLAZER TITLE LIST

Adventure Cycle-Touring Handbook
Adventure Motorcycling Handbook
Australia by Rail
Azerbaijan
Cleveland Way (British Walking Guide) – due 2018
Coast to Coast (British Walking Guide)
Cornwall Coast Path (British Walking Guide)
Cotswold Way (British Walking Guide)
The Cyclist's Anthology

Dales Way (British Walking Guide)
Dorset & Sth Devon Coast Path (British Walking Gde)
Exmoor & Nth Devon Coast Path (British Walking Gde)
Great Glen Way (British Walking Guide)
Hadrian's Wall Path (British Walking Guide)
Himalaya by Bike – a route and planning guide
Inca Trail, Cusco & Machu Picchu
Japan by Rail

Kilimanjaro – the trekking guide (includes Mt Meru)
Moroccan Atlas – The Trekking Guide
Morocco Overland (4WD/motorcycle/mountainbike)
Nepal Trekking & The Great Himalaya Trail
New Zealand – The Great Walks
North Downs Way (British Walking Guide) – due 2018
Offa's Dyke Path (British Walking Guide)
Overlanders' Handbook – worldwide driving guide
Peddars Way & Norfolk Coast Path (British Walking Gde)

Pembrokeshire Coast Path (British Walking Guide)
Pennine Way (British Walking Guide)
Peru's Cordilleras Blanca & Huayhuash – Hiking/Biking
The Railway Anthology
The Ridgeway (British Walking Guide)
Sahara Overland – a route and planning guide
Scottish Highlands – Hillwalking Guide
Siberian BAM Guide – rail, rivers & road
The Silk Roads – a route and planning guide

Sinai – the trekking guide
South Downs Way (British Walking Guide)
Thames Path (British Walking Guide)
Tour du Mont Blanc
Trans-Canada Rail Guide
Trans-Siberian Handbook
Trekking in the Everest Region
The Walker's Anthology
The Walker's Anthology – further tales
The Walker's Haute Route – Mont Blanc to Matterhorn
West Highland Way (British Walking Guide)

For more information about Trailblazer and our
expanding range of guides, for guidebook updates or
for credit card mail order sales visit our website:

www.trailblazer-guides.com

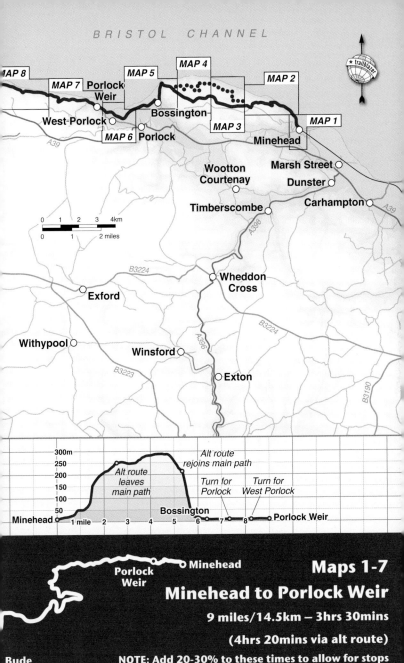

BRISTOL CHANNEL

★ trailblazer

MAP 8
MAP 7
MAP 5
MAP 4
MAP 2
MAP 1
Porlock
Weir
Bossington
MAP 3
West-Porlock
MAP 6   Porlock
Minehead

A39

0   1   2   3   4km
0   1   2 miles

Wootton
Courtenay

Marsh Street
Dunster

Carhampton

A39

Timberscombe

A396

Wheddon
Cross

B3224

Exford

B3224

Withypool

Winsford

A396

B3223

Exton

B3190

300m
250
200
150
100
50

Alt route
rejoins main path

Alt route
leaves
main path

Turn for
Porlock

Turn for
West Porlock

Minehead   1 mile   2   3   4   5   Bossington   6   7   8   Porlock Weir

Porlock
Weir   Minehead

Maps 1-7

Minehead to Porlock Weir

9 miles/14.5km – 3hrs 30mins

(4hrs 20mins via alt route)

Bude   **NOTE: Add 20-30% to these times to allow for stops**

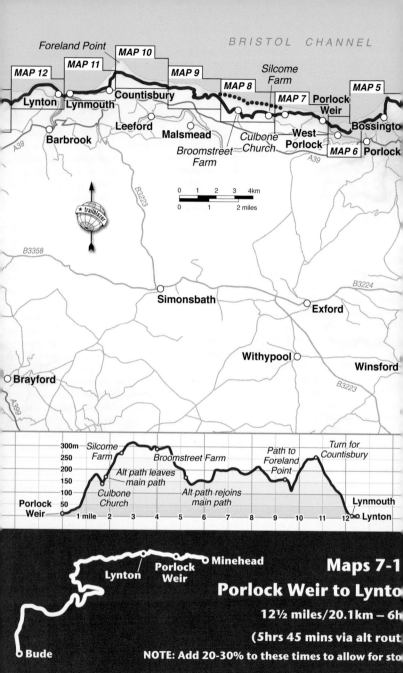

BRISTOL CHANNEL

MAP 12
MAP 11
MAP 10
Foreland Point
MAP 9
Silcome Farm
MAP 8
MAP 7 **Porlock Weir**
MAP 5

Lynton
Lynmouth
Countisbury
West Porlock
Bossingto

Barbrook
Leeford
Malsmead
Culbone Church
Broomstreet Farm
MAP 6 **Porlock**

A39
B3223
A39

0 1 2 3 4km
0   1   2 miles

★ trailblazer

B3358

Simonsbath
B3224
Exford

Withypool
Winsford

Brayford
B3223

A399

300m *Silcome Farm*   *Turn for Countisbury*
250
200   *Broomstreet Farm*   *Path to Foreland Point*
150   *Alt path leaves main path*
100   *Culbone Church*   *Alt path rejoins main path*   Lynmouth
50   Lynton
Porlock Weir
1 mile — 2 — 3 — 4 — 5 — 6 — 7 — 8 — 9 — 10 — 11 — 12

Minehead
Lynton   Porlock Weir
Maps 7-1
Porlock Weir to Lynto
Bude
12½ miles/20.1km – 6h
(5hrs 45 mins via alt rout
NOTE: Add 20-30% to these times to allow for sto

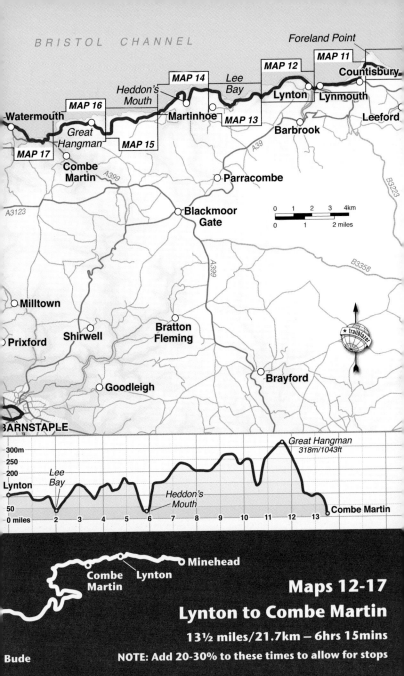

BRISTOL CHANNEL

Foreland Point

MAP 11

MAP 12

Countisbury

MAP 14

Lee Bay

Lynton

Lynmouth

Heddon's Mouth

MAP 16

Martinhoe

MAP 13

Leeford

Watermouth

Great Hangman

MAP 15

Barbrook

MAP 17

Combe Martin

Parracombe

A399

A39

B3223

A3123

Blackmoor Gate

A399

B3358

Milltown

Bratton Fleming

Prixford

Shirwell

Brayford

Goodleigh

BARNSTAPLE

Great Hangman 318m/1043ft

300m
250
200

Lynton

Lee Bay

Heddon's Mouth

50

Combe Martin

0 miles   2   3   4   5   6   7   8   9   10   11   12   13

0   1   2   3   4km

0   1   2 miles

★ trailblazer

Minehead

Combe Martin   Lynton

Bude

Maps 12-17
Lynton to Combe Martin

13½ miles/21.7km – 6hrs 15mins

NOTE: Add 20-30% to these times to allow for stops

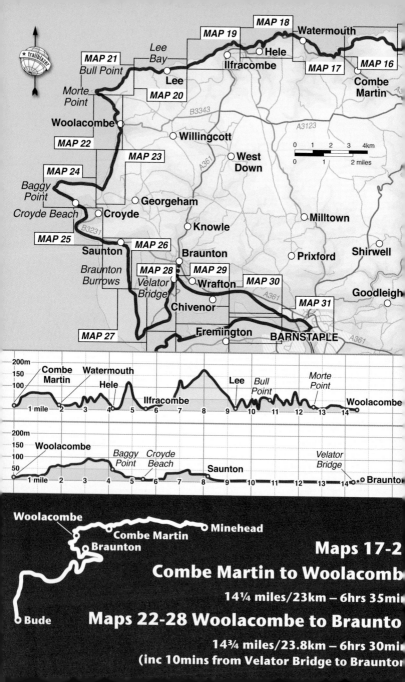

MAP 18
Watermouth
MAP 19
Hele
MAP 21
Lee Bay
Bull Point
Ilfracombe
MAP 17
MAP 16
Combe Martin
Morte Point
Lee
MAP 20
Woolacombe
MAP 22
Willingcott
West Down
A3123

0 1 2 3 4km
0   1   2 miles

MAP 23
MAP 24
Baggy Point
Georgeham
Milltown
Croyde Beach
Croyde
B3231
Knowle
Prixford
Shirwell
MAP 25
Saunton
MAP 26
Braunton
Braunton Burrows
MAP 28
Velator Bridge
MAP 29
Wrafton
MAP 30
Goodleigh
Chivenor
MAP 31
MAP 27
Fremington
BARNSTAPLE
A361

200m
150
100
Combe Martin
Watermouth
Hele
Lee
Bull Point
Morte Point
Ilfracombe
Woolacombe
1 mile 2 3 4 5 6 7 8 9 10 11 12 13 14

200m
150
100
50
Woolacombe
Baggy Point
Croyde Beach
Saunton
Velator Bridge
1 mile 2 3 4 5 6 7 8 9 10 11 12 13 14 Braunton

Woolacombe
Combe Martin
Minehead
Braunton

Maps 17-2
Combe Martin to Woolacomb

Bude

14¼ miles/23km – 6hrs 35mi

Maps 22-28 Woolacombe to Braunto

14¾ miles/23.8km – 6hrs 30mi
(inc 10mins from Velator Bridge to Braunton

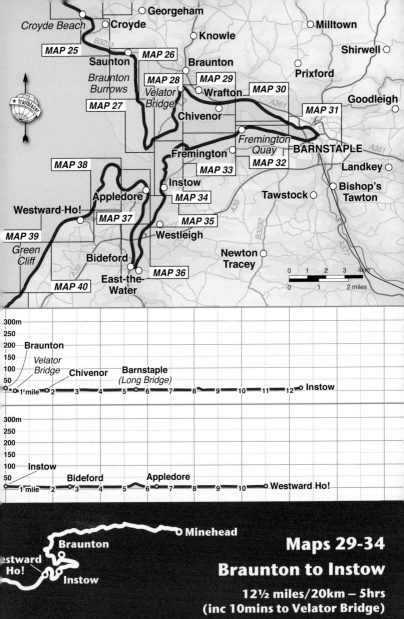

MAP 25

MAP 26

MAP 28

MAP 29

MAP 30

MAP 31

MAP 27

MAP 38

MAP 33

MAP 32

MAP 37

MAP 34

MAP 39

MAP 35

MAP 40

MAP 36

Georgeham

Croyde Beach — Croyde

Milltown

Knowle

Shirwell

Saunton

Braunton

Prixford

Braunton
Burrows

Velator
Bridge

Wrafton

Goodleigh

Chivenor

Fremington
Quay

BARNSTAPLE

Fremington

Landkey

Instow

Bishop's
Tawton

Appledore

Tawstock

Westward-Ho!

Westleigh

Bideford

Newton
Tracey

Green
Cliff

East-the-
Water

0 1 2 3 4km

0   1   2 miles

300m
250
200
150
100
50

Braunton

Velator
Bridge

Chivenor

Barnstaple
(Long Bridge)

Instow

1 mile 2   3   4   5   6   7   8   9   10   11   12   Instow

300m
250
200
150
100
50

Instow

Bideford

Appledore

1 mile 2   3   4   5   6   7   8   9   10   Westward Ho!

Minehead

Braunton

estward
Ho!

Instow

Bude

Maps 29-34

Braunton to Instow

12½ miles/20km — 5hrs
(inc 10mins to Velator Bridge)

Maps 34-39, Instow to Westward Ho!

11 miles/17.6km — 4hrs 50mins

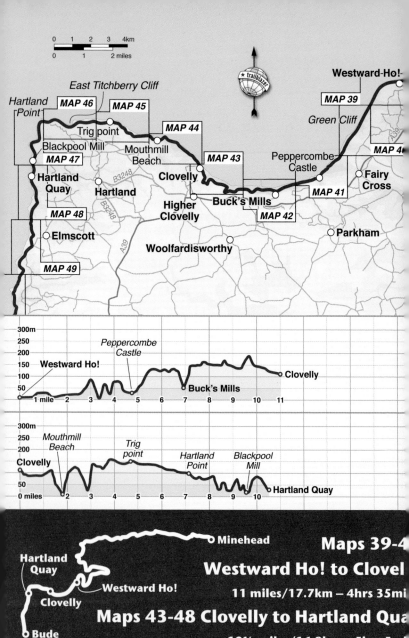

0 1 2 3 4km
0   1   2 miles

Westward-Ho!-

Hartland | MAP 46 | MAP 45 | *East Titchberry Cliff*
Point

MAP 39

Hartland
Point

Green Cliff

MAP 44

A39

Trig point

MAP 4

Blackpool Mill

MAP 47

Mouthmill
Beach

MAP 43

Peppercombe
Castle

Hartland
Quay

B3248

Clovelly

Buck's Mills

MAP 41

Fairy
Cross

Hartland

MAP 48

B3248

Higher
Clovelly

MAP 42

MAP 42

Elmscott

A39

Woolfardisworthy

Parkham

MAP 49

300m
250
200
150   *Peppercombe*
         Castle
100 **Westward Ho!**
50   **Clovelly**
                           Buck's Mills
     1 mile 2   3   4   5   6   7   8   9   10   11

300m
250   *Mouthmill*
200   *Beach*   *Trig*
                         point   *Hartland*   *Blackpool*
     Clovelly   *Point*   *Mill*
50   **Hartland Quay**
   0 miles   2   3   4   5   6   7   8   9   10

Hartland
Quay

Minehead

Maps 39-4

Westward Ho! to Clovel

Westward Ho!

11 miles/17.7km – 4hrs 35mi

Clovelly

Maps 43-48 Clovelly to Hartland Qua

Bude

10½ miles/16.9km – 5hrs 5mi

NOTE: Add 20-30% to these times to allow for sto

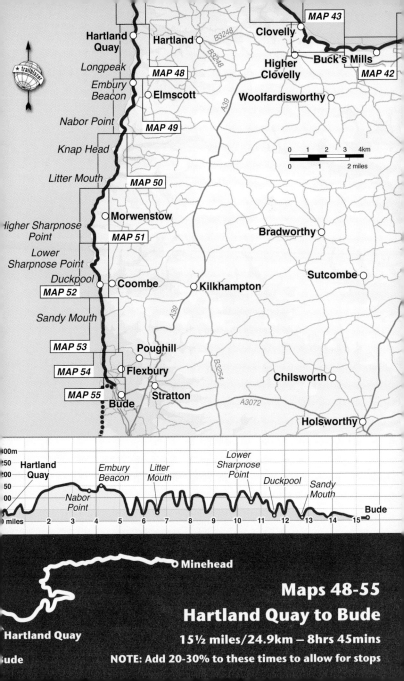

MAP 43

Clovelly

MAP 48

Hartland
Quay

Hartland

Longpeak

*Embury
Beacon*

Elmscott

Nabor Point

MAP 49

Knap Head

MAP 50

Litter Mouth

MAP 51

Morwenstow

*Higher Sharpnose
Point*

*Lower
Sharpnose Point*

Duckpool

MAP 52

Coombe

Sandy Mouth

MAP 53

MAP 54

Poughill

Flexbury

MAP 55

Bude

Stratton

Buck's Mills

MAP 42

Higher
Clovelly

Woolfardisworthy

Bradworthy

Sutcombe

Kilkhampton

Chilsworth

Holsworthy

0 1 2 3 4km
0   1   2 miles

Minehead

Hartland Quay

Bude

Maps 48-55
Hartland Quay to Bude
15½ miles/24.9km – 8hrs 45mins
NOTE: Add 20-30% to these times to allow for stops

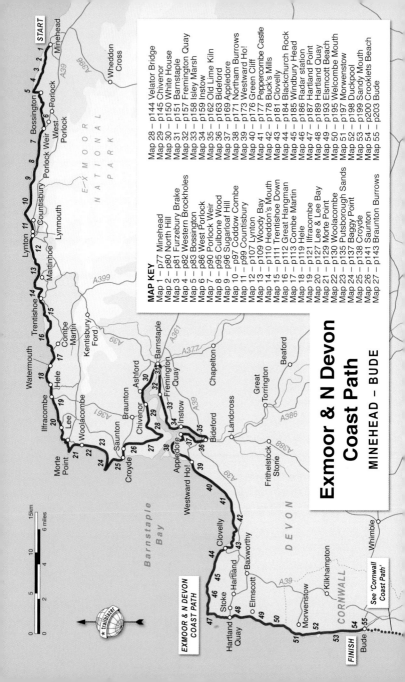

Exmoor & N Devon Coast Path
MINEHEAD – BUDE